Beyond Donkeys and Elephants

Beyond Donkeys
and Elephants

Minor Political Parties in
Contemporary American Politics

Edited by Richard Davis

University Press of Kansas

Published by the University Press of Kansas (Lawrence, Kansas 66045),
which was organized by the Kansas Board of Regents and is operated and
funded by Emporia State University, Fort Hays State University, Kansas
State University, Pittsburg State University, the University of Kansas, and
Wichita State University

Library of Congress Cataloging-in-Publication Data

Names: Davis, Richard, 1955– editor.
Title: Beyond donkeys and elephants : minor political parties in
contemporary American politics / [edited by] Richard Davis.
Description: Lawrence, Kansas : University Press of Kansas, [2020] |
Includes bibliographical references and index.
Identifiers: LCCN 2019042725
ISBN 9780700629275 (cloth)
ISBN 9780700629282 (paperback)
ISBN 9780700629299 (epub)
Subjects: LCSH: Third parties (United States politics) | Political
parties—United States. | United States—Politics and government.
Classification: LCC JK2265 .B47 2020 | DDC 324.273—dc23
LC record available at https://lccn.loc.gov/2019042725.

British Library Cataloguing-in-Publication Data is available.

Printed in the United States of America

10 9 8 7 6 5 4 3 2 1

The paper used in this publication is recycled and contains 30 percent
postconsumer waste. It is acid free and meets the minimum requirements
of the American National Standard for Permanence of Paper for Printed
Library Materials Z39.48-1992.

To the many political activists I have worked with—regardless of political party affiliation—who seek to make their communities, states, and nations better places to live

Contents

Acknowledgments   ix

Introduction   1

PART ONE: NATIONAL AND MULTISTATE PARTIES
1. The Libertarian Party   41
   —*Christopher J. Devine*
2. The Green Party of the United States   64
   —*Steve Lem*
3. The American Constitution Party   82
   —*Edward Lynch*
4. The New York and Connecticut Working Families Party   99
   —*Bilal Sekou*

PART TWO: STATE PARTIES
5. The Peace and Freedom Party of California   121
   —*Joseph Phillips*
6. Third Parties in Vermont   138
   —*Bertram Johnson*
7. New York State's "Multi+" Party System   153
   —*Gerald Benjamin and Michael Catalano*
8. The Independence Party of Minnesota   181
   —*Melanie Freeze*
9. The Independent Party of Oregon   205
   —*Richard A. Clucas*

10. The Mountain Party of West Virginia   223
    —*C. Damien Arthur*
11. The Moderate Party of Rhode Island   238
    —*Emily K. Lynch*
12. The United Utah Party   261
    —*Richard Davis*

About the Contributors   275

Index   279

Acknowledgments

This book began many years ago when, as a new college professor, I became intrigued by minor political parties in a two-party system. What caused people to form these parties and others to run for office on their tickets? Why did minor parties persist in the face of formidable barriers to their existence much less success?

Over time, my curiosity heightened as I saw growing partisan polarization in American politics that spawned more extreme major and third parties but also propelled less ideological candidates, such as Ross Perot, Jesse Ventura, and Angus King, to run and, in the case of Ventura and King, win statewide races. Simultaneously, increasing numbers of voters were telling pollsters they were unhappy with the two major parties and wanted some alternative. Was this public unrest translating into something more substantial than rhetoric? If so, how might that be happening?

It is gratifying to me to take all those musings over time and find them published in this edited volume. In one place, readers can learn about the various contemporary minor parties that exist not only at the national level but also in diverse state settings and answer the questions I raised above. This book would have been useful to me over the years as I discussed minor political parties while instructing students studying American politics. Hopefully, it will help future teachers of American politics.

I want to acknowledge some people who have contributed to this book. I am grateful to the students at several universities and colleges who have stimulated my thinking over several decades of teaching courses on American political parties and elections. They have refined my conclusions but also raised many new questions over the years.

Still another group consists of the many political activists, including party workers, I have associated with as a political activist. Generally, those who volunteer for a campaign or a party are interested citizens who are willing to devote their time and energy to make their community, state, and nation better places for all to live. There is no doubt that they strongly disagree with each other when they work for opposing causes. But they share a similar dedication that is highly admirable, and much needed, in a democratic society.

Certainly, I am thankful to those contributors who have written chapters and made this volume into an informative source for the minor political parties who affect American politics today. I appreciate their interest in making this book better by their contributions.

Finally, my wife, Molina, has been an author's "widow" for many years as I write and write, to test the admonition of Ecclesiastes 12:12: "Of making books there is no end; and much study is a weariness of the flesh."

Introduction

American political history is littered with the corpses of small parties who emerged for a short time and then disappeared. Populists, Constitutional Unionists, and the American Party (Know-Nothings) were examples in the nineteenth century, as were the Progressive, Prohibition, and Reform. The two-party system that emerged in 1860 with the demise of the Whigs and the emergence of the Republicans as the counterpoint to the Democrats has weathered the challenges of these upstart parties through numerous elections over one hundred and sixty years.

However, the endurance of the current two-party system does not mean it has not been seriously threatened at times by other parties. In 1912, a third party—the Progressives or Bull Moose Party—took second place in both the electoral and popular vote, winning six states. That year, the Republican presidential candidate William Howard Taft won only two states— Utah and Vermont—and placed third in twenty-six states.

Another threat occurred in the 1890s with the rise of the Populists (officially the People's Party). In 1892, People's Party presidential candidate James Weaver garnered nearly 9 percent of the vote and won five midwestern and Rocky Mountain states. The Populists promised to be a more potent force four years later in 1896. However, the Democratic Party incorporated the Populists' economic policies, particularly on the "free silver" issue, and nominated a candidate largely aligned with the People's Party—a former Nebraska congress member named William Jennings Bryan. The People's Party also nominated Bryan, which led to the party's absorption. The election produced a realignment of the electorate from the previous North-South division to an economic one, uniting rural midwestern and southern voters against northern industrial and commercial voters.[1]

1

In June 1992, billionaire independent candidate Ross Perot placed first in the Gallup survey, suggesting that a significant number of voters were willing to abandon both major-party presidential candidates for Perot.[2] Perot's odyssey of leaving the race shortly thereafter and then returning a couple of months later made his victory unlikely. Ultimately, he only won 19 percent of the popular vote and no electoral votes. However, he did displace one of the major-party candidates in two states, besting George H. W. Bush in Maine and Bill Clinton in Utah. Perot's bid, like John Anderson's twelve years earlier, was an independent bid. However, unlike Anderson, Perot attempted to institutionalize his candidacy through a new national political party that competed in two subsequent presidential elections.

While these "other" parties have never gained an electoral majority, or even a plurality in presidential elections, they have had more impact on the American electoral system and public policy than their electoral numbers suggest. Other parties have both solidified and weakened the role of the current two major parties—solidified in the sense that their continued failure to fundamentally alter the current system has reinforced the perception of its hegemony and weakened in the sense that the current system has not sufficiently discouraged other parties and, indeed, has signaled that these two major broad-based parties are vulnerable enough to warrant continued threat attempts from other competitors.

One impact of minor parties on each of the major political parties is the attention to issues raised by the smaller parties. For example, the People's Party advanced issues of economic hardship connected to the gold standard that the Democrats incorporated into their 1896 platform. And George Wallace's American Independent Party provoked Republicans to favor anti-integration stances.[3]

It is a fact of American politics that minor parties have formed again and again, regardless of the odds against success. Within the past three decades, new political parties have emerged to run candidates in successive elections—at the local, state, and national levels. For example, the Working Families Party began in 1998 as a labor-oriented, progressive alternative to the Democratic Party. The Green Party of the United States, formed in 2001 by amalgamating various green political organizations under one banner, has run presidential candidates in every presidential election since. The Constitution Party came into existence in 1999, although the organization previously existed as the US Taxpayers Party.

At the state level, the Independence Party in Oregon organized in 2007, and the Moderate Party formed in Rhode Island in 2009. More recently, the American Party started in South Carolina in 2014, and the United Utah

Party formed in 2017. They joined the Independence Party in Minnesota, which had been formed in the 1990s as the Reform Party.

The continual emergence and failure of nonmajor political parties raises questions about why they form and why they fail. The question of failure is a more common question and one that has been given the status of a "law" in political science theory. Duverger's law is considered the standard answer to the question of why third parties fail.

DUVERGER'S LAW AND ELECTORAL SYSTEMS

Maurice Duverger posited that a single-member district, first-past-the-post electoral system will favor two strong parties and therefore disadvantage smaller parties that thrive in proportional representation systems or majority systems with run-off elections. Proportional representation is standard in most European nations, such as the Netherlands, Belgium, or Scandinavia, while France is an example of a majority system with runoffs.[4] These countries develop multiparty systems, resulting in coalition governments or, as in majority system runoffs, still offer smaller parties an incentive to participate since major parties court their support. Hence, unlike in a proportional representation where multiple parties flourish, the electoral system emphasizing simple majorities creates space for only two large parties. According to Duverger, the gap between major parties and minor parties in the American system confirms his "law" that the US electoral system impedes the ability of minor parties to become influential.

Duverger discusses two barriers to the growth of new parties in an electoral system. One is the mechanical effect: the structure of the electoral system that rewards two large parties with majority potential and underrepresents all others. The other is psychological: the individual voter's unwillingness to give his or her vote to a party when it may be wasted. The psychological effect may result in as much as a 20 percent drop in voting for third parties in a plurality system rather than proportional representation. Both of these effects can inhibit party growth.[5]

However, there are some questions that arise from Duverger's law concerning the formation of political parties. One is whether new parties intend to create a multiparty system or whether their founders seek to displace one of the two major parties. Within the US context, new political party organizers may argue that their efforts are contributing to a multiparty system. However, do such parties actually seek to gain and retain the status of one of a set of multiple parties rather than start a new party system?

That status of "one of many" would not gain much traction in the US electoral system unless those parties are all relatively equal in strength. Weak parties in a proportional representation system accrue some rewards for competing without winning a simple majority. They gain seats in legislative bodies. They can become part of governing coalitions and secure cabinet seats in such a coalition government. In some cases, their leader may become prime minister in the case of a grand coalition or a deadlock involving other larger parties. In the US system, none of those rewards exist electorally for a weak party.

One realistic goal, then, is not to seek rewards within a system that will not extend them. Rather, it is to displace a major party and participate in the two-party system. A Libertarian Party presidential candidate explained that his party had "the same opportunity to become a mass party as the Republicans did in the 1850s."[6] The Republicans displaced one of the two major parties at the time—the Whigs—and became a major party.

The other option is to become as strong as the Republicans and the Democrats. That would allow the new party to break through the psychological barrier of the wasted vote. Instead of two competing parties there would be three.

In the past, the duality of the US system has made such a breakthrough difficult. A change in that system would require a rejection by a large segment of the population of both political parties rather than the weakening of one political party, resulting in major-party displacement (as occurred with the Federalists in the 1810s and with the Republicans in the 1850s). Yet, the growth of moderate parties, such as the Moderate Party of Rhode Island, Serve America Movement, and the United Utah Party, suggests that some party founders intend to achieve one of those two objectives—displacing a major party or gaining enough strength to compete effectively with both parties.

At the same time, ideologically moderate parties face disadvantages that ideologically extreme ones do not. First, ideological moderates who are attracted to these parties could return to one of the two major parties and exist on the moderate wings of either party. Second, sociality with like-minded others is not likely to be a major goal since ideological or issue passion are not characteristics of their involvement. Thus, moderates may feel comfortable socializing with moderates in a more extremist major party compared to an ideologue who needs similar ideological companionship and is less likely to find it in the major parties.

Is the formation of a three-party system or the displacement of a major party with a new party a practical objective? At the presidential level, such an effort may be unrealistic. However, is it unrealistic at a subnational level?

Some current forces may not make these potential scenarios as far-fetched as imagined.

One factor is creation of a vacuum at the subnational level in regards to two-party competition. Thanks to gerrymandering of congressional districts, relatively few congressional races are competitive. One party—the majority party—becomes the overwhelming favorite and leads to the degeneration of the losing party. No longer is the losing party a major party because it is not able to compete effectively in elections.

The problem of one-party systems is not limited to congressional districts. It can exist in whole states. States such as Utah, Idaho, and Wyoming have become one-party GOP states, with Democrats only rarely able to win statewide or congressional races and face super-majorities in the legislature. The same is true with Democratic bastions such as Massachusetts, Hawaii, and Maryland.

Could a new party take advantage of the weakness of one of the two major parties to become the second party rather than a third? If the majority party is weakened by various forces, does a disgruntled segment of that party offer an opening for another party? If both of those forces occurred in a one-party state, could a new party capitalize on major-party ineffectiveness?

History does not suggest this scenario is likely. There are only two examples of this phenomenon in US history. One is the emergence of the Whig Party in the 1830s. The Federalists formed in the 1790s but became moribund by 1820 when they failed to even field a presidential candidate and the party had shrunk to a regional organization centered in New England. The Whigs took the Federalists' place as the alternative to the Republican, later Democratic, Party. However, the Whigs were also involved in the second example of major-party disintegration when the party fragmented over the issue of slavery. The demise of the Whigs in the 1850s led to the formation of new political parties in that decade. The best known, and longest lasting, is the Republican Party, which went on to take the Whigs' place as the Democratic alternative.[7]

But the Democrats themselves came close to a permanent splintering when two additional third parties formed out of their ranks in the 1860 election. The Constitutional Union Party, which consisted of opponents of Southern secession, drew from the Whig and Democratic parties. Southern Democrats bolted from the Democratic Party and ran their own presidential candidate that year.[8]

Is it possible for another party to take the place of one of the two major parties as happened previously in American political history? Or is a three-party system possible? What conditions are essential for either of these events to occur?

According to Duverger, a new party must avoid the psychological factor. That is, the phenomenon of voters concluding that casting their vote for a third party is a wasted vote. Clearly, one way to avoid that outcome is to become a stronger party than one of the two major parties. Then, the old major party now is the third party with the spoiler label.[9]

Such takeovers have occurred at the state and local level. The Farmer–Labor Party in Minnesota and the Progressive Party in Wisconsin, as well as the Populist Party in North Carolina, Oregon, and several midwestern states, all won elections at the statewide level. The Socialist Party won the mayoral race in Milwaukee, Wisconsin, several times during the early 1900s.

The theory of a wasted vote works only when there is no prospect that a vote for a non-major-party candidate will, in fact, matter. However, more recent examples undermine that proposition. When Jesse Ventura campaigned for Minnesota's governor, he turned the "wasted vote" theory on its head by arguing that a vote for one of the two major-party candidates was a wasted vote because it would not result in change. But it was Ventura's actual victory that proved the point that success for a non-major-party candidate was possible and a vote for such a candidate was not wasted.

The Ventura example is not a lone one. Others in the past half century at the statewide level include the successful non-major-party gubernatorial candidacies of Walter Hickel (Alaska, 1970), James Longley (Maine, 1974), Lowell Weicker (Connecticut, 1990), Angus King (Maine, 1994 and 1998), and Bill Walker (Alaska, 2014). Still more exist at lower levels—state legislators, mayors, school board members, etc.

Advocates of minor-party voting face an uphill battle in terms of the odds of victory. However, based on historical examples, they are able to argue that there is a chance for the minor party to upset those odds, although that is generally remote. Explaining to voters that the chance exists is not an easy sell.

Nevertheless, psychological barriers can be reduced in certain situations such as the celebrity status of candidates, adequate funding, and the weakness of major-party candidates. Admittedly, that combination of factors is not easy to achieve. Major-party candidates can be weakened by scandal, incompetence, or extremism. But finding well-known or well-funded candidates who are willing to risk their funds on a minor-party campaign is a more difficult task.

The psychological barrier may be present not only in major-party sup-

Table I.1: Minor-Party Supporters' Attitudes on Voting and Their Party

Strongly Agree (%)	Agree (%)	Disagree (%)	Strongly Disagree (%)	Not Sure (%)	Total (%)

Table I.1: Minor-Party Supporters' Attitudes on Voting and Their Party

Strongly Agree (%)	Agree (%)	Disagree (%)	Strongly Disagree (%)	Not Sure (%)	Total (%)
It is better to vote one's conscience than to vote for a candidate because he or she may win.					
51	28	8	5	9	101*
I will vote for a major party candidate if I think he or she can win and I do not want the other major-party candidate to win.					
17	30	25	16	11	99*
I believe in the ideology my political party represents and I do not believe in the ideology of either of the major parties.					
19	36	21	8	16	100
I believe my political party will become a major party in my state or the nation in the next ten years.					
10	24	25	13	28	100

*Rounding error

porters, but also minor-party supporters as well. According to a survey we conducted of major- and minor-party supporters in January 2019, only one-third of minor-party supporters believed that their party would become a major party in the nation or even in their state within the next decade.[10] Another 38 percent said that was not going to happen. (See Table I.1.) Minor-party supporters either are playing a very long game or they expect that their minor-party status will not change and their party will be a largely insignificant electoral force in perpetuity.

Yet, psychological barriers may be less significant in an age of gerrymandering and noncompetitive races. Where gerrymandering has created a lopsided district, supporters for the major party that has become a minority party have a far less than a fifty-fifty chance of their candidate winning the race. Nevertheless, the vast majority of partisans continue to support the party's candidate regardless of the odds. In such cases, even major-party supporters may not be interested in voting rationally (i.e., avoiding the possibility of wasting their vote). At first, they may believe their vote is efficacious. But it is difficult to believe such thinking persists in the face of successive failures. Such voters may believe that they can assist their parties in obtaining a strong showing for the future. But that logic could be similar for the minor-party voter who persists in supporting a political party where the prospect of immediate, or even near future, victory (and avoidance of the "wasted vote") is slim.

PARTY LEVEL: NATIONAL

Minor parties are usually lumped together by scholars. They are considered "third" parties or just the other parties. Yet, one significant differentiation among minor parties is their geographical area of focus.

Scholarly interest has focused primarily on the minor political party that attempts to organize nationally and compete in presidential elections. To gain notice, competition in a presidential election seems to be a prerequisite for a minor party. Some parties have fit that bill. They have organized nationally, typically around a presidential candidate.

The Republican Party is the most successful example, since its membership and influence spread quickly in the 1850s. By the 1860s, the Republican Party not only won the presidency and become a major party, it also gained the majority in Congress. The Progressive Party of 1912 is another example. Theodore Roosevelt waged a national campaign and did well nationally. He won states in the West, Midwest, and Northeast, and placed second in twenty-four additional states in every region of the country. A third example was the Reform Party. The Reform Party sought to compete nationally from its inception. In 1996, the party's presidential candidate, Ross Perot, did not win a single state. However, he received double-digit support in states in the Northeast, the Midwest, and the West, which suggested the national scope of his campaign.

PARTY LEVEL: REGIONAL

The aim for many minor parties is a national presence, but some nascent national parties are really only active in a region of the nation. They become regional parties instead of national ones, even if they run presidential candidates. The Populists (People's Party) of the 1890s succeeded in the Midwest and parts of the South but never became popular in other regions of the country.

The 1948 presidential election saw a short-lived regional minor party. The States' Rights Party (Dixiecrat) was a regional party that lasted only in that election and did not even appear on the ballot in most states outside of the South. But it did prove its ability to garner significant regional support: Strom Thurmond, the party's presidential candidate, won four states.

The American Independent Party that George Wallace formed in 1967, which continued to operate into the 1970s, sought to have a national presence for the 1968 campaign. However, it was successful only in several southern states. Wallace won a majority of the vote in Alabama (his home state) and Mississippi but captured a plurality in three other states (Arkansas, Georgia, and Louisiana) and came in second in three additional states (North Carolina, South Carolina, and Tennessee). But outside of the states of the former Confederacy, Wallace's vote was mainly in the single digits.

PARTY LEVEL: STATE-CENTRIC

The third level—and the one that typically eludes the attention of scholars—is the state-centric minor party. The federal system makes subnational political party competition (and new party formation) possible on a state-by-state basis. While failing at the federal level, some political parties have found success in individual states. The most successful of these state-centric parties was the Farmer–Labor Party, which attempted to become a national party but gained electoral success in Minnesota. The Farmer–Labor Party in Minnesota lasted for twenty-six years before merging with the Democratic Party to form the Democratic–Farmer–Labor Party (DFL) in 1944. The DFL still is the official name of the Democratic Party in Minnesota today. During its existence, the party elected US senators and representatives. At the state level, the party elected three Minnesota governors during the 1930s.[11]

Other examples of briefly successful parties at the state level were the Progressive Party in Wisconsin and the A Connecticut Party. The Progressives elected governors and dominated the legislature briefly in the 1930s. The A Connecticut Party was a state-centric party that revolved around the successful gubernatorial candidacy of former US senator Lowell Weicker in 1990.[12]

The most recent statewide third-party victory was the election of Jesse Ventura in Minnesota in 1998. Ventura was the candidate of Perot's Reform Party and won after a bitter contest that included Republican Norm Coleman and Democrat Hubert Humphrey. Ventura became unpopular quickly and passed on a likely unsuccessful run for reelection.[13]

State-centric parties have been most common in New York where fusion and diversity reward the formation of minor parties. The Liberal Party, the Right to Life Party, and the Conservative Party are examples of New York minor parties that functioned for many years as alternative platforms for major-party candidates. However, during the past three decades, state-centric parties have emerged in other states where fusion does not exist, such as Minnesota, Oregon, and Rhode Island. Some state-centric parties may not start that way. They may have national ambitions similar to the Farmer– Labor Party. However, the party's political appeal limits the party to a specific constituency.

State-centric parties have one of two key traits: either they lack national or even regional relevance or they are the creation of specific politicians seeking statewide impact. An example of the former was the Alaskan Independence Party, which favored a state referendum on secession from the United States. Examples of the latter include the Illinois Solidarity Party in the 1980s and the A Connecticut Party in the early 1990s. These two were the handiwork of two former US senators (Adlai Stevenson III and Lowell Weicker) who were running for governor in their respective states.[14]

Understanding the geographic scope of the party's activity helps scholars gain insights into the party's origins, issue positions, and goals. Unlike the two major parties that operate on all levels simultaneously, minor parties may not attempt to duplicate the Democrats and the Republicans in their national scope. They may limit their activity to a particular geographic electorate based on their goals, as well as their resources. Affecting state policy or furthering a prominent politician's state-focused political career does not require a national party. In fact, such a party would be counterproductive.

Minor parties also may be dynamic in their choice of level, although ending up at a certain level may be less a choice than an unintended outcome. For example, the Farmer–Labor Party sought national status but ultimately appealed only to the Minnesota electorate. Similarly, other parties seeking national recognition were relegated to regional or state-level influence.

Minor parties, then, can move downwards. But can they move upwards? Can a state-centric or regional party become a major party today? Historically, only one such party has done so: the Republicans were a regional party that acquired national status.

The existence of regional and state-centric parties in the twenty-first century speaks volumes about our political system. One lesson is that even in an environment of national media and public attention, the fact that some parties have organized on a state level suggests that federalism and variants in national political culture still matter within the American political system. Another is that hope springs eternal that expansion is possible and the state-centric party of today may become the regional or national party of tomorrow.

LONGEVITY OF THE PARTY: SHORT-TERM MINOR PARTIES

Another cleavage between minor parties is the longevity of their existence in the electoral system. Does the party exist or remain influential for only one or two elections or does it have a more lasting impact on national, regional, or state politics? Historically, nonmajor parties fit within two broad categories: short-term parties and long-term parties.

Short-term parties typically compete for a single election (or perhaps two) and then fade away. They are the vehicles for a public official who has been involved in one of the two major parties but has led a faction of one or both major parties into a third party. The classic example was Theodore Roosevelt who drew progressive Republicans away from the Republican Party with the Bull Moose Party in 1912. Other examples include the candidacies of Henry Wallace, the Progressive Party candidate in 1948; Strom Thurmond, the States' Rights Party candidate also in 1948; and George Wallace, the American Independent Party candidate in 1968. At the state level, an example is Lowell Weicker's A Connecticut Party, which drew moderates from both the Democrats and Republicans in the 1990 Connecticut gubernatorial election but lasted only for a few years. In each national example, the third-party presidential candidate failed to win. Roosevelt came closest by displacing the Republican Party candidate to become the second-place candidate in that election. The others drew away some votes from one or both of the major parties but failed to achieve a majority or even a second place.

Yet, short-term minor parties sometimes receive a significant percentage of the vote. Since the beginning of the two-party system, Roosevelt's 27 percent of the vote in 1912 was the high point. But others have broken double digits. In 1968, George Wallace won 13 percent of the vote and five states in the South. In 1924, Robert LaFollette Sr. won 17 percent of the vote and one state—his home state of Wisconsin.

The two major parties view short-term minor parties as potential threats because they are led by high-profile individuals, they represent significant factions within the party, and they pull away substantial numbers of voters. At the least, this third party could split a major party and elect the candidate of the opposition. At the worst, they could win and displace the party as a major party.

To address the threat, Democrats and Republicans seek to absorb the short-term minor party's issues and supporters. For example, in the wake of the 1968 Wallace candidacy, the Nixon administration instituted a Southern strategy designed to woo Wallace voters to the Republican ticket in

1972 by adopting issues such as antibusing and integration stances important to Wallace voters. The strategy was successful; in 1972, Nixon won all of
the states Wallace had won four years earlier and established Republican
Party control of the South for years to come.[15]

Failure to win a presidential election results in the candidates and the
party supporters of a short-term minor party returning to the party they left
and causing the demise of the party they formed. For example, Roosevelt returned to the Republicans and Wallace the Democrats. Yet, sometimes candidates and supporters move to the other party. Strom Thurmond later became
a Republican.[16] And, as just discussed, Wallace supporters, who had been Democrats, began to shift to the Republican Party in the 1970s and 1980s.

The departure of the candidate leaves the new party that formed around
the candidate in a forlorn position. Shorn of its leader, it collapses. For example, Weicker's A Connecticut Party formed in 1990 for his own gubernatorial bid folded when Weicker forsook a reelection bid.

Moreover, short-term parties often form around a single issue or a small
set of related issues that become prominent in that particular campaign. By
the time the next election comes around, other issues may have displaced
those earlier ones and left the third party without a signature issue. Or,
even if they remain prominent, those issues may be co-opted by a major
party seeking to gain the votes of the third-party supporters.[17]

Short-term minor parties are likely to form out of a failure of one or both
of the major parties to address concerns of a wide swath of the electorate.
For the Bull Moose Party of Roosevelt, it was the conservativism of the Republican Party that worried Republican progressives. In the case of the Wallace candidacy in 1968, the failure stemmed from the Democratic Party's
movement away from the anticivil rights sentiment of southern whites.

But dissatisfaction must be accompanied by the presence of a leader
within one of the two major parties who is willing to bolt and form a third
party. Since such a move against one's party ruins a politician's future career within that party, the act is not taken lightly. Moderate Republican representative John Anderson viewed no future for himself in the Republican
Party when he ran as an independent in 1980. Many political leaders contemplate the move but ultimately shrink from it because of its career effects. For example, Ronald Reagan was recruited to head a new conservative party in the 1970s. Reagan's decision to remain with the Republican
Party ultimately produced his Republican presidential nomination in 1980
and subsequent election.[18]

It is the short-term party movement that attracts the attention of the public, the press, and political scientists.[19] That phenomenon is understand-

able. They feature high-profile political leaders such as Theodore Roosevelt, Bob LaFollette, George Wallace, and Ross Perot. The drama of the political leader bolting from a major party becomes highly newsworthy, and these movements gain a significant number of voters who possess the ability to throw elections in one direction or another.

LONGEVITY OF THE PARTY: LONG-TERM MINOR PARTIES

Long-term minor parties are those that persist over multiple elections and over two or more decades. They are more permanent fixtures of the American political landscape. However, their diminutive size is their weakness. As a result, political scientists have been less interested in researching long-term minor parties. In 1983, Frank Smallwood interviewed leaders of various long-term minor parties at the time, such as the Communist Party, the Socialist Workers Party, and the Prohibition Party. In 1997, Paul S. Herrnson and John C. Green edited a volume that included chapters on long-term minor parties at that time—Libertarians, Greens, and the Reform Party. And some scholars have studied individual minor parties, such as the Communist Party, the Socialist Party, and the Libertarian Party.[20] Yet, long-term minor parties in general are considered aberrations to the two-party system that have minimal effect on electoral outcomes.

Nevertheless, scholars, the press, and the public should pay more attention to them. They have acquired a lasting place in the party system, even if the individual party influence has been minimal. And they constitute an interesting phenomenon—that of organizers, members, and voters supporting a political party that rarely wins elections or, in most cases, even comes close. They gain support from an ardent party base even in the face of likely losses. At the same time, party organizers often are optimistic about their chances to break through the existing two-party system, particularly since a few historical examples have proven that outcome is not impossible.

Besides the commonality of not being one of the two major parties, these two types of minor parties are best understood by their differences. A key distinction is the party leader, who rarely has broad notoriety and cannot bring attention to the party through celebrity status. These parties do not exist because of the efforts of a major-party politician who seeks to win election through other means than association with a major party. Rather, these party supporters are organization oriented rather than individual-oriented.

Another is the relative permanence of competition by long-term minor parties compared to short-term ones. By definition, short-term minor parties emerge quickly and usually disappear suddenly. Long-term minor parties compete in successive elections. For example, the Libertarians have run presidential candidates in each election since 1972. The Greens have done the same since 2000.

Unlike short-term parties, long-term parties receive small percentages of the vote—typically in low single digits. They face the psychological barriers Duverger discusses. Losses can lead typical major-party voters, who may agree with the minor party candidate, to stick with a major party likely to win and make their vote count. However, long-term minor parties also run candidates who possess low name recognition, receive little media attention, and are never invited to participate in the debates offered by the Presidential Debate Commission. Also, they usually do not qualify for federal campaign finance grants. And they are unable to raise sufficient funds to compete effectively against major parties, or even third parties.

Another distinction is the base. Long-term minor-party supporters are usually viewed as so ideological that they can sustain interest in the party and its cause, even in the face of repeated losses. Short-term party voters, however, tend to focus on a single issue or small set of issues rather than an ideology. Once a major party addresses the issue, they are inclined to return to the major party. But long-term minor party supporters reject the two main parties precisely because they do not address the minor parties' issues or they consider them to be too ideologically moderate for their tastes.

Admittedly, long-term minor parties often attempt to become popular. Some long-term minor-party supporters, particularly the more pragmatic segment, long for the vote totals of short-term parties. However, at the presidential level, only the Socialists have come close to bridging the divide. As a party that fielded presidential candidates over several decades, the Socialist Party clearly fit the moniker of a minor party. Yet, the Socialists did win more than a percentage or two of the votes in a couple of elections. In 1912 and again in 1920, Socialist Party candidate Eugene Debs won over nine hundred thousand votes, which constituted 6 percent of the total vote in 1912 and 3 percent in 1920 (following the passage of the Twentieth Amendment extending suffrage to women). Subsequent to the 1920 election, the Socialists returned to the normal vote share as a minor party.

More recently, some long-term minor parties have sought to break through the typical tiny vote percentage threshold, particularly by nominating presidential candidates with some prior name recognition. For the first several elections their candidates competed in, the Libertarians nominated candidates with no electoral experience. However, in 1988, former US representative Ron Paul became the Libertarian Party nominee. But Paul won only 0.05 percent of the vote.[21] The strategy seemed more successful in

2016. Gary Johnson, former New Mexico governor, became the Libertarian candidate that year and exceeded the typical Libertarian vote by gaining over 3 percent of the total vote—or, over 4 million votes. However, when Johnson ran in 2012, he garnered only 1 percent, suggesting the 2016 election dynamics helped the Libertarians more than Johnson's candidacy.

Other parties have adopted the same tack. The Constitution Party recruited a more high-profile candidate in 2012 when it nominated former US representative Virgil Goode. Twelve years earlier, the party attempted to recruit talk show host Alan Keyes as its presidential candidate. Keyes declined at the time.[22] Of course, Ralph Nader's run on the Green Party ticket in 2000 generated attention for the new party.

However, the presence of a well-known outsider candidate can raise tensions within the party, either through factional disputes between pragmatists and purists or concerns the outsider candidate is not sufficiently devoted to the party. When Keyes finally accepted the Constitution Party's offer eight years later, the party rejected his bid because party founder Howard Phillips questioned Keyes's commitment to the party's issue positions.[23] Similarly, Libertarians worried about two high-profile presidential candidates in 1988 (Paul and Native American activist Russell Means) because party loyalists were concerned that neither candidate had long-term association with the Libertarian Party and would use their respective candidacies to promote their own agendas.[24]

CONTEMPORARY MINOR PARTIES

The short-term/long-term dichotomy mainly applies retrospectively since we do not know which contemporary political parties will be short term or long term. But we can create a typology including long-term national parties, short-term national parties, long-term regional parties, short-term regional parties, and long- and short-term state-centric parties that demonstrate the distinctions among minor parties. (See Table I.2.)

Since those earlier studies of minor parties, there have been significant developments in minor party creation. A new development in the twenty-first century is the increasing number of state-specific parties. This book will discuss some of them—the Moderate Party of Rhode Island, the Vermont Progressive Party, the Mountain Party (West Virginia), and the United Utah Party. These parties may have some affiliation with national parties. For example, the Mountain Party is affiliated with the Green Party of the United States. Yet, others are unaffiliated nationally. But even when affiliations exist, the parties have retained their own name, organization, and platform.

Table I.2: US Minor Parties Typology—Level and Longevity Examples

	Long-term	Short-term
National	Libertarian	Progressive (1912)
	Green	Progressive (1912)
	Constitution	Reform (1990s, early 2000s)
Regional	Working Families	Anti-Masonic (1830s)
	Legal Marijuana Now	People's (1890s, early 1900s)
		States' Rights (1948)
State-Centric	Farmer-Labor, MN (1918–1944)	Home Rule, HI (early 1900s)
	Liberal, NY (1944–2002)	Illinois Solidarity (1980s, 1990s)
	Right to Life, NY (1970–2002)	A Connecticut Party (1990s)
	Conservative, NY	
	American Independent, CA	
	Mountain, WV	
	Vermont Progressive	
	Peace and Freedom, CA	

State-centric parties match the federal nature of the US electoral system, but they also reflect the reality of American politics. Starting a national third party is a daunting process. Ross Perot attempted to do it in the 1990s with the creation of the Reform Party. The Reform Party was a centrist party that, thanks to Perot's personal largesse and then-qualifications for federal matching funds for the 1996 and 2000 elections, remained a force at the national level longer than most third parties. The party succeeded in electing Jesse Ventura as governor of Minnesota, but other victories were only local. The party faded into insignificance.

The candidacy of Representative John Anderson, a liberal Republican, was the first to attempt to give a home to moderate voters. Anderson ran as an independent in response to the Republican nomination of Ronald Reagan, who did not appeal to moderate Republicans and represented the success of the antiestablishment right wing within the Republican Party. However, the Democratic Party candidate, incumbent Jimmy Carter, was considered a weak and indecisive president who had offended many elements within his own party.[25] Ross Perot's run twelve years later sought to appeal to a similar set of voters who were unhappy with the choice between incumbent George H. W. Bush and Bill Clinton.

The Reform Party Ross Perot started in the mid-1990s began the era of centrist, nonideologically doctrinaire parties, which have sprung up across the nation. While minor parties traditionally have been single-issue oriented (such as the Prohibition Party and the Right to Life Party) or ideological (Libertarian, Constitution, or Green), these new parties seek to occupy the middle of the ideological spectrum. The Moderate Party of Rhode Island explains that it was designed to appeal to "the moderate middle" while the United Utah Party states it seeks to "focus on practical solutions based on common sense and common ground."[26]

Historically, minor parties occupying the middle of the spectrum have been rare. According to Duverger, the absence of "center" parties in two-party systems is due to the dearth of a real political center. There are only moderates of the left or the right. According to Duverger, "Every centre is divided against itself and remains separated into two halves, Left-Centre and Right-Center. For the Centre is nothing more than the artificial grouping of the right wing of the Left and the left wing of the Right."[27]

Yet, according to our survey, minor-party supporters are primarily moderates. Fifty-three percent of them self-identified as ideologically moderate, 25 percent were very liberal or liberal, and only 22 percent very conservative or conservative. (See Table I.3.) That belies the image of minor-party adherents as extremists. Their moderation contrasts significantly with the ideology of Democrats and Republicans. Sixty percent of Democrats self-identified as liberal or very liberal, while 68 percent of Republicans identified as conservative or very conservative. The large number of moderates among minor-party supporters might suggest that these voters are seeking some alternative to the extremism they see in the two major parties.

Recent attempts to form a national minor-party of the middle have failed or are still in nascent stages. After Perot's run in 1996, the Reform Party nominated a known strong conservative columnist, former Nixon White House aide and former GOP presidential candidate Patrick Buchanan, in 2000. Buchanan won less than 1 percent of the vote. (Ironically, Donald Trump briefly entered the Reform Party presidential nomination contest that year.) America Elect, organized in 2010, sought to form a national third party around a presidential nominee in 2012 by holding a national online primary. The bipartisan organization obtained general election ballot access in a majority of states, but no presidential candidate met the group's requirements for the nomination ballot.[28]

Currently, the Serve America Movement (SAM), formed in 2017, has attempted to create a new national third party based on centrism. The party was started by former Republicans and Democrats who have sought to attract moderate Republicans as well as centrist Democrats. The party won ballot access in New York state in 2018 when its candidate, a former mayor of Syracuse, won slightly less than 1 percent of the vote.[29]

Table I.3: Minor- and Major-Party Supporters Compared

	Minor Party (%)	Democrat (%)	Republican (%)	Unaffiliated (%)
How long affiliated?				
Less than 1 year	20	6	5	N/A
1–5 years	40	22	24	N/A
6–10 years	14	11	11	N/A
Over 10 years	26	61	61	N/A
How voted in 2016?				
Donald Trump	27	6	83	30
Hillary Clinton	25	82	6	29
Jill Stein	8	1	1	4
Gary Johnson	17	3	2	8
Darrel Castle	0	0	0	0
Evan McMullin	3	0	1	4
Other/DN	19	7	6	24
Ideology				
Very liberal	10	19	1	3
Liberal	15	40	3	13
Moderate	53	34	27	63
Conservative	17	5	44	15
Very conservative	5	1	25	6

Another effort is technically not a political party, although in some respects it has acted like one. Unite America has sought to form a national organization by recruiting and supporting independent candidates throughout the United States. Initially formed as the Centrist Project in 2013, Unite America endorsed several independent candidates in 2018 for US Senate or governor, although none exceeded single-digit vote percentages.[30]

Jacob Lentz has termed these new moderate parties "pragmatic-utilitarian" parties due to their focus on pragmatism over ideology.[31] These parties eschew—in fact, inveigh against—doctrinaire ideology that characterizes the typical minor parties: Socialists, Greens, Libertarians, among others. They view the Republican and Democratic parties as new carriers of such ideological dogmatism. According to Lentz: "If a third party can avoid being constrained by an ideology or set of issues and instead embraces a wide-ranging pragmatic approach to government, it positions itself for electoral success."[32]

Are minor parties growing in number and significance? Is there more of a future for minor parties today than in the twentieth century? Will these new parties be different—more grassroots, more state oriented? And will they be parties of the center rather than ideological parties such as the Libertarians or the Greens?

COMPARATIVE MODELS OF MINOR-PARTY DYNAMISM

Are these questions even legitimate? Is the two-party system so entrenched that significant minor-party role—or even displacement of a major party— is impossible to contemplate? One answer may come from other examples of minor-party dynamism. The cases of Britain and Canada may provide models of how a two-party system can be transformed into a multiparty system without electoral structure adjustment.

Britain

In 2010, Britain formed its first coalition government since World War II when the Conservatives and the Liberal Democrats combined to acquire a parliamentary majority. Then, another coalition (albeit a more limited one) was formed in 2017 between the Conservatives and the Democratic Union Party of Northern Ireland. These coalitions involving a major party and a minor party were emblematic of the dramatic shifts in UK party politics that had occurred in the intervening half century. Britain had moved from a system where the two parties monopolized the vote to a multiparty system. All of this occurred despite the fact that Britain's electoral system fit Duverger's law for a two-party system.

Since the success of the Labour Party in the 1920s that displaced the Liberal Party, Britain's electoral system had been a contest between the Conservative Party and the Labour Party. That duopoly was shaken in 1981 when a new party—the Social Democrats—formed. The party, formed by Labour Party moderates, created an alliance with the Liberals in the next two elections and then combined as a new party: the Liberal Democrats.[33] The party won 25 percent of the vote in the first national election after its formation and 23 percent in the second but, due to the first-past-the-post system, was unable to translate that vote count into more than a relative handful of Parliamentary seats. Yet, the party's formation signaled a shift in the duopoly of British politics.

It was shaken again with successive new parties. The Scottish Nationalist Party became a potent force in British politics when it gained a majority of seats in the Scottish Parliament in 2007 and elected nearly every member from Scotland to the British Parliament in 2010. The party's power in Westminster declined by 2017, but it still ruled in Edinburgh.[34]

In 1993, the United Kingdom Independent Party (UKIP) was created by dissidents from the Conservative Party. The Euro-skeptic party had little traction in British politics for twenty years until it won seats in local elections in 2013, garnered nearly 13 percent of the vote in the 2015 general election, and achieved its goal of winning the Brexit referendum in 2016. The party lost badly in the 2017 election but had made its mark through Brexit.[35]

The rise of smaller parties has impacted public support for the two major parties. Over a forty-year period up to 2015, the share of the vote for the two major parties steadily fell, although it did rise again in 2017. One scholar concluded that: "It does not seem too strong to talk about the end of duopoly."[36]

The crises in Britain may not be applicable to the United States. There is no serious devolution movement toward autonomy in the United States, as is true with Scotland. There was no Brexit referendum. Yet, there are similarities in the sense that national crises have challenged the two-party system, and voters considered the traditional large parties incapable of addressing those crises. For example, in the UK, neither the Labour nor Conservative Party addressed the anti–EU feeling that the UKIP capitalized on. Nor could they have advocated Scottish nationalism, even though large numbers of Scottish voters supported that outcome. As far as the role of the Liberal Democrats, their existence was due to the growing concern that the Labour Party was out of touch with UK voters.

Canada

For nearly a century of Canadian history, Canada was a two-party system with power alternating between the Liberals and the Conservatives.[37] Other parties, such as the Social Credit Party in Alberta and the Progressive Party in Manitoba gained traction at the provincial level. But they were unable to become a federal major party.

The New Democratic Party (NDP) formed in 1961 and transformed Canada into a two-and-a-half-party system. For thirty years, the NDP received less than 20 percent of the vote and typically received less than 10 percent of the Parliamentary seats. It did form governments in one province (British Columbia) during that period.

However, the past thirty years of Canadian politics have tipped upside down the two-and-a-half-party system. With five parties competing at one time, Canada is a much more complex system. Since 1993, minor parties have become major parties in Canadian politics, if briefly. A brand new political party, formed by former members of the Progressive Conservative Party (PC) who felt their former party was not conservative enough, decimated the PC in the 1993 elections to become the third parliamentary party. The Reform Party eventually formed an alliance with the Progressive Conservatives to create the Conservative Party. The Bloc Quebecois was the second largest parliamentary party for four years in the 1990s because of the fragmentation of the political parties in the rest of Canada. The New Democrats also served as the second largest parliamentary party from 2011 to 2015. The Green Party polled at 10 percent in the run-up to the 2019 federal elections.

Minor parties have also flourished at the provincial level. They currently control four of the ten provinces: Alberta, British Columbia, Saskatchewan, and Quebec. And, in British Columbia, two minor parties—the NDP and the Greens—control the province in a coalition.

The two-and-half-party system collapsed for various reasons. They boil down to regionalism, ideology, and leadership. One aspect of regionalism was the growing sentiment in Quebec for separation, or at least greater autonomy, which fostered the growth of the Bloc Quebecois at the federal level and the Parti Quebecois and the Coalition Avenir Quebec. Neither the Liberals nor the Conservatives effectively addressed this sentiment. Another factor, also geographical, was the 1990s split within the Conservative Party that produced the western-based Reform Party, a party that expressed the concerns of western Conservatives that the PC Party was ignoring them.

Canada's reputation as a multicultural, socially tolerant society embraced by Liberals and accepted by the PC was challenged by the Reform Party. Reform Party supporters viewed the PC as failing to address the concerns of Canada's social and economic conservatives. When the two parties joined in 2003, the new Conservative Party was decidedly more conservative than its predecessor, the PC.

Party leadership has also been a factor. Increasing leadership control of party organizations has heightened the importance of a leader in a party's electoral fortunes. Leader debates that have included minor parties have reinforced the salience of leaders but also offered minor-party leaders an opportunity to demonstrate leadership qualities before a national audience. The NDP's own dynamic leader, Jack Layton, briefly propelled the party to second-party status. However, leadership also moved the pendulum in the other direction when Layton died in 2013 and Justin Trudeau emerged as an energetic new leader for the Liberal Party.

RECENT FACTORS AFFECTING MINOR-PARTY GROWTH AND IMPACT

Britain's and Canada's electoral systems differ from that of the United States in significant ways that this treatment of their changes is not intended to gloss over. However, the point of potential transformation of a party system remains. The US system, similarly, is a more dynamic entity than is generally realized. Shocks to the system have occurred and may yet occur.

Ross Perot's 1992 candidacy unsettled the electoral system. As a non-major-party candidate, Perot received the largest percentage of the popular vote since Theodore Roosevelt in 1912. What was remarkable about Perot's candidacy was the breadth of his support, as opposed to the typical regional or demographic base of twentieth-century candidates. Perot did poorly among minority voters, but he performed as well with younger voters as he did with middle-aged ones. His worst performance came with older voters, who may have held closely to their long-term party affiliation. Middle-class voters and poor voters supported him in nearly equal numbers.[38]

Perot emerged from the middle of the political spectrum rather than its fringes. In fact, he was difficult to define ideologically. He was not intending to be more conservative than the Republican or more liberal than the Democrat. His approach was pragmatic: fix the deficit, protect the American economy, implement direct democracy. His message was particularly appealing to voters who self-identified as independent because it was nonpartisan.

Academics also responded with a plethora of books and articles on the party system in the United States. Steven J. Rosenstone, Roy L. Behr, and Edward H. Lazarus wrote about why the major parties were failing to address citizens' concerns and the conditions under which minor parties could emerge. Paul S. Herrnson and John C. Green's edited volume examined several of the existing minor parties in the late 1990s—Reform, Libertarians, and Greens, as well as the long-standing multiparty system in New York State. J. David Gillespie went further in detailing a range of smaller parties extant in the 1990s that occupied the periphery of the party system. Debates ensued about whether the nation was on the verge of a three-party system, and whether that would be a good thing.[39]

In the past twenty-five years, no presidential candidate has emerged like

Ross Perot, even though several minor-party candidates have run. One (Ralph Nader) was even credited with playing kingmaker by inadvertently helping George W. Bush win in 2000. Does that mean minor parties have become unimportant again? The 2016 presidential election suggests otherwise.

The 2016 presidential election was dramatic in its outcome—the surprise election of Donald Trump. However, another surprise outcome was the increasing share of the vote won by minor parties and independent candidates. Gary Johnson, the Libertarian candidate, garnered 3.3 percent of the vote. That was the best performance by a minor-party candidate since Perot's 1996 Reform Party bid. Jill Stein, the Green Party candidate, won 1 percent of the vote.

The combined vote for all minor-party and independent candidates was over 6 percent. By contrast, in the three preceding presidential elections, other candidates garnered less than 2 percent of the presidential vote. The 2016 vote for other parties and candidates was the highest total for non-major-party candidates since 1996 but also the first time since 1912 that two minor-party presidential candidates won that high a percentage of the vote.

The 2016 election may be an aberration. However, the persistent talk of a 2020 presidential campaign emerging outside the two major parties suggested it may not be. In 2019, several prominent politicians, including former senator Jeff Flake of Arizona, businessperson Mark Cuban, and former Ohio governor John Kasich, were publicly considering independent runs while business executive Howard Shultz was actively soliciting support as an independent presidential candidate. Ultimately, such talk faded as these potential candidates considered the enormity of the task as well as the possibility of splitting the anti-Trump vote and helping reelect the president.[40]

According to our survey of voters, a large proportion of minor-party supporters recently rejected other parties. While 28 percent of Democrats and Republicans said they had been affiliated with their party for five years or less, 60 percent of minor-party supporters had been in their parties that short a time. (See Table I.3.) Also, while the vast majority of major-party supporters said they had not been affiliated with any other party in the past other than the one they were in now, two-thirds of minor-party supporters said they had been major-party supporters previously.

Minor-party supporters seem to be willing to stand by themselves. When asked if other family members belonged to their party, only 31 percent said that was true. And 54 percent said they were not a Republican or Democrat because they wanted to lodge a protest against the two major parties.

At the state level, the rejection of the two major-party candidates in some places was even more profound. In three states, the non-major-party candidates combined won over 10 percent of the vote. (In Utah, independent presidential candidate Evan McMullin won 21 percent of the vote. That was the largest percentage for a non-major-party presidential candidate in a state since 1992.) In twenty-five states, the "other" candidates beyond Trump and Hillary Clinton combined earned over 5 percent of the vote. In one-quarter of the states, the vote totals of the other candidates prevented either major-party candidate from winning a majority of the vote in that state.

The vote totals for other candidates in that particular election may be attributed to widespread dissatisfaction with the two major-party candidates. Both Trump and Clinton had higher unfavorable ratings than favorable among the general public.[41] No two major-party presidential candidates had been so widely disliked among voters since public opinion polling began.

But other evidence suggests the two major parties may be facing new and serious challenges to their dominant electoral position that precede and extend beyond the 2016 presidential election. Voters in some states are increasingly electing candidates who do not belong to either of the two major parties. Currently, there are two independent members of the US Senate: Bernie Sanders of Vermont and Angus King of Maine. Sanders was elected in 2006 as an independent and has been reelected twice since. Despite the fact that both formally caucus with the Democratic Party, their independence is so important that they have resisted an attempt by the Democratic National Committee urging them to register with the party rather than as an independents when they run for reelection, although Sanders changed his affiliation in order to run for president in 2020.[42]

As mentioned earlier, Alaska elected an independent governor, Bill Walker, in 2014, although Walker, a former Republican, also received the Democratic Party nomination. His running mate was a Democrat. Walker withdrew from his reelection bid in 2018 and backed the Democratic candidate.

In 2016, David Zuckerman was elected lieutenant governor of Vermont. Zuckerman belonged to the Vermont Progressive Party, a state-centric minor party. He also won the Democratic Party nomination that year.

No nonmajor parties are represented in Congress currently. However, minor parties are represented in various state legislatures. Ten Vermont legislators belong to the Vermont Progressive Party, while three state legislators in New Hampshire belong to the Libertarian Party—two (one in Connecticut and one in New York) are affiliated with the Working Families

Party and one (Maine) belongs to the Green Party. The Libertarians claim 166 elected officials across the country, while the Greens say they have 156. However, these include many offices that are not partisan, such as mayors, city councilors, special commission members, and school board members who would not have been elected specifically as Libertarian or Green Party candidates.

Over the past half century, minor-party candidates running for federal and statewide office typically have received only 2 or 3 percent of the vote in an election. That result usually assures the party continued spots on the ballot but demonstrates a distinct lack of support within the electorate. However, some races within the past five years have bucked that trend and confounded the conventional wisdom about the electoral strength of minor parties.

Non-major-party candidates have done better than expected in recent statewide races. In 2014, an independent candidate won nearly 12 percent of the vote for governor of Hawaii. That same year, the Moderate Party of Rhode Island's candidate for governor won 21 percent of the vote, while a US Senate candidate in South Dakota garnered 17 percent and an independent candidate for governor in Kansas captured 43 percent. Two years later, the Libertarian Party candidate for US Senate in Alaska won 29 percent of the vote. In 2018, a United Utah Party candidate for Congress won 12 percent of the vote.

What factors might explain this new phenomenon of a larger-than-usual percentage of voters casting their votes for non-major-party candidates, either at the presidential or state levels?

Public Dissatisfaction with Major Parties

The growth of minor political parties is driven by a mounting perception that public opinion has created space in the electoral spectrum for alternatives. Approximately two of five Americans consider themselves independent of either major political party when measured on a three-point partisan scale. According to the Pew Research Center, independent voters have been the largest voting bloc since 2008, with that group gradually increasing in size.[43]

At the same time, when measured on a seven-point scale, the percentage who identify as purely independent drops precipitously, suggesting that few Americans are completely detached from political parties. Most independents do identify themselves as independent Democrats or Republicans and seek to fit themselves within the two-party paradigm. However, the percentage who self-assess as "leaning independent" has generally grown over several decades.[44] Nevertheless, the large number of Americans with weak partisan attachments suggests a vacuum that the two major parties may not be filling.

Polls show a large majority of Americans favor the formation of a third party. Our survey found that 67 percent of respondents felt a third party was needed, while 33 percent believed the two parties did an adequate job. Support for a third party has existed for several years. Since 2013, around three-fifths of Americans have expressed the need for a third-party option. Young people are even more supportive. In a 2017 NBC News/GenForward poll, 71 percent of millennials reported they wanted a third party formed.[45]

That support varies considerably, however, depending on party affiliation. According to our survey, 49 percent of Republicans saw the need for a third party compared with 64 percent of Democrats. Minor-party supporters, not surprisingly, were most supportive: 84 percent!

Another indication of the uncertainty of the electorate regarding the two major parties is the presence of significant attitudinal shifts among younger voters. They are moving toward lower agreement with their political parties on key issues. For example, younger Republican voters tend to be more environmentally conscious than older Republicans. Millennials are generally more liberal than previous generations.[46]

Millennials are more likely to detach themselves from a political party than older generations. According to the Pew Research Center, half of millennials consider themselves political independents compared to one-third to two-fifths of older generations. And, compared to other generations, millennials are more likely to say there is "hardly any difference" between the two major parties.[47] In our survey, minor-party supporters were slightly younger than major-party supporters. Fifty-three percent of those who affiliated with a minor party were under forty-five compared with 47 percent of Republicans and 46 percent of Democrats.

According to our survey, Democrats and Republicans are willing to vote for a minor-party candidate under certain circumstances. Eighty percent said they were at least somewhat likely to do so if the candidate agreed with "my views on issues important to me." Half of those who said that indicated they were "very likely" to do so. Another factor was candidate viability. Three-fifths said they were at least somewhat likely to vote for a minor-party candidate if they were "polling close enough to the major-party candidates to win." And 53 percent said they were at least somewhat likely to vote for a minor-party candidate if they had "met the candidate."

The lack of media coverage of minor-party candidates leads to the lack of name recognition, which in turn contributes to the perception of lack of viability. This is a vicious cycle. Nearly half of our survey respondents said they would be at least somewhat likely to vote for a candidate if they had "heard a lot about the candidate in the media." But the odds they will hear much about a minor-party candidate are low. Few non-major-party candidates win extensive name recognition. In 1992, Ross Perot was one exception. At the state level, Jesse Ventura achieved significant name recognition in 1998 in Minnesota. Those cases are rare. Voters will not go out of their way to look beyond traditional media coverage. In our survey, 52 percent of voters said they "rarely or never" seek out information about candidates other than those from the two major parties. Only 12 percent of these major-party supporters said they do so "very often" in an election year.

Voters often give themselves more credit for openness than they actually demonstrate in the voting booth. In our survey, 43 percent of major-party supporters said that if they were unhappy with the candidate of their own party, they would vote for a non-major-party candidate. One-fourth said they would vote for the other major-party candidate, while nearly one in three said they simply would not vote for anyone for that office.

Yet, the tendency of these same voters to support their own party is high. Eighty-four percent of major-party voters in our survey said they vote for the candidate of their own party "most of the time" or "always," while 32 percent said they always do. And 85 percent said they "rarely or never" voted for a candidate other than one from a major party. Only 25 percent of major-party supporters said they were at least somewhat likely to vote for a minor-party candidate in the 2020 election, with only 7 percent saying they are "highly likely" to do so.

Even minor-party supporters are drawn to the two major parties. In our survey, 79 percent of minor-party supporters at least agreed (with 51 percent strongly agreeing) that it is better to vote one's conscience than to vote for a candidate because she or he may win. And 54 percent said they do not believe in the ideology of the two major parties. That would suggest a tendency to vote for their own party's candidate regardless of viability. Yet, 47 percent said they would vote for a major-party candidate to prevent the other major-party candidate from winning, and 52 percent of minor-party supporters admitted that, in 2016, they did vote for a major-party candidate rather than one from a minor party. That lack of support, even for their own party's candidate, suggests the uphill climb minor parties face in even getting the vote of those who affiliate with them. (See Table I.1.)

Public dissatisfaction with the two major parties has not yet translated into minor-party support. Voters are not yet conducting a widespread search for other candidates from other parties. Nor has it resulted in voting patterns rejecting the two major parties. This presents a problem for minor political parties in breaking through the behavior of voting for the major-party candidate, even if a minor-party candidate is on the ballot.

Utilizing Traditional Media and Social Media

Traditional news organizations rarely cover minor parties or their candidates, particularly in comparison with the attention devoted to major-party candidates. Yet, traditional news media coverage today is not out of reach. Minor parties have become savvy in their use of media, particularly in the choice of candidates. Celebrity candidates gain greater recognition for the party and draw in voters.

Jesse Ventura's background as a professional wrestler, as well as his malapropisms, gave him more-than-typical news coverage for a non-major-party candidate.[48] News media coverage of the novelty of the presence and activity of the new political party and its candidates has become the focus of party- and candidate-generated news. In the case of Ventura, news media organizations focused on the novelty of his campaign rather than his more controversial background.[49]

Another example is the nomination of television actor Cynthia Nixon by the Working Families Party in the New York gubernatorial race. Nixon's nomination became newsworthy when Nixon lost the Democratic Party nomination but potentially remained on the ballot through her endorsement by the Working Families Party. Ultimately, Nixon withdrew and the party endorsed the Democratic candidate, Governor Andrew Cuomo, but her possible candidacy gained attention for the party as it decided whether to stick with Nixon or turn back to Cuomo in the general election.[50]

However, another tool exists today that was not available to minor political parties a quarter century ago. Prior to the internet and social media, minor political parties, like interest groups and social movements, faced a high barrier to organizing—the cost of communicating with members and supporters. Other forms of communication such as newsletters, magazines, and direct mail were costly for minor parties relying on shoestring budgets.

Today, those costs have been lowered dramatically. Minor parties can create websites for a fraction of the cost of direct mail campaigns. Social media platforms can take the messages of minor parties viral. Even without sharing with hundreds of thousands or even millions of voters, social media provides reinforcement and mobilization for at least the thousands or tens of thousands of supporters of minor parties. Indeed, our survey found that minor-party supporters were significantly more likely to get their news about party activities from social media than were major-party supporters, and they were less likely to gather such information from traditional media than were major-party adherents.

How are minor parties utilizing social media? Has the presence of social media affected the formation, organization, and messaging of minor parties? Will it affect electoral outcomes of the future?

Financing Minor-Party Campaigns

Minor parties are vastly outspent by major parties. This is true not only at the presidential level but also in state and local campaigns. The financial difference is particularly evident in advertising. As mentioned above, social media can reduce advertising costs since ads on Facebook or other social media platforms cost a tiny fraction of the amount for broadcast television advertising. But such advertising is limited in reach compared to television. And minor-party candidates rarely possess sufficient funds to advertise on television—an expenditure that still constitutes the bulk of candidate spending.

However, public financing policies have grown in number at the state and municipal levels. The acceptance of public financing has not been without setbacks. Some states, such as California and Wisconsin, have repealed public financing programs due to lack of legislative or public support. Nevertheless, twelve states currently use some form of public financing in partisan statewide or legislative races. Five of those states have initiated these programs since the mid-1990s. Three states—Maine, Arizona, and Connecticut—offer full funding.[51]

Public financing includes minor-party candidates, although they still must qualify for the funds. The treatment of minor parties in these programs has varied across states. Maine and Arizona have not distinguished between major- and minor-party candidates. However, Connecticut's law requires minor-party candidates to jump through additional hoops, such as receiving 10 percent of the vote in the previous election or gathering petition signatures equaling 10 percent of the votes cast in the prior election.[52]

At the presidential level, minor parties have gained some benefits from public financing, although the operation of the system has advantaged major-party candidates over minor-party candidates. For example, the threshold for receiving a general election grant is 5 percent in the previous election.[53] Since the beginning of federal campaign financing, only Ross Perot gained the necessary qualification for general election funds. Moreover, general election grants for minor-party candidates are granted only after an election. However, the grant can be used by the party for the next election.

Minor-party candidates do qualify for primary election-matching funds. Presidential candidates for the Libertarian, Green, Reform, and Natural Law Party have been awarded primary matching funds. In 2016, Jill Stein, the Green Party candidate, was awarded nearly half a million dollars, while Ralph Nader received nearly $900,000 in 2004. In presidential races, these amounts are miniscule compared to those awarded to major-party candidates. And the gap between major and minor parties has grown with the abandonment of federal primary matching and general election funds by serious major-party contenders. For example, in 2016, only one major-party presidential candidate took primary matching funds, and none received the general election grants.[54]

At the state level, financial assistance for a minor-party candidate can be significant as well. In Minnesota, Reform Party gubernatorial candidate Jesse Ventura was able to qualify for $326,000 in public money. Twelve years later, Independence Party candidate Tom Horner received $346,000 in state campaign funds.[55]

The trend in state public financing raises questions about the effects on minor parties. Has the growth of public financing programs in the past two decades helped minor-party candidates compete? If more states turn to public funding in the wake of concerns over the nexus between wealthy individual donors and corporations, will minor parties be discriminated against or will new programs be more minor-party friendly?

Fusion

Fusion has helped minor political parties by allowing them to gain the attention of major parties through ballot coalitions. Through fusion, a minor political party can influence a major party's nomination, influence the decisions of candidates concerning which issues to press in order to gain a minor party's nomination and boost their electoral chances, and influence the outcome of an election by either enhancing the winning candidate's voting percentage with a cross endorsement or electing an opposing candidate by splitting the vote between a major party and the minor party.

The party also may be more successful in obtaining its legislative agenda if it has cross-endorsed a successful candidate who owes their election (or at least not their defeat) to the efforts of the minor party. Such an outcome allows the minor party to gain credibility as a political player in the larger political environment rather than remaining a minor party without power. The minor party can claim credit that enhances its legitimacy with its own supporters.

Even better for the party is the possibility that a party supporter allies with a wing of a major party and wins that nomination as well. One example is the Vermont Progressive Party, which, through fusion, has elected candidates in tandem with the Democratic Party and placed its own supporters in elective office. As stated earlier, the current lieutenant governor of Vermont is a member of the Progressive Party who also won the Democratic Party nomination.[56]

At the same time, fusion has a long history of harming minor parties.[57] Fusion was a factor in the People's Party's relationship with the Democratic Party when Democrats fused their own candidates with the Populist Party. This increased the likelihood of Populist support among Democrats, but split off Republican-leaning Populists who were hostile to the Democrats.[58] The most dramatic case of fusion involving the Populists was the 1896 presidential campaign fusion between the Democrats and the Populists in support of William Jennings Bryan. That fusion led to the decline of the Populists.

The best example of fusion's effect on the party system is New York's model. Minor parties have been successful in gaining and maintaining ballot access through fusion. They have acquired a place in the political landscape as major-party politicians often court the endorsement of minor parties in order to strengthen their own major-party bids. This model has been advocated for other states' electoral systems as well.[59]

Most states ban electoral fusion. However, its availability in New York is an indication that minor parties can use it to advance the party's purposes. Vermont's Progressive Party has employed it there to cross-list progressive candidates with the Democratic Party.

Moreover, efforts to enact fusion have been attempted in several states in the past decade, including New Jersey, New Mexico, Virginia, Arizona, and Minnesota. At the same time, Connecticut has limited the applicability of fusion voting, and New York legislators have considered banning the practice altogether.[60] Either way, fusion is likely to affect minor parties for some time to come.

Debate Rules

One of the indicators of legitimacy in a race for a third- or minor-party candidate is the ability to participate on the same debate stage as the major-party candidates. For example, Ross Perot's inclusion in the 1992 presiden-

tial debates, which Perot was credited as winning, helped him gain credibility as a presidential candidate. Even more significantly, the League of
Women Voters' inclusion of Jesse Ventura in the 1998 gubernatorial debates offered him an opportunity to compete effectively and win that year's
gubernatorial election.[61]

For several decades following the reintroduction of debates in political
campaigns during the 1960s and 1970s, debate sponsors sought to exclude
such candidates on the grounds that their presence would confuse the electorate with too many choices or limit the time each candidate had to answer
questions. Another complaint is that minor-party candidates plan to woo
voters primarily through the debates rather than conduct their own active
campaigns.

However, organizers of debates have faced increasing pressure to lower
their participation thresholds to allow non-major-party candidates to debate.
The Presidential Debate Commission set a threshold of 15 percent. Only
one non-major-party candidate, Ross Perot in 1992, has met that threshold
to date. But the commission has faced lawsuits and advertiser pressure to reduce the thresholds to allow minor-party candidates to participate.

Some debate sponsors have responded to that pressure by lowering
thresholds beyond those set by the Presidential Debate Commission. The
Utah Debate Commission, formed in 2013, set a threshold of 10 percent.
The Indiana Debate Commission allows any candidate qualified to appear
on the ballot to participate in its debates.

Lowering the thresholds means more inclusion of minor-party candi-
dates and a better opportunity to gain public exposure and legitimacy.
Perot was viewed as the winner of at least one of the 1992 debates. Similarly,
Ventura was widely praised for his debate performances in 1998.

Have new policies regarding debate inclusion offered new opportunities
for minor-party candidates that did not exist a quarter century ago? Will
minor parties' candidates' debate performance gain the attention of voters,
particularly in a political context of public dissatisfaction with major-party
choices?

Future Developments: Multimember Districts and Ranked-Choice Voting

Various electoral reforms have been proposed that could reshape the two-
party system. These include majority (rather than plurality) elections, easy
ballot access, or even increasing the size of Congress.[62] Obviously, propor-

tional representation could achieve that result since minor parties might receive some electoral reward for their efforts. But that possible reform has not gained traction.

Two innovations already exist in nonpartisan races that, if applied to partisan races, could affect the electoral status of minor parties. One is multi-member districts.[63] Such districts already exist in municipal races. Members of a city council are elected on an at-large basis, thus allowing a voter to choose more than one candidate at a time.

This could be applied to partisan races for a state legislature by creating multimember districts where several legislators jointly represent a district. Legislators could be elected together from a city or county. The same could be true of Congress. However, such a change would necessitate a revision in statutes at the federal level. But multimember districts at the state level might be accomplished by state statute or constitutional amendment.

Another innovation also being currently applied in some areas is ranked-choice voting. Ranked-choice voting reduces the "wasted vote" argument since voters can rank-order their preferences rather than having to choose only one option. Their second choice, if no candidate wins a majority on the first round, may win on the second round. And that second choice is likely to be a third, moderate-party candidate they can support more readily than the opposing major party. Hence, voters would feel that a vote for a non-major-party candidate is not wasted, and they could vote their true preferences.[64]

SUMMARY

Despite the pressure of the electoral system, ballot access rules, traditional voter affiliations, and campaign financing rules, minor parties still exist in the two-party system of the United States. As this book will demonstrate, new minor parties are still being created while longer-term parties have acquired a niche they are attempting to expand. In fact, developments in electoral politics over the past two decades have affected or are affecting the operations, messaging, and electoral fortunes of minor parties. Through the following case studies, this book addresses these developments and their impact on minor parties in contemporary American elections.

NOTES

1. R. Hal Williams, *Realigning America: McKinley, Bryan, and the Remarkable Election of 1896* (Lawrence: University Press of Kansas, 2010).

2. Gallup, Gallup Poll, USGALLUP.322002.Q01 (Ithaca, NY: Roper Center for Public Opinion Research, iPOLL, June 1992), accessed December 19, 2018.

3. Steven J. Rosenstone et al., *Third Parties in America: Citizen Response to Major Party Failure* (Princeton, NJ: Princeton University Press, 1984), 67–75; Daniel Mazmanian, *Third Parties in Presidential Elections* (Washington, DC: Brookings Institution, 1974), 82–87.

4. Maurice Duverger, *Political Parties: Their Organization and Activity in the Modern State* (New York: John Wiley & Sons, 1954).

5. Duverger, *Political Parties*, 225–227; Andre Blais and R. K. Carty, "The Psychological Impact of Electoral Laws: Measuring Duverger's Elusive Factor," *British Journal of Political Science* 21 (January 1991): 79–93.

6. Frank Smallwood, *The Other Candidates: Third Parties in Presidential Elections* (Hanover, NH: University Press of New England, 1983), 187.

7. Richard P. McCormack, *The Second American Party System: Party Formation in the Jacksonian Era* (New York: W. W. Norton, 1973).

8. J. David Gillespie, *Politics at the Periphery: Third Parties in Two-Party America* (Columbia: University of South Carolina Press, 1993), 56–60.

9. Duverger, *Political Parties*, 225–228. See also William H. Riker, "The Two-Party System and Duverger's Law: An Essay on the History of Political Science," *American Political Science Review* 76 (December 1982): 753–766.

10. A national survey of registered voters was conducted in October 2018 of 1,885 registered voters throughout the United States. The Qualtrics survey included oversampling from select states (New York, California, Minnesota, Vermont, and Connecticut) where minor parties are more popular in order to oversample minor-party supporters. The survey examined major-party supporter attitudes toward minor parties, as well as minor-party supporters' attitudes about their own parties and the major parties.

11. Gillespie, *Politics at the Periphery*, 241–252.

12. Gillespie, 52–56, 252–255; and J. Gold Howard, "Explaining Third-Party Success in Gubernatorial Elections: The Cases of Alaska, Connecticut, Maine, and Minnesota," *Social Science Journal* 42 (2005): 523–540.

13. Jacob Lentz, *Electing Jesse Ventura: A Third-Party Success Story* (Boulder, CO: Lynne Rienner, 2002); Jodi Wilgoren, "Governor Ventura Won't Seek Re-election," *New York Times*, June 19, 2002.

14. Kate Zernike, "A Palin Joined Alaskan Third Party, Just Not Sarah Palin," *New York Times*, September 3, 2008; Gold, "Explaining Third-Party Success," 523–540; Thomas Hardy, "Solidarity Party Gets Reprieve," *Chicago Tribune*, September 25, 1987.

15. Joseph A. Aistrup, *The Southern Strategy Revisited: Republican Top-Down Advancement in the South* (Lexington: University Press of Kentucky, 1996), 32–37.

16. Jack Bass and Marilyn W. Thompson, *Strom: The Complicated Personal and Political Life of Strom Thurmond* (New York: Public Affairs, 2005).

17. Daniel Mazmanian, *Third Parties in Presidential Elections* (Washington, DC: Brookings Institution, 1974).

18. Jonathan Riehl and David Frisk, "The Third-Party Trap," Politico, December 30, 2013.

19. Mazmanian, *Third Parties*; Rosenstone, *Third Parties*; Gillespie, *Politics at the Periphery*; Donald J. Green, *Third-Party Matters: Politics, Presidents, and Third-Parties in American History* (Santa Barbara, CA: Praeger, 2010).

20. Smallwood, *The Other Candidates*; Paul S. Herrnson and John C. Green, *Multiparty Politics in America* (Lanham, MD: Rowman & Littlefield, 1997); Fraser M. Ottanelli, *The Communist Party of the United States* (New Brunswick, NJ: Rutgers University Press, 1991); David A. Shannon, *The Socialist Party in America* (New York: Macmillan, 1955); Ira Kipnis, *The American Socialist Movement, 1897–1912* (New York: Columbia University Press, 1952); Leonard B. Rosenberg, "The 'Failure' of the Socialist Party of America," *Review of Politics* 31 (July 1969): 329–352; Joseph M. Hazlett II, *The Libertarian Party and Other Minor Political Parties in the United States* (Jefferson, NC: McFarland, 1992).

21. Hazlett, *Libertarian Party*, 99–101.

22. Tucker Carlson, "Will Keyes Go Fifth Party," *Weekly Standard*, June 5, 2000.

23. Jo Mannies, "At KC Convention, Constitution Party Picks Pastor for President," *St. Louis Post-Dispatch*, April 26, 2008; W. James Antle III, "Out of Keyes," *The American Spectator*, April 28, 2008.

24. Hazlett, *Libertarian Party*, 99–100.

25. Rosenstone, *Third Parties*, 116–119.

26. http://www.moderateparty.org and http://www.unitedutah.org.

27. Maurice Duverger, *Political Parties: Their Organization and Activity in the Modern State* (New York: John Wiley & Sons, 1954), 215.

28. Adam Nagourney, "Reform Bid Said to Be a No-Go for Trump," *New York Times*, February 14, 2000; David Weigel, "Nobody for President: The Inevitable, Glorious, $35 Million Failure of Americans Elect," *Slate*, May 15, 2012.

29. Shane Goldmacher, "Stephanie Miner to Make Independent Bid to Challenge Cuomo," *New York Times*, June 18, 2018; Michelle Breidenbach, "Stephanie Miner Wins Ballot Line for New Serve America Movement in NY Governor Race," Syracuse.com, November 7, 2018; Chris Baker, "What Is Serve America Movement? Obscure New Party Backs Stephanie Miner for Governor," Syracuse.com, June 19, 2018; and http://www.joinsam.org, accessed November 28, 2018.

30. Kyle Stewart, "Centrist Project Charts Course for Electing Independents," Roll Call, July 12, 2017.

31. Lentz, *Electing Jesse*, 119–123.

32. Lentz, *Electing Jesse*, 119.

33. For a discussion of the Social Democratic Party, see Ivor Crewe and Anthony King, *SDP: The Birth, Life, and Death of the Social Democratic Party* (Oxford: Oxford University Press, 1995).

34. James Mitchell, Lynn Bennie, and Rob Johns, *The Scottish National Party: Transition to Power* (Oxford, Oxford University Press, 2012); Gerry Hassan, "After

the Landslide: Scotland Still Marches to a Different Politics, Only Slightly Less So," *Political Quarterly* 88 (July–September 2017): 375–381.

35. Matthew Goodwin and Caitlin Milazzo, *UKIP: Inside the Campaign to Redraw the Map of British Politics* (Oxford: Oxford University Press, 2015); David Cutts et al., "Defeat of the People's Army? The 2015 British General Election and the UK Independence Party (UKIP)," *Electoral Studies* 48 (August 2017): 70–83; Tim Niendorf, "UKIP—Still a Third Party in a Two-Party System," in *The End of Duopoly: The Transformation of the British Party System*, eds. Klaus Detterbeck and Klaus Stolz (Augsburg: Wissner-Verlag, 2018), 76–98.

36. Alistair Clark, "Changing the Rules of the Game? Continuity and Change in the UK Party System," in *The End of Duopoly: The Transformation of the British Party System*, eds. Klaus Detterbeck and Klaus Stolz (Augsburg: Wissner-Verlag, 2018), 71.

37. For a discussion of Canada's political party system, see Alain-G. Gagnon and A. Brian Tanguay, eds., *Canadian Parties in Transition*, 4th ed. (Toronto: University of Toronto Press, 2017).

38. "How Groups Voted in 1992," Roper Center for Public Opinion Research, Cornell University, accessed December 19, 2018, https://ropercenter.cornell.edu /polls/us-elections/how-groups-voted/how-groups-voted-1992/.

39. Rosenstone, *Third Parties*; Herrnson Green, *Multiparty Politics*; Gillespie, *Politics at the Periphery*; Theodore J. Lowi and Joseph Romance, *A Republic of Parties? Debating the Two-Party System* (Lanham, MD: Rowman & Littlefield, 1998).

40. "Who Are the Independents Who Might Run for President in 2020," CBS News, November 6, 2017; Steve Peoples, "Prominent Anti-Trump Republican Jeff Flake May Challenge Trump with a Presidential Run in 2020," Associated Press, March 16, 2018; Michael Scherer, "Budding Independent Howard Schultz Aims Most of His Ire at Democrats," *Washington Post*, January 30, 2019.

41. Karen Yourish, "Clinton and Trump Have Terrible Approval Ratings. Does It Matter?" *New York Times*, June 3, 2016.

42. Lisa Hagen and Ben Kamisar, "DNC Resolution Pressures Sanders to Join Democrats," The Hill, October 28, 2017.

43. "A Deep Dive into Party Affiliation," Pew Research Center, April 7, 2015.

44. "Party Affiliation," Gallup, accessed December 3, 2018, https://news.garo sellup.com/poll/15370/party-affiliation.aspx; "Guide to Public Opinion and Electoral Behavior," American National Election Studies, accessed December 3, 2018, http://anesold.isr.umich.edu/nesguide/gd-index.htm.

45. R. J. Reinhart, "Majority in U.S. Still Say a Third Party is Needed," Gallup, October 26, 2018, accessed December 3, 2018, https://news.gallup.com/poll/244 094/majority-say-third-party-needed.aspx; Hannah Hartig and Stephanie Perry, "Millennial Poll: Strong Majority Want a Third Political Party," NBC News, November 29, 2017.

46. Cary Funk and Meg Hefferon, "Many Republican Millennials Differ with Older Party Members on Climate Change and Energy Issues," Pew Research Center,

May 14, 2018; "Millennials in Adulthood: Detached from Institutions, Networked with Friends," Pew Research Center, March 7, 2014.

47. "Millennials in Adulthood: Detached from Institutions, Networked with Friends," Pew Research Center, March 7, 2014.

48. Lentz, *Electing Jesse*, 87–88.

49. Lentz, 91–95.

50. Jesse McKinley, "Cynthia Nixon, Battling Cuomo, Wins Endorsement of Progressive Die-Hards," *New York Times*, April 14, 2018; Jon Campbell, "Andrew Cuomo Accepts Working Families Party Nod, Clears Cynthia Nixon From Ballot," *Democrat and Chronicle*, October 5, 2018.

51. "State Public Financing Options 2015–2016 Election Cycle," National Conference of State Legislatures, accessed December 20, 2018, http://www.ncsl.org/Portals/1/Documents/Elections/StatePublicFinancingOptionsChart2015.pdf; Robert M. Stern, "Public Financing in the States and Municipalities," in *Public Financing in American Elections*, ed. Costas Panagopoulos (Philadelphia, PA: Temple University Press, 2011), 62–123; Juhem Navarro-Rivera and Emmanuel Caicedo, "Public Funding for Electoral Campaigns," Demos, accessed December 20, 2018, https://www.demos.org/publication/public-funding-electoral-campaigns-how-27-states-counties-and-municipalities-empower-sma.

52. Mark Pazniokas, "A Primer on Public Financing of Campaigns in Connecticut," *CT Mirror*, July 2, 2014; "How Clean Funding Works," Citizens Clean Elections Commission, accessed December 20, 2018, https://www.azcleanelections.gov/en/run-for-office/how-clean-funding-works; "Maine Clean Elections Act," Maine Commission on Governmental Ethics and Election Practices, accessed December 20, 2018, https://www.maine.gov/ethics/mcea/.

53. "Public Funding of Presidential Elections," Federal Elections Commission, accessed December 20, 2018, https://www.fec.gov/introduction-campaign-finance/understanding-ways-support-federal-candidates/presidential-elections/public-funding-presidential-elections/.

54. "Public Funding of Presidential Elections," Federal Elections Commission, accessed December 20, 2018, https://www.fec.gov/introduction-campaign-finance/understanding-ways-support-federal-candidates/presidential-elections/public-funding-presidential-elections/.

55. Lentz, *Electing Jesse*, 81–86.

56. Nicole Higgins DeSmet, "Zuckerman Wins Race for Dems Lt. Governor," *Burlington Free Press*, August 9, 2016.

57. Bernard Tamas, "Does Fusion Undermine American Third Parties? An Analysis of House Elections From 1870 to 2016," *New Political Science* 39 (2017): 609–626.

58. Peter H. Argensinger, *The Limits of Agrarian Radicalism: Western Populism and American Politics* (Lawrence: University Press of Kansas, 1995), 9–21.

59. Mazmanian, *Third Parties*, 115–132.

60. "State Elections Legislation Database," National Conference of State Legis-

latures, January 10, 2017, http://www.ncsl.org/research/elections-and-campaigns /elections-legislation-database.aspx; Richard Winger, "Connecticut Legislature Passes Bill Outlawing Fusion for New and Small Parties," *Ballot Access News*, June 4, 2013; Yancey Roy, "End to Oft-Criticized 'Fusion Voting' Could Be on the Table," *New York Daily News*, November 25, 2018.

61. Lentz, *Electing Jesse*, 86–87.

62. Scott Schraufnagel, *Third Party Blues: The Truth and Consequences of Two-Party Domination* (New York: Routledge, 2011), 94–103.

63. Schraufnagel, *Third Party*, 96–98.

64. Arend Lijphart, "The Political Consequences of Electoral Laws, 1945–1985," *American Political Science Review* 84 (June 1990): 481–496.

PART ONE

National and Multistate Parties

CHAPTER 1

The Libertarian Party

Christopher J. Devine

INTRODUCTION

The Libertarian Party (LP) proudly claims to be "America's third largest political party."[1] And it is, in fact. In 2016, for example, Libertarian Gary Johnson was the only minor-party presidential candidate to appear on all fifty state ballots, and he won 3.28 percent of the national popular vote—three times more than the nearest competitor, Jill Stein of the Green Party, and more than any other minor-party candidate since 1996. The LP's pre-eminent status among minor parties also extends beyond presidential elections; in 2016, it nominated 52 percent of all minor-party candidates for the US House,[2] and it had more registered voters (approximately five hundred thousand) than any other minor party.[3]

Indeed, the Libertarian Party portrays itself as *the* third choice for Americans who find themselves dissatisfied with the two-party system—not a fringe group of small-government radicals but a mainstream alternative to the Democratic and Republican parties with broad electoral appeal and the potential to emerge as a major party in its own right. Central to the LP's messaging strategy is its claim to represent an *ideological* alternative to the current two-party system, one that essentially splits the difference between left (Democratic Party) and right (Republican Party) on economic versus social issues. That is to say, Libertarians are "fiscally conservative and socially liberal." And, the argument goes, those Americans who identify as the same should find their home in the Libertarian Party.

For instance, during the 2016 presidential campaign, Gary Johnson cast himself, and the Libertarian Party in general, as a sensible, mainstream alternative that married the best that the Democratic and Republican parties had to offer—as evidenced in this exchange on MSNBC's *Morning Joe*:

> Willie Geist: For people who don't know a lot about you and haven't had a chance to hear and learn where you stand on the issues, what is the lane for the Johnson-Weld ticket between Donald Trump and Hillary Clinton? What do you bring that's different from those two?
> Gary Johnson: Well, I think there's a big six-lane highway down the middle that encompasses 60 percent of Americans. And broadly speaking, fiscally conservative, socially inclusive, skeptical when it comes to our military intervention. . . . So, I think that encompasses about 60 percent of the electorate and I think that the two-party system has really, really got to the fringes on both sides.[4]

Likewise, a June 2016 interview on NBC's *Meet the Press* began with this, from host Chuck Todd: "All right, you say you believe the great middle of this country is Libertarian. How do you convince the great middle of this country that they are?" Johnson's response: "Just the notion that most people, I think, are fiscally conservative and socially liberal. And most people, I think, recognize that our military interventions, for the most part, are having the unintended consequence of making things worse, not better."[5]

Johnson and his running mate, former Massachusetts governor William Weld, repeated this message, in various formulations, throughout the campaign. When asked to describe Libertarians at a CNN "town hall," Johnson responded: "What is a Libertarian? In broad brushstrokes: fiscally conservative, socially accepting, tolerant."[6] At another town hall, Weld explained: "We were two of the most fiscally responsible (i.e., conservative) governors in the United States when we served together back in the [19]90s. . . . We are socially inclusive, tolerant, whatever word you want."[7] And on Fox News's *Special Report*, Johnson described himself as "being fiscally conservative, over the top, and being socially, uh, tolerant—liberal."[8]

The Libertarian Party often uses the same message in its public outreach. For example, a December 2018 tweet from the party's official Twitter account asked, "Are you #Libertarian?," with an accompanying graphic that included five boxes. In the center was a box labelled "Libertarian Positions," while on the far left and far right were boxes labelled "Left Positions" and "Right Positions," alongside symbols of the Democratic and Republican parties, respectively, highlighting positions with which Libertarians "Disagree." The center-left and center-right boxes highlighted positions with which Libertarians "Agree" with the political left or right, labelled "Personal Freedom" and "Economic Freedom," respectively. The implication was clear: Libertarians represent the mainstream (i.e., center) of American politics, while Democrats and Republicans represent the ideological extremes (i.e., far left and far right, respectively). And next to the party's logo was this message: "Libertarian: Fiscally Responsible[,] Socially Accepting."[9]

"Fiscally conservative and socially liberal," or some variant thereof, are convenient shorthand descriptions of Libertarian Party politics or libertarianism as an ideology. Indeed, it is one that political scientists often adopt; one leading textbook, for instance, describes libertarians as "conservative on economic issues, liberal on social issues"[10] and "those who are conservative economically and liberal socially."[11] But are these descriptions accurate? And is it the case, as LP candidates and officials often imply, that Libertarians simply "agree" with the political left, or the Democratic Party, on social issues and the political right, or the Republican Party, on economic issues—in essence, splitting the ideological difference between them? Or, is the Libertarian Party significantly *more* conservative on economic issues and *more* liberal on social issues than either of the major parties, thus placing it well outside the mainstream or centrist position that it often claims to hold in American politics?

In this chapter, I present a comprehensive analysis of the Libertarian Party, focusing on its historical background, electoral performance, organizational structure, policy positions, and future prospects. As part of this analysis, I aim to answer the questions presented above: first by examining the LP's official policy positions, as described in its platform, and second by examining the policy preferences of its mass constituency (i.e., its party members or party voters), as reported in the 2016 Cooperative Congressional Election Study.

BACKGROUND

The Libertarian Party was founded by David Nolan—a former Republican and Young Americans for Freedom activist, who lived in Denver, Colorado—in 1971. Nolan made the decision to start a new political party after watching then-President Richard Nixon announce on August 15 of that year that the US government would institute wage and price controls and abandon the gold standard.

On December 11, Nolan and seven associates met at a home in Colorado Springs to begin contacting customers from the mailing list for his libertarian-themed button business in hopes of building a base of support.[12] Soon afterward, Nolan began promoting the new party through articles and advertisements in libertarian magazines.[13] On January 31, 1972, he held a press conference to announce the formation of the Libertarian Party. It attracted widespread media coverage, even appearing on the front page of the *New York Times*.[14]

The Libertarian Party was founded for ideological rather than electoral purposes and with long-term rather than short-term goals in mind. According to the *New York Times*, "Mr. Nolan had no illusions that the Libertarians would ever become powerful in raw votes. But he hoped the party's participation in elections would simply expose Americans to libertarian views as a means to effect change."[15] Also, he hoped that it would provide an ideological alternative for disaffected Republicans and Democrats. The major parties, in his view, would never advocate libertarian ideals because doing so might jeopardize their chances of winning elections in the short term; "a third party, in contrast, can take a long-range approach—running candidates with no intention of immediate victory."[16]

Nolan's conception of the party as a vehicle for promoting libertarian ideals points to an important distinction: the Libertarian Party and *libertarianism* are not one and the same. Indeed, libertarianism is an ideology that long predated the party founded in its name. For many years, adherents to what we now call libertarianism referred to themselves as "classical liberals." When it became clear, around the midtwentieth century, that "liberalism" had become synonymous with Democratic Party politics, many adherents began calling themselves "libertarians." By the 1960s and 1970s, the label had become widespread.[17]

So, what is libertarianism? David Boaz, executive president of the libertarian Cato Institute, provides this definition:

> Libertarianism is the view that each person has the right to live his life
> in any way he chooses so long as he respects the equal rights of others.
> . . . Libertarians defend each person's right to life, liberty, and
> property—rights that people possess naturally, before governments are
> created. In the libertarian view . . . the only actions that should be
> forbidden by law are those that involve the initiation of force against
> those who have themselves used force—actions like murder, rape,
> robbery, kidnapping, and fraud.[18]

Because it purports to operationalize a political ideology, the Libertarian Party always has been fraught with tension: the party must negotiate the parameters of libertarianism, as an ideology, and the policies required to faithfully enact it while remaining unified and expanding its appeal to the broader public in order to win elections, or at least win enough votes to attract attention and spread its message. This tension is exacerbated by the very nature of libertarianism. As Brian Doherty, author and senior editor at *Reason*, notes: "The most significant thing about libertarianism, the element that distinguishes its unique place in modern American thought, is that it is *radical*."[19]

This is why many libertarians resisted the formation of the Libertarian Party, and many reject it to this day. Anarchist libertarians, for instance, often believe that the movement should focus on *enacting* its principles rather than electing someone to do so—that "libertarians needed to show-not-tell how markets and liberty made the world a better place, that they didn't need to wait for the state to go away, or even convince lots of people that it *ought* to go away, to start 'living liberty,' as the movement saying goes, right now."[20] Also, many libertarian purists believe that widespread electoral success cannot be achieved, at least in the near-term, without compromising libertarianism's integrity. As Gary Greenberg, the party's nominee for governor of New York in 1978, put it: "The very idea of worrying about the LP becoming a major force is essentially selling out, because hard-core libertarianism *has no mass constituency*."[21]

Tensions between the Libertarian Party and the libertarian movement, writ large, seem to have gotten worse, not better, over time. According to Doherty, in the party's early years, "major libertarian intellectuals . . . would show up at the LP conventions as interested parties, delegates, or platform members." But, he says, those days "are over" and "a fresh purely political class has dominated since the 1990s." This has caused "a general sense of embarrassment from many of those who see themselves as the serious professional libertarians about the LP." For their part, "LPers can often sense that contempt, so resentment often runs back."[22] As usual, when it comes to libertarian politics, these disputes boil down to a fundamental question of identity and legitimacy: Is the Libertarian Party *really* libertarian?

Disputes over this very question have been central to the Libertarian Party's history, and to this day they have a profound—and often detrimental—effect on the party. Indeed, the LP's ideological base of support, which is relatively small to begin with, is not unified behind its mission but is, in fact, quite divided and prone to infighting. This, in turn, often leads the LP to seek support outside of its ideological base, by emphasizing its mainstream appeal—that is, nominating former Democratic or (usually) Republican officials with relatively high name recognition but questionable libertarian credentials or advertising the party as an anodyne, "fiscally conservative and socially liberal" alternative to the two major parties. But, in doing so, the LP only exacerbates the tension between those who advocate pragmatism versus purity as a means of furthering libertarian ideals.

ELECTORAL PERFORMANCE

The LP's status as "America's third largest party" mostly derives from its performance in elections—specifically, in terms of the number of elections that its candidates contest and the vote share won by those candidates. However, no Libertarian ever has won a presidential election, even in one state, nor a seat in the US Congress. Libertarians have won a limited number of seats in state legislatures, but none since 2000. Instead, Libertarians who attain public office usually are elected at the local level.

Presidential Elections

The Libertarian Party nominated its first presidential and vice-presidential candidates—philosopher John Hospers, of California, and television producer Tonie Nathan, of Oregon—at its June 1972 national convention, in Denver. Hospers and Nathan appeared on the presidential ballot in two states, Colorado and Washington, and won only a few thousand votes nationwide. The ticket's most notable accomplishment, however, came when a libertarian elector in Virginia, Roger MacBride, defied his state's voters, who supported the Republican ticket by a two-to-one margin, and cast his electoral vote for Hospers and Nathan. It was the first—and, to date, the only—electoral vote ever cast for a Libertarian presidential ticket and the first one cast for a woman or a Jewish person (Nathan) in US history.

In 1976, the LP nominated MacBride for president, alongside running mate David Bergland, of California. This ticket appeared on the ballot in thirty-two states but won only 0.21 percent of the national popular vote. In 1980, however, the Libertarian Party had its best performance yet, and for many years to come, it achieved ballot status in all fifty states and won 1.06 percent of the national popular vote.

The LP's 1980 presidential nominee was Ed Clark, an oil company lawyer who had won 5 percent of the vote as an independent candidate for governor of California in 1978. But perhaps the key to the ticket's success was its vice-presidential candidate David Koch—co-owner of Koch Industries and one of the wealthiest businesspeople in the United States. As a candidate, Koch was able to make unlimited contributions to the Libertarian presidential campaign without violating the maximum individual contribution limits set by the Federal Election Campaign Act of 1974. Indeed, David Koch was a critical source of financial support for the Libertarian Party throughout the 1970s; according to Doherty, during that time, "the Libertarian Party . . . [was] largely Koch financed and/or 'controlled' by people who were."[23] Koch contributed $2 million to the 1980 Libertarian Party presidential campaign—out of $3.5 million raised, in total—which, among other things, enabled the LP to run its first television advertisements.[24]

In 1984, the LP was divided between purists, who favored Bergland for president, and pragmatists, who favored Earl Ravenal, a former foreign policy adviser to the Kennedy and Johnson administrations. Bergland won the nomination by only one vote, prompting Koch and other pragmatist leaders to leave the LP, for good.[25] With the party divided and underfunded, its presidential ticket performed poorly in the 1984 election—winning only 0.25 percent of the national popular vote and appearing on thirty-eight state ballots.

The same divisions were apparent in 1988, when the LP nominated former Republican US representative from Texas Ron Paul for president over the purists' favorite, Native American activist Russell Means, by only three votes. Paul and his running mate, former Alaska state legislator Andre Marrou, managed to get on the ballot in forty-six states but won only 0.47 percent of the national popular vote. As the LP's presidential candidate in 1992, Marrou also appeared on forty-six state ballots but won only 0.28 percent of the vote.

In the next three elections, the LP turned back toward purity by nominating presidential candidates—Harry Browne in 1996 and 2000, and Michael Badnarik in 2004—who had no political experience and little appeal beyond the party's ideological base. While Browne won ballot access in all fifty states, he won only 0.50 percent of the national popular vote in 1996 and 0.36 percent in 2000. Badnarik made the ballot in forty-five states and won 0.32 percent of the vote.

In 2008, the LP reversed course again, in the direction of pragmatism, when it nominated Bob Barr—a former Republican US representative, from Georgia—for president. Barr's libertarian credentials were suspect, at best. In Congress, he had sponsored the Defense of Marriage Act and a ban on medical marijuana use in Washington, DC, he voted for the USA PATRIOT Act and a constitutional amendment banning flag desecration, and he helped lead the impeachment efforts against President Bill Clinton. As a national political figure, the LP apparently hoped that he would attract significant media attention and enough Republican voters to expand its electoral coalition. But Barr barely performed better than Badnarik in 2004, winning only 0.40 percent of the national popular vote while appearing on forty-five state ballots.

Gary Johnson was a more credible choice for the LP's presidential nomination in 2012, and again in 2016, given his reputation for fiscal conservatism and social liberalism while serving for two terms as governor of New Mexico, from 1995 to 2003. However, the fact that Johnson had served as a Republican and also sought that party's presidential nomination in 2012 invited criticism from many libertarians that he was merely "Republican-lite." Johnson's selection of former Massachusetts governor Bill Weld as his running mate in 2016—a relative moderate and former Republican who had endorsed Barack Obama for president in 2008 and would later return to the Republican Party to seek its presidential nomination in 2020—only exacerbated these concerns. Indeed, at the LP's 2016 national convention, Johnson and Weld failed to win their party's nominations on the first ballot.

In addition to winning ballot access in all fifty states, in both elections, in 2012 Johnson won the highest vote share of any LP presidential candidate since Ed Clark (0.99 percent), and in 2016 he tripled Clark's previous record by winning 3.28 percent of the national popular vote. In some respects, though, Johnson's candidacy was disappointing: his strong performance in early polling declined dramatically over the course of the campaign, perhaps due to some high-profile gaffes, including his infamous "Aleppo Moment," and he failed to gain entry into the presidential debates.[26]

Congressional Elections

It bears repeating that no Libertarian Party candidate ever has been elected to the US Congress—although some members of Congress have self-identified as libertarians (e.g., Justin Amash) or have been closely associated with the LP (e.g., Ron Paul). Nonetheless, Libertarians frequently appear on congressional ballots, and occasionally they win a substantial percentage of the vote.

Figure 1.1 presents the percentage of US House and Senate elections in which a Libertarian candidate appeared on the ballot, from 1982 to 2018.[27] The data show that at least 39 percent of Senate races since 1992 and 25 percent of House elections since 1996 have featured a Libertarian candidate. LP participation peaked in 2000, when it contested 70 percent of Senate elections and 56 percent of House elections. After a steep decline in subsequent years, Libertarians contested a record 71 percent of Senate

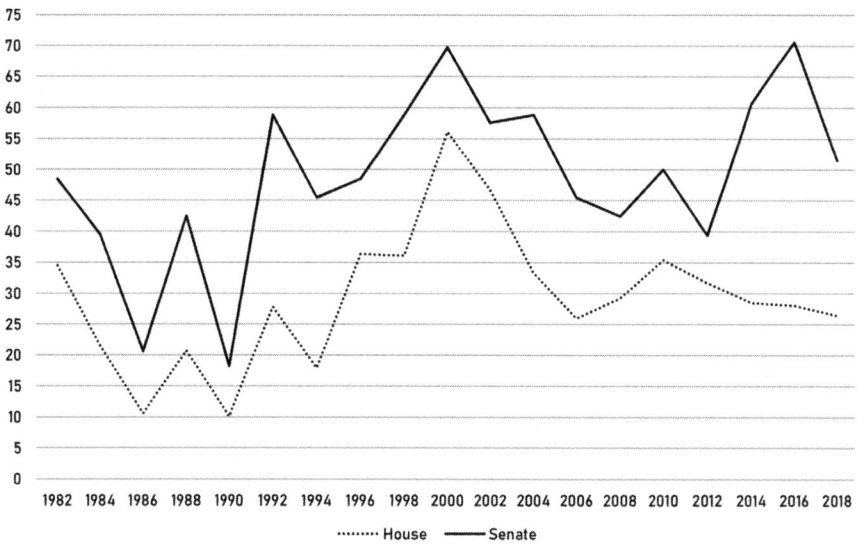

Figure 1.1: Percentage of US House and Senate elections with Libertarian Party candidates, 1982–2018. Federal Election Commission, https://transition.fec.gov /pubrec/electionresults.shtml.

elections in 2016 but only 28 percent of House elections. In 2018, the LP ran far fewer candidates for the Senate (52 percent) and slightly fewer candidates for the House (26 percent). In general, Libertarians have appeared on more congressional ballots over time; but the data show a great deal of fluctuation, including in the most recent elections, rather than a clear trendline.

Figure 1.2 presents the average vote percentage won by Libertarian candidates when running for the US House and Senate, from 1982 to 2018. The data show that Libertarians' vote share in congressional elections increased rather steadily from 2004 to 2016. Indeed, Libertarians performed particularly well in 2016, winning an average vote share of 3.8 percent in Senate races and 4.9 percent in House races—their best and second-best performances in the time series, respectively. The Senate figure is particularly impressive, given that 2016 also was the year that Libertarians appeared on the highest percentage of Senate ballots (70.6 percent). But in 2018, LP support collapsed at the congressional level, with its average vote share in House races reduced by half, to 2.4 percent, and by a full percentage point in Senate races, at 2.7 percent.

Since 1982, of the 132 Libertarian candidates who won 10 percent of

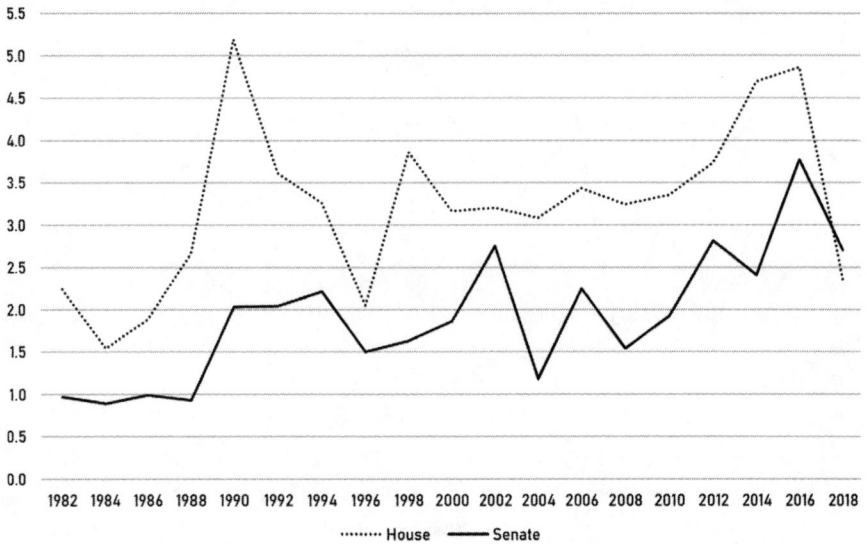

Figure 1.2: Mean vote share won by Libertarian Party candidates when running for US House and Senate, 1982–2018. Federal Election Commission, https://transition.fec.gov/pubrec/electionresults.shtml.

the vote in congressional elections, only five did so while running against opponents from *both* major parties. Since 2000, this has happened only in one House and one Senate race—both in Alaska, in 2016. Jim McDermott finished third in Alaska's at-large House race, with 10.31 percent of the vote. Joe Miller, on the other hand, finished second in the race for Alaska's Senate seat, with 29.2 percent of the vote, ahead of Democrat Ray Metcalfe (11.6 percent) but well behind Republican Lisa Murkowski (44.4 percent). This makes Miller—who had defeated Murkowski for the Republican nomination to the same seat six years earlier, only to lose to her in the general election as a write-in candidate—the only Libertarian congressional candidate since 1982 to win more votes than a major-party opponent.

State and Local Elections

Libertarian Party candidates have been elected to state and local offices only. In 1977, Libertarians were elected to local office for the first time— Elaine Lindsey to the Circleville, Ohio, City Council and Norman Betros Jr. to the Haldane, New York, Board of Education. In 1978, a Libertarian state legislator was elected for the first time—Dick Randolph, to Alaska's House

Table 1.1: Libertarian Party State Legislators, 1972–2018

Year(s)	State	Chamber	Legislator	Elected as LP?	Reelected as LP?
1979–1982	Alaska	House	Dick Randolph	Yes	Yes (1980)
1981–1982	Alaska	House	Ken Fanning	Yes	No; defeated for reelection
1985–1986	Alaska	House	Andre Marrou	Yes	No; defeated for reelection
1991–1994	N. Hampshire	House	Cal Warburton	No; switched from Republican	Yes (1992)
1991–1994	N. Hampshire	House	Finlay Rothaus	No; switched from Republican	Yes (1992)
1993–1994	N. Hampshire	House	Andy Borsa	Yes	No; defeated for reelection
1993–1996	N. Hampshire	House	Donald Gorman	Yes	Yes (1994)
1995–1996	N. Hampshire	House	Jim McClarin	Yes	No; retired
1999–2000	Vermont	House	Neil Randall	Yes	No; reelected as Republican
2001–2002	N. Hampshire	House	Steve Vaillancourt	Yes	No; reelected as Republican
2011–2012	Rhode Island	House	Daniel Gordon	No; switched from Republican	No; retired
2016	Nevada	House	John Moore	No; switched from Republican	No; defeated for reelection
2016	N. Hampshire	House	Max Abramson	No; switched from Republican	No; defeated for governor
2016	Utah	Senate	Mark Madsen	No; switched from Republican	No; retired
2016–2018	Nebraska	Senate	Laura Ebke[a]	No; switched from Republican	No; defeated for reelection
2017–2018	N. Hampshire	House	Caleb Dyer	No; switched from Republican	No; defeated for reelection
2017–2018	N. Hampshire	House	Brandon Phinney	No; switched from Republican	No; defeated for reelection
2017–2018	N. Hampshire	House	Joseph Stallcop	No; switched from Democrat	No; defeated for reelection

Source: Compiled from *LP News* archives, accessed February 1, 2019, https://lpedia.org/LP_News.

[a]Nebraska's legislature is unicameral and officially nonpartisan. Ebke was a registered Republican at the time of her election. In June 2016, she registered as a Libertarian.

of Representatives. Over the next forty years, many more Libertarians would be elected to local offices but very few to state legislatures.[28]

Table 1.1 provides a complete list of state legislators who were elected to or served in office as members of the Libertarian Party, through 2018.[29] Of these eighteen officials, ten were elected to their first term, or a subsequent term after switching parties, as Libertarians. However, no state legislator has been elected as a Libertarian since 2000. While eight have served as Libertarians since 2011, each did so after being elected as a Republican (seven) or as a Democrat (one) and then switching parties. None of these legislators were reelected as Libertarians; five were defeated for reelection, one was defeated for governor, and two retired.

The Libertarian Party claimed 176 elected officeholders as of January 1, 2019, of whom 57 were elected on a partisan basis (i.e., identified on the ballot as a Libertarian).[30] Each elected official served at the local, rather than state or federal, level. This includes ten mayors (two of whom were elected on a partisan basis) and fifty-seven council members (e.g., city, town, county, neighborhood, village, community, borough). Other Libertarians elected to partisan offices included a town judge, a county attorney, a justice of the peace, a constable, and members of the Board of Education and the Solid Waste Management Commission. And those elected to nonpartisan offices included a municipal court judge, a county supervisor, a town meeting representative, and members of the Community College Board of Trustees, the Fire Protection Board, the Library Board, and the Soil and Water Conservation District.

ORGANIZATION

According to Article 2 of its bylaws, the national Libertarian Party exists for the following purposes:

- To function as a distinct libertarian political identity
- To elect Libertarians and "move public policy in a libertarian direction"
- To charter and support Libertarian Party affiliates throughout the US
- To nominate presidential and vice-presidential candidates
- To engage in "public information activities."[31]

The Libertarian Party also has state-level affiliates in all fifty states. The state parties, in turn, have the power to charter local party affiliates.

The national Libertarian Party is led by four elected officers, including the chair, who operates as the party's chief executive officer, "with full authority to direct its business affairs," and who presides at national meetings and conventions; the vice chair, who performs duties as directed by the chair; the secretary, who keeps minutes for all party meetings and conventions; and the treasurer, who provides annual financial reports and oversees all financial matters.

The Libertarian National Committee (LNC) is responsible for overseeing the party organization and implementing its policies. The LNC is composed of twenty-seven members, including the four party officers; five at-large members, elected at national party conventions; and eighteen additional members (nine voting members and nine alternates) representing the state parties. Only official members of the Libertarian Party are eligible to serve on the LNC.

Members of the Libertarian Party are required to certify, in writing: "I do not believe in or advocate the initiation of force as a means of achieving political or social goals." Also, they may purchase a lifetime party membership for $1,500, or become "sustaining members" by paying twenty-five dollars per year. Prior to 2006, the LP required dues payments as a condition of membership. In 2017, membership dues accounted for approximately one-third of the party's total annual revenue. The LP claimed 18,908 official members at the beginning of that year.[32]

POLICY: PARTY PLATFORM

The Libertarian Party's platform is a radical document, uncompromising in its emphasis on liberty and individual rights.[33] According to its Statement of Principles: "We hold that all individuals have the right to exercise sole dominion over their own lives, and have the right to live in whatever manner they choose, so long as they do not forcibly interfere with the equal right of others to live in whatever manner they choose." In elaborating upon these principles, the LP casts itself in opposition to state power ("We . . . challenge the cult of the omnipotent state") and to those political parties that enable it ("Within the United States, all political parties other than our own grant to government the right to regulate the lives of individuals and seize the fruit of their labor without their consent"). For its part, the LP denies government the right to infringe upon individual rights to "life," "liberty of speech and action," and "property," and endorses the free-market system as "the only one compatible with the protection of individual rights."

From there, the platform describes the LP's policy positions within three categories, labelled personal liberty, economic liberty, and securing liberty. The first and second categories correspond to what are usually called social and economic policy, respectively. The third category corresponds, in part, to what is usually called foreign policy, while also addressing migration, civil rights, and election law.

First, with respect to personal liberty (or social policy), the platform states: "Individuals are inherently free to make choices for themselves and must accept responsibility for the consequences of the choices they make." To that end, the platform affirms various rights, including freedom of expression and religion as well as parental and LGBTQ+ rights. In terms of specific policies, the platform opposes government access to third-party email, medical, and library records; marriage licensing; capital punishment; all restrictions on firearms; and all regulation of "crimes without victims" such as gambling, prostitution, and drug use of any kind. The platform also rejects all legal restrictions on abortion ("government should be kept out of the matter") but goes out of its way to "recogniz[e] that abortion is a sensitive issue and that people can hold good-faith views on all sides."

Second, with respect to economic liberty (or economic policy), the platform states: "Each person has the right to offer goods and services to others on the free market. The only proper role of government in the economic realm is to protect property rights, adjudicate disputes, and provide a legal framework in which voluntary trade is protected." To that end, the platform condemns all government efforts to redistribute wealth and regulate trade. In terms of specific policies, the platform opposes eminent domain; civil asset forfeiture; wage and price controls; government guarantees on bank deposits and student loans; inflationary monetary policies; legal tender laws; occupational licensing; "all government control of energy pricing, allocation, and production"; and all forms of government subsidies. The platform also endorses a free market health-care system, the replacement of Social Security with "a private voluntary system," a balanced budget amendment to the US Constitution, and "any initiative to reduce or abolish any tax."

Third, with respect to securing liberty (or foreign policy and other matters), the platform states: "The principle of non-initiation of force should guide the relationships between governments." While supporting "the maintenance of a sufficient military to defend the United States against aggression," as well as "adequate intelligence to detect and counter threats to domestic security," the platform categorically rejects foreign military intervention. In terms of specific policies, the platform opposes compulsory national service, torture, foreign aid, trade tariffs, and "unreasonabl[e]" constraints on migration. This section also condemns bigotry in various forms but recommends that it be corrected through private rather than governmental means. And, with respect to election law, this section denounces all campaign finance laws and the exclusion of "alternative candidates and parties" via ballot access laws and gerrymandering.

At least, that is what the Libertarian Party stands for *on paper*. But what does it stand for *in practice?*

POLICY: INDIVIDUAL-LEVEL DATA

Past research provides only a limited indication of Libertarians' actual policy preferences. The most relevant evidence comes from survey-based analyses of *ideological* libertarians, one of which finds that self-identified libertarians score significantly higher than liberals or conservatives on "personal liberty" and "economic liberty" scales.[34] But, to my knowledge, no previous study has directly and systematically analyzed policy preferences among Libertarian Party members or voters.

This gap in the political science literature is at least partly—if not primarily—attributable to the fact that most surveys do not include enough Libertarians (or other minor-party respondents) to permit meaningful statistical analysis of their policy preferences. Indeed, many leading election-related surveys, such as the American National Election Studies, typically include no more than 2,000 respondents. And Libertarians constitute only a small fraction of the electorate in any given year—less than 0.5 percent of registered party voters and, prior to 2016, no more than 1 percent of voters in presidential elections.

The 2016 Cooperative Congressional Election Study (CCES)[35] provides an extraordinary opportunity to analyze Libertarian policy preferences, for two reasons in particular. First, the 2016 CCES features an exceptionally large (and nationally representative) sample of 64,600 respondents. Second, in 2016, the Libertarian Party won its greatest share of the presidential vote (3.28 percent) and had its greatest share of national party registrants (0.44 percent), to that date.[36] Another advantage is that the CCES uses public records to validate whether or not respondents voted in the 2016 presidential election ($n = 35,829$) and with which party (if any) they were registered ($n = 19,970$). In total, the 2016 CCES includes 1,266 Libertarian Party "voters" (i.e., validated voters who reported choosing Gary Johnson) and 165 Libertarian Party "members" (i.e., respondents who were officially registered as members of the Libertarian Party in their state). I conducted separate analyses of party voters and members, since both represent credible-yet-limited indicators of partisan identity.[37]

The 2016 CCES includes numerous measures of economic, social, and foreign policy preferences, many of which directly correspond to policy positions stated in the Libertarian Party platform. First, in terms of economic policy, the LP platform opposes all tax increases, minimum wage laws, government regulation of health care, and government control of energy production. The corresponding CCES items measure support for increasing taxes (versus cutting spending) to achieve a balanced budget, increasing the federal minimum wage to $12 per hour, repealing the Affordable Care Act (ACA), and allowing the Environmental Protection Agency to regulate carbon dioxide emissions. Second, in terms of social issues, the LP platform opposes same-sex marriage bans and all government restrictions on abortion, while supporting the repeal of all drug laws. The corresponding CCES items measure support for legal recognition of same-sex marriages, legalized abortion in all circumstances, and eliminating mandatory minimum sentences for nonviolent drug offenders. Finally, in terms of foreign policy, the LP platform categorically rejects foreign military intervention and economic sanctions. The corresponding CCES items measure support for US military intervention to protect oil supplies, disrupt terrorists, stop genocide or civil war, spread democracy, protect allies, or uphold international law (or none of the above); and instituting economic sanctions against Iran.

I use these measures to determine whether Libertarians generally agree with the Libertarian Party platform and whether they—like the platform itself—represent a radical ideological alternative to the two major parties. In other words, I ask: Are Libertarians *more* economically conservative, socially liberal, and noninterventionist in foreign policy than their Democratic and Republican counterparts? Or, as public discourse usually suggests, do Libertarians simply "agree" with Republicans on economic policy and with Democrats on social policy (and foreign policy, for the most part)?

Figure 1.3 plots the 2016 CCES respondents' average position on economic, social, and foreign policy, for Libertarian versus Republican or Democratic presidential voters (top row) or party registrants (bottom row). To derive these scores, I began by coding each policy measure on a 0 (most liberal position) to 1 (most conservative position) scale. Then, I calculated each respondent's average position across all measures within a given policy dimension. Finally, I calculated the average policy position for all respondents within a given partisan group of voters or registrants.[38]

The evidence in Figure 1.3 suggests that Libertarians are, in fact, "fiscally conservative and socially liberal." That is to say, on average, Libertarians are to the right of center on economic policy (0.61 for party voters, 0.74 for

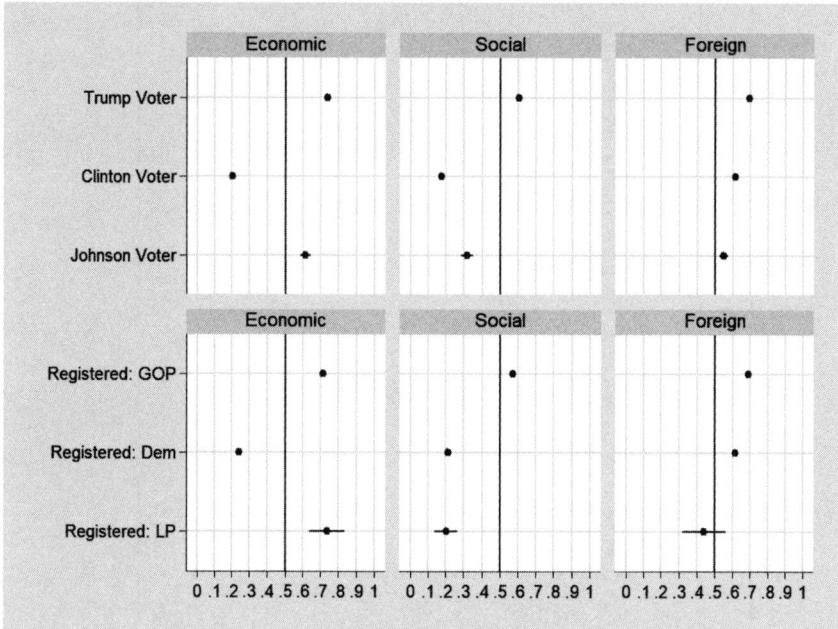

Figure 1.3: Mean economic, social, and foreign policy positions by 2016 presidential vote choice (top) and party registration (bottom). Economic policy includes government spending, minimum wage, health care, and environmental regulation. Social policy includes same-sex marriage, abortion, and drug sentencing. Foreign policy includes military intervention and economic sanctions. Scores represent respondents' mean positions on issues within each category, with 95 percent confidence intervals. *Source:* 2016 Cooperative Congressional Election Study, https://cces.gov.harvard.edu.

party members) and to the left of center on social policy (0.32, 0.20). In neither case do Libertarians represent an ideological extreme. Comparing across party voters, Libertarians are less conservative on economic policy than Republicans and less liberal on social policy than Democrats. These differences are statistically significant at $p < 0.05$. Comparing across party members, Libertarians are slightly more conservative than Republicans on economic policy and slightly more liberal than Democrats on social policy, on average. But neither of these differences is statistically significant.

Only in terms of foreign policy are Libertarians significantly more extreme than the two major parties. Yet they hardly qualify as extreme in this regard—or even "noninterventionist," really. Instead, Libertarian party vot-

Table 1.2: Percentage of Libertarians Whose Policy Preferences Align with the Libertarian Party Platform

Policy	Platform Position	LP Voters (%)	LP Members (%)
Economic Policy			
Balanced budget	Cut spending only (no tax increases)	11.9	29.8
Minimum wage	Don't increase federal minimum wage	53.9	71.5
Health care	Repeal Affordable Care Act	70.8	81.8
Environment	Don't allow EPA to regulate CO_2 emissions	45.0	69.7
Overall	Economic policies, combined	8.4	28.2
Social Policy			
Gay rights	Same-sex marriage should be legal	76.6	84.2
Abortion	Abortion should be legal in all cases	57.3	63.6
Drug crime	No mandatory minimums for nonviolent offenses	75.0	86.1
Overall	Social policies, combined	41.3	50.9
Foreign Policy			
Military intervention	No intervention in any circumstance	13.0	22.0
Economic sanctions	No sanctions against Iran	25.9	35.2
Overall	Foreign policies, combined	6.4	13.6
Overall Policy	Economic, social, foreign policies, combined	1.0	4.0

Source: 2016 Cooperative Congressional Election Study, accessed February 1, 2019, https://cces.gov.harvard.edu.

Note: The 2016 CCES validates respondents' voter turnout and party registration. The data include 1,266 validated voters who reported voting for Gary Johnson in the 2016 presidential election ("LP Voters") and 165 validated Libertarian Party registrants ("LP Members").

ers are positioned slightly to the right of center, at 0.55, and party members slightly to the left of center, at 0.44, on average.

Libertarians, it would seem, are not nearly as radical as their party platform. To confirm this impression, in Table 1.2, I present the percentage of Libertarian respondents whose policy preferences align with LP platform positions on a given policy or combined across a given set of policies. Indeed, fewer than one-third of party members and one-seventh of party voters endorse the party's most radical platform planks by opposing all tax increases and foreign military intervention. An overwhelming majority of Libertarians do not adopt the platform positions on economic or foreign policy, generally, while a bare majority of party members and less than half of party voters do so on social policy. Only 1 percent of Libertarian voters and 4 percent of members agree with the party platform on all nine issues. Nonetheless, on most issues, the majority of Libertarians agree with their party—for instance, on the minimum wage, the ACA, same-sex marriage, abortion, and criminal sentencing for drug offenders. In short, Libertarians *are* fiscally conservative and socially liberal—but not radically so.

A LIBERTARIAN FUTURE?

The apparent disconnect between the Libertarian Party's platform and its constituents' policy preferences—essentially, between radical and mainstream versions of what the LP stands for—is reflective of the tension between forces of purity and pragmatism, respectively, that have always divided the party and limited its growth. Furthering this sense of an identity crisis is the fact that party elites (e.g., organizational leaders and elected officials) seem conflicted as to whether purity or pragmatism is the best way forward.

In many cases, party elites advocate a pragmatic messaging strategy. For instance, Mark Rutherford, formerly the party's national vice chair and later its nominee for secretary of state in Indiana, has said that he discourages LP candidates from using broadly ideological arguments, such as "taxation is theft," when communicating with voters. Instead, he recommends: "Just say taxes are too high and let's get rid of these specific taxes, cut this specific spending."[39] Likewise, Jeff Hewitt—perhaps the LP's most prominent officeholder at present, having won election as mayor and, in 2018, a seat on the Riverside County, California, Board of Supervisors—reports reassuring skeptical voters: "I'm not the guy to get rid of all your taxes or pull us out of Libya or stop the border wall. I don't deal with any of that."[40] Then, of course, there are the efforts of the national Libertarian Party and its most prominent candidates, such as Gary Johnson, to brand the party as a "fiscally conservative and socially liberal" mainstream alternative to the two major parties.

At the same time, party leaders continue to approve a radical platform and, in many cases, denounce or "purge" those who do not abide by it. For example, in October 2016, the Executive Committee of the Libertarian Party of Nevada unanimously voted to censure state assembly member John Moore—one of four Libertarians serving in state legislatures at that time, nationwide—for voting in favor of two tax increases. In a press release, the state party denounced Moore for "his betrayal of principles," which "shattered the [party's] confidence and [its] credibility."[41] According to Austin Petersen, who left the Libertarian Party after finishing second in the LP's 2016 presidential nomination contest, the same dynamics are evident at the national level. He said, in 2017: "It appears as if they [the national LP] are kind of back to their old tricks of, rather than building, they seem to be more willing to purge and destroy—which is kind of the natural tendency of libertarians, in general, more than just the party." He added: "I think that the problem with the party structure is that they see the party platform as the ideology. . . . It's very difficult to dwell in the areas of nuance that are necessary for the winning of elections, which is what parties are *supposed* to be for—rather than it being a philosophical club, which is what some people want it to be."[42]

Perhaps Peterson should be dismissed as embittered and unfair in his assessment, having lost his bid for the LP's presidential nomination and defected to the Republican Party. But party leaders also seem to recognize that Libertarians these days are divided and prone to recriminations, if not "purging." Reflecting upon the party's performance in the most recent midterm elections, and its future prospects, national chair Nicholas Sarwark saw fit to issue this admonition in the December 2018 issue of the *LP News*:

> Be good to each other. Don't fight or bicker, don't rush to attack our fellow Libertarians. Hostility and disrespect for each other will drive out those we need to be working with to set our communities free and make work harder for all of us. If we want a politics that focuses on freedom for everyone, the way we treat each other sends a powerful message to those we are recruiting to join our cause.

In the same column, Sarwark celebrated signs of party growth—including a 40 percent increase in the number of Libertarian candidates running for office from two years prior and more widespread ballot access than the LP ever had achieved coming off of a midterm election. And he set a positive agenda for the year to come: "In 2019, we will continue to develop strong state affiliates, recruit and train candidates, and gain ballot access as early as possible . . . in all 50 states and D.C. in 2020."

Indeed, there is reason to believe that the Libertarian Party will grow stronger in the near future. According to Bernard Tamas, minor parties in general are "poised for political revival" due to increasing polarization in the two-party system and increased access to campaign resources via the internet and social media—this, notwithstanding institutional barriers to their election, such as plurality voting and single-member districts.[43] As the nation's third largest political party—far outpacing its competitors in presidential and congressional elections and in party registration—the Libertarian Party is in the best position to exploit this potential "rebirth of American third parties." But, Tamas cautions, this may require significant internal restructuring: "To the degree that the Libertarian and Green Parties' organizations have been institutionalized and an old guard of third-party activists dominate them, they may be unable to innovate in ways that a rapidly shifting political situation dictates."[44]

One such innovation might be to shift decisively toward a more pragmatic strategy for growth, by revising the Libertarian Party's platform so as to better reflect the views of its constituents and appeal beyond its ideological base within the libertarian movement. As ever, such a strategy risks fragmenting the party's base and alienating its most dedicated supporters, whose primary goal is to advance libertarian principles and not simply to win power. But the change that they seek may never come if Libertarians continue to win only the most votes among losing parties. In the words of Jeff Hewitt, whose election to city and county offices has afforded him the opportunity to enact libertarian principles into policy, even if incrementally so: "You change things by being elected."[45]

NOTES

1. The Libertarian Party, "The Official Twitter of the Libertarian Party, America's Third Largest Political Party. We Promote Free Markets, Civil Liberties, and Peace," Twitter, accessed February 1, 2019, https://twitter.com/LPNational.

2. Bernard Tamas, *The Demise and Rebirth of American Third Parties: Poised for Political Revival?* (New York: Routledge, 2018), 3.

3. Richard Winger, "Early 2018 Voter Registration Totals," Ballot Access News, March 1, 2018.

4. Ryan Teague Beckwith, "Read the Interview Where Gary Johnson Asked What Aleppo Is," *Time*, September 8, 2016.

5. "Meet the Press," NBC News, June 5, 2016.

6. Gary Johnson, "Who Is Gary Johnson?" interview by Chris Cuomo, *Libertarian Presidential Town Hall*, CNN, June 23, 2016.

7. "Transcript: Libertarian Town Hall Meeting," CNN, August 3, 2016, accessed February 1, 2019, http://transcripts.cnn.com/TRANSCRIPTS/1608/03/se.01.html.

8. Gary Johnson, "Gary Johnson on Immigration, Domestic and Foreign Policy," interview by Bret Baier, *Special Report*, Fox News, June 6, 2016.

9. Libertarian Party, "Are you #Libertarian?" Twitter, accessed February 1, 2019, https://twitter.com/LPNational/status/1074776339545243648.

10. Elizabeth A. Theiss-Morse, Michael W. Wagner, William H. Flanigan, and Nancy H. Zingale, *Political Behavior of the American Electorate, Fourteenth Edition* (Thousand Oaks, CA: CQ Press, 2018), 111.

11. Theiss-Morse, *Political Behavior*, 163.

12. Douglas Martin, "David Nolan, 66, Is Dead; Started Libertarian Party," *New York Times*, November 22, 2010.

13. Brian Doherty, *Radicals for Capitalism: A Freewheeling History of the Modern American Libertarian Movement* (New York: Public Affairs, 2007), 391.

14. Doherty, *Radicals for Capitalism*, 392.

15. Martin, "David Nolan."

16. Raffi Khatchadourian, "The Third Man: Bob Barr's Libertarian Run for the White House," *New Yorker*, October 27, 2008.

17. David Boaz, *Libertarianism: A Primer* (New York: The Free Press, 1997), 25.

18. Boaz, *Libertarianism*, 2.

19. Doherty, *Radicals for Capitalism*, 15.

20. Doherty, 399.

21. Doherty, 594.

22. Doherty, 593.

23. Doherty, 410.

24. Doherty, 412.

25. Doherty, 421.

26. Kyle C. Kopko and Christopher J. Devine, "#TeamGov: On the Political Experience, Campaign Messaging, and Electoral Performance of Johnson-Weld 2016," in *Studies of Communication in the 2016 Presidential Campaign*, ed. Robert E. Denton Jr. (Lanham, MD: Lexington, 2018), 163–188.

27. Congressional elections data came from "Election Results," Federal Election Commission, accessed February 1, 2019, https://transition.fec.gov/pubrec/electionresults.shtml. The available congressional elections data begin in 1982.

28. Arthur DiBianca, "1971–2011: The Libertarian Party's 40th Anniversary," LP News, December 2011.

29. Compiled from "LP News," LP News archives, accessed February 1, 2019, https://lpedia.org/LP_News.

30. "Elected Officials," Libertarian Party, accessed January 1, 2019, https://www.lp.org/elected-officials.

31. "Libertarian Party Bylaws and Convention Rules," Libertarian Party, July 2018, accessed February 1, 2019, https://www.lp.org/wp-content/uploads/2018/07/2018_LP_Bylaws_and_Convention_Rules_w_2016_JC_Rules.pdf.

32. Brian Doherty, "The Libertarian Party's Paid Membership Numbers Take a Dive," *Reason*, September 15, 2017.

33. "2018 Platform," Libertarian Party, accessed February 1, 2019, https://www.lp.org/platform.

34. Ravi Iyer, Spassena Koleva, Jesse Graham, Peter Ditto, and Jonathan Haidt, "Understanding Libertarian Morality: The Psychological Dispositions of Self-Identified Libertarians," *PLOS One* 7 (August 2012): 1–23. The data used in this study, however, do not come from a nationally representative respondent sample. Therefore, these findings may not be generalizable to the US population as a whole.

35. Stephen Ansolabehere and Brian F. Schaffner, "CCES Common Content, 2016," Harvard Dataverse, accessed February 1, 2019, https://doi.org/10.7910/DVN/GDF6Z0.

36. Winger, "Early 2018."

37. Specifically, many Johnson voters probably saw him as the least objectionable presidential candidate and were not "Libertarian" in any meaningful or lasting sense. Party registration provides a more general indication of partisan identity, but only thirty-one states register voters by party.

38. In doing so, I used the CCES postelection weights for validated voters (voters) or the full sample (registrants).

39. Doherty, "Libertarian Party's."

40. Steven Greenhut, "California Libertarian's Victory Could be a Roadmap for Others," *Reason*, December 21, 2018.

41. Patsy McFadden Choat, "Libertarian Party of Nevada Censures Assemblyman John Moore (L)," Libertarian Party of Nevada, October 17, 2016.

42. Austin Petersen, interview with author, August 29, 2017.

43. Tamas, *Demise and Rebirth*.

44. Tamas, 182.

45. Greenhut, "California Libertarian's."

CHAPTER 2

The Green Party of the United States

Steve Lem

In the 2000 presidential election, Republican candidate George W. Bush controversially defeated Democratic nominee Al Gore. Although Bush received fewer nationwide votes, he held a narrow Electoral College majority that hinged upon Florida's highly contested presidential race. After two recounts and a United States Supreme Court decision to end that process, Bush won Florida by just 537 votes, which assured his move into the Oval Office.

In the aftermath of the election, analysts explored a variety of scenarios and their impact on the presidential outcome, with many claiming that Green Party candidate Ralph Nader's participation in the election "spoiled" Gore's victory over Bush. Nader pulled 2.8 million votes (2.74 percent) nationwide, six to seven times more than the other minor party candidates. Perhaps most consequently, Nader won 97,488 votes in Florida: significantly more than Bush's margin of victory. If Nader had dropped out of the election, so the thinking goes, his supporters would have chosen Gore, which would have reversed the outcome of the election.

Concerns about the Green Party spoiler effect were also prevalent in the 2016 presidential election. When asked about Stein during a Republican rally, Donald Trump remarked, "I think a vote for Stein would be good. . . . Because I figure anyone voting for Stein is gonna be for Hillary."[1] Clinton's campaign also acknowledged this possibility in their voter mailings, simply and boldly stating that a vote for Stein is a vote for Trump. The aftermath, much like Bush versus Gore, saw Trump win a majority of Electoral College votes, whereas Clinton received a larger share of the popular vote. Once again, Democrats pointed the finger at the Green Party for spoiling the election.[2]

The prominent role of the Green Party in American politics evokes several questions. How did a small meeting of academics and activists in 1984 lead to a political party that could exert such a great deal of influence in national elections? How well do Green candidates perform in other elections at the local and state level? Who votes Green and what policies do they offer to the voters? Do they really spoil elections by siphoning away votes from Democratic candidates? What may the future hold for Green and major-party politics? This chapter explores the answers to these questions.

FROM A GRASSROOTS MOVEMENT TO A NATIONAL PARTY

The Green Party of the United States shares its origin with its sister parties in Europe. For the first half of the twentieth century, division between economic classes defined party politics. Fueled by Marxist concerns, the political debates of Western democracies were dominated by disagreements over resource scarcity: labor unions mobilized in the quest for state-sponsored policies promoting job security, higher wages, and better working conditions, whereas land and capital owners tended to mobilize behind parties that were willing to implement policies aimed at expanding businesses and profits.

The two decades following World War II ushered in political change. Postwar reconstruction produced an unprecedented level of economic growth, which, in turn, facilitated a boom in postsecondary education.[3] Combined, these factors provided the opportunity for new political thought: baby boomers expanded their concerns beyond the materialist interests of their ancestors. Political movements opposing the use of nuclear weapons specifically and nuclear energy generally grew from the 1960s through the 1970s. Antiwar protests and peace movements became popular on college campuses—particularly in the United States following its involvement in Vietnam during the Cold War. Baby boomers also championed for social inclusion and justice for women and minority groups, and they came to sympathize with the impoverished citizens of developing countries following major powers' colonial exit.

The rise of these "postmaterialist" issues created new patterns of political behavior, as interest groups and new political parties emerged to capitalize on what was eventually dubbed the New Left movement.[4] The first political parties to campaign on a predominately environmental platform materialized in Europe and New Zealand in the early 1970s, but it was not until the German Green Party's (Die Grünen) surprising win of 5.7 percent of the vote and twenty-seven seats in the 1983 German parliamentary election that

Green parties received national prominence and international recognition. Founded in January of 1980, Die Grünen established the four pillars of its platform, which would be adopted by future Green parties: 1) grassroots participatory democracy, 2) social justice, 3) ecological sustainability, and 4) peace and nonviolence.

Inspired by the burgeoning Green movement in Europe, Green politics began to take shape in the United States in 1984.[5] Following several grassroots campaigns to shut down Maine's sole nuclear power plant, seventeen people met in January to officially establish the first state-level Green Party in the United States.[6] Coincidently, and quite independently, a national Green movement was simultaneously underway. Academics and environmental activists from the Midwest and West Coast organized the founding conference for a national political organization to be held in August, although through some unfortunate circumstances, the newly established Maine Green Party did not receive an invitation.[7]

The conference produced two major outcomes. First, participants were divided on how Green politics should be structured. Although some favored the creation of strong state organizations and a national party, others insisted that centralization was antithetical to the core pillar of grassroots activism. The compromise was the creation of the Committees of Correspondence (later renamed the Green Committees of Correspondence), an inter-regional organization that would be used to network and coordinate state and local groups. Second, the conference was instrumental in developing the movement's "Ten Key Values," which originally included ecological wisdom, grassroots democracy, personal and social responsibility, nonviolence, decentralization, community-based economics, postpatriarchal values, respect for diversity, global responsibility, and future focus.[8]

The Green movement expanded significantly over the rest of the decade. Activists continued to hold conferences to discuss electoral strategies and to develop a national political platform, although as Green participation grew so did the division between movement purists and party mobilizers. At the state level, Green organizations ran successful campaigns against radioactive waste and environmentally harmful corporate behavior in Maine and California.[9] Green candidates also contested local elections across several states, picking up victories in Wisconsin, Massachusetts, and North Carolina for positions in school, town, and county governance.[10]

By the fourth national Green Gathering held in 1991, most of the necessary planning for a national political party had already been completed, but tension between the Greens' two factions remained high. The outcome of the meeting was the creation of the Greens/Green Party of the United

States (G/GPUSA), which was designed to unify the movement and party under a single organizational umbrella. However, fundamental questions remained over how much political activity members were expected to complete, what type of dues structure would be required to sustain the national organization, and how this change would impact the state and local Green organizations.[11] Consequently, some state parties—most notably in Hawaii and California—did not affiliate with G/GPUSA.

Following the conference, Green politics continued to flourish at the state and local level. In California, the party qualified for statewide ballot status in 1992 by registering over one hundred thousand Green voters. The party's relatively strong performance (3.8 percent) in the 1994 election for secretary of state would also ensure it retained its ballot status for the 1996 presidential election.[12] Green politics in New Mexico were also exceptionally noteworthy. In 1994, Green candidates participated in a wide range of elections and received significant vote shares in many of those contests (e.g., 33 percent for state treasurer, 28 percent for a seat in the state House of Representatives, and 10 percent for governor). As a result, the Greens were the first third party to achieve "major party" status in the state of New Mexico.[13]

Nationwide, Green parties competed in ninety elections across fourteen states in 1994, contesting positions for all levels of government (e.g., city council, state House of Representatives, governor, US Senate, etc.). Their efforts paid off, particularly in five states where Green candidates received enough votes to achieve party ballot status: in addition to California and New Mexico, Greens did well in Alaska, Maine, and Rhode Island. With their ballot status secured, these state parties could turn their attention to running a candidate for the 1996 presidential election.

THE PUSH FOR THE PRESIDENCY AND THE GREEN SPLIT

Successfully running a presidential candidate requires not only strong state parties but also a good deal of coordination between them. After all, these parties would have to agree on a candidate, run aggressive campaigns in most states to get his or her name on the ballot, and then get out the vote. Due to their disagreements with G/GPUSA, however, several state parties opted to coordinate separately through the creation of a new organization, the Green Politics Network (GPN). Ultimately, the GPN would be the precursor for more significant change to national Green politics following the 1996 election.

The Greens found their candidate when Ralph Nader, who had appeared in a handful of presidential primaries in 1992, expressed interest in running for the presidency. Nader, a self-proclaimed independent, criticized both Republicans and Democrats; he was particularly opposed to then-President Bill Clinton's moderate policy platform, which he attributed to the influence of corporate America.[14] In late 1995, the Green Party of California capitalized on his progressive interest and recruited him as their candidate for their January presidential primary. By early 1996, Maine's Green Party had followed suit, and the GPN launched an extensive national campaign to get Nader's name to appear on the ballot.

In August, representatives from the state parties met for the first Green presidential nominating convention. Each state party that had successfully placed Nader on the ballot provided a report of their experiences, and both Nader and his running mate, Winona LaDuke, delivered acceptance speeches.[15] By the election in November, Nader was ballot-qualified in twenty-two states and finished fourth with 685,297 votes (0.71 percent).

The Green's first foray into presidential politics showcased both the organization's strengths and its weaknesses. Unsurprisingly, the state parties were the nexus of Green politics. Working with local groups, they were the ones responsible for running candidates in local, state, and congressional elections. Additionally, these parties coordinated and executed Nader's presidential campaign. On the other hand, the national organization, G/GPUSA, played a far less important role. Since state parties placed Nader's name on the ballot and many did not affiliate with G/GPUSA, the national organization never formally nominated him. G/GPUSA also did little to build the party platform or contribute to individual Green candidate campaigns. Consequently, based on the 1996 electoral cycle, the Federal Election Committee (FEC) concluded that G/GPUSA did not meet the criteria to qualify as a national committee of a political party.[16]

The most consequential shift away from G/GPUSA occurred ten days after the 1996 election, when state party and GPN leaders met with the explicit purpose of unifying the state parties and establishing a federally recognized national party. Together they founded the Association of State Green Parties (ASGP), which, through its bylaws, unequivocally established itself as a politically and electorally motivated organization. By doing so, ASGP stood in direct competition with G/GPUSA, and the two groups would spend the rest of the decade competing for members. By 1999, however, most state parties affiliated with ASGP, which dwarfed the number of local activists who remained in G/GPUSA.

In late 1998, ASGP moved to recruit a presidential candidate and contacted numerous potential nominees, including Nader. ASGP officially selected him as their candidate at their nomination convention in the summer of 2000. At the meeting, delegates also ratified the party's first national platform that reflected the original four pillars of the movement: democracy, social justice and equal opportunity, environmental sustainability, and economic sustainability.[17] The manifesto, much like Nader himself, the Greens hoped, would offer the American voter an ideologically progressive and electorally viable alternative to both major parties.

Nader and the Greens embarked on a significantly more aggressive campaign than in 1996, and their efforts were rewarded. Nader appeared on the ballot in forty-three states and Washington, DC—twice the number than in the previous election. He also received nearly three million votes, which ensured the Green Party would retain ballot status in places where they already had it and helped achieve it in several new states. The party also ran candidates in 286 state, local, and congressional contests, nearly tripling their nationwide presence compared to 1996.[18]

After a final attempt to unite the two Green organizations failed (ASGP approved the proposal but G/GPUSA did not), ASGP changed its name to the Green Party of the United States (GPUS) and requested national party status from the FEC in 2001. G/GPUSA attempted to block the process by arguing that its organization had long been recognized as the "Green Party" and ASGP's use of the name was a fraudulent affair. However, numerous state parties and Green leaders supported ASGP's bid, and the FEC recognized GPUS as the national committee of the Green Party in November of that year. Consequently, G/GPUSA continues to coexist alongside GPUS, although it has largely abandoned its electoral agenda in favor of education and advocacy.

GREEN ELECTORAL SUCCESSES AND CHALLENGES

The Green Party, like all other third parties, faces the difficult challenge of contesting elections in an electoral system that favors Democrats and Republicans. More than half a century ago, Maurice Duverger formulated his now famous "law" in political science that states that single-member district plurality (SMDP) elections—those in which the highest vote recipient is awarded the single position that is being contested—tend to produce a two-party system.[19] These electoral rules tend toward two parties, in part, due to what he referred to as the "mechanical effect," which is simply how the process converts the distribution of votes into seats. Specifically, since only the plurality winner receives a seat, all other party/candidate votes are essentially wasted.

This mechanical effect is reinforced by a psychological one. Political actors, aware of the distortion in SMDP elections, adapt their behavior accordingly. Instead of casting their ballot for a party/candidate that is unlikely to be successful, strategic voters often shift their support to a major-party one that has a shot at winning the election. Similarly, candidates who are motivated to win office are often better off using their resources under a major-party label or otherwise avoiding the election completely.[20]

Economist Anthony Downs expanded upon this expectation by noting that, in SMDP elections, a candidate is assured victory with a minimum vote share of 50 percent plus one.[21] Office-seeking candidates, therefore, have a strong incentive to compete for the "median voter" by moderating their policy positions toward their interests, which, in theory, would lead the parties to converge in the center (notably, this was Ralph Nader's criticism of the Democratic Party under Clinton). If additional candidates entered the election, they would have to flank one of the two parties at the center, which would split the vote between themselves and their closest major-party competitor. Splitting the vote, however, benefits the opposing candidate, which makes both the flanking and neighboring major party worse off.

Most state and federal elections fall under this winner-take-all framework. Elections for the majority of state legislatures and the US House of Representatives use SMDP. The map of each state is divided into discrete geographic territories such that each district represents one seat in the legislature. The candidate who receives the highest percentage of the vote is declared the winner and representative of the people that reside within the district's boundaries. Statewide elections (e.g., governor, US Senate) function similarly, except that the entire state constitutes the district. Finally, with the exception of Maine and Nebraska, a state's Electoral College votes for the presidency are awarded through a winner-take-all system based on the statewide popular vote.

Given the strength of the party duopoly, it is not all that surprising that the Green Party enjoys most of its electoral success at the local level. First, party identification is one of the strongest predictors of an individual's vote choice, since party affiliation acts as a simple proxy for the ideological disposition of a candidate. This heuristic cue, in essence, reduces the need to collect additional information about candidates for voter decision-making.[22] Unlike the vast majority of federal- and state-level elections, nonpartisan ballots—those where candidates' political affiliations are not listed next to their names—are often used for county and municipal office. In these elections, the relationship between party identification and vote choice disappears, since voters must rely on alternative information to cast their vote.[23] Thus, the use of nonpartisan ballots neutralizes the psychological effect against third-party voting.

Second, local elections operate on a smaller scale than federal and state ones and, as a result, tend to attract fewer candidates. Entrenched major-party incumbents or lopsided partisan composition of the electoral unit (e.g., county, ward, precinct, etc.) may lead the opposing major party to forgo running a candidate in that contest. After all, major-party candidates are strategic actors who recognize that their limited resources are better spent in competitive electoral contests than the ones they are likely to lose. Minor parties that run candidates in what would otherwise be uncontested elections provides them the opportunity to serve as the major opposition, which should significantly increase their vote share compared to when they serve as a third option against the two major parties.

Finally, some municipal and county offices may have multiple vacancies and, therefore, eschew SMDP electoral rules in favor of at-large elections. In small cities, for example, it may not be practical to divide the city's geography into separate political units and run individual elections for a council member from each ward. Instead, in at-large elections, all of the candidates are pooled into a single election, and the available seats are awarded to the corresponding number of top-vote recipients.

Greens benefit from the structure of local elections, and even though the party has expanded its efforts into higher profile races, nearly all of its wins occur in these types of contests. Their earliest victories in the mid-1980s, for instance, were in nonpartisan elections for the county board of supervisors in Wisconsin and nonpartisan, multiseat elections for school committee in Massachusetts. Furthermore, nearly 30 percent of all Green victories to date have been in nonpartisan and multiseat elections for city council or school/education board.

Even their higher profile victories for mayor conform to these third-party-friendly principles. In 1991, Kelly Weaverling became the party's first mayor after winning office by fifty-one votes on a nonpartisan ballot in Cordova, Alaska, a small fishing town hit hard by the Exxon Valdez oil spill of 1989.[24] In a set of more recent elections, Steve Arnold picked up a Green Party mayoral victory in 2015, serving as the then-incumbent's only challenger in Fitchburg, Wisconsin, a small twenty-five thousand-person suburb of Madison. Similarly, Bruce Delgado scored wins in 2014 and 2016 for mayor of Marina, California, where he was one of two candidates on a nonpartisan ballot.

Greens have had more limited success in elections for state offices, although the party has picked up a handful of wins. Although major parties tend to dominate state legislative elections, districts often have disproportionate partisan leanings. This has played to the Green Party's advantage, as it achieved all of its legislative victories in heavily Democratic districts and elections that lacked a Republican challenger. Audie Bock, the first Green elected to a state legislature in 1999, won a special election to the California State Assembly after placing second against four Democratic candidates in the first round of voting, and then defeating her Democratic opponent in the second-round run-off. Similarly, Jon Eder in Maine (2002 and 2004) and Richard Carroll (2008) and Fred Smith (2012) of Arkansas won seats in elections against a single Democratic challenger.[25]

Green candidates have participated in a plethora of other state elections, but the party has failed to capture any of these offices. Gubernatorial elections are high-profile, high-cost, and high-reward affairs that are heavily contested by the major parties. Unsurprisingly, voters tend toward the major parties when selecting a governor, and, when coupled with partisan ballots and the option for a straight-party vote, down-ticket offices (secretary of state, auditor, etc.) also favor the election of major-party candidates. Thus, in the vast majority of cases, the Green Party's vote share for these positions has been in the single digits.

The party has fared no better in federal elections, despite consistently fielding candidates for Congress since the 1990s. Since 2000, Greens have contested elections in about fifty districts for the US House of Representatives and run around ten Senate campaigns each biennial election cycle. In House elections with multiple candidates, the Greens typically receive less than 3 percent of the total vote; candidates may, however, receive significantly more if the election lacks a major opponent challenger. Rodolfo Cortes Barragan, for instance, served as Democratic incumbent Lucille Roybal-Allard's sole challenger in California's solidly Democratic Fortieth Congressional District, where he pulled nearly 23 percent of the vote in 2018. Similar to their performance in heavily contested House elections, Green candidates generally pull only 1 to 2 percent of the vote in Senate races.

At the presidential level, the Greens have been unable to match the electoral success of Nader's 2000 campaign. The efforts of David Cobb (2004) and Cynthia McKinney (2008) were both disappointing follow-ups, with each candidate receiving less than two hundred thousand votes—around one-tenth of a percentage point—nationwide. Jill Stein did only slightly better in 2012. She finished with just under five hundred thousand votes (around 0.36 percent), although she did receive enough campaign contributions to qualify for matching federal funds—a first for a Green candidate since Nader. Stein's second presidential effort in 2016 did noticeably better by pulling in more than 1.4 million votes (1.07 percent), which was about half the number of votes separating Donald Trump and Hillary Clinton.

RUNNING TO LOSE? PARTY BUILDING AS AN ELECTORAL GOAL

Green candidates roughly win only one out of every five elections they contest, and their foray into statewide and federal elections seems irrational given their tepid vote shares and inability to win office. However, unlike the Democratic Party, which can trace its heritage back to the anti-Federalists in 1787, and the Republican Party, which solidified itself around Abraham Lincoln's presidency in 1860, the Green Party of the United States has existed for less than twenty years, and its existence as a national political organization is not assured. Instead, Greens must establish their presence in an entrenched two-party system. To do so, they need to sustain their party status and relevance, even if this means running candidates in elections they are almost certainly guaranteed to lose.

It is often said that Democrats and Republicans rarely agree, but they both dislike third parties. Since the Constitution dictates that state legislatures determine how elections are administered, and because major parties control those bodies, third parties often have a difficult time participating in elections because state governments limit their ability to appear on the ballot.[26] Petition requirements vary, but most states require that new parties demonstrate a sufficient level of political support by collecting voter signatures, which in some places may be over one hundred thousand.[27] Parties that qualify for the ballot then need to maintain it in subsequent elections. This is usually achieved by receiving a defined percentage of the vote in a statewide election.

State Green Parties, which are currently qualified in over twenty states, have spent a great deal of effort to get on the ballot. Fielding candidates for high-profile state offices are more about party visibility and securing enough votes to maintain their status than winning office. The same rationale applies to federal elections. To continue to be recognized as a political party by the FEC, GPUS must demonstrate sufficient activity on a national level by, in part, nominating candidates for various federal offices in numerous states. Similarly, running a presidential candidate is not about winning, although garnering 5 percent of the vote would make the party eligible for matching federal funds in the next election cycle. Drawing attention to their issues and their potential impact on the election are more modest and realistic goals. Both Nader and Stein accomplished this by picking up significant media coverage prior to their respective presidential contests, which propelled them into mainstream politics.

RED, BLUE, OR GREEN? THE ELECTORAL BASE

Although Green candidates typically receive only a small fraction of the vote, their participation can have widespread impact, especially in close major-party contests. This effect, however, depends largely on how they draw votes away from the major parties. If, for instance, Greens draw proportionately (say, 1 percent each) from both parties, the net effect would be zero. On the other hand, if the majority of Green Party voters would have otherwise chosen Democrats, the election could be tilted in favor of the Republicans.

GPUS is the fourth largest political party, with approximately two hundred and fifty thousand registered voters nationwide, and generally pulls support from about 5 percent of the electorate (based on prepolling and actual electoral outcomes), although the latter varies from election to election. This implies that very few Green voters are the ones that belong to the party; rather, the majority of supporters must be drawn from the two major parties or independents. Building a demographic profile of Green voters, however, is surprisingly difficult. Since Greens operate at the margins of mainstream politics, there have been virtually no studies that systematically examine third-party vote choice or affiliation.[28] Instead, major polls and surveys (e.g., Pew, American National Election Studies, General Social Survey) typically lump non-major-party responses into the "Independent" or "Other" categories.

Despite these challenges, Green Party success in other democracies has warranted a closer examination of their parties' supporters in order to yield insights for the United States.[29] First, age, education, and income tend to be the strongest and most consistent predictors of Green voting. This is unsurprising, given Greens promote a progressive, postmaterialist agenda. Young voters, especially those in college, are less attached to the established parties and therefore more likely to voice their support for an alternative option.[30] Similarly, those with graduate degrees and high incomes are more likely to support the Greens' platform of social and environmental justice. Second, gender, race, and family status also matter, although the supporting evidence is mixed. Women tend to support Greens slightly more than men, as do ethnic minorities and those with children. Once again, these findings square with the key values of social and environmental justice, postpatriarchal values, and future focus.[31]

These findings can be corroborated, at least in part, with data from the United States. Although most national studies do not ask questions about the Greens specifically, they do survey attitudes about the environment. The General Social Survey (GSS), for instance, asks respondents about whether the country spends too much, too little, or about the right amount on improving and protecting the environment. An analysis of demographic variables produces results that are largely consistent with the literature on Green Party support.[32] Age, education level, gender, and race were all significant predictors of environmental attitudes, with young, better educated, female, and minority respondents all more likely to state that more should be done. Income was also significant in the model, but its effect highly correlated with education levels.

Green supporters and Democrats share similar demographics, and the party has enjoyed most of their success in predominantly blue states like California, Connecticut, and Massachusetts. However, Greens also tend to be more educated and have higher incomes, which are more characteristic of Republican voters. To that end, Nader stated in his autobiography that exit polls showed 25 percent of his voters would have supported Bush, 38 percent would have chosen Gore, and the rest would not have voted at all.[33]

POSTMATERIALISM AND THE ELECTORAL APPEAL OF THE GREENS

The relationship between political parties and social groups has been an enduring question for political scientists. In their seminal work, Seymour Lipset and Stein Rokkan argue that parties in Western Europe organized around four societal divisions after the Industrial Revolution.[34] First, parties may reflect the division of church and state, where religious and secular voters form distinct political blocs. Second, the center—those occupying the state's economic, political, and cultural capitals—may come in political conflict with those in the periphery, who push for decentralization and regional autonomy. Next, parties may represent divisions between urban and rural interests, which historically arose over state support of the industrialized urban centers at the expense of rural landowners. Finally, and perhaps most evidently, parties solidified around economic interests reflected in Marxist class conflict between workers and owners.

In the United States, the major parties combine multiple groups to form two durable voting coalitions. On one side, the Democratic Party draws most of its support from the nation's population-dense urban cities by championing the interests of the poor and working class through increased centralization of federal programs (e.g., health care). Democrats also strongly advocate for the social and political acceptance of nontraditional (i.e., secular) social behaviors, including modern interpretations of marriage and family. The Republican Party, on the other hand, performs electorally better in rural areas and is supported by a coalition of religious voters who prefer traditional interpretations of social norms; small-business owners; and wealthy, upper-class citizens. As such, their political agenda has consistently pushed for decentralized decision-making in favor of empowering state governments to determine the best course of action for their constituents.

Given these voting blocs, can the Green Party appeal to Republicans? The tentative answer is yes, although it requires that the Greens fundamentally disrupt conventional major-party politics. Specifically, political conflict is often defined along a single spatial dimension that most people commonly refer to as *left-right*. The terminology originated during the French Revolution to reflect the distribution of seats in the National Assembly; those who supported the revolution and social change sat on the left of the president, and those who were loyal to the King and aristocracy sat on his right. Today, left-right still largely reflects those distinctions. Liberals, the left, tend to represent the lower economic and social classes and advocate for progressive reforms aimed at reducing societal inequities. Conservatives, on the other hand, occupy the right and tend to represent the interests of the upper or dominant groups in society, which tend to be better off under older, more traditional political and social arrangements.

The dominance of the two major parties in the United States automatically constrains partisan conflict to a single dimension, but left-right itself is a manufactured construct. If a third party offered policies that appealed to, say, urban ethnic minorities and rural farmers, they could essentially "unpack" left-right and create a new bundle of issues that appealed to some voters of both major parties. Additionally, they could encourage nonvoters— who, due to their conflicting ideology, do not align with either major party—to show up at the polls. Finally, new parties may introduce issues that were not part of political discourse when the voting coalitions for the major parties were formed. This would provide a new wave of voters with a partisan outlet for these concerns, which would be to the electoral detriment of established parties.

For the most part, this is what the Greens have done. Their platform is fairly comprehensive, and many of their positions mirror the Democrats. Their first platform (2000) included typically left issues, such as increasing taxes on the wealthy and redistributing money through social programs, creating a universal health-care system, reducing military spending, and supporting policies that open immigration. However, Nader and the Greens were also very critical of Bill Clinton and what they perceived as large corporate influence. Consequently, their platform also called for the end of commercial farming in favor of family-operated farms, support of small businesses through increased availability of capital and reduction in bureaucratic oversight, and the rejection of Clinton-era trade agreements such as NAFTA. These policies surely appealed to some Republican voters.

The other major appeal of the Greens is that their platform introduces postmaterialist issues to political discourse, which include ecological, post-patriarchal (feminist), and quality-of-life matters. [35] As the party has developed its manifesto, they have adopted specific and progressive stances on nuclear energy and waste management, gender equality and identity, and re-empowering the people over large businesses. These policies in particular appeal to the increasing group of young, well-educated middle-class citizens who may not have developed strong ties to the existing parties or clear ideological placement on left-right. Consequently, the Greens, at least in the European context, have been labeled Left-Libertarian, since they are committed to traditional left issues like redistribution but appear almost anticapitalist in their favor of grassroots participation over corporate bureaucracy.[36]

IMPACT AND FUTURE OF GREEN POLITICS IN THE UNITED STATES

So, did Ralph Nader spoil the election for Al Gore in 2000 and did Jill Stein do the same for Hillary Clinton in 2016, and do the Greens pose a threat to the Democrats moving forward? Although the Green platform appeals to some Republicans, the party draws more heavily from the Democratic voter demographic, and it is probable that if Nader had not run Al Gore would have won the presidency.[37] However, the Greens have been unable to recapture Nader's level of electoral success despite a high level of national visibility. Instead, their biggest impact on American politics is how the major parties respond to their presence. The Democratic and Republican parties are, after all, strategic actors who want to maintain their hegemony.

In an influential work on Green and far-right party entry in Western Europe, Bonnie Meguid argues that dominant parties may combat challenger entry by co-opting the new party's issues. In the United States, both the anecdotal and systematic evidence seem to support this claim.[38] Over the past few decades, the Democrats have adopted postmaterialist issues such as environmental protection, progressive stances on gender identity and equality, multiculturalism and diversity, and other quality-of-life issues. In early

2019, for instance, the Democrats introduced a Green New Deal plan to much media attention and acclaim. Even a few years earlier, such a proposal would have clearly fallen under the ownership of GPUS.

Dan Lee, who has conducted the few systematic studies of third-party entry in the United States, argues that even the mere threat of a third-party challenger will elicit a strategic response from the major parties.[39] He finds that major-party candidates will diverge as they shift themselves to co-opt the positions of flanking third parties. Lee also shows that Congressional incumbents that live in districts with a high risk of third-party entry tend to vote along ideological dimensions other than left-right. This suggests that they are attempting to thwart off challengers like the Greens who introduce new ideological dimensions to the electoral arena. Finally, he and John Aldrich note that the ability for major parties to co-opt third-party issues through their control of the agenda is one of the main reasons for new parties' limited electoral success.

The Democrats' ability to co-opt environmental and other postmaterialist issues showcases what is simultaneously the Greens' biggest strength and biggest weakness. GPUS's roots lie in grassroots activism. Like any political party, they must strike a balance between their office-seeking ambitions and maintaining their core policy preferences; if they stray too far in their efforts to recruit new voters, they risk losing their original supporters who define what the party stands for. As a result, the national committee has remained relatively weak. The strength of the party has always been at the local and state levels, and their rejection of centralization and corporate funding through super political action committees (PACs) limits the party's ability to coordinate and divert resources to a few states or congressional districts where the party could achieve mainstream electoral success. Instead, the loose organization of Green state parties continues to mount more moderate campaigns for state and federal offices across the United States.

Despite these challenges, the history and strength of the Green movement, both in the United States and internationally, has demonstrated its resiliency and will almost certainly play an important political role for the foreseeable future. The number of independent voters continues to outnumber partisan identifiers, and the majority of Americans now believe that a third party is needed.[40] The Green Party of the United States is one of few parties that is currently well-suited to meet these demands, as long as they can reorganize and shift their strategy to be more competitive in a predominately winner-take-all system.

NOTES

1. Harper Neidig, "Trump: A Vote for the Green Party Helps Me," The Hill, July 27, 2016.

2. Eli Watkins, "How Gary Johnson and Jill Stein Helped Elect Donald Trump," CNN, November 25, 2016.

3. Lazerson, Marvin, "The Disappointments of Success: Higher Education After World War II," *The Annals of the American Academy of Political and Social Science* 559 (1998): 64–76.

4. Ronald Inglehart, *Cultural Shift in Advanced Industrial Society* (Princeton, NJ: Princeton University Press, 1989).

5. Two oft-cited mainstream books for jumpstarting the environmental movement are Rachel Carson's *Silent Spring*, which showcased the damaging effects on the environment and of human health by using DDT as an agricultural pesticide, and Paul Ehrlich's *The Population Bomb*, which produced concerns over overpopulation and mass starvation. Rachel Carson, *Silent Spring* (New York: Houghton Mifflin, 1962 [2002]); Paul Ehrlich, *The Population Bomb* (Cutchogue: Buccaneer Books, 1969).

6. John Rensenbrink, "Early History of the United States Green Party, 1984–2001," Green Party US, May 15, 2017

7. Charlene Spretnak and her coauthored book played an important role in the movement toward and activity and actions of the founding conference. Charlene Spretnak and Fritjof Capra, *The Global Promise of Green Politics* (New York: E. P. Dutton, 1984).

8. Resenbrink, "Early."

9. David Reynolds, "The Greens," in *The Encyclopedia of Third Parties in America*, eds. Immanuel Ness and James Ciment (Armonk: M. E. Sharpe, 2000).

10. "Summary," GPUS Elections Database, 2019, accessed January 10, 2019, https://www.gpelections.org.

11. Reynolds, "The Greens."

12. "Green Party of California Ballot Status History," Green Party of California, accessed January 24, 2019, http://www.cagreens.org/history/ballot-status.

13. Reynolds, "The Greens."

14. Ayres B. Drummond Jr, "Ralph Nader Is Nominated for President, but Vows He Will Ignore His Party's Platform," *New York Times*, August 20, 1996.

15. Rensenbrink, "Early."

16. "Advisory Opinion 1996–35," Federal Election Committee, November 18, 1996.

17. "2000 Platform," Green Party of the United States, June 2000, accessed January 25, 2019, https://gpus.org/committees/platform/2000-platform/.

18. "Summary," GPUS Elections Database.

19. Maurice Duverger, *Political Parties: Their Organization and Activity in the Modern State* (London: Methuen, 1954).

20. For further discussion, see William H. Riker, "The Two-Party System and Duverger's Law: An Essay on the History of Political Science," *The American Political Science Review* 76 (1982): 753–766; Gary W. Cox, *Making Votes Count: Strategic Coordination in the World's Electoral Systems* (Cambridge: Cambridge University Press, 1997).

21. Anthony Downs, *An Economic Theory of Democracy* (New York: Harper, 1957).

22. Cindy D. Kam, "Who Toes the Party Line? Cues, Values, and Individual Differences," *Political Behavior* 27 (2005): 163–182.

23. Brian F. Schaffner, Matthew Streb, and Gerald Wright, "Teams without Uniforms: The Nonpartisan Ballot in State and Local Elections," *Political Research Quarterly* 54 (2001): 7–30.

24. "Environmentalist Elected Mayor of Oil Spill Town," UPI, October 3, 1991.

25. The Green Party also obtained representation in the New Jersey General Assembly when Matt Ahearn switched his party affiliation from Democrat to Green.

26. Steve B. Lem and Conor M. Dowling, "Picking Their Spots: Minor Party Candidates in Gubernatorial Elections," *Political Research Quarterly* 59 (2006): 471–480; Barry C. Burden, "Ballot Regulations and Multiparty Politics in the States," *PS: Political Science & Politics* 40 (2007): 669–673; Daniel J. Lee, "Take the Good with the Bad: Cross-Cutting Effects of Ballot Access Requirements on Third-Party Electoral Success," *American Politics Research* 40 (2012): 267–292.

27. Oliver Hall, "Death by a Thousand Signatures: The Rise of Restrictive Ballot Access Laws and the Decline of Electoral Competition in the United States," *Seattle University Law Review* 29 (2005): 407–448.

28. For a review of the literature, see Ingmar Schumacher, "An Empirical Study of the Determinants of Green Party Voting," *Ecological Economics* 105 (2014): 306–318.

29. Martin Spiess and Martin Kroh, "A Selection Model for Panel Data: The Prospects of Green Party Support," *Political Analysis* 18 (2010): 172–188; Diego Comin and Johannes Rode, "From Green Users to Green Voters," Technical Report, National Bureau of Economic Research, 2013.

30. "NBC News Exit Poll: Third Party Candidates Prove a Draw for Some Younger Voters," NBC, November 8, 2016, accessed February 3, 2019, https://www.nbcnews.com/card/nbc-news-exit-poll-third-party-candidates-prove-draw-some-n68 0926.

31. Spiess, "Selection Model."

32. Tom W. Smith, Michael Davern, Jeremy Freese, and Michael Hout, *General Social Surveys, 1972–2016* (Chicago, IL: NORC at the University of Chicago, 2018).

33. Ralph Nader, *Crashing the Party: Taking on Corporate Government in an Age of Surrender* (New York: St. Martin's, 2002).

34. Seymour M. Lipset and Stein Rokkan, "Cleavage Structures, Party Systems, and Voter Alignment: An Introduction," In *Party Systems and Voter Alignments: Cross-National Perspectives*, ed. by S. M. Lipset and S. (New York: Free Press, 1967).

35. Ana Maria Belchior, "Are Green Political Parties More Post-Materialist than

Other Parties? An Assessment of Post-Materialist Forecasts," *European Societies* 124 (2010): 487–492.

36. Herbert Kitschelt, "New Social Movements and the Decline of Party Organization," in *Challenging the Political Order. New Social and Political Movements in Western Democracies,* eds. R. Dlaton and M. Kuechler (New York: Oxford University Press, 1990): 179–208.

37. Christopher S. P. Magee, "Third-Party Candidates and the 2000 Presidential Election," *Social Science Quarterly* 84 (2003): 574–595.

38. Bonnie M. Meguid, "Competition between Unequals: The Role of Mainstream Party Strategy in Niche Party Success," *The American Political Science Review* 99 (2005): 347–359.

39. Daniel J. Lee, "Anticipating Entry: Major Party Positioning and Third Party Threat," *Political Research Quarterly* 65 (2012): 138–150; Daniel J. Lee, "Third-Party Threat and the Dimensionality of Major-Party Roll Call Voting," *Public Choice* 159 (2014): 515–531; John H. Aldrich and Daniel J. Lee, "Why Two Parties? Ambition, Policy, and the Presidency," *Political Science Research and Methods* 4 (2016): 275–292.

40. Lydia Saad, "Perceived Need for Third Major Party Remains High in U.S," Gallup, September 27, 2017.

CHAPTER 3

The American Constitution Party

Edward Lynch

INTRODUCTION

The permanence of the two-party system in electoral politics seems as certain a reality as any in a dynamic political system like that of the United States. The last time that a political party other than the Republicans or the Democrats won any electoral votes for president was more than fifty years ago, when American Independent Party candidate George Wallace won forty-five electoral votes, by virtue of wins in Georgia, Alabama, Mississippi, Louisiana, and Arkansas. Since then, the closest that any third-party candidate has come to winning even a single electoral vote was in 1992, when Reform Party candidate Ross Perot nearly won the second congressional district in Maine, which awards electoral votes on the basis of congressional districts.

Still, it is inaccurate to say that smaller parties have not had a crucial impact on presidential elections. In the photo-finish 2000 election, George W. Bush won Florida by only 537 votes. In the same election, Green Party candidate Ralph Nader won over 97,000 votes in Florida. This means that had only one-half of 1 percent of Nader's voters decided to vote for Democratic candidate Al Gore, the vice president would have won Florida and become the forty-third president of the United States.

In 2016, President Donald Trump's victory was sealed by wins in Pennsylvania, Wisconsin, and Michigan. In the Keystone State, Trump's margin of victory was 44,322 votes, with 49,941 votes going to Green Party candidate Jill Stein. In Michigan, Trump won by 10,704 votes, and Stein garnered 51,463 votes; in Wisconsin, Stein's 31,072 votes more than accounted for Hillary Clinton's loss by 22,748 votes.

In recent elections for the United States Senate, smaller parties have also played a crucial role. In 1986, for example, an unusual set of circumstances gave Republicans hope that they could defeat four-term ultraliberal California senator Alan Cranston, even in a year that boded ill for Republicans. The GOP nominated Silicon Valley congress member Ed Zschau, a moderate on social issues who united California's fractious Republican Party. On Election Day, the Libertarian Party candidate won over 175,000 votes, in an election in which Cranston's margin was 104,000 votes. In 2002, Republicans came within a whisker of defeating Democrat Tim Johnson with rising star John Thune. In this case, even when Libertarian Party candidate Kurt Evans dropped out and endorsed Thune, it was too late to remove Evans's name from the ballot, and he got three thousand votes, more than covering Thune's five hundred-vote loss. In 2016, the Libertarian Party cost Republican senator Kelly Ayotte her reelection bid, taking over twelve thousand votes in a race won by just over one thousand.

More evidence, albeit negative evidence, of the importance of minor parties is the extent to which the two major parties seek to discredit them and dissuade their followers from voting for them. When Wallace ran in 1968, and especially when he showed unexpected strength among blue-collar workers in the Northeast, both Richard Nixon and Hubert Humphrey diverted precious campaign resources to shoring up votes they thought they could take for granted.[1] Both campaigns also found that they could not shore up those votes without risk to their overall chances.

Thus, minor political parties have had a significant influence over elections in the United States and, therefore, over the making of public policy. In this chapter, I will highlight the relevant portions of important theoretical works on political party functions as well as the theoretical characteristics of a classic two-party system. The chapter will then move to a discussion of the history, platform, and campaigns of the Constitution Party, originally the US Taxpayers Party, from its inception in 1991 through its role in the 2016 presidential election. (Rather than chronicle each campaign, I will focus on 1996, the party's most successful run at the presidency and on selected campaigns for other offices.) I will demonstrate that the Constitution Party performs almost none of the classic functions of the political party, and that it may be more appropriate to use other sets of measures to assess its effectiveness.

THEORETICAL BACKGROUND

For G. Bingham Powell Jr., Russel J. Dalton, and Kaare Strom, political parties serve the following functions: political socialization, elite recruitment, citizen recruitment, interest articulation, interest aggregation, and policy-making.[2] John F. Bibby and L. Sandy Maisel present a similar list of political party functions

> If they function well, they make it easier for citizens' views to be converted into public policy. . . . They aggregate the opinions and interests of different elements of society; they socialize new citizens into the political system; they recruit leaders to serve in government; they compromise among competing demands among their followers; they contest elections that in turn legitimize the power of those in government; and they organize the government.[3]

Political socialization can be defined as the process through which actors in a political society introduce the values and attitudes of that society to new members (children, or perhaps newcomers to the society). Political parties in the United States perform their socializing function by identifying their own party platform with the founding principles of America itself. The parties seek to infuse political discussion and debate with a sense of what is proper or appropriate while also seeking to identify certain political attitudes or positions as out of bounds (for example, when 2016 Democratic nominee Hillary Clinton called Trump's supporters "deplorables.")

Elite recruitment is arguably more vital for minor political parties than it is for the major parties, since it is the presumed desire of small parties to become less small. To do so, they have to win elections, which means recruiting candidates, staff, and contributors. Citizen recruitment is important for the same reasons, with the added urgency that comes from being shut out of public events like debates and candidate fora.

Interest articulation is the central raison d'être of most minor parties in the United States. They come into existence because their leaders do not believe that the major parties are articulating the interests that they find most important, or they believe that the major parties are not serious in their commitment to follow through in the area of policy-making. For the most part, the members of minor parties reject the concept of interest aggregation, either in whole or in part. The assembly of a major-party coalition, especially in a large and diverse society, necessarily requires more emphasis on some issues than others.

Minor-party leaders in the United States are fully aware that in a two-party system, the most likely outcome of numerous defections will be a benefit to the other party. It is reasonable to believe that the ninety-thousand-plus Floridians who voted for Nader were not supportive of a Republican presidency, yet that is exactly what they caused. On the other hand, Green Party, Libertarian Party, or other minor-party members would not be surprised if they were confronted with the counterproductive nature of their votes. More likely, they would cast the blame on the failure of one of the major parties to sufficiently take their concerns, interests, and beliefs into account. By causing adequate losses to the major party, minor-party members may hope to "punish" Republican or Democrat leaders and thus "force" them to take the concerns of minor-party voters into account in the next election.

On occasion, there is an almost dialectical pattern of thought among the more dedicated and determined minor-party members. Green Party members, for example, may deliberately contribute to the election of right-leaning Republicans on the assumption that their polices, once enacted, will generate enough disgust with "rightist" government to make Green Party liberalism more attractive.

ORIGINS OF THE CONSTITUTION PARTY

A strong argument could be made that the real founder of the Constitution Party was President George H. W. Bush. When he broke his "Read my lips: no new taxes" pledge in 1990, he enraged conservatives, including Howard Phillips, the president of the Conservative Caucus. Phillips had played the role of conservative purist gadfly even during Ronald Reagan's administration, so it is hardly surprising that he would view the presidency of mainstream Republican Bush with a good deal of skepticism.

A native of ultraliberal Boston and a graduate of Harvard University, Phillips grew up in a political family and got involved in politics at an early age. As a first-year student at Harvard, he was campaign manager for the Republican challenger to House Speaker Tip O'Neill.[4] He was just over thirty years old when he took a position as director of the Office of Economic Opportunity in the Nixon administration. It was also early on that Phillips adopted a hard-line commitment to smaller government and showed a willingness to act on his convictions. After a short time in the position, he resigned as director when Nixon failed to act on campaign promises to defund Lyndon Johnson's Great Society programs.

In 1974, Phillips founded and then spent the next two decades as chairperson of the Conservative Caucus (CC), a nonpartisan public policy advocacy group. The caucus was well known in Washington. Capitol Hill staff members regarded the CC as a no-compromise advocate that was difficult to work with. Even the group's fellow conservatives sometimes tired of Phillips's insistence on the most hard-line position possible.[5]

The CC addressed issues across the board. It lobbied against the 1978 Panama Canal treaties and against the Strategic Arms Limitation Treaty (SALT) signed by President Jimmy Carter in 1979. It also opposed President Ronald Reagan's appointment of Sandra Day O'Connor to the Supreme Court, supported the 1981 Reagan tax cut, and supported the Strategic Defense Initiative (SDI). Phillips's most serious clash with Reagan came in 1982 when Phillips coauthored a letter to Reagan demanding that then-White House chief of staff Jim Baker be fired for watering down the president's conservative agenda. Reagan issued a stern public rebuke for waging a "campaign of sabotage" against Baker.[6]

When Bush reneged on his promise of no new taxes, and did so by proposing the then-largest tax increase in US history, Phillips announced the need for a new party committed to lower taxes. Appropriately enough, the new party was christened the US Taxpayers Party.[7] The new party invited existing state-based conservative parties to affiliate, with the strong suggestion that they change their name to avoid confusion. Phillips was nominated as the party's 1992 candidate for president, and the arduous task of complying with state ballot requirements began. Phillips appeared on twenty-one state ballots and won a total of 43,369 votes, or 0.04 percent of the total. Party leadership also worked to expand their presence by running candidates for office at state and local levels, while also seeking recognition from the Federal Elections Commission (FEC). This recognition was achieved in 1995, allowing the Constitution Party to join Democrats, Republicans, Libertarians, and Greens as officially recognized parties.

The fortunes of the Constitution Party have fluctuated since its founding, at least in presidential elections. Phillips was again the nominee in 1996, and he more than quadrupled his 1992 showing, with over 184,000 votes. In 2000, however, the vote total dropped to just over 98,000, growing to 143,630 in 2004. This was still short of 1996, a total that would not be surpassed until 2008. The party's votes then dropped again in 2012 to 122,389. The party would not top the two hundred thousand mark until 2016.

While the largest surge in the Constitution Party vote, between 1992 and 1996, can be largely attributed to FEC recognition and success in appearing on more state ballots, the 400 percent growth is also due to the high level of dissatisfaction among Republicans with their party's 1996 nominee. Longtime Kansas senator Bob Dole was also a longtime moderate and longtime critic of tax cuts. But with a more reliably conservative GOP nominee in 2000 and 2004, in the person of George W. Bush, the Constitution Party struggled. In 2008, when Republicans once again nominated a US senator with a history of dislike for conservatives (at one point referring to religious conservatives as "agents of intolerance"), the Constitution Party benefitted from the alienation of conservative Republicans. In 2016, widespread distrust of onetime Democrat Donald Trump resulted in a record vote for the Constitution Party.

BALLOT ACCESS

All third parties in the United States face significant obstacles to being placed on electoral ballots. With almost no exceptions, the relevant officials who make decisions about the makeup of ballots are members of the two major parties and are often very partisan and loyal members. County election board members and local registrars have a legitimate reason for limiting ballot access that has nothing to do with party loyalty: preventing voters from being confronted with a confusing ballot. Lengthy lists of choices, at a minimum, make for long lines on Election Day and may even lead to disenfranchising some voters if the lines are so long that they are turned away when the polls close. California's recent experience with ballot initiatives, which has led to pages-long ballots for voters to grapple with, demonstrates the problem confronting ballot decision-makers.

More often than not, the Constitution Party has been successful in its efforts to "crash the party" on Election Day. But the larger parties usually try to set the rules, and sometimes the struggle can become personal. In 1996, for example, the Pennsylvania Republican Party stripped a delegate to the national convention of her credentials for circulating a petition to get Constitution Party founder Phillips on the Pennsylvania ballot.[8] The Constitution Party presidential candidate appeared on thirty-nine state ballots in 1996, a feat the party has not achieved since.[9]

Still, access for the Constitution Party cannot be taken for granted. As recently as 2015, a federal judge used harsh language in a decision requiring Pennsylvania to make way for minor-party candidates. US district judge Lawrence Stengel opined that the rights of third parties to get their message out "had been decimated" by a stringent provision of the commonwealth's election code. The provision forced third parties to submit a much higher number of signatures on nominating petitions than either Republicans or Democrats. The same provision also required minor parties to pay legal fees associated with challenges to their signatures, fees that could go as high as $100,000. Under the rules in place at the time, "independent" candidates had to collect enough signatures to equal 2 percent of the votes cast for the winner in the most recent statewide election. In practical terms, this meant that the Constitution Party had to gather seventy thousand signatures, while Democrats and Republicans only needed about two thousand. The ruling allowed the Constitution Party to run a candidate for president in Pennsylvania for the first time since 2000.[10]

In Alabama, minor-party candidates must amass five thousand signatures to run as independents, which means that while the name of the candidate appears, his or her party name does not appear on the ballot. To have the name of the Constitution Party included, nearly forty thousand signatures are required.[11] In 2016, it took a decision by a US district judge to ensure that Cindy Redburn had her opportunity to run for a seat on the St. Louis County Council. The judge told county officials that they could not enforce a charter provision limiting ballot access to parties that had received the highest two vote totals in Missouri's most recent gubernatorial election.

The same coalition of parties fought a similar battle in Georgia, where Democrats and Republicans barely had to submit signatures at all, while independent parties needed a number of valid signatures equal to 1 percent of the state's registered voters. After a judicial ruling similar to the one in Pennsylvania, Georgia appealed, insisting that independent parties had to show "a modicum of support" to avoid what the state called "voter confusion." The judge's ruling applied only to the presidential race. Down-ballot candidates still have to match 5 percent of the voters in a congressional or state legislative district.[12]

In West Virginia, efforts by the secretary of state's office to remove minor-party candidates from the ballot resulted in a federal judge overruling the state supreme court and directing that seventeen independent candidates' names, including Darrell Castle, presidential nominee of the Constitution Party, be restored. In this case, the candidates' lawsuit was supported by the American Civil Liberties Union (ACLU).[13]

THE CAMPAIGN OF 1996

The Constitution Party hit its peak in the year of the Bill Clinton–Bob Dole election. Given the origins and nature of the party, this is not surprising. As a US senator from Kansas, Dole had championed a large tax increase in 1982 and had proposed several additional tax increases since. Moreover, Dole muted many of his policy differences with incumbent President Clinton, who was anathema to the Constitution Party–faithful not only because of the large tax increase Clinton signed into law in 1993 but also because of his support for government-sponsored health care and his prochoice position on abortion.

Finally, 1996 shaped up to be a good year for the Constitution Party because its voters could be quite certain that their votes would not skew the outcome of the presidential race. While Dole's campaign experienced a surge after he chose tax-cut enthusiast Representative Jack Kemp as his running mate, the Republican nominee spent virtually the entire fall campaign almost twenty points behind Clinton. (There was so little drama on election night that CBS announced Clinton's reelection almost as an afterthought.)

Phillips and other leaders of the Constitution Party had one more reason for high hopes: a secret plan to lure a prominent Republican leader to their side. Phillips held several unannounced meetings with conservative commentator Pat Buchanan, who had challenged Dole in the Republican primaries. Based on these conversations, Phillips decided to hold the Constitution Party's national convention in San Diego, at the same time as the Republican convention.

The plan was for Buchanan, when he addressed the Republican delegates, to announce that he was leaving the Republican Party and joining the Constitution Party. He would then invite disgruntled (or merely unenthusiastic) delegates to join him. In the imagination of the Constitution Party leaders, dozens of delegates would walk out, on national television, and place the Constitution Party on the political map.

In the event, the party was to experience yet another disappointment. Buchanan endorsed Dole the night before the convention. The Constitution Party, for its part, nominated Phillips again. Phillips still did not give up. Phillips suggested that if he won enough Electoral College votes to win, he would direct electors pledged to him to vote for Buchanan.[14]

The party's choice of Herbert W. Titus as vice-presidential nominee also brought complications. First, since both Phillips and Titus were from Virginia, electors from that state would not be able to vote for both. Thus, a stand-in candidate was needed for Virginia. Second, during the campaign, Titus had the distraction of a defamation suit brought against Regent University School of Law after he was forced out of his dean's position by Regent founder and religious broadcaster Pat Robertson.[15]

Through much of the 1996 campaign, Phillips spent much more of his time and energy running against Dole than against Clinton. His campaign literature on abortion, crime, education, and international issues contrasted Phillips's positions with Dole's and made no mention of Clinton.[16] In an interview with the *St. Louis Post-Dispatch*, Phillips touted endorsements from the American Life League, Operation Rescue, the New York State Right to Life Party, and a traditional Catholic newspaper. He told the paper that he wanted, and expected, the Constitution Party to be "the successor party" to the Republicans, as the Republicans were the successors of the Whigs in the 1850s.[17]

The effort began with getting the party on the ballot in as many states as possible. In this regard, 1996 was a great success. His name and party affiliation were on the ballot in thirty-nine states, up from twenty-one in 1992.[18] Still, as late as mid-October, Phillips had to admit that his campaign was "invisible to the naked eye," and he lamented Buchanan's failure to come on board. "There's no doubt about the fact that Pat Buchanan was a name-brand candidate. I am not," he told the Associated Press.[19]

The platform of the US Taxpayers Party revolved around four principles: codifying legal personhood beginning at conception, and thus outlawing abortion for any reason; asserting US sovereignty and withdrawing from international organizations that threaten to weaken that sovereignty, such as the United Nations and the International Monetary Fund; deep cuts in the federal budget, including the elimination of entire cabinet-level departments; and replacing the federal income tax with high tariffs and state contributions to cover those functions the party recognized as constitutional.[20]

Throughout, Phillips suffered the hardships of an underfunded and almost invisible campaign. As one observer put it, "[third party candidates] are forced to run on the cheap, and it's not always easy. On days when Clinton and Dole are resting up in fancy hotel suites, they're stuck in low-budget motels. When Clinton and Dole are on stages speaking to thousands, they're talking to busy shoppers at suburban malls. And when they can afford to fly at all, they fly coach."[21] Maintaining a sense of optimism under such circumstances is not easy, but Phillips managed it. He told a reporter: "We could go from nothing to something overnight. Very few people expected the Berlin Wall to fall as dramatically and quickly as it did."[22] On Election Day, the party had its best showing to date, gaining 184,820 votes, or 0.19 percent of the total. This was far short of the 5 percent needed for federal matching funds but a huge improvement over 1992.

THE PARTY'S 2016 PLATFORM

Twenty years later, The Constitution Party perceived another unique opportunity, given the lack of enthusiasm among many faithful for Democrat Hillary Clinton and Republican Donald Trump. The party compiled its most recent platform in April 2016 at the party's convention in Salt Lake

City and published the platform online. Using boldface type and centering the words on the page, the party immediately invoked America's founding documents: "We declare the platform of the Constitution Party to be predicated on the principles of: The Declaration of Independence, The Constitution of the United States and The Bill of Rights, according to the original intent of the Founding Fathers."[23]

The document then includes elements that are evidently intended to distinguish the Constitution Party from the Libertarian Party, an effort that has animated party leaders since the beginning. The preamble starts with this sentence: "The Constitution Party gratefully acknowledges the blessing of our Lord and Savior Jesus Christ as Creator, Preserver and Ruler of the Universe and of these United States." There follows a prayer that Christ will assist "as we work to restore and preserve these United States."

The platform goes on to include thirty-nine planks, thirty-eight of which are listed alphabetically. The exception is the very first plank after the preamble, which is called "Sanctity of Life." This plank uses the most famous quotation from the Declaration of Independence as its heading: "We hold these truths to be self-evident, that all men are created equal, that they are endowed by their Creator with certain unalienable rights, that among these are Life, Liberty and the pursuit of Happiness." Personhood, for the Constitution Party, comes from God and must be recognized by any legitimate government, from fertilization to natural death, "without exception." The document adds: "No level of civil government may legalize or fund the taking of life without justification."

With regard to the often-cited exceptions of rape and incest, the platform expresses empathy with the victims and "assert[s] the need to provide immediate protection and care in a safe environment." Significantly, the document does not specify what institution should provide this protection and care. It is emphatic, however, in its rejection of abortion as a remedy: "We find it unconscionable to take the life of an innocent child for the crimes of his (sic) father." The party explicitly promises a prolife litmus test for those seeking appointment to "the judiciary, and to other positions of legal and executive authority."

As far as *Roe v. Wade* is concerned, the Constitution Party sees this decision as a violation of Article IV, Section 4, of the Constitution. This provision guarantees that states will have a republican form of government. By striking down existing laws against abortion, as the Supreme Court did in its 1973 decision, the court acted in violation of this guarantee. Thus, the justices' ruling "is binding on the parties to the controversy as to the particulars of the case, [but] it is not a political rule for the nation. Roe v. Wade is an illegitimate usurpation of authority, contrary to the Declaration of Independence and the Constitution." As remedies, the platform urges resistance by civil authorities at all levels and calls upon Congress to use its authority under Article 3, Section 2, to limit the appellate jurisdiction of the federal courts on the issue of abortion.

The platform also draws distinctions between the Constitution Party and the Libertarian Party on the issue of drug laws. This part of the 2016 platform includes the text of the 10th and 4th Amendments to the Constitution (in that order). The document goes on to defend the rights of states and localities to restrict the use of and access to drugs. It also endorses blocking the entry of illegal drugs into the United States from foreign countries, consistent with the party's belief that providing for national security is a core government function.

The same plank, however, notes the dangers in actually enforcing the laws that the Constitution Party endorses one paragraph above. It adds: "We will take care to prevent violations of the Constitutional and civil rights of American citizens. Searches without probable cause and seizures without due process must be prohibited." In addressing the issue of drug abuse in this way, the Constitution Party may be trying to attract both voters interested in morality and Libertarian Party voters. The latter is famous for its laissez-faire attitude toward drugs.

The effort to distinguish itself from the Libertarian Party continues in plank twenty-one of the 2016 platform, titled "Pornography, Obscenity & Sexually Oriented Businesses." Here, the party quotes Samuel Adams: "While the people are virtuous they cannot be subdued; but once they lose their virtue they will be ready to surrender their liberties to the first external or internal invader."[24] Nor is pornography just a personal issue. Rather, the "distortion of the true nature of sex" that pornography and obscenity represent "results in emotional, physical, spiritual and financial costs to individuals, families and communities."

The plank goes on to link pornography with "increasing crime rates, specifically rape and molestation, in addition to the loss of dignity belonging to all human beings," as well as reduced property values. The party acknowledges that government action may be needed in this matter, noting that "government plays a vital role in protecting all citizens, particularly our most vulnerable, women and children, from exploitation."

In short, the Constitution Party issues a qualified and conditional invitation in its platform to libertarians. While making no mention of the rival party in its 2016 document, no one from either party could fail to see the significant overlap between the two party platforms.

THE 2016 CAMPAIGN

The Constitution Party's national convention nominated Darrell Castle, a sixty-seven-year-old Tennessee lawyer who had been the party's vice-presidential nominee in 2012. His signature promises during the campaign were to get the United States out of the United Nations, to quit the North Atlantic Treaty Organization (NATO), to abolish the Federal Reserve, and to cut taxes and spending. Castle's biggest advantage in 2016 was the record-low approval ratings of Trump and Clinton. He was also buoyed by a Gallup poll showing that 57 percent of voters believed that a third major political party is needed in the United States. At the same time, the number of self-identified independent voters was also at a record high.[25] The downside of these phenomena for Castle, however, was the number of third-party campaigns that were better funded, better advertised, and better organized than his own, such as Gary Johnson for the Libertarians, Jill Stein for the Green Party, and independent candidate Evan McMullin.

His biggest boost occurred when radio talk show host Glenn Beck endorsed Castle in October. Beck had been a vocal critic of Trump and rejected him completely after the release of the *Access Hollywood* tape that showed Trump speaking disparagingly about women. Even in this case, Beck's endorsement of Castle seemed an afterthought. The talk show host originally posted on Facebook that, in light of the *Access Hollywood* revelation, a vote for Hillary Clinton would be "a moral, ethical choice." Concluding soon afterward that Clinton was also morally unacceptable, Beck threw his support to Castle.[26]

The party's lack of national organization was clear in the confusion over the ballot in Idaho. Rather than send delegates to the national convention in Salt Lake City, Idaho's Constitution Party held a statewide primary, won by Reverend Scott Copeland. Having won the primary, Copeland successfully sought certification from the secretary of state. Later, Castle decided to try to get on the ballot as well, and ran as an independent. The state party chairman said of the party's national nominee, "Mr. Castle is the insider, or the party elite of the establishment, if you will, in the Constitution Party."[27] In the end, Castle received 4,403 votes in Idaho to Copeland's 2,356.[28] Nationwide, the Constitution Party appeared on twenty-five state ballots and received 203,010 votes, 0.15 percent of the total.[29]

OTHER CONSTITUTION PARTY CAMPAIGNS

One of the keys to the success of the fledgling Republican Party in the 1850s was the breadth of its ambition. Put differently, the first Republicans did not just appear in the presidential election. Such a strategy consigns a new party to almost complete invisibility three out of every four years. Rather, the Republicans presented candidates in state and local elections, and they were especially sedulous in doing so after 1856, the year of their first presidential ballot appearance. Thus, when the party held its nominating convention in Chicago in 1860, the event drew tens of thousands.

By contrast, the Constitution Party has had little success in running candidates for state and local elected offices, let alone getting their members elected. It is worth noting, in this regard, that at their 2016 convention, their seventh national convention, the Constitution Party drew only 142 delegates. This is an extraordinary record of neglect, given the claims by Phillips and others that the party is the natural successor to the GOP. Even the party's own website lists only a few dozen candidates nationwide.

Such a paucity of aspirants points to the lack of grassroots support for the Constitution Party, a lack that appears even in strongly conservative states. A spokesperson for the South Dakota party chapter noted that the party had about one hundred members statewide, at a time when the state's population was about seven hundred and fifty thousand. The spokesperson went on: "Our main effort right now is to get more members and figure out how to raise more money. At this point, we just need more people, and that's difficult."[30] The party's US Senate candidate in New York voiced a similar reality just before Election Day, saying, "Most of the people don't know we exist. When you're a third-party candidate, many people think you're a fringe person."[31] The same year, only four Constitution Party candidates ran in all of North Dakota, another state that should be considered prime territory for the party.[32]

As often as not, down-ticket Constitution Party candidates are disgruntled Republicans who have concluded that the Republican Party is no longer committed to constitutional principles. One such example is a state legislative race in Montana in 2000. Three-term representative Rick Jore announced in February that he would quit the Republican Party and file as a candidate from the Constitution Party. He announced his new party affiliation, saying, "I don't see any change in direction as far as restoring constitutional principles [in the Republican Party]." He added, "My concern is that the Republican Party simply takes conservatives for granted. The inclination is generally to compromise toward the Democrats. The conservatives are simply left out in the cold." Jore promised to persuade other legislators to follow him to the new party but seemed doubtful that he would have much success in doing so. Like other Constitution Party candidates, Jore faced difficult ballot access requirements. He had to gather at least five thousand signatures statewide, which had to include at least one hundred and fifty signatures from thirty-four of the one hundred House districts in the state.[33] (He ended up being defeated for reelection that year.)

Jore's example points to the usefulness of the Constitution Party as a threat to establishment Republicans. If dozens of legislators were indeed to follow Jore's example, the goal of pushing the Republican Party to the right would probably be achieved. A more specific version of this overall goal was visible in the threat issued by one prominent Republican later in 2000. Alan Keyes, who had twice run for the GOP presidential nomination, said he would quit the GOP and join the Constitution Party if delegates to the Republican national convention that year softened their prolife position or if then-presumptive nominee George W. Bush chose a running mate who was not reliably prolife.

A Keyes spokesperson said that the party change would indicate that Keyes had "[exhausted] all of his mental energy in trying to get the Republican Party to do the right thing." Constitution Party leaders, for their part, immediately promised to welcome Keyes to the party and even make him their candidate for president.[34] In the end, Bush chose prolife champion Dick Cheney for vice president, the prolife plank was not revised, and Keyes remained in the GOP. Without a high-profile defection, prospects for the party, even on the congressional, state, and local level, remain bleak.

CONCLUSION

The most relevant question about the Constitution Party for political analysts is not whether or not the party has a chance to become a major factor in American politics, but rather whether or not the organization should be considered a political party at all. Of the necessary functions of political parties listed by G. Bingham Powell Jr., Russell J. Dalton, and Kaare Strom, which have been adapted by other scholars, only one can be clearly identified with the Constitution Party, and that is interest articulation. The party has staked out a clear set of positions, and these positions have changed very little since the first campaign by the US Taxpayers Party in 1992.

However, by any other measure, the Constitution Party comes up short. Their efforts at publicity have been unsuccessful enough that they can make no claim to influence political socialization. As noted above in the cases of Pat Buchanan and Alan Keyes, they have had spectacular failures in the area of elite recruitment. I have noted examples above of Constitution Party spokespeople themselves admitting that their efforts at citizen recruitment have also been largely unsuccessful. As far as interest aggregation is concerned, the founding rationale of the party is a rejection of interest aggregation. And having never elected a member of Congress and only a handful of other officials, the party can make no claim to a role in policy-making.

Thus, what is called the Constitution Party is really more of an interest group. Like other interest groups, it adheres to a firm set of policy preferences. It seeks to find space for those policy preferences in political discussions. It seeks to persuade elected officials, while at the same time threatening those officials with political reprisals if the interest group is not satisfied. Most of all, the Constitution Party takes the hard-line positions that it does as a counterweight to opposing positions, with the ultimate hope of moving the needle of political discussion in its direction.

One scholar compared third parties in the United States to bees.[35] While their stings can be painful, and rarely fail to attract attention, they are fatal to the bees themselves. Normally, this fatality occurs when a major party adopts the positions of a third party and causes the third party to disappear. This fate is currently beyond the reasonable aspirations of the Constitution Party.

NOTES

1. Paul F. Boller Jr., *Presidential Campaigns from George Washington to George W. Bush* (Oxford: Oxford University Press, 2004), 324.

2. G. Bingham Powell Jr., Russell J. Dalton, and Kaare Strom, *Comparative Politics Today: A World View* (London: Pearson Publishing, 2014), ch. 6.

3. John F. Bibby and L. Sandy Maisel, *Two Parties—Or More?* (Boulder, CO: Westview Press, 1998), 4

4. Shelley Donald Coolidge, "The Other Men Who Would Be President Series: The 1996 Campaign," *Christian Science Monitor* 22 (October 1996): 10.

5. I was with some of those conservative groups in the 1980s, and this summary is based on my own interactions with Phillips and with those who attempted to work with him. Even the undoubted legislative victories of the Reagan years usually left Phillips insisting that a greater victory would have been possible if only there had not been premature and unwarranted compromise.

6. Phil Gailey and Warren Weaver Jr., "Briefing," *New York Times,* June 5, 1982, A8.

7. The party would change its name to the Constitution Party in 1999.

8. Anick Jesdanun, "Pennsylvania GOP Ousts Buchanan Delegate from National Convention," Associated Press, August 7, 1996.

9. "Facts about the U.S. Election November 5," Reuters, November 4, 1996.

10. Ben Finley, "Judge: PA Code Unfair to Third-Party Candidates," *Philadelphia Inquirer,* July 25, 2015, A1. In the event, the Constitution Party was on the ballot in Pennsylvania in 2016 and garnered 0.4 percent of the votes.

11. Philip Rawls, "Alabama Law Makes Ballot Access Difficult for Third Parties," *Associated Press*, July 2, 2000.

12. Kristina Torres, "Election 2016: Ruling Eases Way for Third-Party Hopefuls," *Atlanta Journal-Constitution*, April 2, 2016, A1.

13. "Judge Orders 17 Independent Candidates Must Remain on Ballot," *Associated Press*, September 24, 2016.

14. Jennifer Loven, "U.S. Taxpayers' Party Wants Pat Buchanan—Whether He Likes It or Not," *Associated Press*, April 3, 1996.

15. "Virginians Run for President, Vice President," *Associated Press*, August 22, 1996.

16. Susan Hegger, "Third Parties Clamoring for Attention, Votes," *St. Louis Post-Dispatch*, October 30, 1996, A8

17. Hegger, "Third Parties," A8.

18. Had Pat Buchanan agreed to be the party's presidential candidate, ballot access might actually have been more difficult due to "sore loser" laws. Such laws prevent the loser in a primary to run on a different party ticket in the general election.

19. "Taxpayers' Party Candidate Encouraged by Greater Ballot Access," *Associated Press*, October 21, 1996.

20. Jo Mannies, "Taxpayers' Party Candidate Says God Guides Platform," *St. Louis Post-Dispatch*, September 25, 1996, 5B.

21. Mimi Hall, "Dim Odds Don't Daunt Third-Party Candidates," *USA Today*, October 9, 1996, 7A

22. Hall, "Dim Odds," 7A.

23. "2020 National Platform," Constitution Party, accessed January 10, 2019, https://www.constitutionparty.com/assets/2016-2020_National_Platform.pdf.

24. This quotation is taken from a letter to James Warren, dated February 2, 1779.

25. Byron Tau, "Longshot Names Are Historically Strong," *Wall Street Journal*, November 8, 2016, A10. It is worth noting that, even on Election Day, minor parties were relegated to the back pages of major newspapers.

26. Ben Rosen, "Glenn Back Offers up Another Gradation of the Not-Quite-Endorsement," *Christian Science Monitor* 11 (October 2016).

27. "Idaho to Have Different Constitution Party Nominee," *Associated Press*, August 21, 2016.

28. "Official 2016 Presidential General Election Results," Federal Election Commission of the United States of America, accessed February 13, 2019, https://transition.fec.gov/pubrec/fe2016/2016presgeresults.pdf.

29. "Official 2016," Federal Election Commission.

30. "Party Trying to Beef up Membership in State," *Associated Press*, June 7, 2000.

31. Anny Kuo, "Third Party Candidates in Senate Race Just Want to Be Heard," *Associated Press*, November 4, 2000.

32. Dale Watzel, "June Statewide Primary Ballot Is Whole Lotta Blankety-Blank," *Associated Press*, April 23, 2000.

33. "Conservative Lawmaker Says He'll Bolt GOP, Push Constitution Party," Associated Press, February 15, 2000.

34. Douglas Kiker, "Keyes Might Leave GOP if Party Weakens Anti-abortion Platform," Associated Press, May 23, 2000.

35. Tau, "Longshot Names," A10.

CHAPTER 4

The New York and Connecticut Working Families Party

Bilal Sekou

INTRODUCTION

The winner-take-all voting system and the lack of a parliamentary system or proportional representation makes access to the ballot line difficult for minor parties in most states, strongly tilting the American political system in favor of the two major political parties, the Democrats and Republicans.[1] Given the structural limits to ballot access third parties face, by the 1990s, many activists on the left and leaders of the labor movement believed that the best strategy to exercise influence in the political system was to work within the Democratic Party and use primary elections to move it to the left rather than attempt to build an alternative left-wing political party.[2]

However, others on the left and in the labor movement felt the Democratic Party had shifted so far to the right since the 1960s that an alliance with Democrats was unpalatable. Some wanted to simply create a left alternative and challenge the Democrats. Dan Cantor, the labor coordinator for the Jesse Jackson campaign in 1988, believed that there was a third option. Cantor coauthored a paper with Joel Rogers, a political scientist and law professor at the University of Wisconsin, titled *Party Time*. In the paper, Cantor and Rogers advocated for both an inside and outside strategy. They wrote, "We propose a cross between the 'party within the party' strategy favored by some Democratic Party activists and the 'plague on both your houses' stance adopted by some critics of both major parties."[3]

The Working Families Party (WFP) was founded in the state of New York in 1998 by Cantor and a coalition of labor unions, politicians, community organizations, key staff from the now-defunct national New Party (NP), and advocacy groups such as the Association of Community Organizations for Reform Now (ACORN) and Citizen Action of New York.[4] The party has a full-time staff of forty people in New York. The number of paid canvassers swells from thirty-five during nonelection years to five hundred around Election Day (this does not include the thousands of volunteers who work for the party during the final weeks of the campaign). By comparison, the WFP's noncanvassing staff is larger than the staff of the Democratic party in every other state. The party employs less than a dozen staff outside of New York.[5] This chapter is about how the WFP in two states—New York and Connecticut—uses its access to the ballot to work within the Democratic Party in an attempt to move it to the left and fight for the passage of legislation the party considers essential to support the needs and interests of working-class people.

The WFP's strategy is straightforward: with a spot on the ballot, the party is able to exercise leverage over politicians who want to run, as well as those who run on its own line. Fusion voting is a process where two or more parties (typically a major party and a minor party) endorse the same candidate for the same office during the general election. Other names for fusion voting are *electoral fusion, cross endorsement, multiple-party nomination, multiparty nomination, plural nomination,* and *ballot freedom.* Electoral fusion was once popular in the United States in the early twentieth century. However, as minor political parties increasingly used it with success, lawmakers from the two major parties in most states banned its use. Currently, fusion voting is legal only in New York, Connecticut, and six other states.[6] States that ban electoral fusion either prohibit multiple-party endorsement or require that candidates be members of the party that nominated them.[7]

In multiple-party nomination states, the candidate must either seek the cross endorsement or accept it if unsolicited. In Connecticut, New York, and Oregon, the candidate's name appears on the ballot as many times as they are nominated by a political party, with the total number of votes the candidate receives on each ballot line added up together.[8] In those states that allow plural nominations, minor parties are able to potentially influence election outcomes and public policy.[9]

THE NEW YORK WORKING FAMILIES PARTY

In 1990, Cantor and Rogers helped found the NP. The NP was to be a left political party that would work both "inside" and "outside" the Democratic Party. They thought that fusion was the way to help the NP exercise influence in the Democratic Party; by winning progressive votes for Democrats on the NP ballot line, the party could pressure Democratic candidates to move left to win its support.[10] Getting more states to adopt fusion voting was crucial to their strategy. But, at the time, only six states allowed cross-party endorsements. For the next seven years, the NP only ran candidates for office with good chances of winning and mounted legal challenges to state laws blocking fusion. The party ran its first candidates in 1992. Over the years, it was able to accumulate a record of impressive accomplishments: NP candidates won offices at the local level, mostly city council and school board seats; roughly half its candidates were women and more than one-third of its candidates were people of color.[11]

However, in 1997, the US Supreme Court ruled in a 6–3 decision, *Timmons v. Twin Cities Area New Party*, that states could ban electoral fusion.[12] After the *Timmons* decision, the NP and its various chapters around the nation started to fade. Cantor and a few key staff members moved back to New York, a state that allowed cross-party endorsements, and began laying the groundwork for a new political party, the Working Families Party.

New York has a long history of minor political parties exercising influence disproportionate to their size in the state; first, there was the Liberal Party in the 1930s, and then the Conservative party in the 1960s. In 1992, the Right to Life Party helped Alfonse M. D'Amato win reelection to the Senate, and in 1994, George E. Pataki defeated three-term incumbent Governor Mario Cuomo with the support of the Conservative Party.[13]

Currently, there are six minor parties in New York with statewide memberships: the Conservative Party, the Green Party, the Independence Party, the Libertarian Party, the Serve America Movement (SAM) Party, and the Working Families Party.[14] According to Article 6, Section 128, of the Consolidated Laws of the State of New York, to launch a minor party and qualify for a ballot line, an aspirant party must first collect fifteen thousand voter's signatures (at least one hundred people have to sign in one-half the congressional districts in the state) via nomination petitions. If the organization's gubernatorial candidate receives fifty thousand votes, the organization will be recognized in the state as a political party, earns a dedicated spot on the ballot for the next four years, and can nominate candidates for future offices without having to collect signatures. The second step is to form state and county committees, prepare rules for governing the party, and file party rules with the board of elections before the next election. To maintain party status, the party must continually nominate a candidate for governor who wins at least fifty thousand votes in each gubernatorial election.[15]

For the founders of the Working Families Party, the creation of the WFP was to counter what they saw as the rightward drift of political parties, including the Democrats. "We saw all these parties pulling the debate toward the interests of the wealthy, or Christian right, but no one was pulling the debate toward working people or progressive ideas," said Bob Master, the political director of the Communications Workers of America for New York and New Jersey and one of the key organizers of the party.[16]

Worried that Pataki would win reelection in 1998, union leaders wanted to energize their members who did not believe that the Democrats fought hard enough to prevent Pataki's 1995 budget cuts and his attempt to reduce workers' compensation rates.[17] The WFP was born at a time when the Democratic Party was weak in the state of New York. Pataki was easily cruising toward reelection, Republicans had control of both chambers of the legislature, and Rudy Giuliani was in his second term as mayor of New York City.[18]

The Local Level

In 2001, the WFP cross-endorsed New York City councilman Peter Vallone Sr., the Democratic Party nominee for governor. Vallone, at the time the second most powerful person in the city, was selected the first speaker of the city council in 1986. The Vallone endorsement was controversial; he was not a progressive. Mostly an exercise in pragmatism, the move paid huge dividends. The party picked up 51,325 votes on the WFP ballot line with Vallone at the top of the ticket (the party needed fifty thousand votes to guarantee a spot on the ballot over the next four years). After earning a place on the ballot, the party was now able to grow in the state. Cantor became the executive director, and several of the state's largest private-sector unions joined the WFP, including 32BJ and 1199 of the Service Employees International Union.[19]

Whereas some of the groups behind the formation of the Working Families Party were mostly concerned with winning statewide offices, others saw the party as a vehicle to win local races. In New York City, the party was also a means for settling a long-running feud with Raymond B. Harding, the chairman of the Liberal Party, who had endorsed Rudy Giuliani in 1989 and 1993. Guiliani ran as a fusion candidate of both the Republican and Liberal Parties against the Democratic Party nominee David N. Dinkins.[20]

In 2009, the WFP became involved in races for seats on the New York City Council. The party started recruiting potential candidates for the council back in 2007. In 2009, nine of the ten candidates it backed were elected.[21] One endorsed candidate, Letitia James, who was running for reelection on city council, became the first candidate for public office in the state of New York to win, running solely on the WFP ballot line.[22]

The group formed a progressive caucus on the council and promoted three top priorities: paid sick days for workers, an inclusionary zoning ordinance that would require that developers build "affordable" housing units in exchange for building permits, and a citywide "living" minimum wage that would include workers on projects that receive money from the city. For the next three years, the caucus pushed their issues. Their persistence paid off when council speaker Christine Quinn finally allowed a vote on the issue in 2013. A paid sick bill was passed over the veto of mayor Michael Bloomberg. Companies with more than fifteen employees would have to provide at least one hour of sick time for every thirty hours an employee works, with a maximum requirement of forty hours of sick time to an employee each year (the law was revised in 2014 to cover employers with more than five workers).[23]

In 2010, the WFP recruited, trained, and, in 2013, endorsed candidates for thirteen seats on the city council. The party campaigned on ending the city's notorious police practice of stop and frisk and raising the wages of fast-food workers. Twelve of the thirteen were elected to the council, dramatically expanding the progressive caucus.[24]

With its influence in local politics growing with each election, the party came under attack for allegedly violating campaign finance laws. The party had created a for-profit campaign arm, Data and Field Services, to provide campaign services to candidates—such as offering contact lists and get-out-the-vote efforts on Election Day—and was accused of funneling unreported illegal campaign contributions to candidates it liked by discounting those services violating New York's public campaign financing laws.[25] The United States attorney's office in Manhattan issued subpoenas seeking campaign documents from the WFP and candidates who contracted services with the party in 2009.[26] A three-year investigation by the US attorney's office and the state's Election Commission ended with no charges.

For a number of years, the party had its eyes on the mayor's office. The party finally found who they believed to be the right candidate in 2013. The WFP endorsed and then helped Bill de Blasio get elected mayor of New York City. Prior to running for mayor, de Blasio was a member of the city council from 2002 to 2009 and had been the public advocate for the city from 2010 to 2013 (the WFP helped him get elected to both offices).

The mayor had strong ties to the WFP; he was present at the founding of the party. And he and Dan Cantor had been friends for about thirty years, first meeting when they were graduate students at the School of Interna-

tional and Public Affairs at Columbia University. When de Blasio was on the
city council, he and Cantor unsuccessfully fought to block then-Mayor
Bloomberg's effort to change the city's term-limit law so that he could run
for a third term. Soon after their defeat, de Blasio decided to run for city
advocate with the backing of the WFP.[27]

While the WFP did not endorse de Blasio during the Democratic mayoral primary (the groups affiliated with the WFP were deeply divided about
who to support in the hotly contested primary), once he secured the nomination, the party quickly got behind his run for mayor.[28] Throughout his
campaign, the candidate talked passionately about the need to address economic inequality. Given his long history with the WFP, it should come as no
surprise that the party's agenda became the new mayor's agenda. Under de
Blasio, the city has increased the minimum wage for workers, expanded the
city's paid sick leave law, created a new photo ID card so that the city's large
population of undocumented immigrants can access city services and
banks, stopped arresting people with small amounts of marijuana, scaled
back the police policy of stop and frisk, implemented tougher rent control
laws, and more than twenty thousand units of affordable housing has either
been built or preserved.[29]

The State Level

In 2010, five statewide candidates ran on the WFP's ballot line: the governor, the attorney general, the comptroller, and both candidates for the US
Senate. All five won their races. However, the party's decision to back Andrew Cuomo for governor was controversial. He ran a conservative campaign and held off accepting the party's endorsement until it agreed to his
platform in which he promised to cap local property taxes and reduce state
spending, including money that goes to unions representing teachers.
Party leaders argued that a Cuomo endorsement was necessary because the
party needed to secure at least fifty thousand votes to gain a spot on the ballot for the next four years. With Cuomo at the top of their ticket, the party
received 155,000 votes.[30]

It may come as no surprise that tension between the WFP and Governor
Cuomo had flared up again by 2014 when he first ran for reelection. The
governor faced a challenge in the primary from a political activist and associate professor of law at Fordham University, Zephyr Teachout. Party leaders were seriously flirting with the idea of endorsing Teachout in the primary.[31] WFP and labor leaders met with Cuomo to talk about their
grievances and try to find common ground.

For many in the WFP, reconciliation with Cuomo depended on his willingness to work with Democratic leaders in the legislature to create a program that would fund elections with the public's money, a top priority for good government groups and liberal activists for years. The governor, on the other hand, was proud of his record of progressive policy accomplishments and was not pleased with being pressured to support a program for the public financing of elections.[32] Eventually, New York City mayor de Blasio brokered a deal between the governor and his WFP critics that resulted in the governor appearing in a video in which he promised to prioritize a Democratic Party takeover of the state senate, legislation raising the minimum wage, and campaign finance reform.[33] While the party did not endorse Teachout, she challenged the governor in the primary and won a third of the vote.[34]

Election night failed to deliver a Democratic Party takeover of the state senate. To some, the governor did not work as hard as he should have to help Democrats take the chamber. Rather, he spent more energy on building support for the Women's Equality Party, a minor party he helped create. In a press release, the WFP's political director, Bill Lipton, voiced his disappointment: "Governor Cuomo promised to take back the State Senate. Instead, he squandered millions on a fake party, and left millions more in his campaign account as New York Democrats in the legislature and in Congress withered on the vine."[35]

Roughly four years later in April 2018, although the race for the Democratic nomination for governor of New York had barely begun, the WFP endorsed Cynthia Nixon over the two-term incumbent governor.[36] Nixon, an actress—best known for her role on the romantic comedy-drama television series *Sex and the City*—and educational activist, was making her first attempt at public office. The actress had been teasing the possibility of her running for governor for months.[37] The endorsement would give Nixon a ballot line in November. But first, Nixon would have to defeat the governor in September's Democratic primary.[38]

The Nixon endorsement did not come as a surprise. Months before the primary, the party had been mulling over whether to endorse Cuomo or nominate their own candidate for governor. Leaders of the party, liberal activists, and some labor union allies had grown increasingly frustrated with the governor—a level of frustration that had been building for years.[39]

While the governor's previous two terms had seen progressive and proworker policies and programs signed into law—legalizing same-sex marriage, enacting stronger gun laws, implementing a free college tuition program, increasing paid family leave, and raising the minimum wage to fifteen dollars an hour—many in the party and some Democrats in the legislature believed the governor was too selective in choosing which progressive issues to put the weight of his office behind. Moreover, some thought that he was too conservative on fiscal issues; for example, he lowered corporate taxes, exempted some multimillion-dollar estates from paying inheritance taxes, froze the wages of employees working for the state, reduced the retirement benefits of newly hired state workers, and placed a cap on increases in local property taxes.[40]

Another reason some in the WFP distrusted Cuomo was his acquiescence to the Independent Democratic Conference (IDC). After Republicans took control of the state senate in 2010 with a razor-thin two-seat majority, and just hours before Cuomo was to deliver his first state of the state address, four Democrats decided to break with their party and form the Independent Democratic Conference and work with Republicans. During the previous year, senate Democratic leaders had been embroiled in investigations of casino bidding and lawmaker earmarks and lost the confidence of some in the Democratic caucus. In a press conference, Senator Jeffrey Klein of the Bronx, one of the four Democrats who broke away, said, "Let me be clear. We are Democrats, but we could no longer in good conscience support the present Democratic leadership."[41]

The IDC would eventually grow into a group of eight senators who helped solidify the Republican's hold on the state senate. Progressive groups believed the IDC stood in the way of Democrats retaking the senate and the successful passage of bills such as marijuana legalization and universal health care. Even after the Democrats won control of the senate in 2012, the IDC stayed in place. It would not be until early 2018 when, facing primary challenges, the group would decide to formally disband and end its alliance with Republicans. During the primaries, six of eight members of the IDC—including Jeffrey Klein—were defeated by candidates endorsed by the WFP.[42]

Responding to the Nixon threat, the governor and his allies were prepared for a potential WFP defection and struck first. The governor's emissaries summoned some of the party's top leaders and labor unions (some of the biggest funders of the party) to a meeting at the Manhattan headquarters of the United Federation of Teachers. The party leaders were advised to stay neutral in the governor's race and were warned that if Nixon got the WFP nomination, but lost the primary and remained on the ballot, she would take votes from the governor and help the Republican nominee. Although he was not at the meeting, the governor reportedly encouraged labor groups to stop giving money to liberal community groups backing

Nixon—specifically, Citizen Action of New York, Make the Road Action, and New York Communities for Change. After the meeting, two powerful unions dropped out of the WFP: Local 32BJ of the Service Employees International Union and the Communications Workers of America District 1. Some labor leaders aligned with the governor threatened to form an alternative labor party to compete with the WFP.[43]

About three weeks after the drubbing Nixon took on primary day, the WFP endorsed Cuomo for reelection. The governor beat Nixon with 65 percent of the vote after spending twenty-eight million to do so. Fresh off of his victory, he accepted the WFP endorsement. Rescinding Nixon's endorsement and throwing their support behind the governor was a practical move. Although many members of the party wanted her to stay on the ballot, party leaders did not want to divide the vote in November. And in order to maintain their ballot status, the party needed to receive at least fifty thousand votes on its line, something Nixon might have been able to do given that she had received more than five hundred thousand votes; however, such a move would have likely angered the governor. Cuomo would also appear on two other ballot lines: the Independence Party and the Women's Equality Party.[44] The governor and his allies had created the Women's Equality Party back in 2014, some suggested at the time, to damage the WFP when it was holding back endorsment for reelection.[45]

Over the years, the reoccurring dispute within the party over whether or not the WFP should or should not endorse Cuomo for governor exposed fundamental tension in the party between its liberal wing, comprised of progressive activists who thought the governor was too fiscally conservative and could not be trusted, and the pragmatic wing of the party, comprised mostly of labor union leaders who believed that the governor was going to be reelected and wanted to be in the best possible position to work with him on their top priorities.[46]

The falling-out between some labor groups and WFP leaders, started in 2014 over disagreements about endorsing Governor Cuomo, has carried over into national politics. During the 2016 Democratic presidential primary, most of the state's biggest unions backed former first lady and former US senator from the state of New York, Hillary Clinton. Several of these unions withdrew their financial support from the WFP over the party's endorsement of Bernie Sanders.[47] Some of the tensions in the party may resurface during the 2020 presidential election cycle.

CONNECTICUT WORKING FAMILIES PARTY

Connecticut has a long history of minor parties, some at the local level and some with statewide memberships. Connecticut minor parties have ranged from Communist to Libertarian, and some are one-town or one-issue parties.[48] An example of a minor party exercising influence disproportionate to its size in the state was the A Connecticut Party (ACP), named in such an unusual way to give it placement at the top of the ballot. In 1990, the ACP was a minor party created by former Connecticut Republican senator Lowell Weicker to support his gubernatorial bid. Weicker was elected governor and served one term. Two years after Weicker became governor, the ACP endorsed more than one hundred candidates for the general assembly (the party cross-endorsed mostly Democrats and a few Republicans, and ran sixteen candidates under the banner of the ACP). The party endorsed Weicker's lieutenant governor, Eunice Groark, for governor in 1994, but she lost. Without the charismatic leader it was organized around, the party faded by the end of the decade.[49]

Currently, there are four minor parties with statewide enrollment privileges: the Green Party, the Independent Party, the Libertarian Party, and the Working Families Party.[50] According to the Connecticut General Statutes, Section 9-372(6), to launch a minor party, the first step is to run a candidate using a nominating petition (i.e., collect the signatures of either 1 percent of the votes cast for that office during the previous election or the signatures of seven thousand five hundred voters) with a party designation. If the party receives 1 percent of the vote cast for that office, the party can nominate a candidate for that office without having to collect signatures at the next election. The second step is to file party rules with the office of the secretary of the state before nominating someone for that office in the next election. Last, to maintain minor-party status, the party must continually nominate a candidate for that office in subsequent elections. Failure to do so will result in the loss of minor-party status for that office.[51]

The Connecticut Working Families Party (WFP) was founded in 2002 by a group of labor unions and a community-based organization. The founding executive committee consisted of the American Federation of State, County, and Municipal Employees Council 4; the Communications Workers of America Local 1298; the United Food and Commercial Workers Union Local 371; and ACORN.[52] At the time, Connecticut had a divided state government. While the Democratic Party controlled both chambers of the Connecticut General Assembly, Republican John G. Rowland was governor. The founding members of the party said that they were frustrated with what they perceived as a Democratic Party that had moved to the right and a Republican governor hostile to the needs of working people. The party planned to fight for issues it believed were important to working and poor families in Connecticut, including worker rights, a livable wage, universal health care, property tax reform, public financing of elections, and corporate responsibility.[53]

Jon Green was the Connecticut WFP's first director. Shortly after assuming leadership of the party, Green traveled across the state recruiting candidates to run for seats in the general assembly. The party ran candidates in twenty-five electoral districts in its first year, fielding more candidates than any other minor party in the state. The party's goal, however, was not to win those seats. They were fine with losing as long as their candidate got at least 1 percent of the vote, which would guarantee the party a spot on the ballot without petitioning in the next election. Then, candidates the WFP endorsed in the future would appear twice on the ballot, on either the Democrat or Republican line and the party's line.[54] Although many of their nominees got clobbered on Election Day, all twenty-five of their candidates won at least 1 percent of the vote, putting the party on the ballot in those districts in 2004.[55]

The pragmatic strategy of qualifying for as many ballot lines as possible paid off when in 2006, then-Democratic state senator Chris Murphy defeated incumbent Republican Congress member Nancy Johnson. Because the WFP had fielded a candidate that lost to Johnson in the Fifth Congressional District in 2004, the party was able to cross endorse Murphy in his bid to unseat her two years later. Murphy received an extra 5,794 votes on the WFP ballot line. The party spent about $100,000 and targeted about twenty-eight thousand unaffiliated voters with direct mailings, phone calls, and door-to-door canvasing.[56]

By 2008, the party had gained a line on every ballot in Connecticut. Amazingly, of the 1.5 million registered voters in the state, only fifteen were members of the WFP, which did not even include Green.[57] The leaders of the party were okay with that. What really mattered to them is that the WFP had its ballot line. According to Green, like the WFP in New York, the party's success in Connecticut would come "from making strategic decisions about how to use their ballot line and from doing very good grassroots work."[58] He believed that the party tapped into a huge reservoir of disillusioned voters who trembled at the prospect of having to vote for a candidate of either the Democratic or Republican Party. But, "it's a protest vote that actually counts," he said.[59] Voting for a candidate on the WFP ballot line should have given voters a legitimate option. Green did not want the party's candidates to be seen simply as spoilers, or ideologically pure candidates without a chance to win. "The vote sends a message, but at the same time they don't feel they're wasting it on some kind of Pollyannaish candidate," he added.[60]

When it comes to electing candidates to office to advance its progressive agenda, the Connecticut WFP follows two strategies. At the local level, the party runs its own candidates for office. At the state level, it typically does not run its own candidates—it primarily cross endorses candidates.[61]

The Local Level

While not all of their nominees win, Connecticut WFP–endorsed candidates have run in competitive local races for mayor, board of education, and city council in cities and towns across the state, winning offices in 2018 in Windham/Willimantic, Hartford, Bridgeport, and Norwalk.[62] According to party director Lindsey Farrell, the WFP has made inroads "where there are a lot of unaffiliated voters who don't feel like they are represented by the two major parties."[63] The party has gained its strongest foothold in local politics in Hartford and Bridgeport, benefiting from a quirk in Connecticut law. Many Connecticut municipalities have a rule that prohibits one-party control of locally elected boards and requires minority-party representation. For the city council in Hartford, the city election law says that parties can only nominate six candidates. Voters may only vote for a total of six candidates. But the top nine candidates that receive the most votes are elected. All seats are at-large.[64] In 2007, WFP members Wildaliz Bermudez and Larry Deutsch received more votes than the Republican Party-endorsed candidates and were elected to the city council. In addition to seats on the city council, the quirk in the law has also helped WFP candidates capture a seat on the school board and one of Hartford's registars of voters was elected on the party's ballot line.[65]

On election night in 2011, the WFP expanded by one the number of council seats it controlled in Hartford, capturing all three seats set aside for the minority party, leaving the GOP with no representation. Cynthia Jennings was elected to the council while Bermudez and Deutsch were re-elected.[66] While the rules in Connecticut make it easier for a minor party to have success at the municipal level, party members attribute their victories to the WFP message. "People rally around the Working Families Party because it does specifically address the needs of the regular working families that need to get their voices heard," Jennings said. "The issues that affect whether people can feed their families and breathe clean air and live without having to work two or three jobs. These are all issues that resound with voters. That's the only way a minor party could come in and take seats away from a major political party."[67]

In Democratic-controlled Bridgeport, two-party-endorsed candidates won seats on the Bridgeport Board of Education in 2009. One of those candidates, Maria Pereira, became the city's first WFP chairperson. However, Pereira resigned from the party in 2014 because the party endorsed the incumbent governor, Dannel Malloy, for reelection. The governor was instrumental in a state takeover of the city's public schools, which the courts eventually ruled was illegal—for her, it was an unforgivable overreach of power by the Malloy administration. Although it does not have many registered members in Bridgeport, Pereira acknowledges the invaluable election support the party gave her and other candidates in the city. "They're good at all the requirements of filings, paperwork," she said. "And they're [*sic*] use of current technology—Facebook, Twitter, phone banking—is something the average municipal campaign is not great at."[68]

The State Level

In 2010, the party endorsed Democratic Party nominee Dannel Malloy for governor. The newly elected governor received 26,308 votes on the Working Families Party's ballot line, helping him win his race against the self-funded Republican candidate, Thomas C. Foley, a former United States ambassador to Ireland under President George W. Bush. The election secured ballot access for the WFP.[69] For the first time, the Connecticut WFP helped a candidate win statewide office. Most importantly, in the party's view, the new governor was a strong supporter of the signature issue that the WFP had been organizing around since its founding in the state: paid sick leave.[70]

The WFP typically endorses Democratic candidates through cross endorsements it thinks it can work with. However, if the party identifies a more progressive candidate than the one endorsed by the Democrats for a seat in the legislature, the party has to run its own candidates. In a special state senate election held in February 2015, Edwin A. Gomes became the first candidate in the nation to win a legislative seat, running solely on the WFP line.[71]

Gomes had previously held the same seat in the senate but as a Democrat. A retired union official and an early backer of the WFP when it was being formed in Connecticut, he first won the seat in 2005 in a special election, succeeding the former senator Ernest Newton who went to jail on corruption charges. Gomes was badly defeated in the Democratic primary in 2012 by Andres Ayala.[72]

His former seat reopened after Ayala resigned to become the commissioner of motor vehicles. Gomes was denied the Democratic Party's nomination after a controversial vote but won the five-way race by 542 votes, capturing nearly 50 percent of the vote.[73] Upon returning to the legislature, Gomes once again caucused with the Democrats.[74]

By fall 2016, the alliance between the WFP and Governor Malloy had become shaky. While the governor was a reliable ally to progressives in the state on many social issues, he was more moderate on fiscal matters. He closed a big budget deficit by laying off state workers rather than raising taxes on corporations and the wealthy, and he offered large tax breaks and other financial incentives to corporations to get them to either locate their businesses in Connecticut or prevent them from leaving the state.[75]

The relationship between the WFP and the Democratic Party in general was shakier. On August 9, 2016, all five of the WFP-endorsed candidates who vowed to support the party's proworker agenda in the legislature beat establishment Democrats in primaries to advance to the general election in November. Notably, two incumbent state senators and WFP-endorsed candidates, Gomes and Marilyn Moore, defeated their primary challengers despite each failing to receive the Democratic endorsement (Moore clobbered the candidate selected by the Democrats by a margin of 63 to 37 percent, and both won reelection by comfortable margins that November).[76]

Seizing the moment, a week after the primary, the WFP launched an ambitious prolabor campaign that, if successful, would require major corporations such as Walmart and McDonalds to pay their employees fifteen dollars an hour or be charged a fee to offset the costs to the state when their employees utilize public services. Framing the issue as corporate welfare, the idea behind the low-wage workers fee was quite simple: either companies pay their workers a living wage or they should help cover the cost of public services their workers use.[77]

To kick off the campaign for the low-wage workers fee, dubbed the "Walmart Bill," the WFP asked the public to watch a video and sign a petition.[78] The petition drive was part of a larger effort by the WFP to pressure Governor Malloy to support taxing the rich more, increase the state's minimum wage to fifteen dollars an hour, and establish paid family and medical leave.[79] Connecticut's working poor who work at least 40 hours a week earn less than $19,968 per year, which is roughly $384 per week."[80] Despite being one of the wealthiest states in the nation, roughly one-third of Connecticut residents struggle to cover the cost of food, rent, and other basic needs.[81] "Right now, large profitable corporations are systematically underpaying employees and offering few or no benefits," says Connecticut WFP executive director Lindsay Farrell. "Their workers are forced to rely on public aid programs and as taxpayers, we are subsidizing their profits."[82]

Joshua M. Hall, the party's nominee in a special election held on April 2017 for Connecticut State House District 7, became the second candidate in the nation to win a legislative seat running solely on the ballot line of the Working Families Party.[83] Hall's run reflected a willingness on the part of the WFP to break with the Democrats and run when they deemed more progressive candidates for office were necessary. The party had already registered its discontent with the Democratic-controlled state government over budget cuts enacted in the previous legislative session by backing Joshua Elliot in his challenge of House Speaker J. Brendan Sharkey in the primary. Sharkey chose not to seek reelection and Elliot won the seat.[84]

Hall, a former treasurer for the Democratic State Central Committee and a vice president of the Hartford Federation of Teachers (HFAT), is a strong supporter of the city's beleaguered public school system, a defender of the right of public employees to collectively bargain, and an opponent of austerity budgeting. He defeated Rickey Pinckney Sr., the Democratic-endorsed candidate, and Kenneth P. Green, a petitioning former state legislator trying to make a political comeback.[85]

Hall, a registered Democrat, had tried to win the party's endorsement for the open seat but lost it to Pinckney. The race deepened some of the growing tension between the WFP and the Democratic Party. Pinckney, who had the strong backing of both the Hartford Democratic Party and the State Democratic Party, hit Hall with a mailer produced by a Connecticut-based Democratic campaign consulting firm, the Vinci Group. "Working Families Party? Not on our watch," said the Vinci Group-produced mailer. "There are only 26 registered Working Families members in our district. Only 26. Don't let them steal our seat." On the other side was a picture of President Barack Obama with the statement: "Proud to be a Democrat."[86]

Marc DiBella, the Hartford Democratic Party chairman, expressed his frustration with the WFP challenging their endorsed candidates in a party primary: "They want to have both their cake and eat it, too. . . . There is some bad blood between the Working Families Party and the Democratic Party in Hartford—and some other places." Lindsay Farrell, executive director of the WFP replied: "Ultimately, we are an independent organization. We feel, when the Democratic Party has gotten it wrong, we'll do our own thing. This is one of those times. I can't speak to whether or not that's going to hurt our relationship. It's up to them whether that hurts our relationship. That's up to them."[87] After joining the legislature, Hall caucused with the Democrats.[88]

As a sign of the party's growing strength in state politics, in 2018, WFP-endorsed candidates won big on election night. All candidates that ran with the WFP through cross filing won their statewide office. Moreover, the Democratic Party picked up seats in both the state house and the senate. In the senate, WFP-endorsed candidates won thirteen out of twenty races. In the house, of the seventy-five candidates the party backed, fifty won their seats.[89]

As usual, party activists and volunteers hit the streets, knocking on doors and making turnout calls in each district and across the state. The party also launched a new digital organizing tool, sending over two hundred and fifty thousand texts to potential voters. Going into the 2019 legislative session, the party hoped to exercise more influence than ever in its history; the state senate had more WFP-endorsed Democratic senators than Republican senators.[90]

CONCLUSION

In an article titled "Build an Independent Political Organization (But Not Quite a Party)," published in 2012, Dan Cantor spelled out his vision of the Working Families Party: "(1) build durable, electorally oriented organization and power at the state level; (2) knit that organization and power together across state lines into a national network; and (3) use it all to pull, prod, yank, and compel the Democrats to move in a more progressive direction."[91]

While the full scope of the WFP's success in moving the Democratic Party "in a more progressive direction" is difficult to measure, Cantor's vision of the party expanding outside of New York is being realized. There are state chapters or local branches in New York, Connecticut, Oregon, New Jersey, Washington, DC, Maryland, Pennsylvania, Wisconsin, Rhode Island, New Mexico, West Virginia, Texas, South Carolina, Colorado, Nevada, Ohio, Washington, Louisiana, and Georgia.[92] In states that allow cross endorsements (fusion voting is legal in Connecticut, New York, and Oregon, and in each the party has statewide ballot access), candidates are reaping the benefits of the WFP endorsement without having to give up their status as a member of a major party.

NOTES

1. Elizabeth A. Theiss-Morse, William H. Flannigan, Nancy H. Zingale, and Michael W. Wagner, *Political Behavior of the American Electorate* (Washington, DC: CQ Press, 2018).

2 Harold Myerson, "Dan Cantor's Machine," *The American Prospect*, January 6, 2014.

3. Myerson, "Dan Cantor's."

4. Amy Waldman, "New Party Is Courting Liberal Constituencies," *New York Times*, November 1, 1998; "About Us," Working Families Party, accessed January 20, 2019, http://workingfamilies.org/about-us/.

5. Myerson, "Dan Cantor's."

6. "Fusion Voting," Ballotpedia, accessed September 28, 2019, https://ballotpedia.org/Fusion_voting.

7. Terrance Adams, "Cross-Endorsing Candidates," Connecticut General Assembly, January 16, 2013, accessed January 24, 2019, https://www.cga.ct.gov/2013/rpt/2013-R-0046.htm.

8. Adams, "Cross-Endorsing."

9. "Fusion," Ballotpedia.

10. Myerson, "Dan Cantor's."

11. Paul Haber, "Party Time? Building a Progressive Electoral Movement; A Case for the New Party," *Contemporary Justice Review* 2, no. 2 (1999), 143–144.

12. Timmons v. Twin Cities Area New Party (95-1608), 520 U.S. 351 (1997).

13. Waldman, "New."

14. "Ballot Access Requirements for Political Parties in New York," Ballotpedia, accessed January 20, 2019. https://ballotpedia.org/Ballot_access_requirements_for_political_parties_in_New_York#cite_note-nydef-5.

15. NY Cons. Laws, Elect. Law § 6–128 (nd).

16. Waldman, "New Party."

17. Waldman.

18. David Freedlander, "Bill de Blasio Mayoral Win Signals Working Families Party Ascendancy," The Daily Beast, November 5, 2013.

19. Myerson, "Dan Cantor's."

20. Waldman, "New Party."

21. Freedlander, "Bill de Blasio."

22. Myerson, "Dan Cantor's."

23. Henry Grabar, "New York City Passed Paid Sick Leave, and Guess What? It Didn't Kill Any Jobs," *Slate*, September 7, 2016.

24. Myerson, "Dan Cantor's."

25. David W. Chen, "Working Families Party Documents Subpoenaed," *New York Times*, December 16, 2009; Myerson, "Dan Cantor's."

26. Michael Powell, "As Clout Grows, Working Families Party Faces a Question: Has It Reached Too Far?" *New York Times*, January 6, 2010.

27. Freedlander, "Bill de Blasio."

28. Freedlander.

29. Molly Ball, "The Equalizer: Bill de Blasio vs. Inequality," *Atlantic*, November 23, 2015.

30. "Cuomo Accepts Working Families Party Endorsement," CBS New York, September 12, 2010.

31. Susanne Craig and Thomas Kaplan, "Working Families Party Warns Cuomo of a Possible Opponent," *New York Times*, May 30, 2014; Thomas Kaplan and Susanne Craig, "As Antics Subside, Both Cuomo and the Left Claim the Last Hurrah," *New York Times*, June 2, 2014.

32. Thomas Kaplan and Susanne Craig, Cuomo Works to Mend Fences with Liberals," *New York Times*, May 12, 2014; Thomas Kaplan, "Cuomo, Backed by Working Families Party, May Chip Away at Its Clout at the Polls," *New York Times*, November 1, 2014.

33. Ken Lovett, "Major Unions Drop Funding of Working Families Party," NY Daily News, April 18, 2016.

34. Craig and Kaplan, "Working Families."

35. Chris Smith, "How Cuomo Played the Working Families Party," Intelligencer, November 5, 2014.

36. Gregory Krieg, "The Working Families Party Is Ready 'to Pick a Fight.' But First It Has a Decision to Make," CNN, April 13, 2018; Jesse Mckinley and Vivian Wang, "Working Families' Nod to Nixon Ends a Battle, but the War Awaits," *New York Times*, April 19, 2018.

37. Shane Goldmacher, "Democrats in New York State Senate Reconcile After Years of Infighting," *New York Times*, April 4, 2018.

38. Krieg, "Working Families"; Mckinley and Wang, "Working."

39. Kaplan and Craig, "Cuomo Works."

40. Kaplan and Craig.

41. Thomas Kaplan and Nicholas Confessore, "4 Democrats in State Senate Break With Leaders," *New York Times*, January 5, 2011.

42. Shane Goldmacher, "Cynthia Nixon Explores Possible Run Against Andrew Cuomo," *New York Times*, March 6, 2018; David Weigel, "The End of New York's 'Independent Democrats,' Explained," *Washington Post*, April 4, 2018.

43. Shane Goldmacher and Jesse Mckinley, "Flexing Their Support for Cuomo, Key Unions Leave Working Families Party," *New York Times*, April 13, 2018.

44. Jesse Mckinley, "Cuomo Accepts the Working Families Ballot Line, Ending Feud. For Now," *New York Times*, October 5, 2018; Yancey Roy, "Cuomo Accepts Working Families Line, Ends Feud," Newsday, October 6, 2018.

45. Kaplan, "Cuomo, Backed."

46. Smith, "How Cuomo."

47. Lovett, "Major Unions."

48. Frank Juliano, "To Minor Political Parties, Their Message Is Major," *Greenwich Time*, November 9, 2009.

49. Aaron Faust, "Unions, Association Join to Form Workers' Party," *Hartford Courant*, August 14, 2002; Michele Jacklin and Larry Williams, "Party's Future up to

Goark: A Test of Independence," *Hartford Courant*, March 15, 1994; Jonathan Rabinovitz, "Can the Party Survive Without Weicker? New Path or a Lengthened Shadow?" *New York Times*, October 5, 1994.

50. "Minor Parties in Connecticut," CT.gov, accessed January 20, 2019, https://portal.ct.gov/SOTS/Election-Services/Political-PartiesTown-Committe-Rules/Minor-Parties-in-Connecticut.

51. Nominations and Political Parties, Conn. Stat. § 9–372(6) (2018).

52. Faust, "Unions, Association."

53. Faust; Mark Pazniokas, "Tiny Working Families Party A Coalition Pushing Labor Agenda," *McClatchy-Tribune*, August 4, 2008.

54. Mark Spencer, "Working the System; Party Pushes for Political Clout One District at a Time," *Hartford Courant*, November 2, 2006.

55. Aaron Faust, "3rd Party Earns Ballot Places; Candidates Gain Minimum Tally," *Hartford Courant*, November 7, 2002.

56. Spencer, "Working the System"; Pazniokas, "Tiny Working ."

57. Pazniokas, "Tiny Working."

58. Faust, "Unions."

59. Pazniokas, "Tiny Working."

60. Spencer, "Working."

61. Molly Ball, "The Pugnacious, Relentless Progressive Party that Wants to Remake America," *Atlantic*, Janurary 7, 2016.

62. Carolos Moreno, "Dozens of Wins Across CT Show Appetite for Progressive Change," *Working Families*, February 7, 2018.

63. Brian Lockhart and Keila Torres Ocasio, "Working Families Party Claims Big Victory," *Connecticut Post*, March 1, 2015.

64. Richard Winger, "Working Families Party Elected Three Candidates on 3 November 2015," Ballot Access News, December 2, 2015.

65. Lockhart and Ocasio, "Working Families."

66. Winger, "Working Families."

67. Lockhart and Ocasio, "Working Families."

68. Lockhart and Ocasio.

69. Mark Pazniokas, "With Malloy as Governor, Working Families Party Pushing Paid Sick Days," CT Mirror, November 26, 2010.

70. Pazniokas, "With Malloy."

71. Mark Pazniokas, "Ed Gomes Wins Big, Will Resume State Senate Career at 79," CT Mirror, February 25, 2015.

72. Pazniokas, "Ed Gomes."

73. Pazniokas.

74. Pazniokas.

75. Daniela Altimari, "Working Families Party Pushing Malloy On Higher Wages," *Hartford Courant*, August 19, 2016.

76. Alana Semuels, "Can the Working Families Party Keep Winning?" *Atlantic*, August 16, 2016.

77. Altimari, "Working Families "; Semuels, "Can the Working."

78. "Stop Exploiting Workers, Make Corporations Pay," Action Network, accessed January 20, 2019, https://actionnetwork.org/petitions/stop-exploiting-workers-make-corporations-pay; Working Families Party, "Stop Exploiting Workers, Make Corporations Pay," YouTube, August 15, 2016, https://www.youtube.com/watch?v=Z7FpTMUsg00.

79. Daniela, "Working Families."

80. "Stop Exploiting," Working Families Party.

81. Semuels, "Can the Working."

82. "Stop Exploiting," Working Families Party.

83. Mark Pazniokas, "Working Families Wins in Hartford, GOP in Watertown," CT Mirror, April 26, 2017.

84. Mark Pazniokas, "WFP Backs Union Officer over Endorsed Democrat in Hartford," CT Mirror, March 22, 2017.

85. Pazniokas, "Working Families."

86. Mark Pazniokas, "Hartford Special Election Exposes Political Fault Lines," CT Mirror, April 26, 2017.

87. Pazniokas, "Hartford."

88. Pazniokas, "Working Families."

89. "Connecticut Elections," Ballotpedia, accessed February 25, 2019, https://ballotpedia.org/Connecticut_elections,_2018; "CT WFP Wins Big on Election Night," Working Families, November 13, 2018, accessed February 25, 2019, http://workingfamilies.org/2018/11/d-wfp-state-senate-caucus-surpasses-republicans-voters-turned-out-for-progressive-policies/; "CT Working Families Party 2018 Endorsed Candidates," Working Families, accessed February 25, 2019, http://workingfamilies.org/ct-working-families-party-2018-endorsed-candidates/.

90. "CT WFP," Working Families.

91. Daniel Cantor and Anthony Thigpenn, "Build an Independent Political Organization (But not Quite a Party)," *The American Prospect*, November 28, 2012.

92. "State Hubs Archive," Working Families, accessed February 29, 2019, http://workingfamilies.org/states/.

PART TWO

State Parties

CHAPTER 5

The Peace and Freedom Party of California

Joseph Phillips

The Peace and Freedom Party (PFP) was established in 1967 by a group of anti–Vietnam War activists who were frustrated with the Democratic Party's handling of the war.[1] After a brief but high-profile collaboration with the Black Panthers and an attempt at forming a national People's Party with other left-wing parties, it has become a locus of activism, electoral and otherwise, in the state of California. The PFP has never won any elections other than nonpartisan local races, and due to recent changes in California election law, its visibility has decreased. However, the PFP has had a lasting impact on California's political system through serving as a hub for activism and actions in court on behalf of other third parties.

FROM FRUSTRATED NATIONAL AMBITIONS TO STATE ACTIVITY

The PFP's founding can be understood as a means to house New Left party politics under one electoral roof. The New Left was a movement in the 1960s that sought to redefine socialism in two ways. First, earlier socialist movements and parties tended to view struggles for racial and gender equality as outgrowths of class-based oppression, and thus treated them as secondary considerations.[2] The New Left aimed to treat these struggles as legitimate priorities in their own right.[3] Second, a major component of earlier socialist strategy was seeking election to office, something the New Left saw as largely misplaced energy that could go to direct actions such as protest.[4] The activists that founded the party on June 23, 1967, shared these concerns.[5] However, rather than eschew party politics altogether, it sought to dislodge the dominance of the major parties by channeling their updated understanding of socialism into a single competitive entity.[6]

By the beginning of 1968, the Black Panthers saw an ally in the fledgling party. They proceeded to cooperate on a series of initiatives, including a petition to hold a referendum on community policing.[7] Their collaboration culminated in running Eldridge Cleaver for the presidency in 1968 in seven states. However, not all members within the party agreed with his nomination, and so some state affiliates ran comedian Dick Gregory in another eight states. Combined, these candidates won 83,000 votes for the presidency. The party also competed in several down-ballot races that year, running for three state senate seats (California, Hawaii, and New York), eighteen House of Representatives elections (ten in California, four in New York, two in Hawaii, and two in Washington),[8] one lieutenant governor position in Washington, and at least two state representative seats in Washington.[9] Combined, these candidates netted the party an additional one hundred and ninety thousand votes.[10]

Soon after the election, the PFP experienced two pivotal events: 1) its ambitions to become a national force were stymied. With the exception of California, all of its state affiliates either failed to maintain ballot access by not attaining enough votes or failing to elect party leaders, subsequently dissolving; 2) its alliance with the Black Panthers fizzled in the coming years. While it is unclear as to why these groups grew apart, a few key events emerge as possible explanations. First, the Panthers always saw collaboration with the PFP as convenient but temporary.[11] Second, members within the Black Panthers always saw a white leftist party as too conditional of an ally to be trusted. Third, the party was slowly moving away from protest against the Vietnam War and for civil rights in favor of a more general anticapitalist platform.[12]

Despite these setbacks, the party was determined to have national prominence. By 1972, it aligned with other small left-wing parties to form the People's Party.[13] While the People's Party still focused on opposing the Vietnam War, it also began to emphasize a platform of economic justice, including universal health care and increased worker decision-making power in businesses.[14] The party ran pediatrician and antiwar activist Benjamin Spock in 1972 and community activist Margaret Wright in 1976 for president, carrying with them seven to thirteen congressional candidates per cycle. Spock got eighty thousand votes and Wright fifty thousand votes nationwide. However, both the party's down-ballot candidates and voter base were largely confined to California, meaning that even in this time, their national pull was limited.[15]

Shortly after the 1976 election, the People's Party dissolved and it was again relegated to maintaining activity in the state of California, where it has focused its energy since. The only exception to this was the 2012 presidential campaign of Roseanne Barr, who also attained ballot access in Colorado and Florida, but only for her candidacy. Since this time, the party has settled into its current form—a coalition of left-wing activists in the state of California who run candidates for the presidency, Congress, and state legislatures.[16] Most of the time, it has run its own candidates for president— Maureen Smith in 1980, Herbert Lewin in 1988, Ronald Daniels in 1992, Marsha Feinland in 1996, Leonard Peltier in 2004, and Roseanne Barr in 2012. However, it has also served as a ballot line for other left-wing candidates, including Citizen's Party candidate Sonia Johnson in 1984, independent candidate Ralph Nader in 2008, and Party for Socialism and Liberation candidate Gloria La Riva in 2016.

A PLATFORM EMBODIED THROUGH ACTIVISM

The PFP's political platform, which is on the far left of the political spectrum, is part and parcel with its long history of interaction and collaboration with activist groups.[17] Dating to the PFP's collaboration on initiatives with the Black Panthers, the party considers combatting racial discrimination a top priority, including discriminatory hiring and police brutality.[18] Over time, the party has expanded its focus to include combatting issues experienced by the Latinx and Native American communities. For the former, they advocate adding Spanish as an official language, adding protections for rural farm workers, and relaxing immigration laws. For the latter, the party advocates honoring the sovereignty of tribes and their lands as well as freeing Native Americans such as Leonard Peltier, their 2004 presidential nominee, who they see as a political prisoner.[19]

The party has also had a long history of antiwar activism. In addition to their antiracist beginnings, they also began as an anti–Vietnam War group that was well-represented in student protests. This included direct action to ban military recruiters from college campuses.[20] They have continued to resist what they see as senseless violence and oppression in the name of national security, protesting against US intervention in Iraq, opposing arming rebels in the Syrian civil war, and protesting the use of predator drones by blocking entry to an air force base engaging in such activity.[21] To this day, toward the top of the PFP's platform are calls to end US intervention in other countries, end nuclear disarmament, and dismantle the production of weaponry.[22]

While the PFP has never been opposed to conservation efforts, they originally were not a top priority for the party. In 1968, conservation activists approached the party about collaborating on saving People's Park, a student-run makeshift playground that was the target of law enforcement.[23] While some local candidates included preserving the park in their speeches, activity was relatively limited. However, the party has come to see environmental degradation as an act of "the same corporate forces and economic system that exploit and brutalize the world's working class." As such, it now advocates for sustainable planning, restrictions on using genetically modified organisms (GMOs), protecting wild habitats, and ending the practice of putting environmentally unsound factories in poor and minority communities.[24]

Under the umbrella of the New Left was also advocacy for LGBTQ+ rights, referred to in the late 1960s and early 1970s as "gay liberation."[25] As an outgrowth of the New Left, the PFP also championed these ideals. Longtime party members prided themselves on being early champions of gay liberation, running some of the first openly gay candidates in American history.[26] In its platform, the party has come to view discrimination against LGBTQ+ people in marriage, the military, and the workplace as part of the struggle for the working class. Subsequently, it has framed its participation in activism for public education and workers' rights in this way.[27]

The lion's share of the PFP's platform, however, has been dedicated to opposing capitalism and ensuring what it sees as economic justice. They support increased wages and lowered work hours; they combat employment discrimination against women, minorities, and the LGBTQ+ community; they work toward lowering taxes on the working class; and intend to ensure sufficient funding for public education.[28] In recent years, it has backed up this platform with participation in movements like Occupy Wall Street and the annual May Day protests.[29]

They also consider a large part of economic justice to be ending gentrification and instead making sure that housing in urban and rural areas remains affordable and rent-controlled.[30] Gentrification in particular is an issue on which the party sets itself apart from Democrats.[31] Akin to their counterparts in other urban areas like Newark and New York City, Democrats in Venice Beach wanted to attract investors to the neighborhood and, to raise its profile, wished to demolish public housing and discourage homeless people from begging near areas with heavy tourist traffic.[32] In response, the Peace and Freedom Party, among other activists, disrupted town hall meetings to voice opposition and maintain representation in neighborhood housing councils.[33]

ORGANIZATIONAL INFIGHTING:
A PRODUCT OF PARTY STRUCTURE

There are three layers of organization to the PFP: the state central committee, the county central committees, and the state executive committee. The state central committee is tasked with maintaining ballot access for the PFP, ensuring diversity in its candidate pool, promoting the candidate and party to the public, and keeping the party involved in activist work.[34] Any member of the PFP, which is any voter registered under the Peace and Freedom Party name, can become a state central committee member, and those interested simply have to file an intent to run for the position with their local county clerk.[35] Voters then have the opportunity to elect prospective members through California's state primary elections. State committee members are elected as part of California's primary ballot for registered PFP voters. County central committees have the same responsibilities and selection procedures, albeit at the county level.

The other state-level organizational body of the party is the state executive committee, which is designed to continue party operations on a day-to-day basis. Its only explicit task is endorsing candidates who wish to run on the PFP ballot line prior to primaries, though getting this endorsement does not preclude candidates from running for the party.[36] However, the state central committee reserves the right to delegate any tasks it wishes to the state executive committee. It is comprised of all members and officers of the state central committee, as well as delegates from each county central committee. Its meetings take place between state central committee meetings via teleconference, and all decisions made by the body have to be approved by the state central committee at the next meeting.

Since the party's inception, conditions for ballot access in California, in combination with its organizational framework, has left the party vulnerable to interfactional conflict and infiltration. In order for parties to stay on the ballot in California, they have to command 2 percent of the vote in a statewide race or have at least 0.33 percent of registered voters registered under the party name.[37] For most leftist parties like the Socialist Party USA, Workers World Party, or Freedom Socialist Party, this is a difficult figure to clear, especially if those parties are running against one another for the same section of the vote. Instead, these parties do not attempt to achieve separate ballot access in the state of California, opting to register as members of the PFP and use its ballot line to run in elections.[38]

This is not an activity that these parties have to do in secret. In fact, the party encourages such activity through openly allowing the formation of "tendencies," or factions within the party. Nothing in the party's bylaws indicate that there is an official process for forming these tendencies. However, the party does represent these tendencies as entitled to "the expression of various viewpoints," so it is likely that these are informal groups that give like-minded members the opportunity to coordinate advocacy for particular policies and candidates. While tendencies can theoretically be formed on anything, in practice, most of these tendencies are one or a group of these aforementioned leftist parties.[39]

Unfortunately, allowing these tendencies has been a source of instability for the PFP. The reason why multiple leftist parties have proliferated in the first place is due to a long history of party splits over ideological disputes.[40] Though most of the people who engineered these splits are long dead, the mistrust between these small parties is very much alive. Furthermore, the disagreements that have led to these splits are not often huge. For example, the Socialist Workers Party split in 1940 over whether or not to be critical but supportive or critical and unsupportive of the Soviet Union's pact with Hitler.[41]

Longtime activist and former PFP State Central Committee member Casey Peters reports that these disagreements have bled over into their activities within the PFP. Often, these parties support different candidates for presidential and congressional elections. For the most part, this does not impede party business. In 2016, Monica Morehead of the Workers World Party competed with Gloria La Riva of the Party for Socialism and Liberation (which split from the Workers World in 2004) for the party's presidential nomination.[42] Upon La Riva's victory, the party was able to coalesce around her and gain her 66,000 votes. However, 1988 was a different story. That year, the Internationalist Workers Party (a Trotskyist group) wanted to nominate Herbert Lewin, the New Alliance Party (a populist group and psychotherapy movement) wanted to nominate Lenora Fulani, and a third faction made up of the Socialist Party USA and Communist Party USA wanted to nominate a third unknown candidate. These factions were unable to come to a compromise and as a result did not nominate a candidate.

That being said, even if the PFP's arrangement with other parties can lead to instability, it likely has helped the party survive. The requirements for a party to maintain ballot access in California are either to get 2 percent of the vote in a statewide election or have over 0.33 percent of registered voters.[43] For most of its history, the party has failed to achieve the former but has narrowly met the latter benchmark. In an alternate universe where the PFP does not allow other parties to operate in its ranks, they may not have 0.33 percent of registered voters. Even if these leftist parties make up only about 0.1 percent of the California electorate, members of those groups registering with parties other than the PFP would mean the party would fail to maintain ballot access in 1990, 1998, 2004, 2006, 2008, 2010, 2012, 2016, and 2018, in addition to the times it already failed in 2000 and 2002.[44] Failing to be on the ballot that long could have posed an existential threat to the party. Therefore, while not ideal for organizational stability, the arrangement the PFP has secured provides continuity.

On one occasion, the party organization also faced infiltration by nonsocialists—namely, the Libertarians in 1974.[45] While the battle for control of the party turned out to be temporary, during that year, several Libertarians were nominated as PFP candidates for various offices in California. Becoming a member of the PFP only requires registering to vote under the party label. Therefore, if an ideological group wants to control the party's platform, leadership, and candidate nominations, it can simply register new voters and try to take over the leadership at a party convention. The PFP's bylaws give it the right to remove "anti-working class elements" from the party.[46] However, this does not give the party much protection from infiltration, as they cannot preemptively stop nonsocialists from attempting to register with the party en masse.

THE PFP'S SUPPORT BASE

In the PFP's initial years, its support was concentrated among large sections of the New Left, including the organization Students for a Democratic Society[47] and members of the LGBTQ+ community involved in the struggle for gay liberation.[48] It also secured some demographics who are historically well-represented in socialist circles, including the Jewish community and atheists.[49] Indeed, many of its most active members come from the days of New Left activism.[50] However, the New Left has all but vanished as a political force since the 1970s, and the PFP has made inroads with other demographics to maintain its survival.

One section of society that the PFP has drawn from since its past, but even more in recent times, has been a class of workers known as the precariat.[51] The precariat are highly educated people who work jobs that used to be middle class and were secure, usually as a result of union protections. However, those protections have eroded and, as a result, those jobs are increasingly temporary and pay lower wages.[52] Most of the PFP's support base, as a result of its situation, also tend to live in lower-income neighborhoods than their education levels would suggest.

Most of the PFP's early support and activities occurred in the Bay Area of

California, mainly in San Francisco and Berkeley.[53] This also coincides with both cities being hotbeds of New Left activism.[54] Over time, however, registration figures over the last twenty-eight years have indicated a change to uniformity—most counties tend to have 0.3 to 0.5 percent of its voters registered as PFP members. Numerically speaking, however, since the late 1960s, most of its support has shifted from the Bay Area to Los Angeles, and to a lesser extent San Diego.

A HISTORY OF ELECTORAL LOSSES

The PFP has enjoyed almost continuous ballot access since 1968. The only exception to this was from 1998 to 2002, when it lost ballot access because it did not have over 0.33 percent of registered voters, a required benchmark in the state of California.[55] By the time of the 2003 gubernatorial recall election in California, however, it was able to raise its registration figures to over 0.33 percent and has enjoyed ballot access since. It has never won an election, with the exception of some local races (all of which are nonpartisan), but it also prioritizes injecting itself into the policy debate over winning elections outright.[56]

Since its inception, the PFP has always attempted to maintain a presence on the ballot for the highest federal and state offices. With the exception of 1988, when an intense factional struggle made nominating a candidate untenable, and 2000, when the party had no ballot access, the PFP has always run a presidential candidate, either from its own ranks or from another leftist party. Its candidates have attained between 0.2 and 0.8 percent of the vote in California, figures that have waxed and waned over the years.[57] It has also run candidates in every senatorial and gubernatorial election in California since 1968, with the exception of 2002, when the party had no ballot access. In senatorial elections, the party has attained between 0.5 and 3.5 percent of the vote. In gubernatorial elections, it has attained 0.7 and 1.3 percent, with no particular upward or downward trend.[58]

However, the party tends to be more selective in where it runs for seats in the House of Representatives and the state legislature. It tends to marshal its resources to run candidates in Los Angeles, San Diego, Sacramento, and Sonoma Counties.[59] While the party has never won any of these races, candidates at this level, particularly in state legislative races, outperform statewide candidates. Some candidates, particularly if there is only one major-party candidate on the ballot, can get 20 percent of the vote. These candidates include J. Luis Gomez in the Forty-Fifth California Assembly District in 1996[60] and Lee Chauser for the Thirty-Third California Senate District in 2012.[61]

THE PFP'S IMPACT: PROTEST AND LITIGATION

Despite never being able to influence policy directly through membership of an elected body, the PFP has impacted the political system greatly in two ways. The first is in acting as a resource and voice for political activists. In the Venice neighborhood of Los Angeles, the PFP was instrumental in forming neighborhood organizations to combat gentrification and police harassment of the homeless.[62] The party was well-represented in economic justice-oriented protests like Occupy Riverside and May Day (2012). Notable members of the party maintain involvement in protests against continued US intervention in the Middle East. They also protested in solidarity with Native Americans against plans to build an oil pipeline at Standing Rock.[63] While it is certainly not the only party to be involved in protest, its unique role as an organizational hub for left-wing activists remains an asset to networking and coordination.

The PFP has had an impact through its activity in the courts on behalf of parties' rights, namely its involvement in *California Democratic Party v. Jones*.[64] During the 1990s, a referendum passed that altered how California handled its primary elections. Prior to this referendum, each party had what was known as a closed primary, where only voters registered under a party's name can vote in that party's primary. Subsequent to the referendum, voters would all vote in a single primary where all candidates from all parties would be on the ballot, and the highest vote-getter for each party would win the party's nomination and advance to the general election.[65]

The PFP, along with the California Democratic, Republican, and Libertarian parties, sued to make sure this development did not take place. They considered it to be a violation of their first amendment freedom of association because these parties could not ensure that the direction of each party, in terms of which candidates it ran and which officers were in charge of party business, would be in the hands of each party's own members rather than members of other parties who had conflicting interests.[66] While lower courts ruled in favor of upholding the use of this new type of primary, the Supreme Court of the United States ultimately reversed this ruling.[67]

This ruling did not necessarily give parties wide latitude to determine their fates—after all, anyone, including those who did not hold the party's best interests at heart, could become members through registration. This is how Libertarians, despite being nonsocialist, were able to take over the PFP's apparatus in 1974.[68] However, maintaining a closed party represented the ability for each party to have some degree of protection over themselves.

THE PFP'S FUTURE: SURVIVING BUT NOT THRIVING

There are a few key factors that signal that the PFP should be on an upward trend. First of all, the PFP's best result in a presidential election was with its 2016 candidate, Gloria La Riva, who won 0.8 percent of the vote in California. Second, there has been a steady upward trend in the percentage of people open to socialist ideas and organizations. In 2010, a Fox News/Anderson Robbins poll found 20 percent of Americans saw socialism as good and 64 percent as bad.[69] In 2018, those figures were 36 percent and 51 percent, respectively.[70] Since the PFP embraces socialism in their platform, they stand to have a larger ceiling of support than even ten years ago. Third, while the party has always maintained its support from people who are highly educated but work low-wage jobs, this demographic has risen dramatically since the 1970s.[71]

However, the party's growth potential is limited by several factors. The first is that while the precariat and people interested in socialist politics make up increasing proportions of the population, their support is funneled into other parties. The largest socialist organization in the United States, the Democratic Socialists of America, primarily endorses and agitates for left-wing candidates inside the Democratic Party.[72] While democratic socialists such as Bernie Sanders have not yet had success in gaining control over the Democratic Party apparatus, such an option remains attractive to most budding socialists. The Democratic Party has had a long history of winning elections, particularly in the state of California. Furthermore, California Democrats are already some of the most left-wing Democrats in the country, so it does not seem as difficult for socialist ideas to make inroads into the Democrats' platform as it may be for more conservative states.[73]

The other party that is likely limiting the PFP's growth potential is the Green Party. While it is not as left-wing of a party as the Peace and Freedom Party, the Green Party does have a few distinct advantages in recruiting voters compared to the PFP. One factor is that it is a party with a national presence. Even if the PFP is able to win offices regularly in the state of California, its gains will be limited to the state of California. Meanwhile, the Green Party already has a voter base in all fifty states. This means that a surge in Green support can lead to a national victory for left-wing policies. Furthermore, while the PFP's New Left roots may add an air of authenticity to the party's message, the New Left is becoming more of a distant memory among activists. This is particularly reflected in its activists being much older than Green Party activists.[74]

Another factor that limits the potential for the PFP's growth is the rise of California's "top-two" primary. In the June 2010 primary election, California voters passed Proposition 14, which, like Proposition 198 in 1996, changed California's primary system from a closed to a single primary with all candidates on the ballot.[75] Unlike Proposition 198, though, Proposition 14 established that advancers to the general election are the first- and second-place finishers in the primary, not the highest vote-earner from each party. This law went into effect after the 2010 election and remains so at the time of writing.

This change in electoral procedure has negatively impacted the viability of third parties in California. One immediate impact is that third-party candidates have all but vanished as a presence on general election ballots. Most elections have at least one Democrat and Republican, and often multiple candidates from the major parties. Candidates from these parties tend to command considerable percentages of the vote, larger than what third-party candidates tend to muster when competing against both Democrats and Republicans. As a result, there have been plenty of occasions since the top-two primary came into effect, where two Democrats or two Republicans have faced off against one another in general elections, but there are few occasions where a major-party candidate ran against an independent and none where a major-party candidate ran against a third-party candidate.[76]

Absence from a general election ballot, with the exception of the presidential election, hurts the PFP in particular. The PFP does not have a track record of winning elections, nor does it consider winning elections a top priority.[77] However, by placing itself on the ballot in general elections, it can effectively promote its brand among the voting population. Without that presence, though, its goals are frustrated.

It is the case that the PFP candidates could still be present on primary ballots. However, primary elections do not represent fertile ground for outreach on the party's part. Primary elections tend to have more highly polarized electorates, which means that the left-wing voters that could make up the PFP's base might learn of the PFP's existence.[78] However, primary voters are also older, wealthier, and more strictly partisan, the type of voters who would be difficult to sway toward other parties.[79] Furthermore, these voters, due to their place in society, may be at odds with some of the PFP's goals, making primary election participation a particularly difficult method of outreach.

The development of the top-two primary has been discouraging to third parties in California. Because the chances of a third-party candidate securing enough votes to make it to a general election are so low, the leadership of state third parties has had an increasingly difficult time recruiting candidates who see running for office as worthwhile.[80] The PFP has been no exception. In 2010, before Proposition 14 came into effect, twenty-five candidates ran under the PFP banner but by 2012, this figure reduced to eight, with the number of active candidates hovering around this number in subsequent elections.[81] Thus, not only have PFP candidates been relegated to primary elections, which are harder venues to raise awareness, they are raising awareness in fewer venues.

This is not to say that the long-term survival of the party is in jeopardy, however. Even with the setbacks the party has had to endure since the 1990s and in the 2010s, it has been able to keep its registration figures above the 0.33 percent mark. It has also consistently fielded candidates for statewide offices despite difficulties candidates face. However, it does mean that if the party wants to grow more than it has, it has to think about how it can be an attractive option in a way that the Democratic and Green Parties cannot. The party will also likely have to transition to promotion techniques that do not rely on being present in the ballot box or having potential recruits already exist in the activist world.

CONCLUSION

The PFP began its days as a way to channel New Left ideals into partisan politics. While most of the organizations that make up the New Left have disappeared, the PFP has been able to maintain its vitality through intense involvement in activism on behalf of disadvantaged people. The party began its life having national ambitions, but it instead became a state-only party that plays a role vital to democracy: giving a voice to numerous leftist and activist groups that would have had trouble joining the electoral arena otherwise. It is the case that certain factors limit how much the party can grow; parties can grow and change as well as adapt to new circumstances, and the PFP is no exception. For the foreseeable future, however, it will remain a significant fixture of California's party system and of the American left.

NOTES

1. James M. Elden and David R. Schweitzer, "New Third Party Radicalism: The Case of the California Peace and Freedom Party," *Western Political Quarterly* 24, no. 4 (1971): 761–774.
2. Wilson Record, "The Development of the Communist Position on the Negro Question in the United States," *Phylon Quarterly* 19, no. 3 (1958): 306–326.

3. Wini Breines, *Community and Organization in the New Left, 1962–1968* (New Brunswick, NJ: Rutgers University Press, 1989).

4. Shigeo Hirano and James M. Snyder Jr., "The Decline of Third-Party Voting in the United States," *Journal of Politics* 69, no. 1 (2007): 1–16; Breines, *Community and Organization*, 67–93.

5. Todd Gitlin, *The Sixties: Years of Hope, Days of Rage* (New York: Bantam, 1987).

6. David Haldane, "Peace, Freedom Party Still in Fray After 20 Years on Ballot," *Los Angeles Times*, January 11, 1988.

7. Ryan Kirkby, "'The Revolution Will Not Be Televised': Community Activism and the Black Panther Party, 1966–1971," *Canadian Review of American Studies* 41, no. 1 (2011): 25–62.

8. For the presidential and congressional elections of 1968, see "Election Statistics, 1920 to Present," Clerk of the House, United States House of Representatives, accessed November 27, 2008, https://history.house.gov/Institution/Election-Statistics/. Specifically, see pages 5–7 for California, 11 for Hawaii, 30 and 32 for New York, and 48 for Washington.

9. "Electoral Archives," Secretary of State, Kim Wyman, accessed June 7, 2019, https://www.sos.wa.gov/elections/results_report.aspx. While it is plausible and even likely that candidates ran in state legislative races in California, election data for California in 1968 that includes third-party candidates is unavailable.

10. Peter de Rosa, "Where They Stand: The Libertarian Party and Its Competition, 1968–1978," *Journal of Libertarian Studies* 3, no. 4 (1979): 391–403.

11. Eldridge Cleaver, "Revolution in the White Mother Country and National Liberation in the Black Colony," *North American Review* 253, no. 4 (1968): 13–15.

12. Tony Thomas, "Black Nationalism and Confused Marxists," *Black Scholar* 4, no. 1 (1972): 47–52; Todd Donovan, Shaun Bowler, and Tammy Errio, "Support for Third Parties in California," *American Politics Quarterly* 28, no. 1 (2000): 50–71.

13. de Rosa, "Where They Stand," 396.

14. "Other Presidential Aspirants Offer Wide Choice," *New York Times*, October 29, 1972.

15. For the 1972, 1974, and 1976 federal elections, "Election Statistics," see Clerk of the House; "Presidential and Vice-presidential Candidates," Peace and Freedom Party, July 3, 2008, http://peaceandfreedom.org/home/about-us/historical-information/presidential-candidates. In 1972, thirteen candidates ran for Congress (eleven from California, one in Kentucky, and one from New Jersey; see pages 4–7, 17, and 28–29) under the Peace and Freedom/People's Party banner. In 1974, nine candidates ran (all from California; see pages 3–5). In 1976, seven candidates ran (six from California and one from Hawaii; see pages 4–6, 11).

16. Donovan, Bowler, and Errio, "Support for Third."

17. Christian Collet and Jerrold Hansen, "Minor Parties and Candidates in Sub-Presidential Elections," in *The State of the Parties: The Changing Role of Contemporary American Parties*, eds. John Green, Daniel Coffey, and David Cohen, 7th ed. (Lanham: Rowman & Littlefield, 2014); Mildred Schwartz, *Party Movements in the*

United States and Canada: Strategies of Persistence (Lanham: Rowman & Littlefield, 2006), 8.

18. Kirkby, "The Revolution," 26–27, 30, 32; Richard Danielson, "Peace Groups to Protest Sen. Bill Nelson's Comments on NSA and Edward Snowden," *Tampa Bay Times*, June 18, 2013; Andrew Deener, "The Ecology of Neighborhood Participation and the Reproduction of Political Conflict," *International Journal of Urban & Regional Research* 40, no. 4 (2016): 817–832.

19. "Platform of the Peace and Freedom Party," Peace and Freedom Party, March 2014, 3–4, http://peaceandfreedom.org/home/downloads/platform_full _2014-03-23.pdf.

20. Gitlin, *The Sixties*, 309.

21. Breanna Reeves, "Thousands Join Multiple Anti-Trump Protests Down Market Street," *Golden Gate Express*, January 21, 2017;"Peace and Freedom Candidate Supports ANSWER Statement on Syria," Peace and Freedom Party, May 30, 2013, http://www.peaceandfreedom.org/home/national/general/1081-peace-and-free dom-candidate-supports-answer-statement-on-syria; "Peace and Freedom Gubernatorial Candidate Cindy Sheehan Supports Anti-Drone Activists," Peace and Freedom Party, August 22, 2013, http://www.peaceandfreedom.org/home/national /general/1114-article-template-do-not-publish-sp-1910799152.

22. "Platform," Peace and Freedom Party, 2.

23. Eugene N. Anderson, "Radical Ecology: Notes on a Conservation Movement," *Biological Conservation* 4, no. 4 (1972): 285–291.

24. "Platform," Peace and Freedom Party, 5.

25. Breines, *Community and Organization*, xv.

26. Casey Peters, "Peace and Freedom Party from 1967 to 1997," *Synthesis/Regeneration* 12, no. 1 (1997); Justin D. Surran, "Coming Out Against the War: Antimilitarism and the Politicization of Homosexuality in the Era of Vietnam," *American Quarterly* 53, no. 3 (2001): 452–488.

27. "October 7 Actions in California," Peace and Freedom Party, October 7, 2010, http://www.peaceandfreedom.org/home/calendar/past-events/781-october -7-actions-in-california; "PFP Activists in the Streets on May Day," Peace and Freedom Party, May 3, 2017, http://www.peaceandfreedom.org/home/national/gen eral/1349-pfp-activists-in-the-streets-on-may-day.

28. "Platform," Peace and Freedom Party, 1–9.

29. Harvey M. Kahn, "Occupy Riverside Protestors Say They Want Their Country Back," *Colton Courier*, October 20, 2011; Daniel M. Jimenez, "Protesters Call for Action after Chevron Richmond Refinery Fire," *Alameda Times-Star*, September 3, 2012.

30. "Platform," Peace and Freedom Party, 7.

31. Deener, "The Ecology of Neighborhood Participation and the Reproduction of Political Conflict."

32. Manning Marable, *Beyond Black and White: Transforming African-American Politics* (London: Verso, 2009).

33. Deener, "The Ecology," 3–8.

34. "Peace and Freedom Party State Central Committee By-Laws," Peace and Freedom Party, November 8, 2015, 6–7, http://www.peaceandfreedom.org/home /downloads/SCC_bylaws_2015-11-08.pdf.

35. "Committee By-Laws," Peace and Freedom Party, 1.

36. "Committee By-Laws," Peace and Freedom Party, 10.

37. Elections Code § 5100(a), 5151(b-c).

38. Peters, "Peace and Freedom."

39. "Committee By-Laws," Peace and Freedom Party, 7; Peters, "Peace and Freedom."

40. Robert J. Alexander, "Schisms and Unifications in the American Old Left, 1953–1970," *Labor History* 14, no. 4 (1973): 536–561.

41. Martin Abern, I. Bern, James Burnham, and Max Shachtman, "The War and Bureaucratic Conservatism," Socialist Workers Party *Internal Bulletin* 2, no. 26 (January 1940), https://www.marxists.org/archive/cannon/works/1940/party/cho9 .htm; James P. Cannon, "Speech on the Russian Question (1940)," in *The Struggle for a Proletarian Party*, ed. David Holmes. (Broadway, Australia: Resistance Books, 2001), https://www.marxists.org/archive/cannon/works/1940/party/cho8.htm.

42. For the complete statement of the vote for the 2016 presidential primaries in California, see "Statement of Vote," Elections and Voter Information, Alex Padilla, California Secretary of State, 13, accessed June 7, 2019, https://elections .cdn.sos.ca.gov/sov/2016-primary/2016-complete-sov.pdf.

43. Elections Code § 5100(a), 5151(b-c).

44. For party registration figures in the complete statements of the vote for all general elections in California between 1990 and 2018, see "Prior Statewide Elections," Elections and Voter Information, Alex Padilla, California Secretary of State, accessed November 27, 2018, https://www.sos.ca.gov/elections/prior-elections /prior-statewide-elections/.

45. de Rosa, "Where They Stand," 6–7.

46. "Committee By-Laws," Peace and Freedom Party, 6.

47. Riley E. Dunlap, "Politics and Ecology: A Political Profile of Student Eco-Activists," *Youth & Society* 3, no. 4 (1972): 379–397.

48. Dunlap, "Politics and Ecology," 379–397; Peters, "Peace and Freedom"; Surran, "Coming Out."

49. Alan S. Maller, "Notes on California Jews' Political Attitudes—1968," *Jewish Social Studies* 33, no. 2–3 (1971): 160–164; Elden and Schweitzer, "New Third Party."

50. Haldane, "Peace, Freedom," 3.

51. Elden and Schweitzer, "New Third Party"; Steven Segal, Jim Baumohl, and Edwin Moyles, "Neighborhood Types and Community Reaction to the Mentally Ill: A Paradox of Intensity," *Journal of Health & Social Behavior* 21, no. 1 (1980): 345–359.

52. Guy Standing, "The Precariat: From Denizens to Citizens?" *Polity* 44, no. 4 (2012): 588–608.

53. Anderson, "Radical Ecology"; Raymond E. Wolfinger and Fred I. Greenstein, "Comparing Political Regions: The Case of California," *American Political Science Review* 63, no. 1 (1969): 74–85.

54. Breines, *Community and Organization*, 20, 24, 35.

55. Elections Code § 5100(a), 5151(b-c).

56. Glenn Davis, "Peace and Freedom Party Defines Victory by How it Influences Policy—Not by Elections Won," *Independent Voter News*, April 3, 2015.

57. "Prior Statewide," Elections and Voter Information, 1990–2018.

58. Elections and Voter Information.

59. Elections and Voter Information.

60. For the complete statement of the vote for the 1996 general election in California, see "Statement of Vote," Elections and Voter Information, Bill Jones, California Secretary of State, November 5, 1966, 18, https://elections.cdn.sos.ca.gov/sov/1996-general/sov-complete.pdf.

61. For the complete statement of the vote for the 1996 general election in California, see "Statement of Vote," Elections and Voter Information, Debra Bowen, California Secretary of State, November 6, 2012, 45, https://elections.cdn.sos.ca.gov/sov/2012-general/sov-complete.pdf.

62. Deener, "Ecology of Neighborhood."

63. Reeves, "Thousands Join"; Danielle Trubow, "Noted Anti-War Activist Leads 'Tour de Peace' into Toledo," *The Blade*, June 10, 2013; Dennis Banks, "Why We Take a Stand at Standing Rock," *San Francisco Chronicle*, November 6, 2016.

64. *California Democratic Party v. Jones*, 530 US 567, 571, 578 (2000).

65. *California Democratic Party*, § 1.

66. *California Democratic Party*, § 3.

67. *California Democratic Party*, § 1.

68. de Rosa, "Where They Stand."

69. Dana Blanton, "Fox News Poll: Most Voters See No Sign of Economic Recovery, But They're Hopeful," Fox News, August 10, 2012.

70. Dana Blanton, "Fox News Poll: Democrats Maintain Lead in Race for House," Fox News, August 22, 2018. Figures for California specifically could not be found. However, from other polls, it seems California is somewhat more positive and less negative about socialism than the United States as a whole. In a 2010 Pew Research study, 32 percent of Californians saw socialism positively and 54 percent negatively, compared to 29 percent and 59 percent nationally. A similar question in 2011 put those figures at 38 percent positive and 56 percent negative in California, compared to 31 percent positive and 60 percent negative nationally. See Pew Research Center, Poll, "April 2010 Political Futures Survey," USPEW2010-04POL (April 2010), version 2; Pew Research Center, Poll, "December 2011 Political Survey—Future Outlook/2012 Presidential Election," USPEW2011-12POL (December 2011), version 2. See also Arwa Mahdawi, "Socialism Is No Longer a Dirty Word in the US—and That's Scary for Some," *The Guardian*, July 29, 2018.

71. Elden and Schweitzer, "New Third," 765; Segal, Baumohl, and Moyles, "Neighborhood Types," 348; Standing, "The Precariat."

72. Joseph M. Schwartz, "A History of Democratic Socialists of America 1971–2017: Bringing Socialism from the Margins to the Mainstream," July 2017, https://www.dsausa.org/about-us/history/.

73. Robert S. Erikson, Gerald C. Wright, and John P. McIver, *Statehouse Democracy: Public Opinion and Policy in the American States* (New York: Cambridge University Press, 1993), 103.

74. Collet and Hansen, "Minor Parties."

75. Debra Bowen, *Official Voter Information Guide* (Sacramento: California Secretary of State, 2010), 14–20.

76. "Prior Statewide," Elections and Voter Information, 2012–2018.

77. Davis, "Peace and Freedom." There are exceptions to this. One activist mentioned by Haldane states that the party had early hopes to win several important political offices, and that some activists hold out hope that there will come a time where the party will become popular and its candidates win election. See Haldane, "Peace, Freedom."

78. Eric McGhee, Seth Masket, Boris Shor, Steven Rogers, and Nolan McCarty, "A Primary Cause of Partisanship? Nomination Systems and Legislator Ideology," *American Journal of Political Science* 58, no. 2 (2014): 337–351.

79. Karen M. Kaufmann, James G. Gimpel, and Adam H. Hoffman, "A Promise Fulfilled? Open Primaries and Representation," *Journal of Politics* 65, no. 2 (2003): 457–476.

80. Keith Smith, "Proposition 14 and California's Minor Parties: A Case Study of Electoral Reform and Party Response," *California Journal of Politics & Policy* 6, no. 4 (2014): 437–470.

81. "Prior Statewide," Elections and Voter Information, 2010–2018.

CHAPTER 6

Third Parties in Vermont

Bertram Johnson

In 2004, *Burlington Free Press* columnist Jon Margolis expressed what was probably the view of many Vermont Democrats in a grumpy essay entitled "Progressive Party Will Never Win." Progressive candidate Anthony Pollina had lost a recent bid for lieutenant governor, showing, in Margolis's view, the futility of third-party politics. State and national institutions are structured to prevent viable third parties, reasoned Margolis, and "very few people will listen to a politician who has no chance to be elected." The fact that the Vermont Progressive Party persisted in fielding candidates was therefore a sign of a certain kind of pathology: "Left and right, some people disdain compromise. They believe in being pure. They do not want to sully themselves by associating with those less committed to truth, justice, and virtue. So they create their own institutions, impotent but moral." Progressive "self-indulgence" had gone so far as to become "decadence." The party was doomed.[1]

It has not worked out that way. At present, Vermont is home to one of the most successful third-party movements in the country. As of 2019, two statewide office holders, seven members of the state senate (23 percent), and fourteen members of the state House (9 percent) claim affiliation with the Vermont Progressive Party.[2] What is more, the Liberty Union Party has appeared on ballots in Vermont since the 1970s, Libertarians run competitive candidates from time to time, and the newly founded Green Mountain Party ran a candidate for state House in 2018. Although the Democrats and Republicans remain dominant, members of other parties have often held pivotal positons and shaped the direction of state and local politics. Third parties have by no means vanished in the last few decades—in many ways, they are stronger in Vermont than ever before.

A political scientist new to Vermont would quickly identify two potential explanations for this success. First, many of Vermont's legislative districts elect more than one member. Forty-six House districts and ten senate districts elect two or more representatives. According to Duverger's law, multi-member districts are more likely to lead to multiparty systems. Second, Vermont law permits fusion, in which candidates may be endorsed by multiple parties. Fusion laws have also long been associated with the emergence of viable third parties. The Green Mountain State would appear to be a tidy case study of both of these effects.

A closer examination of Vermont's recent history complicates these simple explanations, however. The state's multimember districts are not structured in a way that gives third parties obvious advantages, nor is fusion an easy way for third parties to demonstrate their strength among voters, as is the case in some other states. These structural features may not work against third parties, but they do not support them in the ways that scholarly theories would predict. Instead, the Vermont case shows the importance of local government institutions in generating advantageous "footholds" for third-party organizing. The Vermont Progressive Party, in particular, illustrates the utility of being identified—but not too closely identified—with a unique and successful leader.

In this chapter, I explain how Vermont's local institutions and the power of personalities has shaped the development of the state's third-party politics. I first outline the development of Vermont's state electoral institutions and illustrate why they do not provide direct explanations of third-party success. I then describe the history of the Vermont Progressive Party, showing how local institutions and key leaders have breathed life into the party.

VERMONT'S STATE ELECTORAL RULES

Fusion

Vermont allows fusion, the simultaneous endorsement of a single candidate by multiple parties. However, the system operates very differently from the way it does in Vermont's neighbor to the west, New York. In New York, minor parties have independent ballot lines, meaning that a candidate's name may appear on the ballot multiple times if that candidate is endorsed by multiple parties. This system gives minor parties leverage because they can immediately tell how many voters they delivered to a candidate by tallying up the votes a candidate received under the party ballot line. In Vermont, although a single candidate may receive the nomination of multiple parties, each candidate only receives one ballot line. Candidates may designate which party identification comes first (e.g., "Progressive/Democrat" or "Democrat/Progressive"), but the single ballot line does not allow parties to determine which votes are "from" one party versus another.

This ballot rule stems from what some major-party representatives perceived as an abuse of a New York–like system. Prior to the 1960s, Vermont was a one-party Republican stronghold. No Democrat had been elected governor in over a century, and not even Franklin Roosevelt could pry the state's electoral votes loose from Republican hands in national elections. The 1962 gubernatorial race, which pitted the youthful Democrat Phil Hoff against the even more youthful Republican incumbent F. Ray Keyser,[3] looked to be another easy contest for the dominant party. In reality, as historian Joe Sherman writes, Keyser "sat atop a melting glacier of political power, around the base of which Democrats and wayward Republicans were lighting fires."[4] Some of these wayward Republicans, upset over Keyser's proposals as well as by his inability to lead a divided legislature, were nevertheless reluctant to vote for a Democrat under any circumstances. Two activists hit on a solution: they formed the "Vermont Independent Party" (VIP), gave Hoff the party's endorsement, and (under the rules of the time) thereby granted Hoff an extra, non–Democratic Party ballot line.[5] Hoff won the election by 1,315 votes; he had received 3,282 votes on the VIP line.

It took more than a decade, but in 1977, the Vermont legislature quietly did away with the ballot rules that allowed for such a tactic. Since 1978, the state's election laws state that a candidate's name cannot appear on the ballot more than once for any individual office.[6] For good measure, the law stipulates that no political party can have the word "independent" as part of its name.[7] There would be no more separate ballot lines for the VIP.

Minor parties in Vermont therefore cannot make use of separate ballot lines to demonstrate their strength. As a result, fusion has not been as great a boon to minor parties in the Green Mountain State as it may be in other states, and minor parties have at times been ambivalent or even hostile to its use. In the early stages of the history of the Progressive Party, as I explain below, party leaders soured on fusion and expressly disavowed it as a tactic. Although it played a crucial role in Hoff's election in 1962, fusion cannot explain the success of Vermont's minor parties.

Electoral Districts

Vermont's multimember legislative districts—another potential boon to minor parties—do not operate in a way that would naturally result in viable third parties, by Duverger's law.

Prior to the pivotal US Supreme Court decisions of *Baker v. Carr* and *Reynolds v. Sims*, Vermont's legislature was made up of a lower House of 246 members, each of whom represented a city or town; and a state senate of thirty members, each of whom was elected by a county.[8] As in other states, the Supreme Court's one-person, one-vote standard upended the structure of representation in Vermont. Although the legislature conceded the need to bring representation in line with population, a tenacious culture of localism led to a plan that preserved the territorial integrity of individual towns and cities. Smaller towns simply were granted fewer representatives than larger towns, with some towns grouped together into the same legislative districts. For example, in the new one hundred and fifty-member state House of Representatives, the town of Proctor (population 2,102) had one representative, the combined towns of Middlebury, Weybridge, and Ripton (population 5,866) had two, and Brattleboro (population 11,724) had five.[9]

Today's legislative districting follows the same pattern as the post–*Baker v. Carr* plan. There are one hundred and fifty seats in the state House, but only 104 districts, with forty-six districts that elect two representatives apiece. In the state senate, thirty senators are elected from thirteen districts, with three districts electing one senator, six electing two, three electing three, and Chittenden County, home to the city of Burlington, electing six.

In many contexts, multimember districts are associated with proportional representation, a system that Duverger predicted had an affinity for multiparty systems.[10] Under such a system, each voter typically has one vote, and the number of seats are allocated to the top vote-getters until there are no more seats to allocate. Strategic voters in a two-seat district should therefore see three parties as "viable," leading to sustained three-party politics. Vermont's seats are not allocated proportionally, however. As in the case of proportional representation, the top vote-getters win elections. But in Vermont, each voter has as many votes as there are seats in each district. In a two-seat House district, each voter votes for two candidates. In the Chittenden County state senate district, each voter votes for six candidates. Therefore, rather than a proportional representation system, Vermont's multimember districts operate, in many ways, as a series of parallel first-past-the-post elections.[11] The only difference is that all candidates for all seats are listed collectively on the ballot instead of designating a single seat for which they are running.

This collective ballot listing makes for some interesting party dynamics. Each party has an interest in running a full "ticket," so as to soak up all the votes each voter has. As former Vermont House Speaker Ralph Wright explains:

> I would like to have a dollar for every new candidate who, . . . when I was recruiting Democratic candidates throughout the state, thought it was a plus to be the only Democrat running in a two-member district. How often I heard, "Well that means, if I'm the only candidate, I get every Democratic vote." Maybe that's true, but unless you're from Boston or Chicago, you're not supposed to vote twice for the same guy.[12]

One way to handle this dilemma might be for a candidate to ask voters to vote only once, withholding their second vote—a so-called bullet vote.[13] But such a request is deemed rude and somewhat antidemocratic—akin to requesting that voters stay home on Election Day. Instead, candidates team up with others of the same party to ensure that there are as many candidates for each party as there are seats up for election. That way, copartisans can "soak up" voters' extra votes and prevent them from going to a member of another party. In some cases, a more viable candidate may recruit a noncompetitive placeholder candidate of the same party for this purpose. Independents have even been known to recruit fellow independents to run on the same ticket.

The result is that multimember districts do not have the effect of encouraging third-party politics in Vermont. A simple chi-square test finds no statistically significant relationship between the election of Progressives to the legislature in 2018 and multimember districts ($p = 0.95$); Progressives were no more likely to win elections in multimember districts than in single-member districts. If there are structural features of Vermont's political landscape that encourage third parties, multimember districts do not appear to be one of them.

LOCAL GOVERNMENT AND LARGE PERSONALITIES: A BRIEF HISTORY OF THIRD PARTIES IN VERMONT

If fusion and multimember districts do not account for the success of Vermont's third parties, particularly the Vermont Progressive Party, then what does? In this section, I describe the history of third-party politics in Vermont since the 1970s, arguing that Vermont's system of local governments—particularly town meetings, combined with the prominence of several well-known third-party politicians and their allies—have led to the unusual success of the Vermont Progressives.

The history of modern third-party movements in Vermont begins with the founding of the Liberty Union Party in 1970 by former congressman William Meyer and a group of antiwar activists. Meyer, who voters had ousted after one term because of his advocacy of nuclear arms control and recognition of Communist China, became the new party's candidate for Senate in 1970.[14] Peter Diamondstone, in later years a perennial candidate under the Liberty Union banner, became chief spokesperson for the group, outlining their antiwar views and explaining that the third party sought the support of voters who were "dissatisfied" or even "bored" with the two major parties.[15]

In the fall election, Meyer got less than 1 percent of the vote for Senate, Diamondstone got slightly more than 1 percent for attorney general, and activist Dennis Morrisseau came close to getting 3 percent for US House.

The next year, Bernie Sanders joined the party. As the gubernatorial candidate in 1972 and again in 1976, he helped expand the Liberty Union vote share to 6 percent, a figure that prompted serious conversations about the party's potential to play "spoiler," drawing votes away from the Democratic Party and leading to the election of Republicans. Sanders quit the party shortly after the 1976 election and has remained steadfastly independent ever since, with the exception of his 2016 and 2020 primary runs for president in the Democratic Party. Perhaps he agreed with the views of one ally, who dismissed the Liberty Union Party as a "tiny club of idealists with no interest in gaining political power."[16] Nevertheless, Liberty Union continues to run candidates for most major offices; Sanders's Liberty Union opponent in the 2018 US Senate race received approximately half a percent of the vote.

With Sanders's election as Burlington's mayor in 1981, the origins of the Progressive Party were set in motion. Elected as an independent by a margin of ten votes in a four-candidate race, Sanders faced a hostile Democratic board of aldermen, some of whom viewed the self-proclaimed democratic socialist as an outright Bolshevik. In the early years of his mayoralty, conflicts between the mayor and council took on the air of Chicago's bitter 1980s "council wars" between mayor Harold Washington and his political opponents.

Through local organizing and the construction of mobilizing institutions, Sanders and his allies built an alternative political power base to rival that of the city establishment. Sanders supporters formed the Coalition for Responsible Government, which later changed its name to the Progressive Coalition.[17] Although they never won a majority of the Burlington Board of Aldermen, the Progressive Coalition held six of the thirteen seats on the board by the mid-1980s. Separately, the coalition worked to do an end-run around more conservative interests in city government and in the community at large. Sanders created the Community Economic Development Office to rival the establishment Planning Commission, and Sanders allies pushed through the board of aldermen a proposal, institutionalizing quasi-official neighborhood planning assemblies that gave more authority to pro-Sanders neighborhood associations.

Coalition organizers became better at organizing for electoral politics, focusing on turning out voters from working-class neighborhoods as well as college students at the University of Vermont. A 1984 press account alleged that "the coalition of Sanders supporters has grown increasingly more skilled at waging effective campaigns. This year they have progressed even further, adding a computer to their arsenal, a paid campaign coordinator, and have even shelled out $650 to a political consultant."[18] A frustrated Democratic alderman called it a "very powerful machine" that was "slick, with new techniques."[19]

Meanwhile, grassroots organizers had achieved parallel successes elsewhere in the state. In the spring of 1982, antinuclear activists brought the nuclear freeze campaign to Vermont's town meetings, making use of rules that allowed towns to vote on any issue if citizens gathered the requisite number of signatures. Vermonters overwhelmingly voted for the symbolic profreeze resolutions, with 159 towns backing the measure.[20] Inspired by the freeze movement, the Sanders mayoralty, and the 1984 presidential campaign of Jesse Jackson, left-wing activists gathered together as the statewide Vermont Rainbow Coalition to pressure the Democratic Party into taking a more liberal stance on taxation, social policy, and environmental policy.

The Vermont Rainbow Coalition initially focused on endorsing sympathetic Democratic candidates but soured on this strategy when a number of Democratic legislators reversed course and distanced themselves from the group.[21] Instead, the Rainbow Coalition focused on supporting sympathetic independent candidates, including Bernie Sanders in his unsuccessful run for governor in 1986. When the Rainbow Coalition and the Burlington Progressive Coalition merged to form the new statewide Progressive Vermont Alliance (PVA) in 1990, first on the agenda was organizing county committees[22] and ensuring that the "pre-party formation" had a broad statewide base.[23] Notably, the PVA's bylaws opposed endorsing major-party candidates.[24] Platform planks included calls for bolstering health and education programs, increasing the availability of childcare, election reform, cuts in military spending, and additional environmental policies.[25]

By the mid-1990s, PVA affiliates held up to eight seats on the Burlington City Council, plus a few self-identified "progressive" or independent seats in the state House of Representatives.[26] The dynamics of third-party politics had changed, however, with the demonstration by Bernie Sanders in 1988 that a third-party candidate need not be an obvious spoiler. That year, Sanders (running, as usual, as an independent) came in a close second to Republican Peter Smith, with Democrat Paul Poirier splitting the liberal vote to deliver the race to the Republican.

In the succeeding years, Progressives consolidated their base in Burlington, incrementally improved their position in the state legislature (running more candidates from outside the Burlington area), and tested differing approaches to races for statewide office. Sanders succeeded in winning the 1990 race for Congress, with the Democrat Dolores Sandoval relegated to the role of, as one columnist put it, "pesky bystander."[27] Sanders won with 56 percent of the vote; Sandoval got 3 percent.

In 2000, Progressives finally took the step they had long declined to take: forming an official statewide political party. They quickly achieved "major" party status—a designation based on the percent of the vote received, which requires parties to nominate candidates via primaries rather than by insular party-nominating committees. As Progressives ran more candidates in more places throughout Vermont, they continued to struggle with the spoiler accusation in statewide races, as well as the internal debate about fusion. Anthony Pollina, running as a Progressive, lost the lieutenant governor's race in 2002 and, critics charged, threw the race to the Republican candidate by drawing liberal votes away from the Democrat. In 2004, Peter Clavelle, the Progressive mayor of Burlington, ran for governor as a Democrat against the popular (and ultimately victorious) incumbent Republican Jim Douglas. Clavelle's decision to adopt the Democratic Party label rankled many Progressives, who saw the move as a betrayal of principle.

Recent Progressive successes in winning statewide office as well as expanding the Progressive presence in the legislature have come in the wake of the party's gradual acceptance of a fusion strategy. Senator Tim Ashe, now the majority leader of the state senate, embraced both the Progressive and Democratic Party labels in his 2008 campaign for state senate, after having served as a Progressive city council member in Burlington. Other state senators soon followed. In 2016, state senator David Zuckerman, a longtime Progressive state legislator, won both the Progressive and Democratic Party nominations for lieutenant governor and beat Republican Randy Brock in the general election by a six-point margin. Although there remains some skepticism of fusion among core Progressives—"I worry that it's not a long-term strategy that can build a strong, independent third party," one complains—at least some candidates are embracing the tactic wholeheartedly, especially in statewide races.[28]

WHY HAVE THE PROGRESSIVES SUCCEEDED?

The Progressive Party does not hold a majority in the legislature, it does not now hold the mayoralty of Burlington, nor has it ever controlled the governor's office. Some might dispute a characterization of such a party as successful, but the party has persisted in one form or another over four decades; holds a pivotal position in the state House of Representatives, where Democrats need Progressive votes to override a gubernatorial veto; and holds two statewide offices (lieutenant governor Zuckerman and state auditor Douglas Hoffer). What accounts for this level of persistence and success? Three factors, I argue, are critical.

Strong Leadership—But Not Too Strong

First, as the above narrative illustrates, leftist voters had in Sanders a strong leader with a loyal following and a consistent and inspirational message around which they could rally—but Sanders is not so closely identified with the party as to be the sole reason for its existence. On the contrary, Sanders is not a Progressive, has never declared himself to be a Progressive, and has shunned party attachments since his Liberty Union days.[29] Sanders's prominence kept Progressives vital, but his distance from the formal party apparatus gave the party space to select its own leadership, draft its own platform, and recruit its own candidates.[30] It therefore was able to achieve what other third parties, such as the national Reform Party of the 1990s, could not: an identity independent of one or a few big personalities.

Who Is the Spoiler?

Second, on several occasions, Progressives have demonstrated that the third-party candidate is not always the spoiler. In 1988, Sanders came in second to the Republican candidate for Congress, rendering the third-place Democrat the effective spoiler. A similar turn of events threw the Burlington mayor's race to the Republican in 1993. And, most recently, in 2008, Progressive gubernatorial candidate Anthony Pollina edged out the Democrat Gaye Symington, coming in second to Republican incumbent Jim Douglas. In light of this history, it is not clear that votes for the Progressives are necessarily "wasted"—and a key hurdle for third parties is surmounted.

Permeable Institutions

Third, Vermont's political institutions are unusually accessible to community-based activists. For one thing, voters do not have to register as members of one party or the other—they simply choose a Democratic, Republican, or Progressive Party ballot when they arrive at the polls to vote in a primary. In addition, the state's small scale makes the cost of elections reasonable and makes it possible for a candidate without much funding to win elections simply through determination and shoe leather.

But a key advantage for activists in Vermont is the permeability of local institutions. In the narrative above, the Burlington case looms large. There, it was possible not only for an insurgent candidate (Sanders) to win the mayor's office in a divided race in which people were frustrated with a complacent incumbent, but for allies to win seats on the city council, pressure their representatives through neighborhood planning assemblies, and bypass the establishment via the (newly created) Community Economic Development Office.

It was not just Burlington that was accessible to activists on the left, however. Vermont's robust system of town meeting government has allowed activists to place issue items on local agendas that can mobilize activists and generate enthusiasm and excitement. Petitions to add a resolution to a town meeting agenda require the signature of only 5 percent of the town's voters, a hurdle that is not difficult to overcome. The 1982 nuclear freeze resolutions are described previously, and more recent statewide efforts to take stands on national progressive issues have included resolutions concerning climate change and, in 2007, resolutions in more than three dozen towns calling for the impeachment of President George W. Bush. Critics have called such local votes on national issues a waste of time,[31] but the organization of such efforts has created networks of activists statewide and have aided in boosting liberal causes. These efforts have rarely, if ever, been official efforts of a political party, but they may play a role in reinforcing Progressive Party strength.

TESTING EXPLANATIONS OF PROGRESSIVE PARTY SUCCESS

The above account of Progressive Party success is based on the narrative history of the party, and not all elements of it are statistically testable. In this section, I use election data at the city and town levels to test several hypotheses about what accounts for Progressive Party voting. My dependent variables are the percent of votes for Progressive Party candidate for lieutenant governor David Zuckerman, first in the 2016 Democratic primary election in which he ran against two established Democratic members of the state legislature, and second in the general election in which he ran with both the Progressive and Democratic Party nominations against a Republican.

First, I test the hypothesis that "new Vermonters" are more likely to support the Progressive Party candidate. The newly constructed interstate highway system brought many new arrivals to the state in the 1970s, which many observers claim resulted in more liberal politics. I calculate each town's population growth percentage from this period—from 1960 to 1980—to test for the possibility that these newcomers were not only more likely to be Democrats but also more likely to vote for a Progressive. I also include a variable representing each town's population growth from 1980 to 2000 to test whether more recent new arrivals are similarly more likely to be liberal.

Second, I include two variables that serve as indicators of grassroots organizational strength, one from the 1980s and one from the 2000s. I include each town's percentage of the 1984 Democratic primary vote for Jesse Jackson as a proxy for the areas of the state in which the Vermont Rainbow Coalition, a precursor to the modern Progressive Party, was likely to be organizationally strong. I also include a dichotomous variable coded "1" for each of the thirty-six Vermont towns that passed resolutions calling for the impeachment of President George W. Bush in 2007 as an indicator of more recent liberal grassroots organizing.

Third, as an indicator of Democratic Party strength in a town, I include each town's percent of the vote for President Barack Obama's reelection in 2012. I also control for each town's population.

Results appear in Table 6.1. The data indicate that Progressive support in the 2016 primary election is significantly related to areas of historic organizational strength of the Vermont Rainbow Coalition (as indicated by the significance of the Jackson vote percentage in the first column). No other variable is significant. Each additional percentage of the vote for Jackson in 1984 is associated with a bit less than a third of a percent higher vote for Zuckerman in the 2016 primary.

The general election percent of the vote for Zuckerman is associated with overall Democratic Party strength (as represented by the Obama vote), as well as with pre-1980 population growth and the contemporary organiz-

Table 6.1: Explaining 2016 City- and Town-Level Percentage of
Votes for David Zuckerman

	Percentage of Primary Vote: Zuckerman	Percentage of General Election Vote: Zuckerman
Percentage, Jackson	0.279	0.082
	(3.09)***	(1.43)
Population	–0.000	0.000
	(1.48)	(1.76)*
Pop. growth, 1980	0.498	2.273
	(0.63)	(4.57)***
Pop. growth, 2000	1.666	–0.201
	(0.68)	(0.13)
Percentage, Obama	–0.000	1.065
	(0.01)	(21.50)***
Town voted impeach	–0.656	2.131
	(0.40)	(2.07)**
Constant	41.353	–24.333
	(8.65)***	(8.05)***
R^2	0.06	0.75
N	245	245

Note. Ordinary least squares regressions; standard errors in parentheses.
* $p < 0.1$; ** $p < 0.05$; *** $p < 0.01$

ing effort associated with the 2007 impeachment votes. There is a marginally significant relationship between the Zuckerman vote and larger population size, which we might expect of a candidate whose electoral base is in the heavily populated (for Vermont) Chittenden County region. Because, in the general election, Zuckerman had both the Progressive and Democratic Party endorsements, some of these variables would no doubt have been significant if a nonprogressive Democrat had been running. For example, population growth prior to 1980 may have brought more Democrats to Vermont but, based on the regression results for the primary race, it does not appear to have made it more likely that a community would support a Progressive candidate.

CONCLUSION: THE STATE OF THIRD PARTIES IN VERMONT

This chapter began with an account of a skeptic predicting that the Progressive Party could never win. Although there have been losses, to be sure, and although other Vermont third parties have failed to gain a foothold in legislative and municipal offices, the Progressive Party has established itself as a durable, influential, statewide political party.

This success is not, I have argued, the principal result of the two most obvious explanations: multimember districts and fusion. Because of the way these institutions are structured in the state of Vermont, they have not benefited third parties as much as one might predict. Multimember districts, when voters have as many votes as there are seats, do not make a multiparty system much more likely. Without separate ballot lines, fusion does not have as many advantages for third parties as it does in other states. Vermont's Progressives shunned a fusion strategy for many years, and it remains controversial in some Progressive circles.

In recent years, candidates for state office, notably Progressive lieutenant governor David Zuckerman, have likely benefited from fusion. As Table 6.1 shows, Zuckerman did well in traditionally Democratic parts of the state and clearly benefited from defeating potential Democratic challengers, clearing the field for a two-candidate race between him and a Republican.

But fusion, although it may be an element of the party's future, is not a major component of the party's past. For an explanation of the party's growth and durability, we must look to the circumstances under which it evolved. I argue above that these circumstances involved three key elements: leadership that did not stifle the party's ability to grow, key campaigns that demonstrated that an independent or third party need not be a spoiler, and, crucially, accessible local institutions such as city and town governments and town meetings that gave organizers opportunities to flex their muscles. Far from creating their own "impotent but moral" institutions, Vermont Progressives have used existing institutions to their lasting advantage.

NOTES

1. Jon Margolis, "Progressive Party Will Never Win," *Burlington Free Press*, July 18, 2004, 8C.

2. I include here those legislators who listed their primary party affiliation as "Democrat" but listed "Progressive" as a secondary affiliation. (Below I explain Vermont's approach to fusion.) The number of state senators whose primary party affiliation is "Progressive" is two; the number of state representatives whose primary party affiliation is "Progressive" is seven.

3. Hoff was thirty-eight years old; Keyser was thirty-five.

4. Joe Sherman, *Fast Lane on a Dirt Road: Vermont Transformed, 1945–1980* (Woodstock, VT: The Countryman Press, 1991), 51.

5. Samuel B. Hand, Anthony Marro, and Stephen C. Terry, *Philip Hoff: How Red Turned Blue in the Green Mountain State* (Hanover, NH: University Press of New England, 2011).

6. 17 V.S.A. § 2472, accessed June 25, 2019, https://legislature.vermont.gov /statutes/section/17/051/02472.

7. 17 V.S.A. § 2403, accessed June 25, 2019, https://legislature.vermont.gov /statutes/section/17/049/02403.

8. Because Vermont has fifteen counties, each county was guaranteed one senator, and the others were allocated on the basis of population. See "Preliminary Report of Reapportionment Study Commission," Secretary of State, March 22, 1963, https://www.sec.state.vt.us/media/54105/Reapportionment_Study_Commission _Preliminary_Report.pdf.

9. For the text of the 1965 Redistricting Act, Act 98, see https://www.sec .state.vt.us/media/54143/Act_98_1965.pdf, accessed June 25, 2019. For population figures for Vermont from the 1960 census, see https://www.vermonthistory explorer.org/discover-vermont/facts-figures/census-records/census-by-towns, accessed October 2, 2019.

10. Maurice Duverger, *Political Parties* (New York: Wiley, 1954).

11. Cox's formal generalization of Duverger's law focuses on systems of proportional representation and on multimember districts with a single nontransferrable vote system. Gary W. Cox, *Making Votes Count: Strategic Coordination in the World's Electoral Systems* (Cambridge: Cambridge University Press, 1997), chpt. 5.

12. Ralph G. Wright, *Inside the Statehouse: Lessons from the Speaker* (Washington, DC: CQ Press, 2005), 7.

13. Wright, *Inside the Statehouse*, 15.

14. Scott Mackay and Steven Farnsworth, "Ex-Vermont Congressman William Meyer, 68, Dies," *Burlington Free Press*, December 17, 1983, 1A.

15. "Third Party to Aim for Protest Votes," *Burlington Free Press*, July 3, 1970, 2.

16. Terry Bouricius, *Building Progressive Politics: The Vermont Story* (Madison, WI: Center for a New Democracy, 1993), 5.

17. Bouricius, *Building Progressive*, 10; W. J. Conroy, *Challenging the Boundaries of Reform: Socialism in Burlington* (Philadelphia, PA: Temple University Press, 1990), 8-10.

18. Joshua Mamis, "Mission: Possible," *The Vermont Vanguard Press*, March 4-11, 1984, 1.

19. Joshua Mamis, "Mission Accomplished," *The Vermont Vanguard Press*, March 11-18, 1984, 1.

20. Ted Tedford, "159 Towns Support Nuclear Arms Freeze," *Burlington Free Press*, March 4, 1982, 1B.

21. Bouricius, *Building Progressive*, 16, 25-26.

22. Lisa Scagliotti, "Political Groups Form Alliance," *Burlington Free Press*, May 20, 1990, 1B.

23. Bouricius, *Building Progressive*, 19.

24. Bouricius, 19.

25. "Progressive Alliance Ratifies Its Platform," *Burlington Free Press*, May 20, 1990, 2B.

26. Progressive mayor Peter Clavelle was defeated in 1993 by Republican Peter Brownell. Clavelle was reelected in 1995.

27. Sam Hemingway, "Vermont Primary Yields Few Surprises," *Burlington Free Press*, September 14, 1990, 1B.

28. Terri Hallenbeck, "Vermont's Progressives and Democrats Have Uneasy Ties," Seven Days, August 24, 2016, https://www.sevendaysvt.com/vermont/ver monts-progressives-and-democrats-have-uneasy-ties/Content?oid=3616865.

29. That Sanders bowed to pragmatism and ran in the Democratic primaries in 2016 was a real surprise to some Vermonters.

30. Progressive Party leaders Ellen David-Friedman and Martha Abbott deserve much credit for building the party organization.

31. Frank M. Bryan, *Real Democracy: The New England Town Meeting and How It Works* (Chicago, IL: University of Chicago Press, 2004), 50.

CHAPTER 7

New York State's *"Multi+"* Party System

Gerald Benjamin and Michael Catalano

New Yorkers voting for governor on November 6, 2018, found ten party lines on their ballots: Democrat (D), Republican (R), Conservative (C), Working Families (WF), Green (GRE), Libertarian (LBT), Independence (IND), Serve America Movement (SAM), Reform (REF), and Women's Equality (WEP). However, they were offered "only" five candidates: Andrew Cuomo (D, WF, IND, WEP), Mark Molinaro (R, C, REF), Howie Hawkins (GRE), Larry Sharpe (LBT), and Stephanie Miner (SAM). The situation was similar for the other statewide offices: comptroller (nine parties nominating four candidates), attorney general (eight parties nominating five candidates), and US senator (seven parties nominating two candidates). This difference between the number of candidates and the number of party lines on the ballot is not an anomaly; it has long been the norm in New York State.

Democrats and Republicans combined received a total of 86.03 percent of the total vote for governor (Democrat, Cuomo: 54.53 percent; Republican, Molinaro: 31.5 percent). The eight minor parties garnered a total of 12.04 percent of the vote. A combined 12.53 percent of Molinaro's 2,089,228 total vote resulted from Conservative and Reform Party cross endorsements. Democrat Cuomo got 5.2 percent of his winning 3,393,495 total vote by virtue of the cross endorsements by the Working Families, Independence, and Women's Equality Parties (Table 7.1).

Additionally, the vote for minor-party gubernatorial candidates totaled just under a quarter of a million. Howie Hawkins, the Green Party candidate, got 95,716 votes (1.65 percent). Larry Sharpe, the Libertarian, received 90,816 (1.56 percent). Stephanie Minor, running on the SAM label, received 51,367 (0.89 percent).

Table 7.1: Vote for Governor, 2018

	Vote	%	Third-Party Total	Third/ Candidate
Cuomo				
D	3,158,459	54.53		
WF	106,018	1.83	1.83	
I	63,518	1.1	1.1	
WEP	25,510	0.44	0.44	
Total	3,353,505	57.9		5.82
Molinaro				
R	1,824,581	31.5		
C	238,578	4.12	4.12	
Ref.	26,069	0.45	0.45	
Total	2,089,228	36.07		12.53
Hawkins				
G	95,716	1.65	1.65	
Sharpe				
L	90,816	1.56	1.56	
Miner				
SAM	51,367	0.89	0.89	
			12.04	

Note: Democrat (D), Republican (R), Conservative (C), Green (G), Libertarian (L), Working Families (WF), Independence (I), Reform (Ref.), Women's Equality (WEP), Serve America Movement (SAM).

New York's ballot certainly does not look like that of a two-party system (Figure 7.1). But neither does it resemble the ballot of a conventional multiparty system, with each party offering unique choices to the voter. Rather, the ballot indicates a different type of system, the result of the unintended consequences of the combined effect on politics and political incentives of several separately passed state election laws. We, the authors, characterize this result here as a "multi+ party system." Such a system features not only distinct third parties, but also fusion candidacies, with votes for each party distinctly recorded on the ballot and then aggregated to determine the winner.

Electoral fusion, or cross endorsement, is the practice of two or more parties nominating the same candidate for the same office in a single election. It was common in the United States until late nineteenth century,

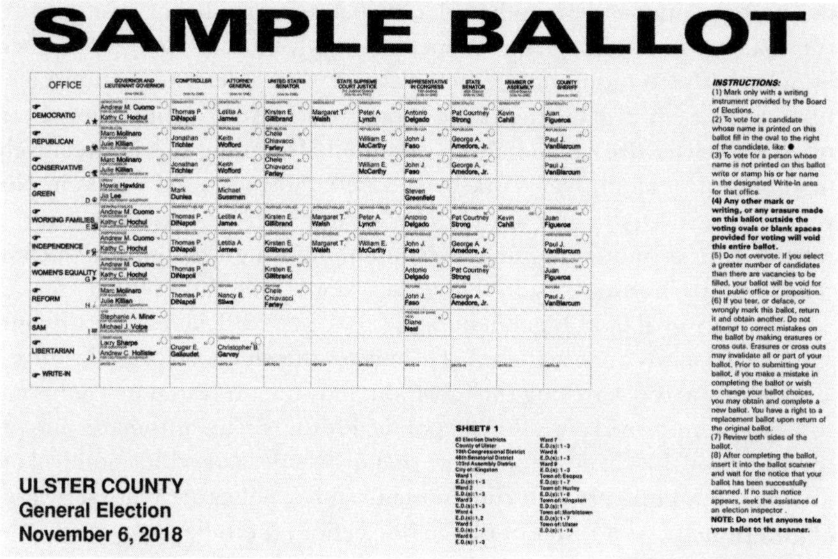

SAMPLE BALLOT

OFFICE	GOVERNOR AND LIEUTENANT GOVERNOR	COMPTROLLER	ATTORNEY GENERAL	UNITED STATES SENATOR	STATE SUPREME COURT JUSTICE		REPRESENTATIVE IN CONGRESS	STATE SENATOR	MEMBER OF ASSEMBLY	COUNTY SHERIFF
DEMOCRATIC A	Andrew M. Cuomo / Kathy C. Hochul	Thomas P. DiNapoli	Letitia A. James	Kirsten E. Gillibrand	Margaret T. Walsh	Peter A. Lynch	Antonio Delgado	Pat Courtney Strong	Kevin Cahill	Juan Figueroa
REPUBLICAN B	Marc Molinaro / Julie Killian	Jonathan Trichter	Keith Wofford	Chele Chiavacci Farley		William E. McCarthy	John J. Faso	George A. Amedore, Jr.		Paul J. VanBlarcum
CONSERVATIVE C	Marc Molinaro / Julie Killian	Jonathan Trichter	Keith Wofford	Chele Chiavacci Farley		William E. McCarthy	John J. Faso	George A. Amedore, Jr.		Paul J. VanBlarcum
GREEN D	Howie Hawkins / Jia Lee	Mark Dunlea	Michael Sussman				Steven Greenfield			
WORKING FAMILIES E	Andrew M. Cuomo / Kathy C. Hochul	Thomas P. DiNapoli	Letitia A. James	Kirsten E. Gillibrand	Margaret T. Walsh	Peter A. Lynch	Antonio Delgado	Pat Courtney Strong	Kevin Cahill	Juan Figueroa
INDEPENDENCE F	Andrew M. Cuomo / Kathy C. Hochul	Thomas P. DiNapoli	Letitia A. James	Kirsten E. Gillibrand	Margaret T. Walsh	William E. McCarthy	John J. Faso	George A. Amedore, Jr.		Paul J. VanBlarcum
WOMEN'S EQUALITY G	Andrew M. Cuomo / Kathy C. Hochul	Thomas P. DiNapoli		Kirsten E. Gillibrand			Antonio Delgado	Pat Courtney Strong		Juan Figueroa
REFORM H	Marc Molinaro / Julie Killian	Thomas P. DiNapoli	Nancy B. Sliwa	Chele Chiavacci Farley			John J. Faso	George A. Amedore, Jr.		Paul J. VanBlarcum
SAM I	Stephanie A. Miner / Michael J. Volpe						Diane Neal			
LIBERTARIAN J	Larry Sharpe / Andrew C. Hollister	Cruger E. Gallaudet	Christopher B. Garvey							
WRITE-IN										

SHEET# 1

63 Election Districts
County of Ulster
19th Congressional District
46th Senatorial District
103rd Assembly District
City of: Kingston

ULSTER COUNTY
General Election
November 6, 2018

INSTRUCTIONS:
(1) Mark only with a writing instrument provided by the Board of Elections.
(2) To vote for a candidate whose name is printed on this ballot fill in the oval to the right of the candidate, like: ●
(3) To vote for a person whose name is not printed on this ballot write or stamp his or her name in the designated Write-In area for that office.
(4) Any other mark or writing, or any erasure made on this ballot outside the voting ovals or blank spaces provided for voting will void this entire ballot.
(5) Do not overvote. If you select a greater number of candidates than there are vacancies to be filled, your ballot will be void for that public office or proposition.
(6) If you tear, or deface, or wrongly mark this ballot, return it and obtain another. Do not attempt to correct mistakes on the ballot by making erasures or cross outs. Erasures or cross outs may invalidate all or part of your ballot. Prior to submitting your ballot, if you make a mistake in completing the ballot or wish to change your ballot choices, you may obtain and complete a new ballot. You have a right to a replacement ballot upon return of the original ballot.
(7) Review both sides of the ballot.
(8) After completing the ballot, insert it into the ballot scanner and wait for the notice that your ballot has been successfully scanned. If no such notice appears, seek the assistance of an election inspector .
NOTE: Do not let anyone take your ballot to the scanner.

Figure 7.1: New York's party line ballot. Each party has its own row. Candidates' names may appear multiple times on the ballot.

when parties prepared their own ballots. Election reform resulted in the use of an official ballot prepared by the government, accompanied by ballot access requirements and (usually) the restriction of candidates to a single ballot line. Later enactments limited candidacies to party members and prevented "sore losers" in a party primary from running on another ticket.[1] According to one 2013 survey, "Laws in 43 states ban fusion voting 1) directly by explicitly prohibiting multiple party nominations or 2) indirectly by requiring that candidates be members of the nominating party. Since candidates can only belong to one party at any given time, the legal effect of these laws is to ban cross-endorsement."[2] New York is one of five remaining states that permits cross-endorsed fusion candidacies. The others are Connecticut, Oregon, South Carolina, and Vermont.[3]

Eight of the ten parties on the 2018 New York State gubernatorial ballot were designated "official," a status that secured their nominees automatic ballot access in the general election. Parties earned official party status by garnering at least fifty thousand votes in the prior gubernatorial election in 2014. From 2015 to 2018, New York's official parties included the Democrat, Republican, Conservative, Working Families, Independence, Green, Women's Equality, and Reform Parties.[4] The Libertarian Party and SAM, designated "independent bodies," had to petition for a ballot position.[5] To run a statewide candidate, an independent body must file petitions signed by at least fifteen thousand registered voters, with at least one hundred of these from each of half the state's (now twenty-seven) congressional districts. Given the size of New York's potential electorate, this is a relatively modest requirement. New York had 12,706,050 registered voters in November 2018, 11,574,222 of these designated "active." Crucially, it is the relative ease of mounting an independent campaign for governor combined with its brand of fusion that makes New York's party system unique.

A primary goal of independent bodies is to gain official party status and sustain this status once achieved. This makes the election for governor essential for survival. Crossing the fifty-thousand-vote threshold in a gubernatorial election provides a valuable political resource: an automatic line on the ballot for the ensuing four years that may be leveraged for political influence, appointments, and commitments in key policy areas at every level of government. As a result of the 2018 election, the Libertarian and SAM parties gained official status, and the Women's Equality and Reform parties lost that status.[6]

As can be seen from the New York sample ballot, a cross-endorsed candidate's name appears multiple times; the number of votes that he or she receives on each line is separately recorded. (Sometimes called "disaggregation," this is also the practice in Connecticut and South Carolina, but not Oregon or Vermont.[7]) The total of all votes cast for each candidate determines the winner of the election. Disaggregation of the vote allows precise measurement of each party's contribution to each candidate's vote total. Contrast this with the treatment of cross endorsement on the sample ballot for Multnomah County, Oregon (Figure 7.2). Each candidate's name appears once, with all parties backing him or her listed next to each name. This method offers no way of quantifying each party's contribution to the candidate's total vote.

The development of cross endorsement in New York is the unintended consequence of the two major parties joining to limit fusion candidacies by empowering a party's governing body in a jurisdiction to control access to its ballot line. As written in 1947, the state's Wilson-Pakula Act bars a person who is not a party member (often the candidate of another party) from running for office as that party's candidate unless that person gets permission from it to enter the party's primary and, if successful, to seek office as its candidate.[8] This has evolved into a process for minor parties to endorse major-party candidates.

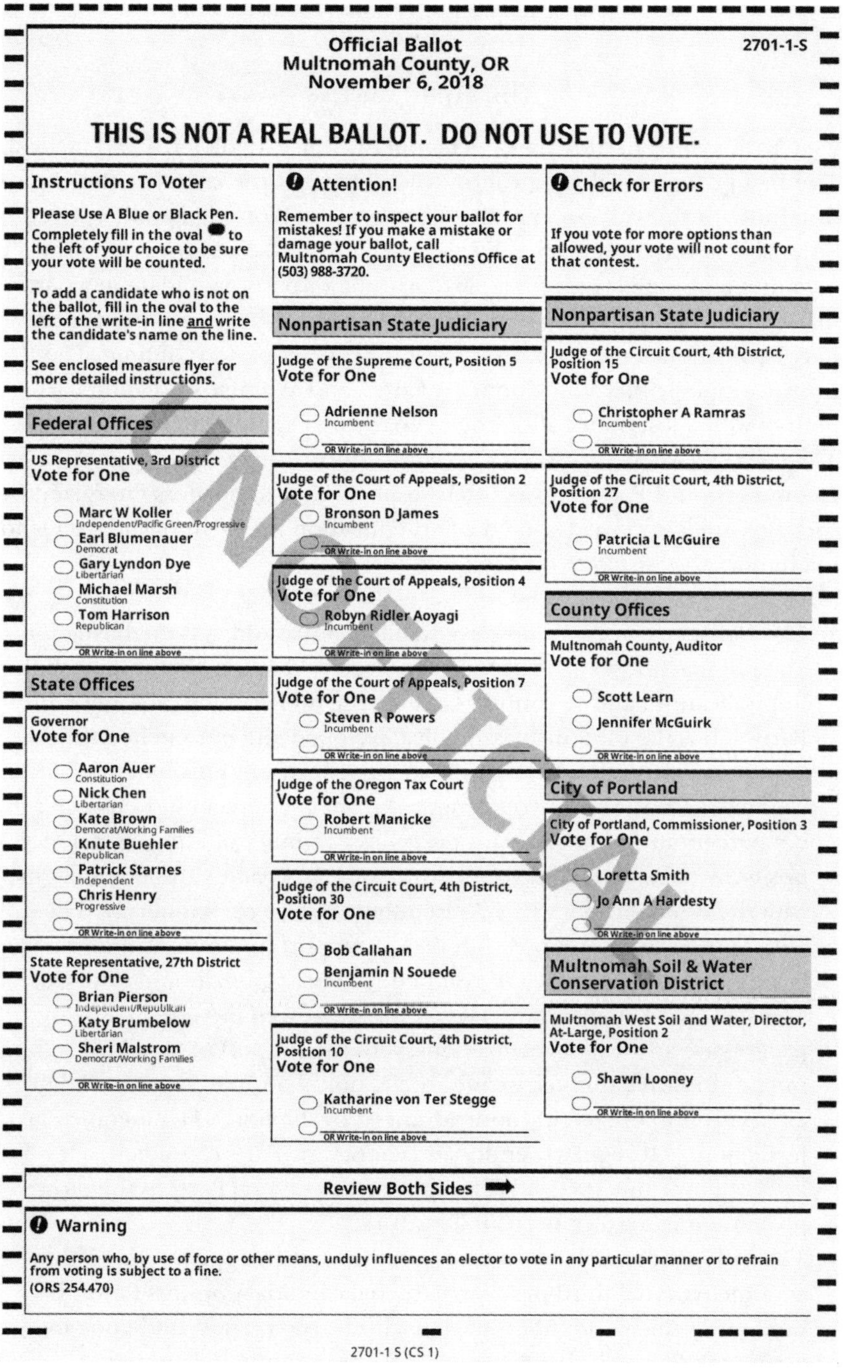

Official Ballot
Multnomah County, OR
November 6, 2018

2701-1-S

THIS IS NOT A REAL BALLOT. DO NOT USE TO VOTE.

Instructions To Voter

Please Use A Blue or Black Pen.

Completely fill in the oval ● to the left of your choice to be sure your vote will be counted.

To add a candidate who is not on the ballot, fill in the oval to the left of the write-in line **and** write the candidate's name on the line.

See enclosed measure flyer for more detailed instructions.

❶ Attention!

Remember to inspect your ballot for mistakes! If you make a mistake or damage your ballot, call Multnomah County Elections Office at (503) 988-3720.

❶ Check for Errors

If you vote for more options than allowed, your vote will not count for that contest.

Federal Offices

US Representative, 3rd District
Vote for One

○ Marc W Koller
  Independent/Pacific Green/Progressive
○ Earl Blumenauer
  Democrat
○ Gary Lyndon Dye
  Libertarian
○ Michael Marsh
  Constitution
○ Tom Harrison
  Republican
○ _____
  OR Write-in on line above

State Offices

Governor
Vote for One

○ Aaron Auer
  Constitution
○ Nick Chen
  Libertarian
○ Kate Brown
  Democrat/Working Families
○ Knute Buehler
  Republican
○ Patrick Starnes
  Independent
○ Chris Henry
  Progressive
○ _____
  OR Write-in on line above

State Representative, 27th District
Vote for One

○ Brian Pierson
  Independent/Republican
○ Katy Brumbelow
  Libertarian
○ Sheri Malstrom
  Democrat/Working Families
○ _____
  OR Write-in on line above

Nonpartisan State Judiciary

Judge of the Supreme Court, Position 5
Vote for One

○ Adrienne Nelson
  Incumbent
○ _____
  OR Write-in on line above

Judge of the Court of Appeals, Position 2
Vote for One

○ Bronson D James
  Incumbent
○ _____
  OR Write-in on line above

Judge of the Court of Appeals, Position 4
Vote for One

○ Robyn Ridler Aoyagi
  Incumbent
○ _____
  OR Write-in on line above

Judge of the Court of Appeals, Position 7
Vote for One

○ Steven R Powers
  Incumbent
○ _____
  OR Write-in on line above

Judge of the Oregon Tax Court
Vote for One

○ Robert Manicke
  Incumbent
○ _____
  OR Write-in on line above

Judge of the Circuit Court, 4th District, Position 30
Vote for One

○ Bob Callahan
○ Benjamin N Souede
  Incumbent
○ _____
  OR Write-in on line above

Judge of the Circuit Court, 4th District, Position 10
Vote for One

○ Katharine von Ter Stegge
  Incumbent
○ _____
  OR Write-in on line above

Nonpartisan State Judiciary

Judge of the Circuit Court, 4th District, Position 15
Vote for One

○ Christopher A Ramras
  Incumbent
○ _____
  OR Write-in on line above

Judge of the Circuit Court, 4th District, Position 27
Vote for One

○ Patricia L McGuire
  Incumbent
○ _____
  OR Write-in on line above

County Offices

Multnomah County, Auditor
Vote for One

○ Scott Learn
○ Jennifer McGuirk
○ _____
  OR Write-in on line above

City of Portland

City of Portland, Commissioner, Position 3
Vote for One

○ Loretta Smith
○ Jo Ann A Hardesty
○ _____
  OR Write-in on line above

Multnomah Soil & Water Conservation District

Multnomah West Soil and Water, Director, At-Large, Position 2
Vote for One

○ Shawn Looney
○ _____
  OR Write-in on line above

Review Both Sides ➡

❶ Warning

Any person who, by use of force or other means, unduly influences an elector to vote in any particular manner or to refrain from voting is subject to a fine.
(ORS 254.470)

2701-1 S (CS 1)

Figure 7.2: Oregon's office block ballot. Third-party endorsements appear under candidates' names, which appear only once on the ballot.

THE THIRD PARTIES

New York's third parties are of two general types: ideological and tactical. The first group has ideological or policy roots; of the current official parties, those in this category are the Conservative, Working Families, Green, SAM, and Libertarian Parties. Parties of the second type are created simply to gather additional votes for a particular major-party candidate in a particular election from persons who are not likely to otherwise support him or her. Tactical third parties tend to exist for shorter periods of time. The Reform (originally the Stop Common Core) and Women's Equality Parties, both of which lost their ballot line in 2018, are examples of tactical parties. They were created in 2014 to attract support for governor for Andrew Cuomo (D) and Rob Astorino (R), respectively, from voters energized by specific issue concerns (women's and education issues, in particular) who might not otherwise vote for them.[9]

- The Conservative Party, now over a half-century old, was established in 1962 in reaction to what its founders regarded as too-liberal Rockefeller Republicanism and to counter-balance the then-influential Liberal Party.[10] It is the most institutionally developed and entrenched third party in modern New York politics. In 2018, county enrollment of registered Conservative voters ranged from 4.3 percent in Rensselaer to 0.7 percent in Tompkins. This party has a number of litmus test policy positions (e.g., antitax, pro–law enforcement, prolife) and often aligns with the Republican Party.[11] As Republican strength has declined in New York in recent years, Conservative support has become increasingly important to achieving GOP competitiveness regionally and statewide.[12]
- The Working Families Party (WFP) was organized in 1998 by progressive advocacy organizations, with the support of New York's public employee unions, to offer social policy positions and candidate alternatives to the left of those advanced by the state's Democratic Party leadership.[13] It regularly endorses Democratic Party candidates at every level of government. The WFP replaced the Liberal Party as the most prominent left minor party in New York.
- The Independence Party came to prominence in 1992 in connection with the national third-party presidential candidacy of Ross Perot. It became a vehicle for gubernatorial runs in 1994, 1998, and 2002 by wealthy Buffalo-area businessperson Tom Golisano.[14] The party advances a government reform agenda. It likely benefits from voter confusion, as those who seek to be independent of the major parties, or

not enrolled at all in a party, sometimes erroneously enroll in the Independence Party because of its name.[15] It does have a very significant voter enrollment base and has the capacity to attract a significant number of votes to its line in statewide elections.

- Newly organized, the Serve America Movement (SAM) is linked to an emerging national third-party effort that seeks to establish a transpartisan coalition of moderates and independents. In New York, it was energized primarily by anti–Andrew Cuomo elements in the state Democratic Party. In anticipation of the 2020 presidential election, its attaining of an automatic ballot line created an important resource in the state.
- The Green and Libertarian Parties are national in scope and the most persistently policy and ideology centered.[16] They seek to use elections to advance policy or ideological goals and are less oriented toward winning. They proudly abjure cross endorsement in favor of offering their own candidates and are most evocative of parties in multiparty systems.

New York politics regularly witnesses third parties that emerge, thrive, decline, and then, after failing to reach the fifty thousand threshold for official status, become inconsequential. Notable among these are the Right to Life Party and the Liberal Party.

- Right to Life was founded in 1970 in reaction to legalization of abortion in the state.[17] Candidates publicly pledged support for prolife policies to attract this party's cross endorsement and to block any potential challenge on its line, even decades after the *Roe v. Wade* decision. The party remained active as an official party between 1978 and 2002.
- The Liberal Party was organized in 1944 by union leader Alex Rose and others as a noncommunist, left-oriented alternative to the American Labor Party (ALP). It was once the most powerful exploiter of fusion opportunities in New York politics.[18] For decades, its cross-endorsement strategies made Liberal Party leaders king makers, especially in New York City. It declined as its leadership aged, the centers of power in New York organized labor shifted, and its focus transitioned from policy goals to patronage gains for party leaders and activists. The Liberal Party ceased to exist in a meaningful way after 2002 when its gubernatorial candidate Andrew Cuomo, a former secretary of the US Department of Housing and Urban Development in the Clinton

administration, withdrew from active campaigning prior to election day and failed to garner the required fifty thousand votes to retain the party's official status.

Inexorably, third parties feel pressures to become more transactional in their attempt to gain and sustain political relevance. Some resist more than others. The balance between ideological and operational purity and effective pragmatism is a persistent and often divisive intraparty issue. This is the dilemma that Dan Cantor and W. F. Mason characterized as whether and when the WFP must be "inside, outside or somewhere in between" in its relationship with the Democratic Party,[19] a challenge that has been most evident in recent years in is fraught relationship with Governor Andrew Cuomo.

In 2014, the WFP endorsed Governor Cuomo for reelection after a divisive internal battle, driven by the anger of many party activists provoked by his working relationship with Republicans and allied dissident Democrats (the Independent Democratic Conference [IDC]) in the state senate, austere fiscal policies, battles with public employee unions, and what many regarded as relative inattention to progressive social policy promises. The WFP's 2018 gubernatorial endorsement of Cynthia Nixon over Cuomo was intended to send a message to the incumbent governor regarding these grievances. However, this stance caused many labor unions, favorable to the incumbent governor, to depart the party.[20]

When Cuomo defeated Nixon in the Democratic primary, she arranged to leave the race by accepting a nomination for an assembly seat (she actually endorsed and campaigned for the incumbent, assembly member Deborah Glick). This allowed the WFP to return to backing Cuomo for governor. The pretext was the need for a united front against President Donald Trump. Of course, in the worst case, the WFP's ballot line might be at stake, a crucial resource in retaining political influence, not only at the state level but in its New York City bastion. Cuomo made them wait before finally accepting.

THIRD-PARTY STRATEGIES

New York's multi+ party system opens a variety of strategies to its third parties for influencing the outcome of elections. In addition to cross endorsement of a major-party candidate, these include running their own candidates straightforwardly, to win the election; staying out of an election to offer indirect support for a major-party candidate; entering an election with an independent candidate to split the vote in a way that favors a major-party candidate; and nominating a major-party hopeful preemptively to influence the major-party nominating process. The presence on the ballot of third-party independent nominees also offers an opportunity for "dirty tricks" by a major-party campaign, designed to draw off votes likely to go to its major-party opponent.

A Separate Candidate

One review of the elections in 2006 and 2008 confirmed that New York third parties rarely run their own candidates for Congress or state offices.[21] The rare occasions when a third-party candidate is competitive in a general election with only one indivisible "prize" (e.g., a single-member district) most often arise when an incumbent is defeated for renomination within one of the major parties. Liberal Republican John Lindsay won reelection for mayor of New York City in 1969 on the Liberal Party line after losing in the Republican primary to John Marchi, a Staten Island state senator. James Buckley gained a US Senate seat a year later as the Conservative Party nominee in a three-way race that included incumbent Republican Charles Goodell, a former Congress member and opponent of the Vietnam War who was appointed by Governor Nelson Rockefeller to fill the vacancy created after Robert Kennedy was assassinated.

In 1990, with the incumbent Democrat Mario Cuomo regarded as virtually unbeatable for reelection to a third term, the GOP had great difficulty in attracting a candidate for governor. Finally, the party settled upon Pierre Rinfret, a wealthy businessperson; he turned out to be a reluctant campaigner and, in general, a disastrous choice. Meanwhile, the Conservative Party nominated Herb London, a conservative professor and prolific public intellectual. London, lively and engaging, campaigned vigorously and almost surpassed Rinfret for second place in the gubernatorial vote totals. The New York State Constitution has required, since 1894, with limited exceptions, that the administration of state and local elections be done by state and county boards headed by an equal number of members (usually two) designated by the two political parties receiving the most and next-most votes in the immediately preceding gubernatorial election.[22] A second-place finish by London would have caused the Conservatives to displace the Republicans in this role, with the loss of hundreds of jobs held by the GOP faithful across the state.

Staying Out

When ideology or activist sentiment within a third party make cross endorsement difficult, or when running on a third-party line is seen by a candidate as a potentially negative signal for his or her major-party voters, third-party leaders may agree to indirectly help that candidate by doing nothing in that race. As we have seen, the Conservative Party far more frequently endorses Republicans rather than Democrats. In the case of former state assembly Democratic majority leader Joe Morelle (Monroe County), Conservatives made no endorsement and ran no candidate. This helped assure that Morelle would regularly run unopposed for his assembly seat. According to one report, "State campaign finance records show donations given to the Conservative Party of Monroe County by both Morelle and various local Democratic Party organizations."[23]

Splitting the Vote

A strong third-party candidacy may make possible the election of a less favored major-party nominee by splitting the opposing vote and reducing the total needed to win. In 1980, Alfonse D'Amato defeated incumbent Republican Jacob Javits in the GOP primary for the US Senate. The Democrat in this contest was state senator Elizabeth Holtzman, winner of a four-way primary in her own party. Nominated by the Liberal Party, Javits stayed in the race. (Under New York's election law, the only ways for a candidate to get off a ballot once nominated is to run for another office, move out of the state, or die.) D'Amato narrowly defeated Holtzman while Javits ran a distant third.

Incumbent Republican governor Rockefeller faced a daunting race for a third term in 1966. The newly formed Conservative Party, created in reaction to his "liberal" record, supported Paul Adams, a professor and dean. Rockefeller's Democratic opponent, New York City Council president Frank O'Connor, was ahead in early polls. A Democratic win seemed likely. But the Liberal Party, which usually cross endorsed the Democrat for governor, nominated Franklin Delano Roosevelt Jr. Allegedly, the Liberal's leader, Alex Rose, decided to take this path because Democrats declined to consider his preferences for their ticket.[24] Roosevelt took enough votes in running third to allow Rockefeller to prevail by a narrow plurality.

This phenomenon of the tail wagging the dog, with third-party leaders exercising disproportionate influence on nominations, occurs at every level, from local town elections to statewide contests. It is the basis of much of the criticism of New York's brand of fusion politics. Third parties, seen as a potential source of the victory margin, make their support at the polls contingent upon selection of their preferred nominee or a place for one of their members on the major-party ticket. This happened at the statewide level in 1994 when, to assure their backing for the party's gubernatorial candidate, state senator George Pataki, Republicans nominated the afore-mentioned Herb London over assembly minority leader John Faso for state comptroller. Pataki won; London lost.

Preemptive Action

Instead of negotiating, a third party may act preemptively in an attempt to influence the major-party choice. The Conservatives did this in 1980, when they nominated Alfonse D'Amato for the US Senate. Liberals did it in 1982, when they selected Mario Cuomo to run for governor on its slate. Both of these third-party-preferred candidates received major-party backing and both won in the general election.

But this approach is not without risks. As noted below, in 2002, the De-mocrats backed Carl McCall for governor despite the Liberal's early nomi-nation of Andrew Cuomo. With no chance to win, Cuomo chose not to campaign. In the ensuing election, the Liberals lost their line on the ballot and subsequently disappeared entirely from New York politics.

Vote Splitting and Dirty Tricks

On occasion in close races, partisans of a candidate of one of the two major parties spend resources on a third-party candidate with whom they do not agree to divide the vote against their favorite. In 2018, the race in New York's Nineteenth Congressional District was among the most hotly con-tested in the nation. Fight for Tomorrow New York, a shadowy political ac-tion committee (PAC) based in Austin, Texas, whose only presence in New York State appeared to be a mailing address at a UPS Store in the small up-state city of Oneonta, spent at least $100,000 on last-minute mailings, robo-calls, and social media advertising, encouraging enrolled Democrats to vote for Steven Greenfield, the Green Party candidate, over Antonio Delgado, the Democrat (see Figure 7.3). The funds were actually provided by New York businessperson Robert Lauder.[25] The hope was that enough votes would be denied Delgado to assure the victory of John Faso, the Republican incumbent. Greenfield wrote: "The messages are not from me, my cam-paign, or any PAC supporting me. They are not from the Green Party or

ON THE ISSUES...

One candidate stands for equality and progressive values

Issues

Steven Greenfield

Antonio Delgado

Medicare For All

Abolish ICE

Support OFF Act
Off Fossil Fuels for a Better Future Act

Length of Residence in District 17 years 1 year

ELECTION DAY: NOVEMBER 6

Pol. Ad paid for by Fight For Tomorrow. Not authorized by any candidate or candidate's committee.

Figure 7.3: Ambiguously named conservative political action committee (PAC) uses liberal arguments to promote the vote for third-party candidate Steven Greenfield in an effort to diminish the vote for Democrat Antonio Delgado and give an advantage to the unnamed Republican John Faso in a very close race for Congress in 2018.

any PAC supporting us. They are from Republicans. I denounce both the message and the messengers. I am as much a victim of this dirty trick as the candidate it purports to undermine."[26] The maneuver did not work; Delgado defeated Faso in a close race.

Fear of the defeat resulting from splitting the vote three ways has motivated major-party candidates to contest third-party nominations. In 2002, incumbent governor George Pataki's campaign registered eighteen thousand people in the Independence Party in anticipation of opposing its expected nomination of Tom Golisano. Golisano fended off the primary challenge but Pataki still prevailed over him and Democrat Carl McCall in a three-way race in the general election.[27]

Cross Endorsement

Fusion candidacies for governor first occurred in New York State in 1854.[28] The last New York gubernatorial election for which there was no cross endorsement was in 1966, over a half century ago. Democrat Mario Cuomo fell short in his bid for a fourth term as governor in 1994 as a result of the votes delivered to his Republican opponent George Pataki, on the Conservative Party line. Republican candidate Michael Bloomberg needed the votes he won on the Independence line to become mayor of New York City in 2001 and later to win his third term in 2009. In that overwhelmingly Democratic jurisdiction, the third-party line gave Bloomberg voters, who would never back a Republican, an alternative place to support him. One study counted 1,569 congressional elections in the state between 1952 and 2014 in which cross endorsement of a major-party candidate by one or more minor parties occurred.[29]

Major-Party Cross Endorsement

When incumbents are entrenched and very popular or a major party is very weak in a constituency (e.g., Republicans for most offices in most places within New York City), one major party may endorse the other's candidate. That candidate then runs on both the Democratic and Republican lines on the ballot. This may make the third-party candidate the only alternative that the voter has when he or she votes. For example, Democratic New York City mayor Ed Koch was also nominated by the GOP in 1981. New York minor parties found a role in the election with the Liberal Party nomination of Mary Codd and the Conservative Party offering John Esposito to voters. Frank Barbaro, a liberal Brooklyn assembly member running on the (independent body) Unity line, outperformed them both. Of course, Koch won.[30]

Strange Bedfellows

Cross-endorsement pragmatics sometimes produce strange bedfellows (or running mates). Ironically, in light of his later career, Republican Rudy Giuliani did not have the endorsement of the Conservative Party when he ran for New York City mayor a second time against Democratic incumbent David Dinkins in 1993. Instead, Conservatives ran their own candidate, George Martin. Giuliani relied upon votes provided by the Liberal Party line to win. In another example of a mixed-party ballot, in 2018, the Reform Party's statewide ticket included Mark Molinaro, the Republican gubernatorial candidate, and Tom DiNapoli, the incumbent Democratic comptroller.

THE PERVASIVENESS OF MULTI+ PARTY POLITICS

Perceptions of the effects of New York's multi+ party system on state politics is ordinarily based upon the publicity given to dramatic, contested statewide nominations and elections. But in fact, these are embedded in the DNA of Empire State politics, with important structural consequences for the electoral process at every level of government: Congress and the state legislature, regional judicial elections, countywide races, and at-large contests for mostly rural town boards.

Legislative Elections

Votes recorded on third-party lines decided two congressional, three state senate, and three state assembly elections in 2016. The two Republican state senators who won assured the GOP control of that house by a one-vote margin. In 2018, the winning margins in five of New York's twenty-seven congressional elections, ten of its sixty-three state senate elections, and five of its one hundred and fifty assembly elections were a result of third-party cross endorsements. Four of the victors in these close state senate races were Democrats who won formerly Republican-held sets; cross endorsement, though not decisive, thus contributed significantly to the historic, decisive Democratic capture of that body. The five assembly members who needed Conservative cross endorsement to win would constitute 12 percent of the minority-party conference in that house.

Table 7.2: Cross-Endorsed State Legislators without a Major-Party Opponent, 2016; with and without Minor-Party Opponent

Chamber	Unopposed	None	D or R+1 minor	One Minor	Two Minors	Three Minors	Cross+ Minor Opponent
Senate	22	1	1	8	3	9	5
Assembly	65	11	2	21	10	21	5

Patterns in the state legislature illustrate that cross endorsement is often less about providing a margin of victory than about establishing or affirming a continuing political relationship. In 2016, sixty-five state assembly members (43 percent) and twenty-two senators (34.9 percent) nominated by a major party ran unopposed by the other major party (Table 7.2). Of these, only one senator and eleven assembly members had no cross endorsement. Two assembly members and one senator ran on the Democratic, Republican, and Conservative lines and had no third-party opponent. Five members in each house unopposed by a major-party candidate had a minor-party opponent. All others ran entirely unopposed but nonetheless secured one or more cross endorsements. The usual pattern was for the Conservative Party to back Republicans and the Working Families and Women's Equality Parties to back Democrats. Independence and Reform were more transactional, attracted to sure winners for the sake of being on their side.

County Executives

New York has fifty-seven counties outside of New York City; eighteen have elected county executives. Races for these offices provide a good window into cross-endorsement practices for the highest-profile local races across the state. Here we see the variety of possible third-party tactics manifest.

In the most recent races for these highly visible local offices, the Conservative Party was the most fully engaged. Only in Long Island's Nassau County was there no cross endorsement. Three Republican incumbents ran unopposed; two of these still got Conservative backing, creating a record of support with the outcome predetermined. In the remaining races, the Conservative Party backed the Republican nine times, the Democrat twice (Albany and Onondaga), and ran its own candidate once (Rockland).

New York has closed primaries; only enrolled party members may vote in

Table 7.3: Cross Endorsement in County Executive Races, 2014–2017

County	Year	D	R	Dem Cross	Rep. Cross	Own Candidate	Cross Decisive
Suffolk	2015	Bellone*	O'Connor	WF, I, WEP	C, Ref.		
Nassau	2017	Curran*	Martins	None	None	G is Lems	
Westchester	2017	Latimer*	Astorino	WF, I, Ref., WEP	C		
Rockland	2017	Porette	Day*	WF, WEP	Ref.	C is Sullivan	
Putnam	2014	Olivario	O'Dell*	None	C, I		
Orange	2017	Davis	Neuhaus*	WF, Ref., WEP	C, I		
Dutchess	2017	Jablonski	Molinaro*	WF, G	C, I, Ref.		
Ulster	2015	Hein*	Bernardo	WF	C, I, Ref.	G is Downie	
Albany	2015	McCoy*	Vitollo	C, I	Ref.	G is Platt	
Broome	2016	Garnar*	Preston	WF, WEP	C, I, Ref.		
Chautauqua	2017	Ferguson	Borrello*	WF, WEP	C, I		
Chemung	2014	Santulli*				Unopposed	
Erie	2015	Poloncarz*	Walter	WF, WEP	C, I, Ref.		
Monroe	2015	Frankel	Dinolfo*	WF	C, I, Ref.	G is Barnabas	
Montgomery	2017	Ossenfort*			C	Unopposed	
Oneida	2015	Picente*				Unopposed	
Onondaga	2015	Shelley	Mahoney*	C, Ref.	I		
Rensselaer	2017	Smyth	McLaughlin*	WF, WEP	C, I, Ref.	G is Foy	Yes
Totals: 18		15	18				

Note. An asterisk denotes the winner. Democrat (D), Republican (R), Conservative (C), Working Families (WF), Independence (I), Reform (Ref.), Women's Equality (WEQ), Green (G).

them.[31] Compared to those for major parties, third-party voter enrollment totals are low, making primary challenges attractive opportunities. In Rockland County, Tom Sullivan defeated county executive Ed Day for the Conservative nomination by registering enough new Conservatives at a time close to the primary vote to control the result. The race was decided by absentee ballots in Sullivan's favor. Day's camp cried foul, alleging Democratic Party meddling and undue influence by development interests in the town of Ramapo, a center of strength for the controversial Hasidic Jewish community. (Interestingly, the Working Families Party accused the Day campaign of seeking to hijack its line in the same election.[32]) Ultimately, these disputes became inconsequential, as Day prevailed in the general election.[33]

County party leaders' reactions to state political dynamics were also sometimes behind less conventional endorsement decisions. For example, in Onondaga, where the city of Syracuse is located, Republican Joanne Mahoney lost Conservative backing largely because of her earlier endorsement of the reelection of Democratic governor Andrew Cuomo.[34]

For its part, the Working Families Party either endorsed Democrats for county executive or remained uninvolved. Women's Equality, created, as noted, to support Cuomo for governor, backed eight Democrats. The Reform Party, created to support Rob Astorino for governor, aligned with Republicans more than Democrats but, remarkably, chose George Latimer (who ran on five party lines!) over Astorino for Westchester County executive.[35] Finally, the Independence Party endorsed more Republicans than Democrats by about the same ratio as the Reform Party (Table 7.3).

Judicial Elections

Judges for New York's Supreme Court, the state's trial court of general jurisdiction, are selected for fourteen-year terms by partisan election in twelve judicial districts. Candidates are nominated at conventions dominated by state and local party leaders, who therefore effectively choose the judges. A state commission appointed by former chief judge Judith Kaye a decade and a half ago found that "in many parts of the State, being on the dominant party's slate is tantamount to winning the elections . . . [because] only four of the State's twelve judicial districts can be considered competitive."[36] One recent example: there were thirty-eight judges elected or reelected in 2016. Twenty-eight won in uncontested races. Thirteen of these ran only on the Democratic line while nine were cross endorsed by the two major parties.

In regions of the state where the outcome is less certain, each major party's county leaders may negotiate among themselves to advance the interests of judicial aspirants from their counties. Then cross-party deals may be made. In the Eighth Judicial District in western New York in 2017, highly regarded Republican appellate division judge Erin M. Peradotto was up for reelection for a second term. She was cross endorsed by the Democrats. At the same time, the Republicans cross endorsed Democrat Lynn Wessel Keane for an open Supreme Court slot. These two candidates were also supported by the Conservative and Working Families Parties, assuring that both would win without opposition (and without having to raise funds for a serious campaign).[37]

Until relatively recently, sitting state supreme court judges seeking a second term were routinely cross endorsed. However, the inclination to make such deals diminishes for the party that thinks it can win all the prizes in a competitive environment. When this is the case, third-party endorsements are sought by the major-party candidates to foster a competitive advantage. Of the ten races for judgeships contested by the major parties in 2016, the Conservative endorsement provided the margin of victory for Republicans in five. New York's former chief judge Sol Wachler has written that, on Long Island:

> Minor parties, such as the Conservative, Independence, Working Family and Reform, . . . manipulate fusion voting . . . [to] tip the balance in selecting judges. By endorsing either a Republican or Democratic candidate, these parties could influence—even determine—who would become Supreme Court justices. The intrusion of fusion voting by minor parties, does not improve the quality of judges; it only increases the number of political bosses who can now pick our judges.[38]

Town Elections

We randomly selected a sample of fifty towns from among a population of 932. We then collected election data from 2014 to 2017 to see how strongly town board elections reflected third-party engagement and influence at the local level. Town elections are generally held in New York in odd-numbered years, but occasional vacancies need filling in even-numbered years. We were able to get data on 366 candidacies for the randomly selected towns. We found that in most town board elections, Republicans prevailed and candidacies tended to be unopposed (Table 7.4). Out of 294 town board and supervisor races, seventeen Democrats and 174 Republicans had no major-party opposition. One Democrat and three Republicans had a minor-party opponent. Additionally, there were three unopposed minor-

Table 7.4: Competition in Sample of Town Elections, 2015–2017

	Dem. (#)	Rep. (#)	Cons. (#)	Indep. (#)	Local (#)	Total (#)	%
Total Candidates	97	256	2	1	10	366	
Major Party Cross Endorsed[a]	23	23				46	
Unopposed by Other Major	17	174				191	
Third Party Unopposed			2	1		3	
Local Party Unopposed					6	6	
Subtotal Unopposed	40	197	2	1	6	246	
Major Opposed by Minor Only	1	3			4	8	
Total: No Effective Opposition						254	69.40
Total: Two Major Party Competitive	56	56				112	30.60

[a]Cross-endorsed candidates counted for each party, for consistency.

Table 7.5: Cross Endorsement in Major-Party Competitive Sample Town
Elections, 2015–2017

	Dem (#)	Rep (#)	Cons (#)	Ind. (#)
Competitive Elections	56	56		
Cross-Endorsed by Third Party[a]	21	42		
Winners	13	42		
Number of Winners Crossed[b]	8	34		
Cross Decisive	4	9	2	1
Times Loser Was Crossed	12	8		

[a]Includes one "other" cross endorsement for a Democrat and two for a Republican.
[b]Includes two "other" cross endorsements for Republicans.

party candidates for town board seats and six unopposed local party candidacies in towns that abjured the conventional party labels. An additional
twenty-three candidates (counted as forty-six candidacies) were cross endorsed by both major parties.

There were fifty-six elections contested by the two major parties in these
towns, out of a total town board election sample size of 294. In these,
twenty-one Democrats and forty-two Republicans were endorsed by at least
one third party (Table 7.5). The cross endorsement was decisive for four
Democrats (7.1 percent) and nine Republicans (16.1 percent). The Conservative Party was most active in cross endorsement at the town level, with
the Independence Party second, and the Working Families Party a distant
third. In addition, two third-party candidates and one Independent candidate won with a margin provided by cross endorsement. Most interestingly,
thirteen candidates that ran on both the Democratic and Republican lines,
seven unopposed Democrats and sixty-four unopposed Republicans had
third-party endorsements. Though these cross endorsements in uncontested races provided no obvious electoral advantage, they do indicate the
importance of multiple nominations to a candidate. We would expect to
see officeholders elected in these circumstances and potentially interested
in reelection to be, at a minimum, solicitous of the views of their communities' third-party leaders.

THE EFFECTIVENESS OF CROSS ENDORSEMENT

Politicians are innately risk adverse. Running on multiple lines both denies
those places on the ballot to actual or potential opponents and contributes,

Table 7.6: Statewide Enrollment and Vote for Governor, 2018

	Enrollment	Vote for Governor	Vote/ Enrollment (%)
D	5,780,030	3,158,459	0.55
R	2,633,776	1,824,581	0.69
C	148,051	238,578	1.63
G	27,581	95,716	3.47
WF	41,853	106,008	2.53
I	442,992	63,518	0.14
WEP	5,845	25,510	4.36
Ref.	2,200	26,069	11.85

Note: Democrat (D), Republican (R), Conservative (C), Green (G), Working Families (WF), Independence (I), Women's Equality (WEP), Reform (Ref.).

they think, votes to their total. One of the difficulties in establishing the effect of cross endorsement in New York politics, however, is the absence of evidence about what would occur under alternative scenarios. While observing the counterfactual is impossible, potential tests of the effects of third-party cross endorsement could come from natural experiments and circumstances that, to some degree, isolate the effects of third-party cross endorsement.

One hint of the value of minor-party endorsement is that, except for the Independence Party, minor parties' statewide vote totals regularly exceed their statewide enrollment, while major-party vote totals fall far short of enrollment totals (Table 7.6). But in addition, there is some solid empirical evidence that, in some circumstances, running also on third-party lines adds to a majority party candidate's vote total. Benjamin R. Kantack looked at fusion candidacies in 1,569 elections for Congress held between 1952 and 2014.[39] He found "fused candidacies" benefited Republicans across the state to a greater degree in nonpresidential than presidential years and Democratic candidates in New York City in presidential years. He concluded that in 5.7 percent (fifty-nine) of the contested house races in the period under study, "fused ballot lines or the absence of a single fused ballot line were critical to the outcome."[40]

A very interesting earlier study took advantage of a quasinatural experiment that arose in two elections for the county legislature in suburban Nassau County. Barbara Johnson was reelected to that body in 1999 with the Independence Party endorsement. She was part of a ten to nine Democratic majority. When Johnson died six month later, her son Craig was nominated to run on the Democratic, Working Families, Independence, and Liberal lines in a special election to succeed her. He won. The Working Families Party made an exceptional, boots-on-the-ground effort for Craig Johnson's election. Through the use of several multiple regression models, the authors concluded that "[The] Working Family Party votes did represent new votes for . . . Craig Johnson, but that there was little evidence that the other minor parties were able to turn out new voters, . . . and they may [have] simply displac[ed] Democratic votes."[41]

PROS AND CONS

Advocates for third parties argue that they give the electorate greater choice, thus enhancing democracy and increasing levels of participation.[42] New York's multi+ party system does afford greater choice at the polls, but there are few pure third-party successes, both in single-member-district plurality-winner elections and those that are conducted at-large with multiple winners. Circumstances are rare in which third-party candidates can offer the legitimacy, gain the resources, and command the visibility to be truly competitive. Those parties in New York that run their own candidates, as is the case elsewhere, primarily seek to add policy views into the political debate, affect priorities, or protest the offerings of the major parties and their governing practices.

Regarding participation, the aforementioned study done of a local legislative race in Nassau County showed that activist third parties can generate greater turnout. But it is not just a matter of an added line on the ballot. The third party must make a serious turnout-the-vote effort to have this effect.[43] Generally, its number of parties notwithstanding, New York has one of the lowest participation rates in the nation.

It is the pervasiveness of cross endorsement that makes New York different. Opponents fear the excessive influence of small numbers of third-party leaders and further political polarization resulting from encouraging third parties. In fact, in New York, third-party endorsement politics does pull the major parties away from the ideological center, reinforcing the effects of the increasingly pervasive and polarizing structural, social, and political factors doing the same.[44] Yet, at the same time, these parties must be pragmatic about retaining their principle resources—their official status and the resulting automatic ballot access—and therefore their influence on government and access to posts in it, both appointed and (occasionally) elected.

A primary function of political parties is to produce governing coalitions. In the American two-party system, this is done within parties in the course of elections; in multiparty systems, this occurs in negotiations between or among parties to form governments after election results are known. Critics fear that encouraging multiparty politics in the United States would damage or undo the current way this function is performed. Because of the availability of cross endorsement, this feared result does not occur in New York. Major parties' governing majorities still emerge from elections. Third parties influence their composition during the nominating and electoral processes.

In elections with a single plurality winner—that is, in most US national- and state-level executive and legislative contests—casting a ballot that will have no consequence, or "vote wasting," is a major argument against third-party voting. This argument has less force in New York. The availability of major-party candidates on minor-party lines allows New Yorkers to reject the Democratic and Republican labels while simultaneously recording a choice for major-party candidates—that is, to protest without wasting their votes.

Ballot length and complexity have been identified as disabilities of multi-party politics. These problems are enhanced in places and election years in which there are a multiplicity of elected offices to fill. New York's layered local government system makes it one of those places. Multiple listings of the same candidate, often with a different combination of candidates—one outcome of cross endorsement in New York—add significantly to ballot length and complexity.[45]

THE FUTURE

In 2013, Democratic state senator Malcolm Smith of Queens, who was briefly that body's majority leader, was convicted of attempting to bribe New York City Republican leaders to give him access to their ballot line under the Wilson Pakula Act for the mayoral race. Smith knew that, if nominated, he would have little chance of winning the mayoralty. But he also knew, as one journalist noted, that "Running for office brings access to the city's six-dollars-for-one, taxpayer-funded campaign-contribution-matching system."[46] Smith went to federal prison for seven years.

The Senator Smith incident precipitated efforts in Albany to revise the election law to block cross endorsement as an anticorruption measure. An alternative approach was to leave cross endorsement in place but end the practice of giving each party a distinct ballot line. Vigorously resisted by third-party leaders, these efforts failed when originally introduced and in subsequent attempts.[47] One idea, not yet considered, is to allow a third party to qualify for a permanent ballot line as a result of its gubernatorial election total and only if the candidate it offers was not a nominee in that election of another party. This would eliminate the tactical use of third-party creation by gubernatorial candidates.

Discussions about the need to eliminate third-party influence in New York elections were renewed in 2018, fueled by the Cuomo/Working Families Party imbroglio.[48] Particular concerns were raised too, as noted, regarding third-party influence on judicial elections. "Forgetting whether it benefits Democrats or Republicans in whatever election," one reform advocate said, the system "empowers some deeply corrupt and non-representative individuals who run these parties and small groups."[49] So, just as newly unified Democratic control of state government in 2018 gave reformers historic wins in their decades-long efforts to ease voter registration and ballot access in New York, some were advocating reducing the range of choice offered to voters.

A commission created by law in the 2019 state budget bill to consider campaign finance reform, a key progressive goal, was also almost, in passing, empowered to write "new election laws" regarding "multiple party camping nominations and/or designations."[50] Third-party leaders sued, arguing that this was an unconstitutional attempt by Governor Cuomo and other mainstream Democrats to eliminate the source of their influence. The immediate goal, they said, was to diminish the impact of the progressive wing of the Democratic Party, with which the WFP is aligned. The law that created the commission also provided that its recommendations would go into effect without a vote in the legislature, where the WFP and Conservative Parties—due to past cross endorsements—have great influence. This process was also challenged as suspect under the state constitution as an unlawful delegation of legislative authority.

Thus New York-style fusion, and the multi+ party system it has nurtured, is under its most serious challenge in decades. Weeks before its decisions were due, the campaign finance commission insisted that the outcomes of its inquiry regarding fusion voting were not predetermined. Perhaps disingenuously, Governor Cuomo declared himself neutral on the question. Given the pervasiveness of third-party influence at every level of New York government, the depth of long-time cross-party personal and political relationships, and the indebtedness of many officeholders to third parties, the laws that sustain New York-style fusion are resilient. Though it has powerful adversaries, the state's multi+ party system may well persist, warts and all. Maybe that is not such a bad thing.

NOTES

Isabelle Hayes, a political science major at SUNY New Paltz and a Cetrino family scholar at the Benjamin Center for Public Policy Initiatives, provided assistance with the tables prepared for this chapter.

1. Howard A. Scarrow, "Duverger's Law, Fusion, and the Decline of American 'Third' Parties," *Western Political Quarterly* 39, no. 4 (December 1986): 638; Peter H. Argersinger, "'A Place on the Ballot': Fusion Politics and Antifusion Laws," *American Historical Review* 85, no. 2 (April 1980): 287–306.

2. Terrance Adams, "Cross Endorsing Candidates," OLR Research Report, Connecticut General Assembly, Office of Legislative Research, no. 2013-R-0046, January 16, 2013, https://www.cga.ct.gov/2013/rpt/pdf/2013-R-0046.PDF. Adams added: "In . . . Idaho and Mississippi fusion voting does not occur in practice." In *Timmons v. Twin Cities Area New Party* (1997), the US Supreme Court held that Minnesota's law limiting a candidate to one ballot line did not violate the federal First Amendment guarantee of the right to association. Timmons v. Twin Cities Area New Party, 520 US 351 (1997), accessed November 23, 2018, http://www.oyez.org/cases/1996/95-1608.

3. This number is variously reported. See Bernard Tamas, "The 2016 Election and the Reemergence of American Third Parties" (conference of the Proceedings of State of Parties: 2016 and Beyond, Ray C. Bliss Institute of Applied Politics, University of Akron, Akron, OH, November 10, 2017). Adams (note 2) says the number is seven.

4. NY Elect. Code § 1–104.3.

5. NY Elect. Code § 1–104.12, 6–136, 6–138. Regarding the Serve America Movement, see "Home," SAM, accessed September 25, 2019, https://joinsam.org/.

6. Howard Scarrow listed the following parties, not otherwise mentioned in this essay, that had official party status in the twentieth century: Prohibition (1892–1922), Socialist Labor (1896–1904), Socialist (1900–1938), Independent League (1906–1916), Progressive (1912–1916), American (1914–1916), Farmer–Labor (1920–1922), Law Preservation (1930–1934), and American Labor (1936–1954). See Scarrow, *Parties, Elections and Representation in the State of New York* (New York: New York University Press, 1983), 75n3.

7. "Notes: Fusion Candidacies, Disaggregation, and Freedom of Association," *Harvard Law Review* 109, no. 6 (April 1996): 1302.

8. These requirements were enacted with the support of both major parties to block unwanted fusion primary candidacies. Targets were the left-wing American Labor Party and, in particular, Harlem congress member Vito Marcantonio. See NY Elect. Code § 6–120 and a sample of the certificate of authorization at http://www.elections.ny.gov/NYSBOE/download/law/authorization.pdf.

9. Joseph Spector, "'Stop Common Core' to Change to Reform Party," Lohud, January 13, 2015, https://www.lohud.com/story/politics-on-the-hudson/2015/01/13/stop-common-core-to-change-to-reform-party/21706463/; Ginia Bellafante,

"Cuomo's So-Called Women's Party," *New York Times*, May 24, 2018, https://www.ny times.com/2018/05/24/nyregion/cuomos-so-called-womens-party.html.

10. J. Daniel Mahoney, *Actions Speak Louder: The Story of the New York Conservative Party* (New Rochelle, NY: Arlington House, 1968).

11. "Home," Conservative Party of New York State, accessed January 6, 2019, http://www.cpnys.org/2018/.

12. Gerald Benjamin, "Political Parties in New York," in *The Oxford Handbook of New York State Government and Politics*, ed. Gerald Benjamin (New York: Oxford University Press, 2012), 49–78.

13. "Home," Working Families Party, accessed January 6, 2019, http://working families.org/.

14. Robert J. Spitzer, "Third Parties in New York," in *Governing New York State*, 5th ed., eds. Robert F. Pecorella and Jeffrey M. Stonecash (Albany: State University of New York Press, 2006), 77.

15. "Home," Independence Party, accessed January 6, 2019, http://www.inde pendencepartyny.org/book.html.

16. Tamas notes that they lately have been the primary sources of third-party candidacies for Congress. See Tamas, "The 2016 Election," 9.

17. Maurice Carroll, "The Unlikely Beginning of the Right to Life Party," *New York Times*, November 25, 1978, https://www.nytimes.com/1978/11/25/archives /the-unlikely-beginning-of-the-right-to-life-party-they-form-a-cadre.html?searchResult Position=1.

18. "Policies and Platform," The Liberal Party, accessed October 6, 2019, http://www.liberalparty.org/policies-and-platform/brief-history-and-platform-of-the -liberal-party/; Bernard Rosenberg, "New York Politics & the Liberal Party," *Commentary*, February 1964.

19. Dan Cantor and J. W. Mason, "Inside, Outside or Somewhere In-Between: Fusion Voting and the Working Families Party," *Social Policy* 34, no. 2 (Winter 2003/ Spring 2004): 53–57.

20. Jimmy Vielkind, "Working Families Party Endorses Nixon over Cuomo," Politico, April 14, 2018, https://www.politico.com/states/new-york/albany/story /2018/04/14/working-families-party-endorses-cynthia-nixon-over-andrew-cuomo -365405.

21. Celia Curtis, "Cross Endorsement by Political Parties: A 'Very Pretty Jungle'?" *Pace Law Review* 29, no. 4 (Summer 2009): 790–791.

22. NY Elect. Code Art. II § 8.

23. Dave Colon, "Is This the Election that Kills Fusion Voting in New York?" *Gotham Gazette*, October 12, 2018, https://www.gothamgazette.com/state/7984-is -this-the-election-that-kills-fusion-voting-in-new-york.

24. Spitzer, "Third Parties," 82.

25. Alex Kotch, "'Dirty Trick': GOP Super PAC Boosts Green Party Candidate in Tight NY-19 Race," Sludge, November 6, 2018, https://readsludge.com/2018/12

/11/mystery-donor-revealed-republican-estee-lauder-heir-spent-100000-to-boost
-green-party-candidate/.

26. "Greenfield Denounces Republican PAC Dirty Trick," Steve Greenfield for
Congress, November 6, 2018, https://stevegreenfieldforcongress.com/republican
-pac-dirty-trick/; Kotch, "'Dirty Trick'"; "Home," Fight for Tomorrow, https://www
.fightfortomorrowny.com/. Note: Fight for Tomorrow's web address (https://www
.fightfortomorrowny.com) has since been taken down. You may find proof of Fight
for Tomorrow's contributions to Greenfeld's campaign through Fight for Tomorrow's Federal Election Commission filings at https://docquery.fec.gov/cgi-bin
/fecimg/?C00549279.

27. Spitzer, "Third Parties," 74.

28. Scarrow, "Duverger's Law," 635.

29. Benjamin R. Kantack, "Fusion and Electoral Performance in New York Congressional Elections," *Political Research Quarterly* 70, no. 2 (June 2017): 292–293.

30. "New York City Mayor 1981," Our Campaigns, accessed January 7, 2019,
https://www.ourcampaigns.com/RaceDetail.html?RaceID=79306.

31. In 2018, the Reform Party opened its primary to registered voters not enrolled in any other party.

32. Michael D'Onofrio, "Working Families Party Says Day Is Seeking to 'Hijack'
Political line," Lohud, September 8, 2017, https://www.lohud.com/story/news
/local/rockland/2017/09/08/working-families-party-says-day-seeking-hijack-polit
ical-line/646788001/.

33. Lanning Taliaferro, "Absentee Votes Push Conservative Insurgent Over Day
in Primary," Patch New City, September 22, 2017, https://patch.com/new-york
/newcity/absentee-votes-push-conservative-insurgent-over-day-primary.

34. Michelle Breidenbach, "2015 Election Takeaways: Comparing Mahoney vs
Magnarelli, Shelley in Races for Onondaga County Executive," Syracuse.com, November 4, 2015, https://www.syracuse.com/politics/index.ssf/2015/11/2015_elec
tion_takeaways_comparing_mahoney_vs_magnarelli_shelley.html.

35. Mark Lungariello, "Latimer Endorsed by Party Astorino Started," Lohud,
August 7, 2017, https://www.lohud.com/story/news/politics/elections/2017/08
/07/reform/537871001/.

36. "Final Report to the Chief Judge of the State of New York," New York City
Courts, accessed January 7, 2018, https://courts.state.ny.us/whatsnew/pdf/Fer-
rickJudicialElection.pdf.

37. Sol Wachtler, "Fix the Way NY Selects State Supreme Court Judges," Newsday, September 30, 2018, https://www.newsday.com/opinion/commentary/end
-how-ny-elects-judges-1.21298066; Cody Cutting, "Who Really Picks New York's
Judges?" Brennan Center for Justice, November 11, 2015, https://www.brennan
center.org/our-work/analysis-opinion/who-really-picks-new-yorks-judges.

38. Wachtler, "Fix the Way."

39. Kantack, "Fusion and Electoral," 291–300.

40. Kantack, 295–297.

41. Melissa R. Michelson and Scott J. Susin, "What's in a Name: The Power of Fusion Politics in a Local Election," *Polity* 36, no. 2 (January 2004): 319.

42. For the arguments against the New York system, see Curtis, "Cross Endorsement." For a view in favor of fusion, and a suggested approach to overcome antifusion laws, see Elissa Berger, "A Party That Won't Spoil: Minor Parties, State Constitutions and Fusion Voting," *Brooklyn Law Review* 70, no. 4 (Summer 2005): 1381; Hendrik Hertzberg, "New York's Third Parties," *New Yorker,* July 30, 2010; Michael Waldman, Miles Rappaport, and Susan Lerner, "Why New York Needs Healthy Third Parties," *New York Daily News,* May 2, 2013.

43. Michelson and Susin, "What's in a Name," 319.

44. Dave Colon, "Is This the Election That Kills Fusion Voting in New York?" Gotham Gazette, October 12, 2018.

45. Ryan Whalen, "WNY Democrats Target 'Fusion Voting,'" Spectrum News Buffalo, May 2, 2018.

46. Bob McManus, "They're All Malcolms," *New York Post,* April 4, 2013.

47. NY Elect. Code § 6-122. See Senate 1166 (2017-2018) (Carlucci) and NYA A00786 (2017) (Preslow), and attendant legislative history.

48. Colon, "Is This the Election."

49. Colon.

50. Vivian Wang and Jesse McKinley, "Did Cuomo Rig a Commission to Sabotage His Political Foes?" *New York Times,* September 25, 2019.

CHAPTER 8

The Independence Party of Minnesota

Melanie Freeze

Turning and turning in the widening gyre
The falcon cannot hear the falconer;
Things fall apart; the centre cannot hold.
—W. B. Yeats, "The Second Coming"

Americans' trust in government has indisputably declined since the 1960s, especially among those at the ideological center.[1] Partially caused by increasing levels of political polarization and accompanying gridlock, deteriorating political trust served critical in opening doors for independent and third-party movements across the United States during the 1990s.[2] Empowered by personal wealth, billionaire Ross Perot ran as an independent candidate in the 1992 US presidential election. Advocating term limits, a balanced budget amendment, import reduction, immigration cuts, and other measures designed to reduce the federal deficit, Perot began to activate, organize, and amplify the public's discontent with the existing political system.[3]

In Minnesota, a state with a legacy of third-party political success, Perot's independent bid was particularly well received. While Perot received 18.91 percent of the popular vote nationwide, he captured 23.96 percent of Minnesota's votes in 1992.[4] However, even before the close of the election, Perot's 1992 independent movement had a significant and long-lasting impact on Minnesotan politics. Perot's erratic campaign triggered the birth of the Independence Party (IP) of Minnesota, one of the most successful third-party organizations the state would experience since the Farmer–Labor Party's victories in the early half of the twentieth century. Drawing on electoral data and elite interviews, this chapter explores how resource availability and party organization influenced the rise and ebb of Minnesota's IP.

THE BIRTH OF MINNESOTA'S INDEPENDENCE PARTY

In July of 1992, Ross Perot suddenly and unexpectedly suspended his campaign despite his favorable poll standing and enthusiastic following.[5] Perot eventually reentered the race in October, but during the seventy-day absence, ambitious activists who had aligned with his movement took steps to fill the vacuum of power. A group of political moderates in Minnesota led by Phil Madsen were frustrated by Perot's withdrawal from the presidential campaign. Cognizant of the latent public energy that Perot's bid had begun to activate, they formally organized the Independence Party of Minnesota on July 22, 1992, in hopes of using it to gain more resources and propel the movement forward in their state.[6] Although the party was formed with the desire to acquire more resources, at that first meeting, no one was aware of what specific resources were available to political parties under existing electoral state laws.[7]

Inspired and motivated by Perot's 1992 presidential bid, Dean Barkley entered the Sixth US House District's 1992 race as an independent candidate. With the hopes of finding a few fired-up and likeminded individuals to volunteer in his campaign, Barkley was also in attendance at this meeting of disoriented Perot supporters in Bloomington where the IP was first formed. After Phil Madsen proposed forming the IP, Barkley stood as the second person to advocate the party route in hopes that party status could help overcome some of the barriers faced by independent candidates. Barkley was the first to donate $100 to the party and would later become a prominent party figure and critical catalyst in the party's development.[8]

Perot's 1992 presidential bid may have sparked the creation of the IP, but the party's relationship with Perot and his movement was tenuous and, at times, even contentious.[9] Only after Perot established the Reform Party in 1995 did Perot and his loyal supporters actively work to bring the IP of Minnesota into their party. On June 22, 1996, the IP agreed to formally affiliate with the Reform Party and adopt the name Reform Party of Minnesota (RPMN).[10] The two groups coexisted for two electoral cycles, but the national party provided little support for the Minnesotan arm and eventually, in 2000, a divorce ensued.[11] The Minnesotan faction, led by Jesse Ventura, left the Reform Party and reclaimed the name—the Independence Party of Minnesota—after losing an internal power struggle with Perot's old allies who aligned with Pat Buchanan. For the purpose of the current research, the names IP of Minnesota and Reform Party of Minnesota will be used interchangeably, especially when referencing events from 1996 to 2000.

The IP sought to replicate the movement of Perot by branding itself as a moderate voice supported by "zealots of the center" who were unhappy with major-party performance and who felt alienated by their increasingly polarized stances.[12] The party roughly mirrored Perot on issues of political reform and fiscal responsibility, as translated to the sphere of state-level issues, but the IP had a more moderate stance on social issues, as it supported abortion rights and the legalization of marijuana.[13] The three main pillars of the IP platform in the early 1990s included fiscal responsibility, honesty in government, and personal liberty.[14]

Unlike Perot, the IP did not emphasize economic nationalism or immigration. To reinforce the image of political honesty, IP candidates did not accept contributions from political action committees (PACs). In 1996, the party emphasized issues of political reform, calling for a unicameral legislature, term limits, a special prosecutor to investigate alleged political use of public resources, and campaign finance reforms.[15] Of course, as a party appealing to moderation and independent political thought, actual issue positions often varied from candidate to candidate within the party. Candidates were only required to agree with 75 percent of the party platform to secure the party's endorsement.[16]

PERFORMANCE OF THE INDEPENDENCE PARTY OF MINNESOTA

During the 2002 electoral campaign, the IP of Minnesota controlled the state's governor's office, had access to millions of dollars in state public finances, endorsed and fielded fifty-five candidates in partisan offices ranging from state legislator to governor, and captured an average of 10 percent of the vote across those elections. The IP reached levels of success rarely seen in modern third-party movements, but "success" can be conceptualized and measured through many different routes. A third-party movement is clearly successful if it can elect its candidates to office. Yet, since the rise of the Republican Party in the 1850s, widespread and enduring candidate victories are rarely seen in American third-party movements.[17] Instead, when considering third parties, scholars tend to follow the definition of success set by Walter Dean Burnham: the ability to win at least 5 percent of the vote.[18] In this section, several indicators are examined to investigate the depth and span of the IP's achievements. The IP's success is most easily and often observed in the few highly salient and viable candidacies that won the plurality or at least garnered respectable shares of Minnesota's statewide vote. Additionally, the party's viability can also be observed in the large number of candidates fielded over a wide range of offices, the robust vote shares captured across the political arena, and its ability to attract campaign funds.

Viable, Salient Candidates

Jesse Ventura, one of the Independence/Reform Party's most dramatic examples of success, broke through barriers that often impede third-party success by winning the 1998 Minnesota gubernatorial election with 37 percent of the vote. A second, less salient IP candidate who managed to win elected office was Sheila Kiscaden, a moderate Republican state senator from District 30 (Rochester and the surrounding areas). In 2002, after being denied the Republican endorsement, she won the seat with 41.56 percent of the district's vote, running as an IP candidate.

Ventura and Kiscaden were the only IP candidates who won their elections and served in Minnesota government; however, other notable and strong performing statewide IP candidates include Tim Penny, Tom Horner, and Dean Barkley. Described as "celebrity candidates," and often recruited by party leaders within the IP, these individuals were relatively well-known political figures with ideologies that did not necessarily align perfectly with the increasingly polarized and homogenous major parties. Tim Penny won 16.18 percent of the vote for Minnesota governor in 2002. Having served as a Democratic Farmer–Labor Party representative from Minnesota's First District from 1983 to 1995, Penny had a record of being a conservative Democrat and later served as an informal advisor to Ventura during his gubernatorial transition.[19] Tom Horner previously affiliated with the Republican Party but later left to join the IP and captured 11.94 percent of the vote when he ran for governor in 2010.[20] Of the individuals who ran for the US Senate, only Barkley, one of the founders and a repeat IP candidate, won over 10 percent of the vote (15.15 percent in 2008).

Higher-profile offices often attract quality candidates with resources enabling them to win, irrespective of party label. For example, Ventura's win can be attributed, in large part, to his impressive name recognition resulting from his celebrity status and entertaining campaign. Not many candidates wear flamboyant yellow feather boas to highlight their prior career as a pro wrestler, produce look-alike action figures, or aired ads where the candidate (and a candidate double) poses nearly nude in imitation of Rodin's "The Thinker."[21] To explore the IP as a party organization and third-party movement separate from candidate-level factors, it is essential to examine its candidacies at all levels of partisan elections in Minnesota, not just a few celebrity candidates' successes under its third-party label. It is also necessary to establish a baseline, or point of reference, to gauge the party's relative success.

Activity and Electoral Performance of Candidates
at Multiple Levels of Government

By considering the number of candidates fielded and share of the vote won by IP candidates over all levels of office and time, we can identify the depth, span, and apex of the party's life. Figure 8.1 displays the 288 candidates running in partisan general and special elections under the IP label in Minnesota between 1994 and 2018, grouped by type of electoral office.[22] In Figure 8.1, the temporal rise and fall of the party's success in terms of candidate volume is seen most clearly in the elections of Minnesota House of Representatives, Minnesota State Senate, and to a lesser degree, the US House.[23] The 2002 general election saw the largest slate of IP candidates run for the state legislature. IP candidates ran for 27 percent of the sixty-seven state senate seats and 19 percent of the 134 state house seats. At the statewide level, for all years except 2004, candidates were consistently fielded for office, especially during gubernatorial election years. Finally, the IP's presence in the US congressional elections varied from cycle to cycle, with a particularly strong showing in 2010 when IP candidates ran for seven of the eight seats.

Efforts inside of the IP organization may have contributed to the upward trajectory in number of IP state legislative candidates at the turn of the century, but it is more likely the increase in IP candidates occurred in an organic manner independent of the formal IP Party organization. On one hand, advances in party organization may have helped increase the number of candidates fielded for state legislature elections. Specifically, a stronger party could recruit more candidates into the party. However, according to Phil Fuehrer (the current state chair of the IP, the 1996 IP candidate for the Minnesota House in District 67B, and an activist who has been involved since the party's founding), most IP candidates running for positions in the Minnesota state legislature tend to adopt the party label with little party outreach. Instead, party recruitment efforts focus primarily on the few US House or other statewide offices and special elections.[24] Therefore, the spikes in the number of candidates running under the IP are more likely indicative of the increasing appeal of the party as a vehicle for candidates to ride outside of the major-party system. Fuehrer noted that, except for a few

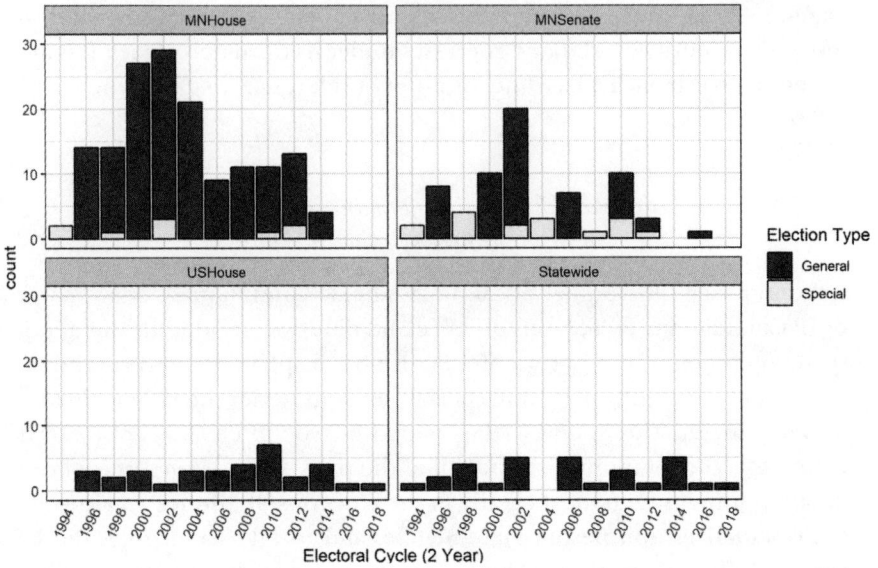

Figure 8.1: Independence/Reform Party of Minnesota candidate counts by electoral cycle, type, and level of office, 1994–2018. State of Minnesota Secretary of State, 2000–2018, Minnesota election results; Minnesota Reference Library, 1994–1998, Minnesota election results.

perennial candidates, most IP candidates running for the lower house were new to the political arena, fueled by frustration with the lack of choices produced by a polarized system and the perception that the system was broken and in need of reform and outsider influence.

The robust number of IP candidates at multiple levels of office provides some evidence of a third-party movement at the level of political elites. But did the IP experience any corresponding third-party movement in the electorate? How viable was the party in the electoral field? Figure 8.2 plots the percent of the total vote won by each of the 288 IP/Reform candidates grouped by electoral cycle and level of office. While electoral performance varies considerably across candidate and office, a clearer picture of the IP's electoral success emerges. On average, candidates consistently garner between 5 and 10 percent of the vote. This was especially true during the late 1990s and early 2000s. The temporal variation in party viability is most apparent in the presence of strong-performing outliers during the early 2000s.

Another burst of viable outlier candidates appears in 2010, but the failure of any statewide IP candidate to win over 5 percent of Minnesotans' votes in 2014 and all subsequent elections signals a clear break and downturn in

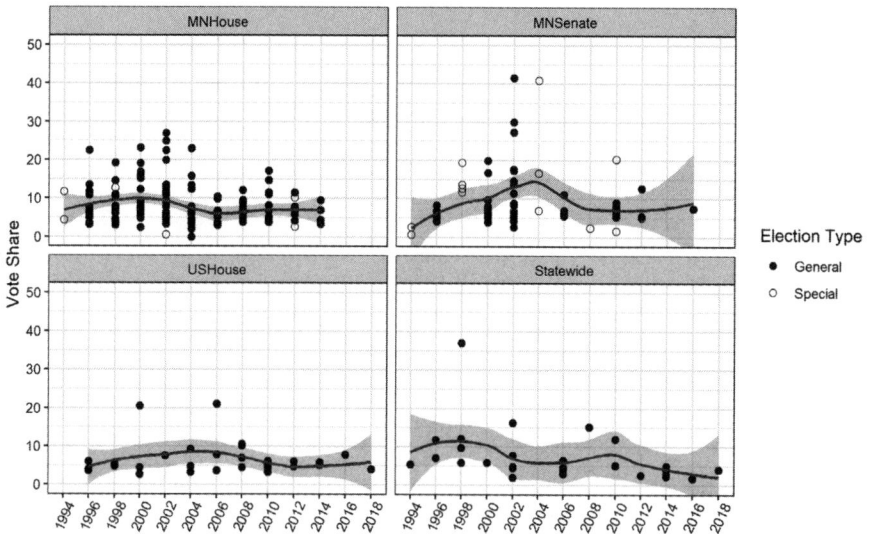

Figure 8.2: Independence/Reform Party of Minnesota candidate vote shares by electoral cycle, type, and level of office with smoothed conditional means and 95 percent confidence intervals, 1994–2018. State of Minnesota Secretary of State, 2000–2018, Minnesota election results; Minnesota Reference Library, 1994–1998, Minnesota election results.

party fortune. After 2014, there were no IP Minnesota State House candidates, and the party's representation in other electoral offices was also sparse. In 2016, an election where the two major-party presidential candidates were burdened with historically low favorability images, the IP decided to endorse long-shot, independent presidential candidate Evan McMullin with the hope he would win over 5 percent of the vote and help jump-start the party's political status.[25] This strategic move failed, as McMullin only won a meager 1.8 percent of the vote. The 2018 election served as another failed attempt by the IP to demonstrate party viability, as the one statewide candidate fielded by the party was unable to win 5 percent of the vote.[26]

Fundraising Performance

Finally, the IP's temporal performance can be assessed by its ability to attract campaign funds. Panel (a) of Figure 8.3 presents the total amount of party funds received by the IP of Minnesota state party committees registered with the Federal Election Commission. Panel (b) of Figure 8.3 displays the percent of total receipts that originated from individual contribu-

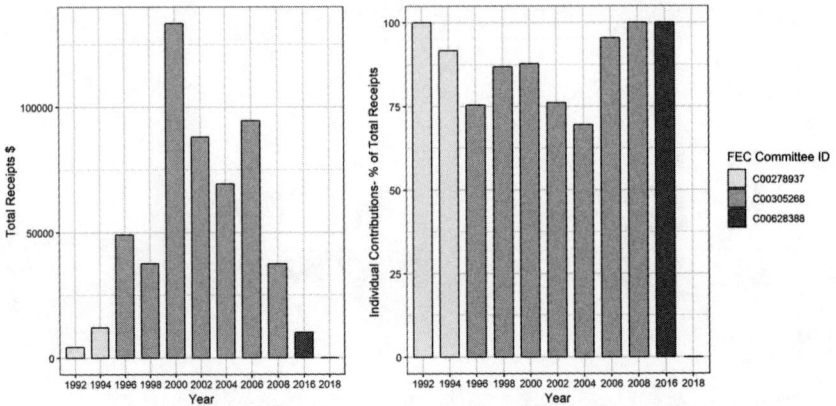

Figure 8.3: Total receipts donated to various party committees associated with the Independence Party/Reform Party of Minnesota, 1992–2018. Federal Election Commission, campaign finance data.

tions. In panel (a) of Figure 8.3, we see a surge in financial resources available to the IP organization that mirrors the temporal candidate volume and vote share trends. The election following Ventura's 1998 gubernatorial victory stands as the party's fundraising peak. In 2000, the IP's party committee raised a total of $133,251, an amount eight times bigger than the combined amount raised by the party during its early years from 1992 to 1996. Although this amount was a relatively large amount for the party, the comparable fundraising committees of the Minnesota Democratic Farmer–Labor and Republican parties raised $8 million and $11.4 million, respectively, in the 2000 election cycle.[27] The data in panel (b) show the party to be very reliant on individual donations, which also serves as another measure of party support in the electorate and indicates the IP movement occurred at the candidate, voter, and donor level. Having established the timeline and magnitude of the IP's success, the following sections explore the role resources played in the party's development and how insufficient resources and brand development contributed to the party's decline.

MINNESOTA'S OPEN INSTITUTIONS, RULES, AND ELECTORAL RESOURCES

One of the most studied and apparent factors impeding third parties' electoral success is the inability to easily garner resources necessary to attract viable candidates, attention, and the support of voters.[28] The two major parties have clearly established ideological brands that, especially in the polarized political climate, help reduce information costs for voters navigating the myriad of candidates in US elections.[29] Major-party campaign finances almost always dwarf third-party opponents, and the general lack of expenditure limits enable major-party campaigns to dominate in terms of spending, especially in the area of advertising. Major-party candidates can also attract and pay for experienced campaign consultants and supporting staff, while third parties often rely on amateur, albeit passionate, volunteers.[30] In addition to these advantages, major parties consistently have greater access to technology and big data, intraparty fund transfers, and significantly greater media access and attention. By comparison, the resources most third parties subsist on are quite meager.[31]

Furthermore, third parties often face greater institutional barriers that stack the decks against them from the start. The winner-take-all system that shapes the vote-to-seat allocation does little to encourage ambitious and experienced politicians to choose to run under the label of a party that tends to come in third or fourth. Also, ballot access requirements in many states force third-party candidates to expend their precious resources to gather signatures or jump over hurdles that major-party candidates automatically bypass. Other electoral laws also diminish the potential of third-party movements. Third-party candidates may energize traditionally disengaged voter populations, but this activation potential may be stunted if electoral laws induce high participation costs in the form of demanding voter registration rules that depress turnout.[32] Described as a "vicious cycle," asymmetric resource access suppresses the third-party presence.[33] Without resources, a party cannot capture public favor or win seats, and without public exposure or power in government, the party is unable to gain resources necessary to compete in the political arena.

Celebrity and self-funded independent or third-party candidates can sometimes break out of the vicious resource cycle. Ross Perot spent over $63 million of his personal wealth on his 1992 independent presidential campaign.[34] With these resources, he captured the attention of the media and public and won a substantial share of the vote. One reason the IP was able to obtain electoral victory and party growth in Minnesota lies in their initial, albeit tenuous, association with the resource-rich Perot movement. A second factor that enabled the party's growth lies in the state's rules and institutions. Small, but consequential, structures in Minnesota statutes dealing with voter registration, major-party status, ballot access, and campaign finance reduced the barriers that often impede the growth of third parties.

Less burdened, the IP rode the Perot wave and was able to produce a political-resource snowball that enabled it to continue to grow into the millennium.

Minnesotan electoral institutions that encourage participation were critical in the initial development of the IP. Successful third-party movements often demonstrate the ability to tap the latent, inactive segment of the electorate who usually fail to vote as a result of major-party disaffection, alienation, or indifference.[35] Therefore, states with less stringent registration requirements provide more fertile ground for third-party movements. In 1974, Minnesota lowered barriers to vote by allowing voters to register on Election Day.[36] And as a result of lower participation costs and other factors, Minnesota historically has higher election turnout compared to other US states.[37]

In addition to these rules that lower the costs of participation, other statutes in Minnesota are quite supportive of viable third-party movements. Major-party status is conferred in Minnesota on any party that has won over 5 percent of the vote (with at least one vote in each county) in a previous statewide election.[38] While major-party status can also be obtained by running a full slate of candidates across the state or securing petition signatures from 5 percent of the statewide electorate, the goal is relatively easy to achieve if the party can get a popular individual to run for a statewide office such as US senator, governor, or secretary of state. And it was through this electoral route that the IP secured major-party status. Dean Barkley, the first candidate to run for US Senate under the IP label, won 5.39 percent of the state's vote in 1994 and catapulted the organization into major-party status.[39]

Major-party status is a third-party's initial goalpost in Minnesota because it is associated with several resource advantages. First, the candidates of major parties are automatically placed on the ballot. In contrast, independent or minor-party candidates must find volunteers or money to obtain signatures before they will be placed on the ballot. It is important to note that by itself, ballot access does not automatically boost a third party's electoral outcomes.[40] Instead, easier ballot access just opens the floodgates, and the most immediate consequence seen is the increase in the number of third-party candidates running for election.[41] When a third party has automatic ballot access, it becomes the logical vehicle of choice for any individuals seeking to run outside of the major-party system.

Ballot access is not the only perk that accompanies major-party status in Minnesota. The second benefit of major party status deals with order candidates are listed on the ballot. Major-party candidates are listed before minor parties on the ballots, with an interesting twist. In addition to being listed first before any other minor-party candidates, major-party candidates are also ordered relative to each other according to their past electoral performance. The major party that fared the worst in the preceding election is placed at the top of the ballot in the subsequent election. For all elections from 1996 to 2014, IP candidate names were the first names read by voters at the polls. Some research finds evidence that while ballot order does not appear to influence outcomes for major-party candidates, minor-party candidates benefit greatly when placed first on a ballot.[42] Third, major-party status helped the IP gain access to public debates.[43] The League of Women Voters, one of the key debate sponsors, used major-party status to determine which candidates to invite to participate in their debates. Other debate sponsors followed suit and often extended invitations to IP candidates due to their major-party status. Debate inclusion contributed to the increased salience of the Independence Party, provided a free communication platform, and led to further free media, as debates are often covered in subsequent press platforms.

Finally, parties with major-party status have access to greater funds within Minnesota's public financing system.[44] Created in 1974 to protect politics from private money of "fat cats," Minnesota's public finance program limits the amount participating candidates can spend in the elections and curtails the amount of contributions allowed from PACS and lobbyists. In return, candidates who submit to these limits and controls can participate in the Political Contribution Refund program and are given public funds (potentially up to 50 percent of a candidate's expenditures) to help them conduct their campaigns.[45]

The Political Contribution Refund program allows Minnesotans who contribute to a registered political party or candidate to apply for a refund of their contribution, up to fifty dollars per person per year. This program was designed to increase individual contributions and belay the effect of PAC money in elections. In 2002, the IP received a total of $280,048 political contribution refunds, only 8 percent of the total $3.4 million contributed through the program. Still, the 2002 contributions obtained by the IP were significantly higher than the funds received in subsequent years. The next highest amount received by the IP was $97,308 in 2006.[46]

The main public subsidy program funds reside in the State Elections Campaign Fund. Within this fund are two accounts: the party account and the general account.[47] The party account draws from money obtained through a tax return's five dollar checkoff.[48] By itself, major-party status did little to immediately boost the amount of funds available from the party account, as any recognized party, major or minor, was listed on the tax checkoff form.[49] However, major-party status did open doors to receiving more public funds from the general account of Minnesota's public subsidy program.

The general account is funded by the taxpayer checkoff program (allocations from taxpayers who choose to distribute money equally to all candidates, not by party) and a set amount allocated from the state budget each election year. To qualify for public funds from the general account, a candidate must be from a major political party (minor parties do not qualify), sign a spending limit agreement, raise a certain amount of individual contributions (threshold varies according to office type), and run opposed in the primary or general election.[50]

IP candidates theoretically had access to general account public funds after they won major-party status in 1994, but it was often too risky to spend money they might not get and extremely difficult to obtain a loan for these potential funds. From 1974 to 2000, general account money was only paid *after* the general election to candidates who had passed a required vote-share threshold.[51] Most IP candidates running in lower offices did not have formal polling figures to help them assess their potential strength and determine the likelihood of capturing the necessary votes needed to recoup campaign expenditures.

Even for viable candidates, securing the loan was very difficult. Jesse Ventura was eligible for $310,000 from the general account, but no major banks would loan him the money.[52] Once in office, Ventura persuaded the legislature to alter this provision to remove the general election performance threshold and require general account funds to be paid immediately after the primary.[53] While Minnesota's public finance program did open the door for third parties and was a critical component in securing Ventura's win, the system was biased in favor of incumbent and major-party candidates, especially before the reforms of 2000.[54]

Major-party status increased the amount of public funds potentially available to the IP, but only viable major-party candidates were able to access general account funds. Party account funds only began to grow after the party captured public attention with the win of Ventura in 1998. Figure 8.4 displays the amounts (in current US dollars) allocated to the Minnesota State Elections Campaign Fund, broken down by major political party and actual tax year.[55] Two important trends emerge in the data. First, the presence of a salient statewide IP campaign appears to influence that year's number of tax checkoffs allocated to the IP. In 1995, the first year the IP was listed as a major party on the tax form, only 3.4 percent of the people allocating funds ($n = 48,820$) chose to send the money to the party. The

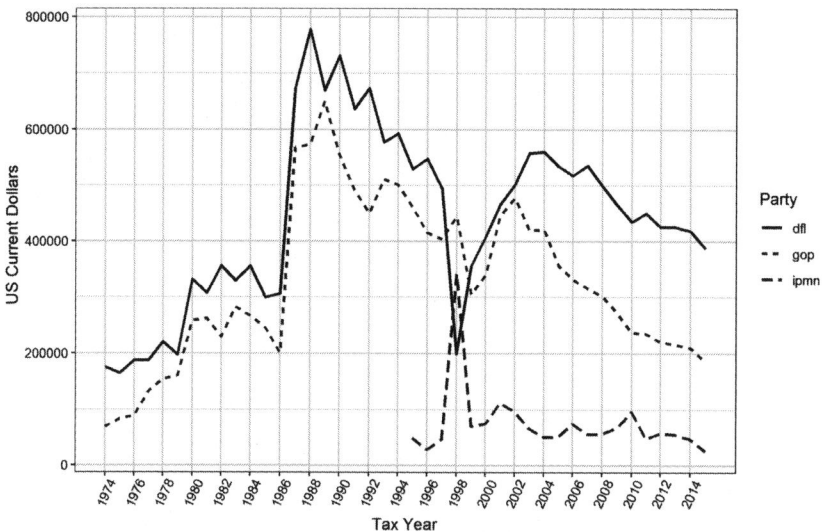

Figure 8.4: Allocation amount (in current US dollars) from Minnesota's income and property tax checkoffs for political parties by tax year and major party, 1974–2015. Minnesota Campaign Finance Board.

party continued to garner little financial support from this program in the next two years, but after the 1998 election, where the IP candidate won Minnesota's governorship, about one quarter of the tax checkoffs ($n =$ 342,480) were allocated to the IP. Second, Figure 8.4 reveals that the burst of IP support in 1998 corresponds to a decrease in the amount of funds allocated to the DFL but there was no decrease in Republican funds. The negative correlation in DFL and IP fund allocation may reflect the negative response of Democrats in Minnesota to the Clinton-Lewinsky scandal that commenced January 17, 1998, and led to the impeachment of Bill Clinton in December of 1998.

It is important not to overstate the effect of Minnesota's public finance program. The program was instrumental in propelling the party forward by providing Ventura much-needed funds for his 1998 gubernatorial campaign, but the public money available to IP candidates was dwarfed by major-party funds, and only a fraction of the funds available were used by the IP. The average IP candidate in 1996 only received about 20 percent of the public subsidies received by an average candidate from one of the two major parties.[56]

In Table 8.1, the public subsidy data for IP candidates running for the state House of Representatives from 1996 to 2004 reveal the low number of

Table 8.1: Public Subsidy Funds Received by Independence Party
Minnesota State House Candidates, 1996–2004

Year	Total Candidates (#)	Candidates Receiving Funds (#)	Amount Paid from Party Account ($)	Amount Paid from General Account ($)	Total Subsidy Received ($)
1996	14	7	699	17,309	18,008
1998	13	3	810	4,094	4,904
2000	27	16	22,973	28,519	51,522
2002	26	20	9,987	49,562	59,549
2004	21	12	8,123	39,259	47,382

Source: Minnesota Campaign Finance Board, Annual Campaign Finance Reports.

IP candidates who received public funds. While over 80 percent of the DFL and Republican party candidates running for the lower legislative body received public money in most elections, only 50 percent of the IP Minnesota House candidates received funds in 1996. The participation rates of state House of Representative candidates did not improve until after the party's big win in 1998 and the relaxing of the general account payment requirements in Minnesota statutes. Even in 2002, the IP had the potential of $63,043 available from the party account for state House candidates but was only able to use $9,987 (16 percent) of these public funds due to the low number of candidates fielded. Given that the average amount of expenditures per state House candidate in 2002 was $15,516, and the average amount of public subsidy received by an IP Minnesota House candidate was $2,977 (19 percent of average expenditures), it is likely that, with a few exceptions in state-level offices that captured a larger share of public funds, public financing did not dramatically alter the outcomes of various IP candidacies.[57] The campaign finance system may have increased the appeal of the IP for strategic candidates seeking to enter the political arena outside of the major two-party system. However, the barriers third-party candidates faced in obtaining the public funds subdued their potential role during the early years when IP momentum was building.

THINGS FALL APART; THE CENTER CANNOT HOLD

Ultimately, a party with minimal resources, organization, and brand consistency cannot sustain a political movement. Following the 2014 election,

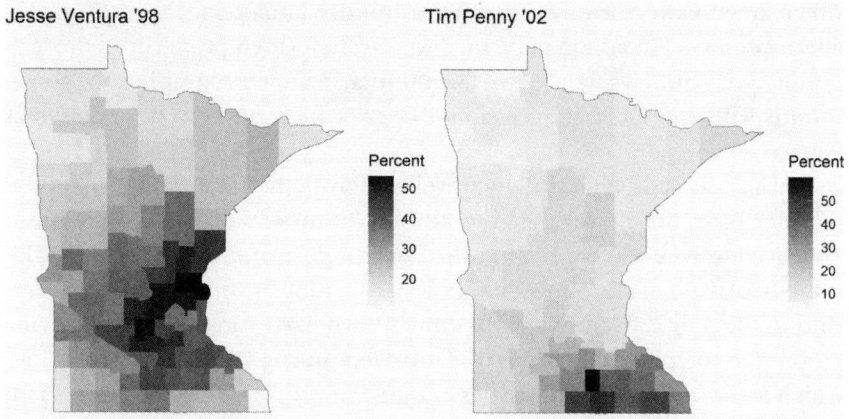

Figure 8.5: County-level general election returns for Independence Party gubernatorial candidates, 1998 and 2002. CQ Press Voting and Elections Collection, Minnesota county-level returns: 1998 governor and 2002 governor.

when not a single IP candidate won more than 5 percent of the statewide vote, the party sank back to minor-party status. Ventura's surprising win in 1998 provided a positive boost for the party, as it generated notable political capital, attention, and resources. However, with no copartisans in the state legislature, Ventura struggled to perform. Apart from some agenda items on which he could agree with the major parties, Ventura was unable to promote policy clearly associated with the IP platform positions.[58] Furthermore, the party's inability to win with a high-quality candidate like Tim Penny sucked the wind out of the movement, resulting in fewer resources allocated to the party and leading to a downward plunge into the "vicious cycle" that haunts third parties. Dean Barkley's 2008 bid for Minnesota US Senator, his strong electoral performance, and involvement in the contentious outcome helped increase public awareness of the party and temporarily sustained the party's life by helping it retain major-party status. However, without a clearly defined and consistent base of voters in the electorate, the IP could not attract the quality candidates, resources, attention, and electoral victories needed to remain viable and sunk back to minor-party status following the 2014 election.

Figure 8.5 displays the county-level vote shares won by the two major IP gubernatorial candidates—Jesse Ventura in 1998 and Tim Penny in 2002. The figure succinctly illustrates the fundamental problem the IP had with attracting a consistent base, not just ephemeral candidate followings. Ventura's support is concentrated in the exsuburbs, such as Anoka County,

which are anywhere from twenty to one hundred miles outside major population centers.[59] In contrast, Penny's wins were located primarily in the less-
populated southeast corner of Minnesota, which geographically corresponds with the First Congressional District he represented in Congress
from 1983 to 1995.

During his campaign, Penny travelled across the state trying to build a
broader base, but he struggled to attract Ventura voters. And while there
appeared to be a three-way tie in the race for governor in several polls, the
tragedy of Paul Wellstone's death in late October produced a significant
shift in the political landscape.[60] Penny's third-party candidacy was virtually
ignored in the partisan dramas that unveiled during Wellstone's memorial,
which activated partisan identities among the public. Without a large campaign budget to wage a full-scale response, no base of donors, no interest
group support, little existing public attachments, and very little party organization to support his candidacy, Penny's inability to win, or at least
come close to winning, the 2002 gubernatorial contest resulted in the critical tipping point for the party.[61]

Although the party never quite recovered from the 2002 loss, the IP's existence left several indelible prints on the Minnesotan political landscape.
First, the IP influenced the nature of the public finance system—general account public subsidy funds became easier to access for viable third-party
candidates as a result of legislation pushed by Ventura following his struggles as a third-party candidate in the public financing system. Second, there
was arguably a diffusion of ideas from IP campaigns to other well-known
third-party candidacies across the country. Dean Barkley served as campaign director for Kinky Freedman's 2006 independent gubernatorial electoral bid and briefly worked on Arianna Huffington's independent campaign in the California gubernatorial election in 2003.[62] Third, while
Barkley in 2008 and Tom Horner in 2010 did not win their respective bids
for elected office, it is possible these IP candidacies played a role in shaping
the outcomes of these incredibly close elections, especially as Barkley and
Horner's issue positions and backgrounds made their candidacies potentially more attractive to Republican-leaning voters. However, it is very difficult to find evidence of the spoiler effect in existing data. A 2008 exit poll
found 13 percent of Democrats and 10 percent of Republicans voted for
Barkley, suggesting Barkley did not pull disproportionately from one party
than the other. However, it is uncertain which candidate the 27 percent of
Independents that voted for Barkley would have voted for if presented with
only two choices.[63] In 2010, Horner had the potential to appeal more to Republicans given his background with the party and public endorsements by

several retired Republican state lawmakers.[64] Yet, a simple analysis drawing on public opinion data from the common content of the 2010 Cooperative Congressional Election Survey of the party identification of Horner supporters uncovers no clear partisan asymmetry in vote choice.[65] Irrespective of whether or not the presence of IP candidacies determined the winners of these two electoral contests, elite and public response reveal a clear belief that IP candidacies influenced the outcomes of the 2008 US Senate race and 2010 gubernatorial election.[66] Following the 2010 election, the Republican Party state central committee voted to ban all members who had endorsed Horner.[67] Even if Horner was not a spoiler candidate, his presence influenced Minnesota politics since it led more moderates to be formally pushed out of the Republican party, reflecting the increasingly polarized landscape in Minnesota.

Could Minnesota see another third-party movement in its future? In the 2018 election, both the Legal Marijuana Now Party and the Grassroots Legalize Cannabis Party garnered over 5 percent of the vote in two different Minnesota statewide races, crossing the threshold needed to earn major-party status. However, it is unlikely these parties will endure, as they compete for similar voter pools and are constructed around only a single issue, which one of the major parties can easily adopt.

For a centrist third-party movement to disrupt the political scene the way the IP did, there first needs to be a critical amount of major-party discontent to generate the necessary pool of candidates and supporters. As party polarization continues to define the current political arena, public discontent with the polarized parties may build and fuel a future third-party movement. However, it is possible the IP's formation and rise during the 1990s was a unique product of early polarization trends. Polarizing parties and shifting political fault lines may have alienated and ideologically displaced unusual amounts of people who were then attracted to the centrist third-party movement. In the recent polarized and sorted climate, identities may have clarified or hardened, reducing the pool of potential supporters and candidates.[68] Second to that, a third-party movement often requires a critical influx of resources to jumpstart the process. In the 1990s, Ross Perot's self-funded electoral bids provided this initial resource outlay. Changing modes of communication may have opened more routes for third-party movements to connect with potential supporters while using less resources.[69] However, in order to attract quality candidates, traditional resources such as money and volunteers remain essential barriers, frustrating most third-party movements.

NOTES

1. Marc J. Hetherington, *Why Trust Matters: Declining Political Trust and the Demise of American Liberalism* (Princeton, NJ: Princeton University Press, 2005), 23; Jack Citrin and Laura Stoker, "Political Trust in a Cynical Age," *Annual Review of Political Science,* 2018.

2. Marc J. Hetherington, "The Effect of Political Trust on the Presidential Vote, 1968–96," *American Political Science Review* 93, no. 2 (1999): 311–326; Bernard Tamas, *The Demise and Rebirth of American Third Parties: Poised for Political Revival?* (New York: Routledge, 2018); Sarah Binder, "The Dysfunctional Congress," *Annual Review of Political Science* 18 (2015): 85–101.

3. Jeffrey Koch, "Attitudes toward Government, Partisan Dispositions, and the Rise of Ross Perot," in *Ross for Boss: The Perot Phenomenon and Beyond,* ed. Ted G. Jelen (New York: State University of New York Press, 2001), 61–86; Walter J. Stone and Ronald B. Rapoport, "It's Perot Stupid! The Legacy of the 1992 Perot Movement in the Major-Party System, 1994–2000," *PS: Political Science and Politics* 34, no. 1 (2001): 49–58; for more on issue voting among Perot supporters, see R. B. Rapoport and W. J. Stone, *Three's a Crowd: The Dynamic of Third Parties, Ross Perot and Republican Resurgence* (Ann Arbor: University of Michigan Press, 2005).

4. Patricia A. Klein, *Federal Election 92: Election Results for the U.S. President, the U.S. Senate and the U.S. House of Representatives* (Washington, DC: Federal Election Commission, 1993).

5. Donald J. Green, *Third-Party Matters: Politics, Presidents, and Third Parties in American History* (Santa Barbara, CA: Praeger, 2010), 91.

6. Jacob Lentz, *Electing Jesse Ventura: A Third-Party Success Story* (Boulder, CO: Lynne Rienner Publishers, 2002), 22.

7. Dean Barkley (former IP leader, former IP candidate, Jesse Ventura campaign chair in 1998, US Senator from Minnesota), phone interview by the author, January 28, 2019.

8. Barkley, phone interview.

9. Jack B. Coffman, "Tug-of-War for Perot Banner Looks Likely," *Saint Paul Pioneer Press* (Minnesota), September 27, 1995, sec. Main.

10. Jack B. Coffman, "Reform Party Keeps Original Agenda; Independence Party Changes Name, Not Goal," *Saint Paul Pioneer Press* (Minnesota), June 23, 1996, sec. Metro; Philip Fuehrer (state chair of the IP of Minnesota), phone interview by the author, November 21, 2018.

11. Lentz, *Electing Jesse,* 85.

12. Ted. G. Jelen, "The Perot Campaigns in Theoretical Perspective," in *Ross for Boss: The Perot Phenomenon and Beyond,* ed. Ted G. Jelen (State University of New York Press, 2001), 6.

13. Jim Ragsdale, "Independence Party Candidates Live Up to Name; Four Very Different Candidates, Each Charting His Own Path, Seek to Carry the Torch Lit by Jesse Ventura," *Saint Paul Pioneer Press* (Minnesota), August 13, 2000, sec. Main. The

current state chair of the IP, Philip Fuehrer, described the party as moderate or slightly conservative during its early years, but he believes it has shifted slightly to the moderate-left in more recent years. See Philip Fuehrer (state chair of the IP of Minnesota), phone interview by the author, November 21, 2018. For current issue positions of the party, see "Our Platform," Minnesota Independence Party, accessed February 19, 2019, http://www.mnip.org/our-values/our-platform/.

14. Barkley, phone interview.

15. Robert Whereatt, "A Little Success Could Translate to a Lot of Clout for the Independence Party; Dean Barkley's Third Party Has Modest Goals in the Coming Elections but Grand Dreams of Being a Major Player in the Minnesota House," *Star Tribune* (Minneapolis, MN), May 27, 1996, Metro ed., sec. News.

16. Barkley, phone interview.

17. Rapoport and Stone, *Three's a Crowd*, 4.

18. Walter Dean Burnham, *Critical Elections and the Mainsprings of American Politics* (New York: Norton, 1970), 28.

19. Tim Penny's conservative ideology is reflected in his moderate, left-leaning DW-NOMINATE score of –0.051. DW-NOMINATE scores measure politicians' ideological positions using their roll-call vote histories. The score can potentially range from –1 (most liberal) to 1 (most conservative). In the 103rd Congress (1993–1995), Penny voted with the Democratic Party only 66 percent of the time while the median House Democrat voted with the party 90 percent of the time. See "Penny, Timothy Joseph (1951–)," Voteview.com, accessed February 6, 2019, https://voteview.com/person/15052/timothy-joseph-penny.

20. Mark Zdechlik, "Independence Party Picks PR Exec Horner for Gov," MPR News, May 8, 2010, sec. Politics, https://www.mprnews.org/story/2010/05/08/horner-ipendorse.

21. The Ventura "no strings attached" action doll that would fight the Evil Special Interest Man was available to buy on the Ventura campaign site and was featured in a television ad. See Marc Fisher, "Jesse 'The Body' Wins Minn. Gubernatorial Race," *Washington Post*, November 4, 1998, sec. Politics.

22. The IP also supported several nonpartisan candidacies that are not included in these data. For example, the IP helped Steve Minn win a nonpartisan Minneapolis City Council seat in 1993. The IP also gained a seat in government when DFL state senator Bob Lessard switched to the party in 2001. For the purposes of this chapter, special elections are grouped together with the general elections in a two-year electoral cycle interval. For example, five IP candidates are recorded as running in the 1994 electoral cycle. However, of these five, only one (Dean Barkley) ran in the 1994 general election. The other four candidates ran in special elections held before the next general election period began. Of the entire 288 IP/Reform candidate list, twenty-five candidates ran in special elections.

23. Minnesota has eight federal congressional districts, 134 state House districts, and sixty-seven state senate districts. General elections for the Minnesota Senate are only held on years ending in zero, two, and six. Election years ending in two

are conducted in newly redistricted districts for all state legislative offices. The statewide category combines candidates running in Minnesota for US president, US senator, governor, attorney general, secretary of state, state auditor, or state treasurer, and as these races vary in timing, IP candidates are more probable during off-cycle years when gubernatorial and most related statewide offices are open to election. While the IP endorsed presidential candidates—Ross Perot in 1996 and Evan McMullin in 2016—the party was fundamentally a state-centric organization, primarily interested in fielding and winning elected office in Minnesota.

24. Philip Fuehrer (state chair of the IP of Minnesota), phone interview by the author, November 21, 2018.

25. Lydia Saad, "Trump and Clinton Finish with Historically Poor Images," Gallup News: Election 2016, November 8, 2016, https://news.gallup.com/poll /197231/trump-clinton-finish-historically-poor-images.aspx.

26. William Denney ran for Minnesota Secretary of State in the 2018 election and won 4.08 percent of the vote.

27. "Minnesota Democratic Farmer Labor Party," OpenSecrets.org: Center for Responsive Politics, accessed February 7, 2019, https://www.opensecrets.org/pacs /lookup2.php?cycle=2018&strID=C00025254; "Republican Party of Minnesota," OpenSecrets.org: Center for Responsive Politics, accessed February 7, 2019, https://www.opensecrets.org/pacs/lookup2.php?strID=C00001313&cycle=2018.

28. Steven J. Rosenstone, Roy L. Behr, and Edward H. Lazarus, *Third Parties in America: Citizen Response to Major Party Failure* (Princeton, NJ: Princeton University Press, 1984), 27–39; Paul S. Herrnson, "Two-Party Dominance and Minor Party Forays in American Politics," in *Multiparty Politics in America: People, Passions, and Power*, ed. Paul S. Herrnson and John C. Green (Lanham, MD: Rowman & Littlefield, 1997), 25–28.

29. Jonathan Woon and Jeremy C. Pope, "Made in Congress? Testing the Electoral Implications of Party Ideological Brand Names," *Journal of Politics* 70 (2008): 823–836.

30. Robin Kolodny and Angela Logan, "Political Consultants and Extensions of Party Goals," *Political Science and Politics* 31 (1998): 155–159; Herrnson, "Two-Party Dominance and Minor Party Forays in American Politics," 29–32.

31. Daniel Kreiss, *Prototype Politics: Technology-Intensive Campaigning and the Data of Democracy* (New York: Oxford University Press, 2016); Damon M. Cann, *Sharing the Wealth: Member Contributions and the Exchange Theory of Party Influence in the U.S. House of Representatives* (Albany: State University of New York Press, 2008); John F. Kirch, "News Coverage Different for Third-Party Candidates:," *Newspaper Research Journal* 34, no. 4 (2013): 40–53; Ron Faucheux and Paul S. Herrnson, "Outside Looking In: Views of Third Party and Independent Candidates," *Campaigns and Elections* 20, no. 7 (1999): 27–33.

32. Benjamin Highton, "Easy Registration and Voter Turnout," *The Journal of Politics* 59, no. 2 (1997): 565–575.

33. Tamas, *Demise and Rebirth*, 147.

34. Herbert E. Alexander and Anthony Corrado, *Financing the 1992 Election* (Armonk, New York: M. E. Sharpe, 1995).

35. Benny Geys, "'Rational' Theories of Voter Turnout: A Review," *Political Studies Review* 4 (2006): 16–35; Dean Lacy and Quin Monson, "The Origin and Impacts of Votes for Third Party Candidates: A Case Study of the 1998 Minnesota Gubernatorial Election," *Political Research Quarterly* 55, no. 2 (2002): 409–437; Gebhard Kirchgässner, "Absentation Because of Indifference and Alienation, and Its Consequences for Party Competition: A Simple Psychological Model," *University of St. Gallen Economics Discussion Paper* (unpublished working paper, 2003), 1–14, http://dx.doi.org/10.2139/ssrn.401882; Alexei V. Zakharov, "A Model of Electoral Competition with Abstaining Voters," *Mathematical and Computer Modelling* 48 (2008): 1527–1553.

36. "Same Day Voter Registration," National Conference of State Legislatures, M.S.A. § 201.061, January 25, 2019, http://www.ncsl.org/research/elections-and-campaigns/same-day-registration.aspx.

37. A comparison of election turnout across states can be found at "Historical Voter Turnout Statistics," Office of the Minnesota Secretary of State Steve Simon, accessed February 7, 2019, https://www.sos.state.mn.us/election-administration-campaigns/data-maps/historical-voter-turnout-statistics/.

38. See 2019 Minn. Stat., § 200.02, subd. 7. Note that as this chapter was being written, a bill had been introduced in the Minnesota State Legislature proposing the required threshold for major-party status be lowered from 5 percent to 1 percent. See Major Political Party Designation Thresholds Modification, S. SF 752/HF708, Rev. 19-1499 (2019–2020).

39. Even when the party changed its name in the 1996 election to indicate alignment with the national Reform Party, it maintained its major-party status won by Barkley.

40. Bernard Tamas and Matthew D. Hindman, "Ballot Access Laws and the Decline of American Third-Parties," *Election Law Journal* 13, no. 2 (2014): 260–276.

41. Barry C. Burden, "Ballot Regulations and Multiparty Politics in the States," *PS: Political Science & Politics* 40, no. 4 (2007): 669–673.

42. Daniel E. Ho and Kosuke Imai, "Estimating Causal Effects of Ballot Order from a Randomized Natural Experiment," *Public Opinion Quarterly* 72, no. 2 (2008): 2.

43. Lentz, *Electing Jesse*, 86; Barkley, phone interview.

44. Minnesota is one of only a handful of states that offer some form of public financing to state candidates. See "Overview of State Laws on Public Financing," National Conference of State Legislatures, accessed February 7, 2019, http://www.ncsl.org/research/elections-and-campaigns/public-financing-of-campaigns-overview.aspx.

45. The Political Contribution Refund Program was not funded from 2010 to 2012 and 2016. See "Public Subsidy of State Election Campaigns," Minnesota Campaign Finance and Public Disclosure Board, accessed February 7, 2019, https://cfb.mn.gov/citizen-resources/board-programs/public-subsidy-of-campaigns/historical-use-of-public-subsidy-program/.

46. "Review of the Political Contribution Refund Program During the Years 2002–2014," Minnesota Campaign Finance and Public Disclosure Board, November 25, 2015, https://cfb.mn.gov/pdf/publications/public_subsidy/historical/report_on_pcr_use_2002_2014.pdf?t=1549132867.

47. On the state tax form, Minnesotans can choose to contribute to a list of qualifying parties at no cost to themselves. Existing taxes are then assigned to each qualifying party according to the proportions of people who selected that party. Amounts allocated to candidates running for state offices are based on complex formula determined by the district's past party performance and the proportion of tax checkoffs for the party that came from that district's county. While most of the party account money is given to candidates running for all levels of office in Minnesota, 10 percent (capped at $50,000) is given to the state committee of a political party.

48. Minn. Stat. § 10A.31, subd. 3a (2018). Parties qualify to be on the tax checkoff form if they are a major or minor political party by July 1 of the taxable year. Only major parties were listed from 1984 to 1995. See "2002 Campaign Finance Summary," Minnesota Campaign Finance and Public Disclosure Board, May 30, 2003, 10.

49. "Tax Checkoff for Political Parties," Minnesota Campaign Finance and Public Disclosure Board, accessed February 7, 2019, https://cfb.mn.gov/citizen-resources/board-programs/public-subsidy-of-campaigns/tax-checkoff-program/.

50. Minn. Stat. § 10A.31, subd. 7 (2018).

51. For statewide elections, the candidate had to win 5 percent of the vote, but state legislators had to win over 10 percent of the general election vote before they could receive funds from the general account. See Peter S. Wattson, "Minnesota's Campaign Finance Law," Office of Senate Counsel and Research for the Minnesota Senate, September 16, 2002, https://www.senate.mn/departments/scr/treatise/campfin.htm.

52. Lentz, *Electing Jesse*, 84.

53. Minn. Stat. § 10A.31, subd. 7 (2001).

54. Patrick D. Donnay and Graham P. Ramsden, "Public Financing of Legislative Elections: Lessons from Minnesota," *Legislative Studies Quarterly* 20, no. 3 (1995): 351–364.

55. The dramatic increase in tax checkoff funds in 1987 reflect a change in the amounts tax payers could check off. The checkoff amount increased from one dollar to two dollars in 1980. In 1987, the amount was increased to five dollars.

56. In 1996, only nine of the twenty-two Independence (Reform) Party candidates filing for office received any public funding payments. The total amount of public subsidy money the party candidates received was $18,268. In comparison, 179 Republican candidates received $1,908,051 and 185 Democratic Farmer-Labor candidates received $2,064,790 of public subsidy money. More comparable numbers are the candidate-level averages of funds received: IP: $2,030; RMN: $10,660; DFL: $11,161.

57. For average Minnesota State House state expenditure in 2002, see "2002 Campaign," Minnesota Campaign, 4.

58. Laura McCallum, "The Political Legacy of Jesse Ventura," MPR News, December 17, 2002, sec. News and Features, http://news.minnesota.publicradio.org /features/200212/17_mccalluml_venturalegacy; Jim Ragsdale, "Swing Voter; Gov. Jesse Ventura Has Hasn't Nurtured the Party That Put Him in Office. Where Will He Stand, and Will He Be Alone?," *Saint Paul Pioneer Press* (Minnesota), February 2, 2002, sec. Main.

59. Barkley, phone interview.

60. Michael Khoo, "Poll: Three-Way Tie in Race for Governor," MPR News, September 17, 2002. sec. News and Features, http://news.minnesota.publicradio .org /features/200209/17_khoom_govpoll/index.shtml; Laura McCallum, "Conflicting Polls Add to Election Confusion," MPR News, November 3, 2002, sec. News and Features, http://news.minnesota.publicradio.org/features/200211/03_khoom _poll/.

61. Timothy Penny, phone interview by the author, January 24, 2019.

62. Barkley, phone interview.

63. "Election Center 2008: Exit Polls, U.S. Senate Minnesota," CNNPolitics .com, accessed February 10, 2019, http://www.cnn.com/ELECTION/2008/results /polls/#val=MNS01p1.

64. Jason Hoppin, "Horner Backed by Handful of Retired GOP Lawmakers," *Saint Paul Pioneer Press* (Minnesota), October 6, 2010, sec. Politics. The former Republican state legislators who endorsed Horner were Peggy Leppik, Neil Peterson, George Pillsbury, Bill Belanger, Dennis Ozment, and Dave Bishop. Former Republican governors Al Quie and Arne Carlson and former US Senator Dave Durenberger also endorsed Horner in 2010. See Joe Kimball, "High-Profile GOP Horner Supporters Punished by State Party because Some Think He Cost Emmer the Election," *MinnPost* (Minnesota), December 6, 2010, https://www.minnpost.com/political -agenda/2010/12/high-profile-gop-horner-supporters-punished-state-party-because -some-think/.

65. Survey-weighted percentages of IP candidate voters broken down by party identification were calculated using 2010 Cooperative Congressional Election Study (CCES) data. Thirteen percent of the 2010 sample reported voting for Horner ($n = 44$). Of these voters, 6 percent ($n = 21$) identified as Democrat or Democrat-leaning Independent. Among Republicans or Republican leaning Independents, 4 percent ($n = 13$) reported voting for Horner. Assuming no difference in turnout, it is impossible to know which way the Independents who report no party tendency would have voted.

66. G. R. Anderson Jr., "Barkley on Senate Recount: 'Fitting End to the Worst Campaign in Minnesota History,'" *MinnPost*, November 21, 2008, sec. Politics & Policy.

67. Mike Kaszuba, "Republicans Defend Ban of 18 Horner Backers; Party Lead-

ers Said They Were Frustrated with Those Who Didn't Support Emmer for Governor," *Star Tribune* (Minneapolis, MN), December 7, 2010, Metro edition, sec. News.

68. Corwin Smidt, "Polarization and the Decline of the American Floating Voter," *American Journal of Political Science* 61, no. 2 (2017): 365–381.

69. Heather K. Evans, Jessica Habib, Danielle Litzen, Bryan San Jose, "Awkward Independents: What Are Third-Party Candidates Doing on Twitter?" *PS: Political Science & Politics* 52, no. 1 (n.d.): 1–6.

CHAPTER 9

The Independent Party of Oregon

Richard A. Clucas

Duverger's law provides the primary scholarly explanation for the prevalence of the two-party system in American states. Yet some scholars have been interested in how third parties are affected by specific provisions in state election law. Their studies have been concerned with understanding how the introduction of the Australian ballot, the use of direct primaries, the ban against fusion voting, and the presence of other electoral rules affect third-party success. In general, most of these studies have dismissed the impact of these legal restrictions on third parties, attributing a far greater weight to Duverger's law. However, a few studies have found evidence that some legal factors can affect third-party success.[1]

Ballot access rules are among the laws that have been of particular interest to these scholars. The ability of parties to get their candidates on the ballot is determined, in part, by how a party is classified under state law. The Democratic and Republican parties are routinely classified as *major* parties. Most third parties are classified as *minor, small,* or *new* parties.[2] The major parties are allowed to place candidate names on the ballot for all partisan offices in every election. The nonmajor parties, however, are not given such a guarantee. Rather, these smaller parties are only granted the right to place candidates on the ballot in individual partisan elections in which they have been able to demonstrate a certain level of public support, such as through the use of signed petitions. Moreover, the smaller parties are required to demonstrate that level of support in every election cycle to continue to place candidates on the ballot for that specific office. This lack of broad and continuing access is one of the challenges often cited for the lack of strong third parties in America.[3]

The Independent Party of Oregon (IPO) is unusual because it is one of the rare third parties in the US that has been able to gain major-party status. Oregon law grants major-status to a political party when at least 5 percent of state voters are registered as members of the party 275 days before the primary election.[4] The IPO was launched in the mid-2000s and then qualified as a minor party in January 2007. Eight years later, it was granted major-party status.[5]

The success of the IPO makes it valuable to study because it has attained the same legal position as the Democratic and Republican parties in the state, enabling it to run candidates in all partisan races. The IPO thus offers the opportunity to examine how a third party is affected when the legal playing field is leveled and it is given the same access to the ballot as the two major parties.

The IPO is also valuable to look at because Oregon offers a political environment in which one would expect a third party to thrive. Oregon voters have long been supportive of an open political system, innovative policies, and maverick politicians. Moreover, the state has had a strong aversion to party politics dating back to the Progressive movement prior to the turn of the twentieth century, along with an enduring streak of populism. [6] Given this support for openness in the political system and the aversion to traditional party politics, one would anticipate that a third party would do well in Oregon, especially once the legal door to greater ballot access has been opened.

The question explored in this chapter is: How has the IPO fared under these beneficial conditions? Has its attainment of major-party status and the existence of the state's open political system enabled it to compete against the two major parties, and thus provide a challenge to Duverger's law? Or, has its significance been limited, as one would expect given Duverger's argument?

A HISTORY OF THE INDEPENDENT PARTY

The history of the Independent Party of Oregon does not follow the same story line of most third parties in America's past. It was not created as a vehicle to gain office by a prominent political figure nor was it part of a strong ideological movement. Rather, it was created as part of a homegrown effort to champion electoral reforms.

The IPO emerged in the aftermath of Ralph Nader's independent campaigns for president in 2000 and 2004. Nader's efforts were consequential because he threatened to be a spoiler in both elections, denying the Democratic Party the state's Electoral College votes. During the 2000 election,

Nader was predicted to enjoy his greatest success nationwide in Oregon, where polls showed him potentially garnering as much as 10 percent of the vote. At the time, support among state voters for the two major political parties and their presidential candidates was closely divided. If Nader—running under the Pacific Green Party label—succeeded in drawing sufficient votes, it would have potentially led to Bush winning the state.[7] As the election neared, the Democratic Party made an all-out effort to convince Nader supporters to vote for Al Gore.[8] Gore ended up beating George W. Bush by fewer than 7,000 votes out of the 1.5 million cast, with Nader receiving 5 percent of the vote. Four years later, Oregon Democrats orchestrated a campaign to keep Nader off the ballot, while a number of conservative groups tied to the Republican Party worked to help him. Ultimately, Nader failed to make the Oregon ballot that year.[9]

Even though Nader was not a spoiler in either election, the experiences spurred Democratic legislators to push legislation, making it more difficult for independent candidates to succeed, a goal that also found support among Republicans. In 2005, two leading members of both major parties cosponsored a bill (HB 2614) prohibiting voters who had cast a ballot in the partisan primaries from later signing nomination petitions for nonaffiliated candidates.[10] The bill quickly passed both chambers and was signed into law by the Democratic governor in July 2005.[11] Opponents of the restriction argued that it doubled the number of signatures needed to get candidate names on the ballot, making it far more difficult for independent candidates to succeed.[12] The legislature also passed a second bill that year, changing the term used on the ballot for candidates who were not affiliated with a political party from "independent" to "non-affiliated."[13]

In reaction to the legislature's actions, two Portland-based political activists began the process for creating a new third party. Leading the effort was Dan Meek, a public-interest lawyer and one of only two individuals to testify against HB 2614. Meek has been an important actor in Oregon politics for two decades, focusing much of his energies on utilities and campaign finance reform. The second activist was Linda Williams, a public-interest lawyer whose legal work has focused frequently on natural resources and civil liberties.[14] The original goal of the two activists was not to displace one of the other major parties or to create a competitive third party. Rather, it was to "provide ballot access for candidates and legal standing in case the legislature decided to make a similar move against the ballot access of Oregon's minor parties" in the future, and to elect candidates to push democratic reform.[15] With the change in state law on how nonaffiliated candidates would be labeled on the ballot, the two were able to use the word "independent" in the title of the new party, which likely would have been denied in the past.[16]

The IPO became recognized as a minor party after submitting more than 30,000 petition signatures in 2007.[17] Once the party was formed, it began to grow rapidly. When it was first listed in the secretary of state's monthly voter registration report in February 2007, the party had 359 members. One year later, it had surpassed the Libertarian Party to become the state's largest third party, with 14,869 registered voters. By February 2011, the IPO's registration was more than double the other third parties combined.[18]

From its beginning, the IPO sought to attract support by downplaying ideology and advocating issues that appealed to voters across the political spectrum. Most of the issues it has supported are good government reforms, such as improving ballot access; instituting new campaign finance regulations; increasing government transparency; and passing improved ethics rules.[19] Rather than targeting Democratic or Republican voters exclusively, it sought support from voters disillusioned with both parties. The diverse constituency in the party can be seen in the 2018 gubernatorial campaign. The leading IPO candidate, Patrick Starnes, barely beat out a write-in campaign by the Republican Party's nominee, Knute Buehler, to gain the IPO's nomination. The Democratic Party incumbent, Kate Brown, also waged a write-in campaign to be cross-nominated by the IPO but received far fewer votes. A week before the election, however, Starnes withdrew from the race. Rather than supporting Buehler, he endorsed Brown.[20]

What has made the party unusual is that many of the policies it has advocated have not come from the party leadership but from surveys of its members. Through these polls, the party has tried to develop specific policy priorities and a party platform that enjoys broad appeal to its diverse constituency. These policies have included increasing vocational training, making college more affordable, and requiring political advertisements to identify sources of funding.[21]

Part of the reason the party has experienced such strong growth in registration has likely been due to this focus on government reform and broadly supported noncontroversial policies, but there are two other factors that have also helped.

One of them was the passage of a bill (SB 326) in 2009, repealing HB 2614.[22] The decision made it easier again for independent candidates to get their names on the ballot. In addition, the bill included a provision allowing multiple parties to nominate the same candidate for office. The passage of this fusion voting law provided a way for third parties to attract members who might otherwise fear that supporting the party's candidates would be a waste of their votes. By nominating the same candidate as one of the two major parties, a third party could appeal to these voters and build its base of support, while establishing its own separate political identity. In addition, fusion voting also encouraged major-party candidates to pay more attention to third parties in order to get the parties' nominations.[23]

The IPO has also benefited from its name. Since gaining minor-party status, the party has been frequently criticized for attracting electors who think they are registering as independent (nonaffiliated) voters when they are actually registering as members of an official party organization. In 2015, the Democratic Party of Oregon conducted a survey of IPO voters. It found that nearly one quarter of IPO members did not realize they were registered with a formal party organization. Another 22 percent thought they were registered with a different party.[24] Many political commentators have also argued that the party's registration has prospered because of the confusion generated by its name. Jeff Mapes, one of Oregon's leading political reporters, wrote, "It's not hard to find voters who thought they registered as small i independents . . . rather than as members of the Independent Party."[25]

With the passage of the fusion voting law, the confusion surrounding the name has likely helped the party further by spurring major-party candidates strategically to seek out the IPO's nomination so that the label of "independent" is also placed on the ballot by their names, as Buehler and Brown did in 2018. With the more prominent major-party candidates seeking the IPO's nomination, it likely helped increase public awareness of the party.[26]

Combined, these different factors helped the party to continue to grow in the second decade of the new millennium. On February 9, 2015, the IPO was granted major-party status by the secretary of state. But the achievement was close. On the date used by the secretary of state to determine majority status, the party needed to have 108,739 registered members. The party exceeded that threshold by just three names.[27] Support reached a new high in October 2018, when the party grew to 125,797 registered members.[28]

THE POLITICAL CONTEXT

There may be justification in discounting the success of the IPO in gaining majority status because of confusion over the party's name. Yet there are reasons to expect the party to do well in Oregon regardless of its name. The political culture that has developed over time in the state has been receptive to innovative policies and maverick politicians. There is a strong populist side to the state, one that has been supportive of an open political system in which there is broad participation. State voters have also been wary of traditional party politics. These characteristics developed early in the state's history but continue to influence state politics today, creating a promising context for a third party to succeed.

The state's innovative and open political culture initially developed during the Progressive movement at the turn of the twentieth century, as the public grew increasingly disillusioned with corruption in the state's government and the dominance of party machines. Led by William U'Ren, the Progressives introduced a series of reforms, which were designed to weaken the political parties, give the voters greater say in the direction of government, and address a wide range of social ills. The most important of these reforms was the introduction of the initiative and referendum process in 1902. Over the next several years, reformers used the initiative extensively to strip the party organizations of their power and to allow residents to vote directly on a myriad of innovative proposals, including direct primary elections, the recall of public officials, the direct election of US senators, and women's suffrage.[29]

The political culture was reinforced five decades later when the state began to be led by a series of independent or maverick politicians. The most prominent of these figures on the national stage were US senators Wayne Morse, Mark Hatfield, and Bob Packwood, all of whom developed reputations for taking independent courses in the Senate. However, there were others in the state who played a central role in creating this environment in Oregon. The most important were Republican Governor Tom Mc-Call and his successor, Democrat Bob Straub. Under their leadership, the state enacted a wide range of innovative policies for which Oregon became known, including bottle recycling, expanded public control of coastal beaches, environmental reform, and the adoption of the state's strong land-use planning rules.[30]

Underlying this openness to innovative policies and maverick politicians is an enduring streak of populism, one that believes in broad public involvement in politics. The Progressive movement grew out of the earlier Populist movement in the state. U'Ren and many other progressive leaders were members of the People's (Populist) Party in the 1890s.[31] Many of the reforms introduced during the Progressive Era were meant to improve representation and open up the political process to a broader segment of the public. This emphasis on opening up the political system can be seen in many of the early ballot initiatives mentioned above. In championing change, progressive leaders declared that reforms were needed to "maintain the people's direct and supreme power." The concern for expanding democracy was so strong that these efforts to bring about changes have been referred to as the "people's rule" movement.[32]

To be sure, Oregon has not always been eager to open the door to all groups. In particular, the state's history is filled with examples of it being intolerant of ethnic and racial minorities and other outsiders. When the state was created in 1859, the state constitution outlawed slavery, but it also banned free blacks from coming to or residing in the state. Those who already lived in Oregon were denied the right to vote, as were Chinese Americans. During the 1920s, the Ku Klux Klan developed a strong following in the state. Until the latter part of the twentieth century, African Americans faced overt racial segregation in the state, including in housing, public accommodations, and jobs. In recent decades, the state has confronted both strong antigay politics and an active skinhead movement.[33]

Despite these caveats, the ideas that there should be broad public participation in politics and that the government should pay attention to the diverse views of voters are ones that are widely ingrained in the culture, even if these ideas have not always been applied to everyone. Not only has this been true in the past, but a streak of populism was a defining characteristic of the state's politics in the last three decades of the twentieth century. Much of the populist rhetoric heard then was voiced by conservative groups, who spoke out for protecting the rights of the people against the government, but many liberal groups also used populist rhetoric to appeal to Oregon voters.[34]

More importantly, the populist streak and antiparty attitudes can be seen in recent efforts to change state election laws and in recent trends in electoral politics. The two most noteworthy changes in election law were the introduction of Vote-By-Mail in the late 1990s and automatic voter registration in 2015. The passage of Vote-By-Mail requires that all Oregon elections are conducted today by mail. The change in voter registration law means that state residents are automatically registered to vote through motor vehicle records. Both laws were designed to improve voter participation rates in a state that already had one of the highest rates in the country. As a consequence of these two laws, Oregon was recently rated as being the easiest state in the nation in which to vote.[35] The decision by the legislature in 2005 to make it more difficult for independent candidates to get listed on the ballot was out of step with this culture, so it was not surprising that the legislature repealed the act four years later.

As for trends in electoral politics, the most important one is the increased number of Oregon voters who are not tied to the two major politi-

cal parties. Not only has IPO membership grown but so has the total number of voters registered for other third parties and for nonaffiliated voters.
In the early to mid-1970s, more than 95 percent of state voters were registered as Republican or Democrats. Since then there has been a steady decline in the percent registered for the two parties. In the first years after the
IPO emerged, the combined registration for Democrats and Republicans
hovered around 75 percent of all registered voters. In 2014, it dropped to
just under 68 percent. In 2018, the total dropped to 61 percent. The most
significant change has been in the number of nonaffiliated voters. Between
November 2006 and November 2014, the number of individuals registered
as non-affiliated increased by more than 108,000 voters. Since 2014, the
number of nonaffiliated has grown by another 340,000, as the new automatic registration system brought in a large influx of voters who did not
register with any party. Nearly 32 percent of voters were registered as nonaffiliated in November 2018. The Democratic Party has also experienced
growth over the past dozen years, expanding from 763,301 registered voters in November 2006 to 977,702 in November 2018. The primary group
that has not seen significant gains has been the Republican Party. The number of registered Republicans has remained relatively constant, rising halt-
ingly from 700,950 to 708,079 over this same period.[36]

These changes in registration indicate that state voters have grown increasingly unhappy with the options provided by the two main parties.
Moreover, this unhappiness can be seen in survey polls in 2000, which suggested that Oregon voters were more supportive of Nader's third-party-bid
for president than voters in any other state.

In evaluating the IPO's success, these recent trends, as well as the state's
broader history, are important to consider because they set the political
context in which the party emerged. The party arose in a state and especially in a time in which one would expect it to thrive. The state has long
been supportive of an open election process, broad representation, and innovation. At the same time, state voters have long been wary of the party system. In recent years, they have grown increasingly unhappy with the system,
foregoing affiliation with the two major parties. By reaching majority status,
the IPO offered disillusioned voters the prospect of a third option, one that
had gained the same legal footing as the two main political parties and that
offered a reform agenda that fit in well with the state's political culture.

Despite this promising context, there are two reasons to be skeptical that
the IPO will flourish. One is that third parties have not fared well in Oregon
since the adoption of direct primaries in 1904. Between the time Oregon
became a state in 1859 and the early 1900s, independent and third-party

candidates were frequently elected to the state legislature. The peak year was 1874, when one-third of the legislators were independents, though the numbers were also high around the turn of the century. In 1903, almost 30 percent of the legislators were from third parties. From 1905 to 1921, a total of eighteen seats were held by independents and third-party candidates. Since then, only seven individuals have served in the legislature who were not affiliated with the two main political parties, and these were all listed as independents.[37] The other reason to be skeptical is Duverger's law.

ASSESSING THE SUCCESS OF THE PARTY

The question that is of particular interest in this study is whether the IPO's ability to attain major-party status has translated into a meaningful challenge to the two-party system. There are four measures I use to assess the party's success: the number of IPO candidates on the ballot, the amount of campaign funds it has raised, the share of the vote IPO candidates have received, and the number of IPO candidates who have been elected.

The number of candidates running for federal and state office under the IPO label grew substantially in the election after the party gained major-party status. From 2008 to 2014, the party ran candidates in a total of fourteen different races (one US Senate, three US House, ten state legislative races), an average of 3.5 races per year. In the 2016 election alone, the party competed in fifteen races (four statewide offices, one US House, ten legislative). The party was less active in 2018, however, running one candidate for governor (the only statewide race that year), two for the US House, and four for the legislative assembly.[38] In addition, the IPO candidate for governor withdrew from the race a week before the election, as discussed above. One benefit the party received in the 2018 election, however, is that its gubernatorial candidate was able to get invited to one of the three gubernatorial debates, bringing statewide attention to his campaign and the party. He was then denied access to the other two debates, which generated additional press.[39]

The IPO's record in running candidates in 2016 and 2018 was slightly better than most of the other prominent third parties. The IPO ran candidates in twenty-two races in 2016 and 2018 combined, out of the 169 elections that took place. Over those same two election cycles, Constitution Party candidates competed in six races and Pacific Green Party candidates competed in eight. The Working Families Party (WFP) nominated two party members for office, focusing its efforts instead on cross-nominating other party candidates under the state's fusion voting law. The Libertarian

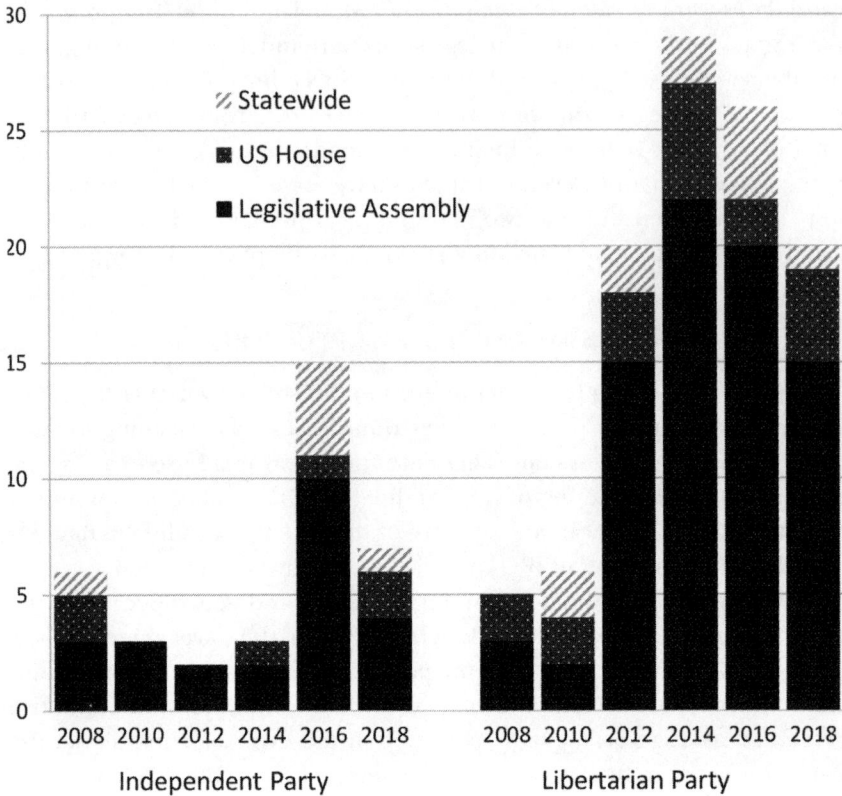

Figure 9.1: Independent Party and Libertarian Party candidates, 2008–2018. Compiled by the author from the Oregon Secretary of State, "Official Results," General Elections, 2008–2018.

Party was far more active than the IPO, however, nominating candidates in forty-six races in both elections combined. It was also considerably more active in 2012 and 2014 (see Figure 9.1).

A second measure we can use to assess the success of the IPO is to look at campaign contributions. One of the challenges facing third parties is the perception that their candidates will not win in partisan races. This perception dampens support at the polls from electors fearful of wasting their votes, and it also makes it difficult for party organization to raise sufficient funds to enable their candidates to compete. The amount of money contributed to a party organization thus provides a rough indicator of the public's willingness to support the party and the potential for the party organization to be involved in election campaigns.

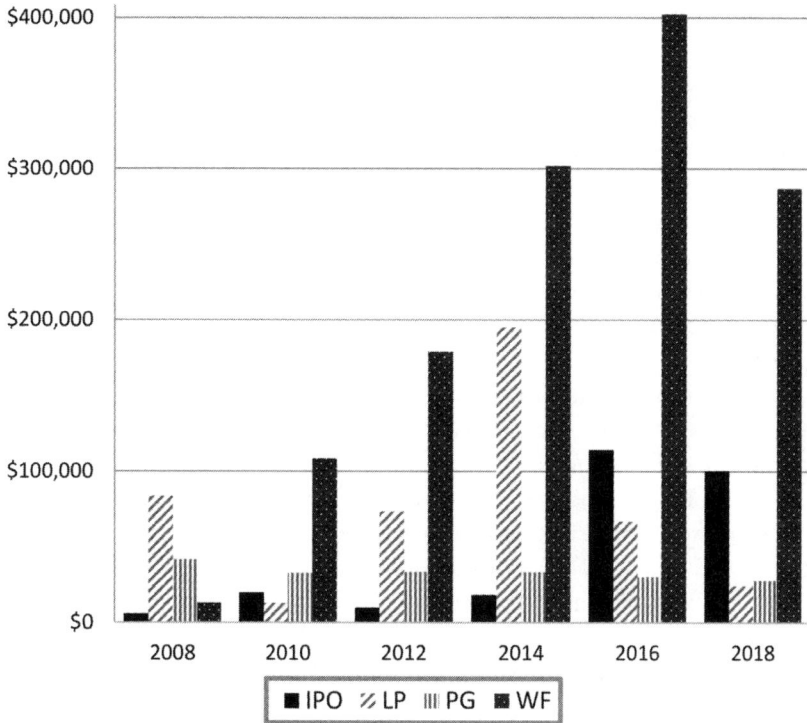

Figure 9.2: Campaign contributions to Oregon third parties by election cycle, 2008–2018. Compiled by the author from the Oregon Elections System for Tracking and Reporting (ORESTAR), 2008–2018.

As with placing candidates on the ballot, the IPO has benefitted from reaching major-party status. The most money it raised as a minor party was $19,680 during the 2009 to 2010 cycle. After becoming a major party, it raised $114,050 in the 2015 to 2016 cycle and $100,395 over the next two years. These figures are better than most of the other third parties. Figure 9.2 shows the contributions received by the other prominent third parties in the state since the 2007 to 2008 cycle, when the IPO first attained minor-party status. The table does not include the Constitution Party, which never raised more than $4,000 in any election cycle during this period. Prior to becoming a major party, the IPO routinely had the lowest contribution levels, with the exception of exceeding the Libertarian Party in 2010. Since becoming a major party, the IPO's fundraising has surpassed that of most other third parties. The one exception is the Working Families Party, which has been by far the most successful third party in raising campaign funds. The

WFP makes an interesting contrast to the IPO. The WFP became a minority party in 2006, shortly before the IPO. However, its main campaign strategy has been to cross-nominate candidates from other parties. The goal of the party has been to push the Democratic Party to the left rather than to place its own members into office. The large campaign contribution figures reflect the support the WFP has received from organized labor.[40]

Even though the IPO has raised more money since becoming a major party, the amount of money it has raised has been minimal compared with the two other major parties. The Democratic and Republican parties raised $2.8 million and $1.4 million, respectively, in the 2017 to 2018 cycle. These figures do not include donations to the party caucus committees, which play the lead party role in funding state legislative races. Thus, while the IPO has benefitted from major-party status, its funding has remained at the level of other minor parties.

Votes for IPO candidates provide a third way to measure the party's success. The party's record at the polls has been considerably stronger than that of other third parties. Looking solely at its record since attaining majority status, the IPO was the only third party to receive more than 4 percent of the vote in any of the sixteen statewide and US House races that were held in 2016 and 2018. The sole exception is that the Libertarian Party candidate received 4.16 percent of the vote in one US House race. The IPO received more than 4 percent of the vote in two US House races, 20 percent in a third, and 9 percent in a state treasurer's race.

The IPO's success at the polls was even stronger in state legislative races. The percentage of votes that any third-party candidate received during those two elections varied considerably depending on whether or not the race included both a Democratic and Republican party opponent. When either of these parties did not field a candidate, then third-party candidates did much better. When both parties fielded a candidate, then the percent of votes received by third-party candidates declined. In the legislative races in which the IPO competed and one of the other major parties did not field a candidate, the IPO candidates received an average of more than 27 percent of the vote per race. The Constitution, Libertarian, and Pacific Green Parties received on average between 9 to 13 percent of the vote in such races. In contests in which the IPO faced competition from both Democratic and Republican candidates, it did not fare as well, receiving an average of 9 percent of the vote per race. The Constitution and Pacific Green Parties did not field any candidates in races in which both of the two large parties were competing. Libertarian Party candidates received 4 percent of the vote on average in these types of races.

Despite its greater ability in attracting voters compared with the other third parties, the IPO has never been able to attract enough support for any of its candidates to come close to obtaining office, the final measure for assessing the party's success. The races in which IPO candidates have received the highest share of the vote have consistently been in districts in which one of the traditional major parties (Democrats and Republicans) so strongly dominates that the other traditional major party has not fielded a candidate. These races are not good indicators of support for the IPO. When one of the two traditional major parties is not competing in a race, voters who support that party are left with two choices: they can sit out the race or vote for a third-party candidate. As such, the total vote for the IPO candidate does not necessarily indicate support for the party. It means instead that the preferred choice for many voters is not on the ballot, encouraging some voters to support an IPO candidate. When candidates from both of the other major parties are running, the IPO still does better than the other third parties, but its vote total is even more limited. If the ultimate measure for gauging the success of the IPO is its ability to elect its members to office, then it remains far from passing that threshold.

CONCLUSIONS

The rise of a third major party in Oregon does not seem all that surprising given the state's political culture and the growing disillusionment among voters with the Democratic and Republican parties in recent years. Oregonians have long been supportive of innovative politics and an open political system. It is part of the state's progressive and populist heritage. The IPO has offered a choice for the large number of voters who have become increasingly disillusioned with the two major parties. It has promised to reform the political system to give voters greater access to and control of government, a promise that has strong appeal in the state's political culture. In other words, the IPO arose at what seems like a particularly opportune time and place for a third party to thrive, offering a platform that fits in well with the state's culture. The lessons one can draw from the party's emergence, however, is not about Oregon politics but the challenges of third parties.

The IPO has surpassed all the other third parties in the state in attracting support, both in voter registration and in votes cast. Yet its achievements have otherwise been modest, at best. When looking at the party's election efforts, there are other third parties that have been more active in nominating candidates and more effective in raising campaign contributions. More importantly, the IPO's success in all the measures examined in this chapter has been poor compared with the Democratic and Republican parties in the state. The IPO may have gained sufficient support to gain majority status, but it has not been competitive with the other two major parties in raising funds, contesting elections, or gaining office. Overall, its performance has been far closer to the other third parties in the state than to the Democratic and Republican parties.

The main lessons one can draw from the story of the IPO is that achieving major-party status is not a guarantee of wider public acceptance or of an ability to compete with the two main major parties on equal terms. The IPO may be unusual because it has attained major-party status, but its experiences are not significantly different from other third parties. Rather than representing a challenge to Duverger's law, and becoming a competitor in the state's two-party system, it has played only a minor role in Oregon politics compared with the Democratic and Republican parties. Given the state's political culture and the growing disillusionment of state voters toward the two major parties, the experience of the IPO in Oregon does not bode well for third parties elsewhere. Oregon offers a political context that seems particularly well suited for third parties, yet the state remains dominated by the Democratic and Republican parties.

As for the future, the IPO's status as a majority party did not look promising in early 2019. With the adoption of automatic voter registration, the number of registered voters in the state expanded considerably, with a large percentage of the new voters being registered as nonaffiliated. As a consequence, the percentage of voters who were registered with the IPO dropped below the 5 percent threshold needed to retain major-party status in 2018, though the legislature allowed it to retain that status through the 2018 election cycle. With that election behind it, the party was expected to revert to minor-party status.[41]

If it loses major-party status, the IPO will not be guaranteed the same access to the ballot as the Democratic and Republican Parties, forcing the party to return to the more difficult task of gathering signatures in each election to gets its candidates on the ballot. The party is also likely to lose much of the media attention it has received as a majority party. The emergence of the IPO as a major party was historic, which brought it considerable media coverage and increased public attention. With a return to minor-party status, the party will no longer enjoy the cachet of its historic position and the attention that has gone along with it.[42] In addition, the party's gubernatorial candidates are not likely to be invited to debates with the other parties, nor will it make the news if the IPO candidates are denied participation in debates, as happened in 2018.

It is difficult to know for certain what the future holds for the IPO, however, given how recent these events have unfolded. Even though the party is expected to lose major-party status, it has been able to attract a surprisingly large number of new members continuously since its inception. To retain major-party status, it will need to increase its membership by more than 10 percent, which may not be impossible given the party's history. One benefit that the party retains is that it still has the word "independent" in its name, which has helped it attract supporters in the past.

Whether the party loses majority status or not, there are two trends that seem fairly certain in the near future. The first is that the IPO will continue to play an active role in Oregon politics, championing changes in the election system and putting forward candidates who support good government reforms, which has been the central focus on the party's agenda. The party may face more challenges in getting its candidates on the ballot if it loses major-party status, but its leaders say they will continue to run candidates and to work for change over the long haul.[43] The second is that the party is unlikely to overcome the challenges generally facing minority parties in state politics. Even if it is able to retain major-party status, the IPO is not likely to replace either of the other two major parties in the state or to compete with them on an equal basis, at least anytime soon. Duverger's law and the other constraints on third parties make that too difficult to achieve.

NOTES

1. Daniel C. Reed, "Ballot Reform and the Decline of Third Parties in State Legislatures," *Representation* 52, nos. 2–3 (2017): 163–177; Bernard Tamas and Matthew Dean Hindman, "Ballot Access Laws and the Decline of American Third-Parties," *Election Law Journal: Rules, Politics, and Policy* 13, no. 2 (2014): 260–276.

2. Elizabeth Bircher, *Election Law Manual* (Williamsburg, VA: Election Law Program, 2008), 3–5.

3. Barry C. Burden, "Ballot Regulations and Multiparty Politics in the States," *PS: Political Science and Politics* 40, no. 4 (2007): 669–673; Marcus Drometer and Johannes Rincke, "The Impact of Ballot Access Restrictions on Electoral Competition: Evidence from a Natural Experiment," *Public Choice* 138, nos. 3/4 (2009): 461–474.

4. Oregon Rev. Stat. 248, § 006 (2017).

5. Hannah Hoffman, "Oregon Is Officially a Three-Party State," *Salem Statesman Journal*, February 10, 2015.

6. Richard A. Clucas and Mark Henkels, "Change and Continuity in Oregon Politics," in *Governing Oregon: Continuity and Change*, eds. Richard A. Clucas, Mark Henkels, Priscilla L. Southwell, and Ed Weber (Corvallis: Oregon State University Press, 2018), 3–18; Richard A. Clucas and Mark Henkels, "A State Divided," in *Ore-*

gon Politics and Government: Progressives and Conservative Populists, eds. Richard A. Clucas, Mark Henkels, and Brent Steel (Lincoln: University of Nebraska Press, 2005), 1–16; Frederick J. Boehmke and Paul Skinner, "State Policy Innovativeness Revisited," *State Politics and Policy Quarterly* 12, no. 3 (2012): 303–329.

7. William Booth, "Naderites Scare Oregon Democrats," *Washington Post,* October 30, 2000; Paul West, "For Gore, a Battle for Green Territory," *Baltimore Sun,* October 24, 2000.

8. John Wildermuth, "Nader Holds Key to Oregon for Gore, Bush/Democrats Struggle to Hold on to State," SFGate, October 31, 2000.

9. "Group: Bush Allies Illegally Helping Nader in Oregon," CNN.com, July 1, 2004; Eric Zuesse, "Ralph Nader Was Indispensable to the Republican Party," Huffington Post, November 11, 2013.

10. Oregon Legislative Assembly, HB 2614, 73rd Legislative Assembly, *Journal of the Oregon House* (February 22, 2005), H-108.

11. "75th Oregon Legislative Assembly: 2009 Summary of Legislation," Oregon Legislative Assembly, Legislative Administration Committee Services, October 2009, 60–61; James Sinks, "State Democrats Enter Legal Dispute," *Bend Bulletin,* December 3, 2006.

12. Sal Peralta, "From Grassroots Movement to Major Party: A Brief History of the Independent Party of Oregon," Independent Voter Network, September 14, 2015.

13. Colin Fogarty, "Independent Party Growing Fast in Oregon," Oregon Public Broadcasting, September 24, 2007; Peralta, "From Grassroots."

14. Jeff Mapes, "Is Multnomah County's Political Contribution Cap Constitutional?" Oregon Public Broadcasting, August 12, 2017; James Nobles, "Meet the Independent Party of Oregon Leadership," *Oregon Outpost,* March 2, 2015.

15. Peralta, "From Grassroots"; Robert Harris, "Opinion: The Independent Party's Longterm Play for Democracy Reform," *Oregonian,* November 14, 2018.

16. Fogarty, "Independent Party"; Jeff Mapes, "Oregon's Independent Party on Cusp of Power, Identity Crisis," *Oregonian,* June 2, 2010.

17. Jim Redden, "Independent Party May Gain Major Party Status," *Portland Tribune,* August 13, 2015.

18. "Voter Registrations by Year and Month," Oregon Secretary of State, February 2007 and February 2011, https://sos.oregon.gov/blue-book/Pages/state/elections/voting.aspx.

19. Nigel Duara, "Oregon's Independent Party Shuns Platforms," *Spokane Spokesman Review,* August 14, 2010; Fogarty, "Independent Party"; Peralta, "From Grassroots."

20. Jeff Mapes, "Cabinetmaker Wins Oregon Independent Party Gubernatorial Nomination," *Oregonian,* June 13, 2018; Connor Radnovich, "Independent Candidate Starnes Drops Out of Oregon Governor's Race, Endorses Kate Brown," *Salem Statesman Journal,* October 30, 2018.

21. Peralta, "From Grassroots."

22. Oregon Legislative Assembly, SB 326, 75th Legislative Assembly, *Journal of the Oregon Senate* (January 16, 2009), S-69.

23. Duara, "Oregon's Independent"; Mapes, "Oregon's Independent."

24. Jeff Mapes, "Independent Party of Oregon Comes Under Fire from Democratic and Republican Parties," *Oregonian*, June 26, 2015.

25. Mapes, "Oregon's Independent"; Fogarty, "Independent Party"; "Our Opinion: Independent Party Must Prove Viability," *Beaverton Valley Times*, August 2, 2018

26. Duara, "Oregon's Independent": Jeff Mapes, "Democrats File Complaint Against Independent Party of Oregon, Question Group's 'Legitimacy,'" *Oregonian*, May 28, 2010.

27. Jeff Mapes, "Independent Party of Oregon Earns Major-Party Status; Looks Forward to State-Run Primary," *Oregonian*, February 9, 2015.

28. "Voter Registrations by Year and Month," Oregon Secretary of State, October 2018, https://sos.oregon.gov/blue-book/Pages/state/elections/voting.aspx.

29. Clucas and Henkels, "Change and Continuity"; George H. Haynes, "'People's Rule' in Oregon, 1910," *Political Science Quarterly* 26, no. 1 (1911): 32–62.

30. Clucas and Henkels, "Continuity and Change."

31. Gordon B. Dodds, *Oregon: A Bicentennial History* (New York: W. W. Norton, 1977).

32. Haynes, "'People's Rule,'" 33.

33. Elinor Langer, *A Hundred Little Hitlers* (New York: Henry Holt, 2004); *The History of Portland's African American Community: 1805 to the Present* (Portland, OR: Portland Bureau of Planning, 1993); George T. Nicola, "Oregon's Other Gay Record: A Recent History of Anti-Gay Ballot Initiatives from Around the State," *Portland Street Roots News*, May 6, 2014.

34. Clucas and Henkels, "A State Divided."

35. Quan Li, Michael J. Pomante II, and Scot Schraufnagel, "Cost of Voting in the American States," *Election Law Journal: Rules, Politics, and Policy* 17, no. 3 (2018): 234–247.

36. "Voter Registrations by Year and Month," Oregon Secretary of State, various editions, https://sos.oregon.gov/blue-book/Pages/state/elections/voting.aspx.

37. Oregon Legislative Assembly, *Chronological List of Oregon Legislators* (Salem: Legislative Committee Services, 2008); "Oregon Legislators and Staff Guide," Oregon Secretary of State, various years, https://sos.oregon.gov/archives/Pages/records/legislators_guide.aspx.

38. These nomination numbers do not include candidates from other parties who were cross-nominated by the IPO.

39. Paris Achen, "Final Two Governor Debates Shove Independent Candidate Aside," *Portland Tribune*, October 4, 2018.

40. Jeff Mapes, "Minor Party Candidates Gain Clout with New Oregon Law," *Oregonian*, July 6, 2009; "Oregon Working Families Party: Minor Party Strives to be a Major Player in Oregon," nwLaborPress.org, September 29, 2015.

41. Robert Harris, "Opinion: The Independent Party's Long-Term Play for Democracy Reform" *Oregonian*, November 14, 2018.

42. Harris, "Opinion."

43. Harris, "Opinion."

CHAPTER 10

The Mountain Party of West Virginia

C. Damien Arthur

The creation of the Mountain Party was possible because of the peculiar nature of politics in the Mountain State. West Virginia was birthed in controversy—emerging during the Civil War in an attempt to increase the number of states opposed to slavery.[1] In an inaugural prayer at the official ceremony of statehood, Reverend J. T. McClure said West Virginia was "born amidst tears and blood and fire and desolation."[2] In some ways, West Virginia's birth saved the Union, prevented the ruin of a human experiment in self-rule, and helped to abolish one of humanity's most dehumanizing and grotesque institutions.

In the same vein, the Mountain Party believes their creation will save the state and its citizens through their robust progressive agenda, which aims to eradicate the bondage of the state's poverty, stop the exploitative extraction industry, and propel folks into the American dream. The story of the Mountain Party is the story of speaking truth to power and the opposition toward that power, and the opposition to the West Virginia Democratic Party and their cozy relationship with the extraction industry and the Republican Party.

West Virginia is unparalleled in natural beauty and exploitation; its mountain cliffs are covered with the most luxuriant and valuable trees. Beneath those mountains is a world of treasure: black rock—bituminous coal, which enabled the state to be exploited for dozens of decades for its resources. Just after the Civil War, "over 30 billion board feet of lumber" was removed from the state and sold by a few eastern financiers.[3] By 1915, the Mountain State was producing 23 percent of the national coal market.[4]

During the time of this extraction of one of her greatest assets, no severance tax was paid to the state by these absentee companies until the 1970s, an irrevocable and irreparable loss that would define generations of West Virginians. As only a few people owned nearly the entire state, none of the wealth remained in West Virginia; it was never invested there, in the people, or any real capital improvements.[5]

During most of the time period of this economic exploitation of West Virginia and her resources (the period between 1861 and 1932), Republicans dominated state government.[6] However, the Democrats did have control during some of the time directly after the war, between 1871 to 1895. With the Great Depression raging, the miners were further exploited. Yet, in 1933, with Roosevelt's election to the presidency and the New Deal, the workers of West Virginia began to unionize, improving their working conditions and their economic prospects. Unions played a major role in West Virginia politics until the Reagan revolution of decentralization in the 1980s, and the New Democratic neoliberalism in the 1990s, decimated their power.

The New Deal ushered in complete Democratic Party control of most of West Virginia's government until 2014. According to the *New York Times,* "In politics, West Virginia is synonymous with Democrats."[7] The house of delegates was Democratic controlled from 1930 until 2014, when the Democrats lost their majority during the midterm elections. The upper chamber in the legislature was controlled by the Democrats from 1933 until the Republicans took power in January 2015.

Democratic Party control had been statewide, in nearly every major office since 1933. For instance, during the electoral statewide offices from 1933 through 2014, eighteen governors were elected; all but four of them were Democrats—five if you count the current governor who was elected as a Democrat in November 2016 and switched his party affiliation to Republican during his first year in office. The four Republican governors were only two men, Cecil Underwood and Arch Moore, who were elected to four different nonconsecutive administrations. The governors of West Virginia tend to be more conservative than their liberal counterparts in other states where Democrats are the executive of the state.[8]

The same contrast exists for the statewide office of secretary of state. Of the last fourteen office holders, nine of them were Democrats. Yet, it is even more telling that over the last eighty-six years, Republicans have only held this office for twelve years. Perhaps the most dramatic version of Democratic control of statewide offices is that of the office of the attorney general. Every attorney general since 1933 has been a Democrat, with the exception of the current one—a very conservative Republican who just lost a race for a US Senate seat in 2018.

Despite the previous Democratic stronghold on political power in West Virginia, the party certainly was not a bastion of liberalism or even a mirrored representation of the national Democratic Party's values and policies. In terms of the differences between the national party and West Virginia Democrats, the distance is somewhat stark. For the national Democratic Party, Project Vote Smart's National Political Awareness Test (NPAT), a survey measure of ideal points of political ideology, is near negative one from a total of negative two, the most liberal, and the West Virginia Party score is just above zero.[9]

Figure 10.1 highlights this contrast, suggesting that West Virginia Democrats are no closer to being either liberal or conservative compared to the pooled congressional party medians of their national party. By 2002, the Democratic Party in West Virginia was as moderate as any other state in the union, on average. According to Boris Shor and Nolan McCarty, West Virginia was on par with the United States as a whole but severely out of step with Democrats and "liberals" from other more progressive states, such as California, Massachusetts, or New York.[10]

The changes in party strength and loyalty in West Virginia were somewhat notable from the beginning of the Clinton era in 1992 to the end of the first term of the second Bush administration in 2005.[11] In 1992, the West Virginia Institute for Public Affairs (WVIPA) surveyed residents on their strength of party affiliation. Just under 22 percent of Democrats claimed to be "Strong Democrat," and just under 10 percent of Republicans identified as "Strong Republican."[12]

The WVIPA did the same survey again in 2005 and found striking changes in the strength and solidification of party identification. For instance, just under 25 percent of Democrats were now "Strong Democrat" and just under 25 percent were now "Strong Republican." Many of the changes came from those who had identified as "Independent" in 1992 and were now affiliated with a party in 2005. For instance, independents in West Virginia decreased by half, while at the same time, moderates decreased by 8 percent. Yet, the most telling ideological trend during this period comes from those who identified as "Conservative," increasing by nearly 10 percent.

Therefore, policy compromises move rightward rather than leftward, by sheer volume of members with moderate and conservative views. Such a reality creates a ripe environment for a progressive or liberal third party, as those with leftward-leaning ideological positions are made to feel as though they have no real choice in their candidates for political office. A few of those with progressive predilections have broken from the West Virginia

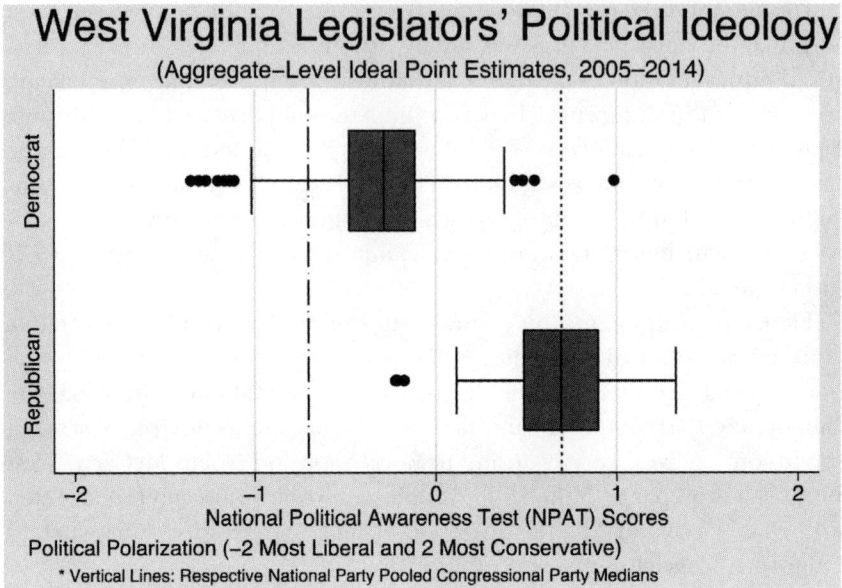

West Virginia Legislators' Political Ideology
(Aggregate–Level Ideal Point Estimates, 2005–2014)

National Political Awareness Test (NPAT) Scores
Political Polarization (–2 Most Liberal and 2 Most Conservative)
* Vertical Lines: Respective National Party Pooled Congressional Party Medians

Figure 10.1: A visual, detailed picture of the distance between the median ideal points of party ideology in West Virginia's legislators. Boris Shor, "Aggregate State Legislator Shor-McCarty Ideology Data, May 2018 update," Harvard Dataverse, V2, https://doi.org/10.7910/DVN/BSLEFD.

Democratic Party. This has occurred despite the party's attempts to make it legally more difficult to create a new party by increasing the threshold of signatures needed for official recognition. Out of frustration with the Democratic Party and its lack of substantial differences from state Republicans, the Mountain Party was born, heralding, in their own words: "West Virginia, you do have a choice!"

THE BIRTH OF THE MOUNTAIN PARTY

In 1999, at a time when the Democrats outnumbered Republicans two-to-one in party registration at the state level, the Democratic Party-controlled legislature created a law that required the number of signatures on the ballot be increased by 100 percent, hoping to discourage any further party factions in the state. Denise Giardina, local author of *Storming Heaven*, a fictionalized novel about the mine wars in southern West Virginia that culminated in the Battle of Blair Mountain, the largest armed uprising since the Civil War, became completely disillusioned with the Democratic Party's relationship to the coal industry, an industry she believed was bad for West Virginia, its people, and its land.[13]

For Giardina, the lack of differences between the state's Democrats and Republicans was too obvious and concerning. She knew that the state Democrats looked nothing like the national Democratic Party, and she especially wondered what the party would look like with the new standard bearer Al Gore at the helm. For her, the Democrats just refused to take on the coal industry and oppose mountaintop removal.

Having grown up in a coal camp, she watched the schools deteriorate rapidly for decades, while the coal industry continued to fight the meager severance tax it paid. They lobbied to have it reduced year after year once it was enacted. Giardina withdrew her support from the Democratic Party after hearing the industry's continued pleas to the media, the legislature, and the citizenry that the severance tax eliminated jobs, while at the same time using machines and virtually no personnel to explode the tops of mountains and remove coal without miners. This procedure, known as mountaintop removal, employs "mammoth machines (and relatively few workers) to literally move whole peaks to get at the coal." Giardina called it "environmental destruction."[14]

In an act of defiance and opposition to the state's Democratic Party, Giardina founded the Mountain Party with the support of a few other defectors. It was a party concerned primarily with the environment, a one-issue movement. Giardina refused to believe that environmental protection and sound economic policy were mutually exclusive. For her, the coal company rhetoric was a tactic to exploit West Virginians and their labor.

The environment was a major policy issue at the time for many West Virginians and others across the country, as Al Gore had been pushing for the reduction of greenhouse gas emissions through endeavors such as the Kyoto Protocol.[15] As noted by the *New York Times*, "The word 'environmental' is often followed here [West Virginia] by 'extremist' when describing Mr. Gore, whose remedies for global warming—including a significant reduction in carbon dioxide emissions—are seen as a body blow to the coal industry."[16] His candidacy was the culmination of ideological splintering of the Democratic Party in West Virginia, a highlighted difference between the national- and state-level Democrats. It came at a perfect time for the Republicans and signaled West Virginia's trend toward support for the Republicans it currently supports. This fueled Giardina's desire to challenge the Democratic Party establishment and create a local party: the Mountain Party.[17]

Nevertheless, the official Democratic Party in the state sued to keep her from accessing the ballot. She was able to secure over 13,000 signatures, ensuring her access to the ballot and the governor's election in 2000. Under West Virginia law at the time, if she obtained 1 percent or more of the total vote, her new Mountain Party could run more candidates in the 2002 election—becoming an officially recognized party in West Virginia.

Giardina only spent around $20,000 total for her campaign. The official stance from the party, then and now, is to refuse any corporate or special-interest campaign money. Her two major party opponents spent tens of millions of dollars, as is typical. The Democratic Party candidate Bob Wise argued during the campaign that candidates polling less than 15 percent should not be allowed to debate, as it would distract the voters within the state from the stark choices between himself and his Republican opponent.[18]

Congress member Wise maintained that he agreed with 85 percent of what Republican governor Cecil Underwood had done while in office but that 15 percent was of paramount concern to West Virginians. Wise refused to participate in the debate if Giardina was there, claiming that adding a candidate from the newly formed Mountain Party would keep the voters from deciphering the differences and the importance of that 15 percent in their choice for whom to vote.[19]

Ellender Stanchina, president of the West Virginia League of Women Voters, the group who sponsored the debates, said, "In West Virginia it is very difficult to get on the ballot. Once you are on the ballot you have a right to participate in the debate. That's what democracy is."[20] The Giardina campaign tried to place Wise's refusal to debate her in the context of the issues.

Congressman Wise's campaign responded that "Denise is in a position of being nowhere in the polls with no substantial support—she has to make sensational statements like that in order to breathe life into what has otherwise been a failing campaign."[21] Giardina was not invited to the debate, as Wise would refuse to participate if she were included.

Giardina's campaign manager, the only paid campaign staff member, argued, "And we expect lots of people to vote who wouldn't otherwise, because this time there is a real choice."[22] The notion of "a real choice" is the bedrock of the birth of the Mountain Party in West Virginia. When the election was over, Giardina received 10,416 votes in the 2000 general election for governor, failing substantially to garner enough votes to overcome the Democratic Party's stronghold in West Virginia. Wise received 324,822 to Governor Underwood's 305,926. In total, Giardina received 1.6 percent of

the total vote, which gave legal authority for the Mountain Party to participate in other elections on the ballot in 2002. They have been on the ballot
in every election since.

Since this election, and its exclusion from the debates, the Mountain
Party has made debate inclusion for other parties and candidates a major
part of its mission. Subsequent candidates for governor on the Mountain
Party ticket have tried to sue to get access to the debates, especially in 2004
and 2008. They lost those court battles.[23] The party claims their lack of success in the courts is because those courts and the judges are part of the
Democratic Party establishment. Even currently, the argument from the
Mountain Party is that they should be given access to the debates between
the major-party candidates. They finally polled over 5 percent, a moving
target, in 2016, high enough to participate in the gubernatorial debates.

THE FORMATION OF TODAY'S MOUNTAIN PARTY

West Virginia has unquestionably become more polarized since 2005. In
2002, it was the second least polarized state, behind Vermont, with West Virginia Democrats significantly more conservative than the average national
Democrat and West Virginia Republicans equal to the average national Republican.[24] Interestingly, exit poll surveys in 2008 suggested that half of Democrats in West Virginia were severely dissatisfied with the direction of the
national Democratic Party, especially if Obama were to win the nomination.

With his election to the presidency, Obama brought large Democratic
majorities to Congress. He was able to push through a great deal of policies
most Democrats wanted in the first years of his administration, particularly
the Affordable Care Act; the Dodd-Frank Wall Street Reform and Consumer Protection Act; the American Recovery and Reinvestment Act; the
Matthew Shepard and James Byrd Jr. Hate Crimes Prevention Act; the
Don't Ask, Don't Tell Repeal Act; the Lily Ledbetter Fair Pay Act; and most
important for West Virginia, the president's Climate Action Plan, which was
designed to reduce greenhouse gas emissions significantly.

The slogan "Obama's War on Coal" was established, and he was demo-
nized by many in the state as being the sole reason for the decline in coal
production and consumption and not market demands, as economists
argue. This was such an issue in the state that many Democrats, including
the governor, Earl Ray Tomblin, did not even attend the 2012 Democratic
National Convention in Charlotte, North Carolina, for fear that they would
be accused of being an "Obama Democrat."

Democratic governor Joe Manchin, while running for the US Senate seat of the deceased Robert C. Byrd, took a high-powered rifle and fired a shot through a literal paper copy of Obama's proposed cap-and-trade bill. He said, "I'll take on Washington and this Administration to get the federal government off of our back and out of our pockets. I'll cut federal spending and I'll repeal the bad parts of Obamacare. I sued EPA and I'll take dead aim at the cap-and-trade bill, [shot fired] because it is bad for West Virginia." After that commercial, as governor, Manchin sued the Environmental Protection Agency and the Obama administration because of their "attempts to destroy the coal mining industry."[25]

The stark differences between the national Democratic Party and the West Virginia Democratic Party were front and center through the actions, and the person, of President Obama, which furthered the divide between West Virginia Democrats and the national party. The two looked substantially different in the past, but they were nearly unrecognizable at the end of the Obama presidency.

While these changes were playing out nationally and locally, the Mountain Party continued to participate in state elections, challenging Democrats for statewide offices—mostly focusing on the governorship and the US Senate. They tried to expand their constituencies by joining the Green Party of the United States, adopting much of its platform and moving beyond a one-issue (mountaintop removal) party label and openly embracing more progressive policies, such as marijuana legalization.

They nominated Bob Henry Baber to run against Governor Manchin for the vacated senate seat of Byrd in 2012. He obtained just under 3 percent of the total vote. The candidate for governor, Jesse Johnson, received over 2.5 percent of the vote—keeping them eligible for the next election. They also nominated Jill Stein for president in 2012 and 2016. She received less than 1 percent of the vote in 2012 and over 1 percent in 2016.

Historically, the Mountain Party has not been a down-ballot party. Their attempts at elective office have concentrated on statewide races. They hoped statewide elected office would give them more control and power to oppose the extraction industry. Fundamentally, they had hoped for national representation in the Senate and state-level representation, which is slightly odd, however, given that the state had fairly liberal representation in the Senate, comparatively speaking, for a long time.

For instance, West Virginia's longest serving senator, Robert C. Byrd, former majority leader and chairman of the Senate Appropriations Committee, voted with congressional Democrats anywhere from 80 percent in the 106th Congress to 90 percent in the 111th Congress.[26] With a Dynamic Weighted Nominal Three-Step Estimation (DW-NOMINATE) score of negative 0.309, that ensures that he was more liberal than 68 percent of the US Senate. Yet, he was still more conservative than 52 percent of the Democrats in the same Congress.

Nevertheless, the Mountain Party began to regularly run three to five down-ballot candidates per election beginning in 2008—a total of twenty-three candidates from 2008 to 2016—out of hundreds of elections. In some of the races, they did much better there than their statewide candidates had done in terms of the total vote percentage. For instance, in a House of Delegates race, Raymond V. Davis III received just over 13 percent in District 5, mostly in Wetzel County, near Morgantown and the flagship university of the state. Mark Myers, in District 11, a city just north of the state capital, received nearly 19 percent of the vote in 2014. In the same year, Daniel P. Lutz Jr. received over 22 percent of the vote in a district in the more liberal eastern panhandle of the state.

In only two elections did the Mountain Party candidate theoretically make a difference in the electoral outcome. In 2012, in a House of Delegates race, if every person who voted for the Mountain Party candidate had voted for the Democrat in the race, the Democrat would have won by forty votes. The same was true for a state senate election in 2016. The Democrat would have won by 512 votes. In the other races, the Democrat either won or lost so badly it would not have mattered whether or not there was a Mountain Party candidate on the ballot.

For all of this, the Mountain Party has never received enough votes to come close to winning a statewide campaign.[27] All the while, in each election since 2000, the party has received over 1 percent of the total statewide vote, ensuring its access to the next election. Their hopes changed a bit after 2014, however. This seeming lack of publicity and inevitable defeat changed during the 2016 race for governor.

TODAY'S MOUNTAIN PARTY

Just prior to the 2016 race, the Mountain Party had around 1,700 registered members with no major statewide candidates elected to office. To that point, only three elected officials—the mayor of a small town, Richwood, and two state conservation officers—identified with the Mountain Party. And, they were elected in nonpartisan elections.

Such an absence of electoral success for a statewide party begs the question: Why are they active? It is readily apparent and indicative from the slogans the party employs, such as "West Virginia, you do have a choice!" and "Support West Virginia's ONLY progressive political party."

For the Mountain Party, West Virginia's Democratic Party is too conservative and aligned too closely with their Republican counterparts ideologically. Their continued political activity is bolstered by the hope that West Virginia might be a prosperous state—a state that is not continually exploited for its natural resources but rather a state in the Union that is welcoming for all.[28] Their continued participation in West Virginia politics is not simply about party ideology per se—especially on the national versus local level, but rather, it is essentially about a few specific policy issues and the tone and emphasis by which the parties address them.

Their current party chair, Denise Binion, said the party simply does not trust the Democrats. The party believes that the West Virginia Democratic Party has no place for the inclusion of Mountain Party policy positions.[29] So, rather than exist in the left wing of the party, as more liberal members do in other states, those more liberal members have decided to create and maintain a new party in West Virginia.[30] However, Binion said the younger members of the Democratic Party are constantly approaching the Mountain Party, seeking reunion, but for her the distrust is too deep for reconciliation.

The Mountain Party obviously seeks electoral success, but given the Democratic Party stronghold in the state, and absent that success, they have been content to advocate policy issues that are important to progressivism.[31] But, with the continued voice of the Mountain Party in the electoral process, there is a chance that the state's political agenda will be further pushed leftward on issues such as the legalization of cannabis and the use of cannabidiol (CBD) oil, as the West Virginia Democratic Party platform currently "supports decriminalization and legalization of cannabis (medical, industrial and recreational—like Colorado) . . . hemp farming and manufacturing hemp products here in WV."[32]

Such policy issues are popular in other states and in West Virginia to some extent. The Mountain Party's push for implementation of their policy platform has helped with their visibility and drawing folks to their party. At the end of 2018, the Mountain Party had 2,220 registered voters across fifty-five counties in West Virginia, which is just under 0.2 percent of the entirety of registered voters. This is in contrast to 520,541 registered Democrats in the state and 406,332 Republicans.[33]

The Mountain Party seems to be gaining members from the Democratic Party, as registration numbers in 2016 were different, although not dramatic.[34] For instance, there were 1,901 registered at the end of 2016, up a few hundred from 1,776 after the 2016 general election. This is no doubt a mechanism of the Democrats nominating a former and now current Republican to lead the party as much as it is the former Democratic Party nominee, Charlotte Pritt, heading the ticket for the Mountain Party. Yet, it is a noticeable change, a 25 percent increase in registered membership, but not significant in terms of the overall voting power of the party.

The Democrats had 569,091 registered voters.[35] Starting with the Trump era, West Virginia Democrats have lost just over 8.5 percent of their registered voters. It appears most of those have changed to the Republican party, which had 398,959 voters. As the Democratic Party in West Virginia struggles to keep its members and embrace the changes in the national party, they are in a catch-22 of sorts, losing members to gain members and gaining those members causes them to lose other members.

THE FUTURE OF THE MOUNTAIN PARTY

The hope of the Mountain Party moving toward 2020 and beyond, especially as expressed in the post-2016 general election interviews that the Mountain Party gubernatorial candidate, Charlotte Pritt, made across the state, is to try to move beyond the labels of "party" and focus on policy issues—issues that they believe will resonate with West Virginians. It appears that in doing so, the Mountain Party hopes to pull some of the disaffected Republicans to their side, those Republicans that reject the Trumpism within the party.[36]

Moreover, Mountain Party officials think their lack of electoral success is due to their exclusion from the debates with the major parties, which hinders their ability to raise their name recognition and push their policy positions to the forefront. Pritt claimed that West Virginia's dual-party control is really just two parties that want the same thing in terms of policy. She has called for the inclusion of all parties that exist in West Virginia to be included in the debates, despite their lack of official ballot access.

The Mountain Party is taking steps to move beyond 2016 and 2018. Yet, in the 2018 midterm election, Daniel P. Lutz Jr. ran as the Mountain Party candidate in the Second Congressional District of West Virginia. This district mostly encompasses Kanawha County, the county with the highest number of registered Mountain Party voters, only two hundred and eighty. Interestingly, Lutz received 3 percent (6,277) of the total vote. More importantly, however, there were only three other Mountain Party candidates, out of 256 state-level candidates with a party affiliation, running for office in the 2018 election.[37]

Jess Johnson, the former Mountain Party state chairman, and Denise Binion, the current chairwoman, want to focus on getting more Mountain

Party candidates elected to the state legislature rather than trying to win the governorship or a US Senate seat.[38] Binion even expressed dismay at running presidential candidates. This appears to be a more reasonable strategy for completing their mission of focusing on the issues. If they can elect members of their party to the legislature, they might be able to shape state policy in a substantive manner, rather than symbolically through agenda-setting.

Although the Mountain Party has not traditionally been a down-ballot party, the official direction of the party will be to try this approach in the future.[39] Johnson believes that there are enough disaffected members in the Democratic and Republican Parties across the state that can be won for the Mountain Party in 2020 and beyond.[40] Democrats are losing registered voters and the Mountain Party is gaining them. So, Johnson sees hope in the future. He said, "We stuck to our guns about issues. We're genuine in fighting for the people, fighting for labor, fighting for women, fighting for families, children, fighting for the environment. We don't take corporate money or interest into play. We've had a consistent, solid message that resonates with the people."[41] By certain standards, the Mountain Party is the most electorally potent offshoot of the Green Party federation of all the other states in the Union. It is certainly the longest existing third party in West Virginia. Yet, it is somewhat doubtful that the Mountain Party can maintain an approach that continues to get a 6 percent statewide vote showing as it did with Pritt's campaign in 2016. Their most reasonable hope is for those voters who enthusiastically supported Bernie Sanders in the 2016 West Virginia Democratic primary to defect to the Mountain Party. If they do not join the party per se, at least these new voters could help them with policy-issue adoption, such as marijuana decriminalization and legalization.[42]

Trump's support was, and still is, overwhelming in West Virginia, as news outlets sang the praises of that approval and support in the state for months after the general election. What does not get talked about often, however, is the support Senator Sanders received in the state. Sanders received 123,860 votes, which was only 51.4 percent of the total vote, and Hilary Clinton received 86,354 votes, 35.8 percent of the Democratic vote. Interestingly, in that primary election, Sanders received only twenty-six thousand fewer votes than Trump. Trump received 156,245 votes, which is 77 percent of the total Republican Party primary—giving him thirty of the thirty-one delegate votes. Ted Cruz was the next closest vote getter, with 18,208, just 9 percent of the total votes.

If it is reasonable to assume that Sanders would get all, or nearly all, of

Clinton's nearly eighty-seven thousand votes, he would have well over two hundred thousand votes, besting Trump significantly in the primary. Most importantly, this speculation is rendered moot when thinking about whether or not it would transfer to a general election between Sanders and Trump in West Virginia, especially given the state's conservative shift. Nevertheless, the Mountain Party thinks, and hopes, it will.

Many of their members changed their party affiliation to work on his campaign—oddly, they were not as excited about their Green Party candidate.[43] Either way, the Mountain Party appears to be thinking that the future of the Mountain State is resting on what Abraham Lincoln wrote to Congress before the people of West Virginia were even granted their statehood: "Winter closes in on the Union people of Western Virginia, leaving them masters of their own country."[44]

NOTES

1. Eric Foner, *The Fiery Trial: Abraham Lincoln And American Slavery* (New York: W. W. Norton, 2011).

2. Senator Robert C. Byrd, "Happy 140th Birthday, West Virginia," *Congressional Record* 149, no. 92 (June 20, 2003): S8319–S8320.

3. R. D. Eller, *Miners, Millhands, And Mountaineers: Industrialization of the Appalachian South, 1880–1930* (Knoxville: University of Tennessee Press, 1982).

4. Eller, *Miners, Millhands.*

5. Ronald L. Lewis, "Railroads, Deforestation, and the Transformation of Agriculture in the West Virginia Back Counties, 1880—1920." In *Appalachia in the Making: The Mountain South in the Nineteenth Century,* eds. M. B. Pudup, D. B. Bilings, and A. L. Waller (Chapel Hill: University of North Carolina Press, 1995).

6. Richard A. Brisbin et al., *West Virginia Politics and Government,* 2nd ed. (Lincoln: University of Nebraska Press, 2008).

7. Janet Battaile. "The Campaign: West Virginia; Gore Is Trying to Catch Up in Democrat-Dominated State," *New York Times,* November 5, 2000.

8. William D. Berry, Richard C. Fording, Evan J. Ringquist, Russell L. Hanson, and Carl E. Klarner, "Measuring Citizen and Government Ideology in the US States: A Re-appraisal," *State Politics & Policy Quarterly* 10, no. 2 (2010): 117–135.

9. Adam Bonica, "Mapping the Ideological Marketplace," *American Journal of Political Science* 58, no. 2 (2014): 367–386.

10. Boris Shor and Nolan Mccarty, "The Ideological Mapping of American Legislatures," American Political Science Review 105, no. 3 (August 2011): 530–551.

11. Brisbin, *West Virginia.*

12. Brisbin, *West Virginia.*

13. David Case, "West Virginia's Mountain (Party) Mama," Mother Jones, February 15, 2017.

14. Case, "West Virginia's."

15. D. P. Daniels, J. A. Krosnick, M. P. Tichy, and T. Tompson, "Public Opinion on Environmental Policy in the United States," *The Oxford Handbook of US Environmental Policy* (Oxford: Oxford University Press, 2012), 461–486.

16. Battaile, "The 2000 Campaign."

17. Battaile, "The 2000 Campaign."

18. Case, "West Virginia's."

19. Case.

20. Case.

21. Case.

22. Case.

23. Ronald Hardy, "Jesse Johnson Sues Debate Organizers," Green Party Watch, October 4, 2008.

24. Shor and Mccarty, "Ideological Mapping," 530–551.

25. Nick Wing, "Joe Manchin Shoots Cap-and-Trade Bill with Rifle in New Ad (VIDEO)," Huffington Post, accessed March 11, 2019, https://www.huffingtonpost.com/2010/10/11/joe-manchin-ad-dead-aim_n_758457.html.

26. Jeffrey B. Lewis, Keith Poole, Howard Rosenthal, Adam Boche, Aaron Rudkin, and Luke Sonnet, "Congressional Roll-Call Votes Database," Voteview, accessed January 14, 2020.

27. Parker Richards, "West Virginia's One Progressive Party," The American Prospect, accessed March 11, 2019, https://prospect.org/article/west-virginia%E2%80%99s-one-progressive-party.

28. Denise Binion, phone interview by author, March 8, 2019.

29. Binion, phone interview.

30. Binion, phone interview.

31. Richards, "West Virginia's."

32. Binion, phone interview.

33. All voter registration and official election data can be found at "Elections Division," West Virginia Secretary of State Mac Warner, accessed October 10, 2019, https://sos.wv.gov/elections /Pages/default.aspx.

34. Richards, "West Virginia's."

35. All voter registration and official election data can be found at "Elections Division," West Virginia Secretary of State Mac Warner, accessed October 10, 2019, https://sos.wv.gov/elections/Pages/default.aspx.

36. Richards, "West Virginia's."

37. All voter registration and official election data can be found at "Elections Division," West Virginia Secretary of State Mac Warner, accessed October 10, 2019, https://sos.wv.gov/elections/Pages/default.aspx.

38. Binion, phone interview.

39. Binion, phone interview.

40. Richards, "West Virginia's."

41. Richards.

42. Richards.

43. Richards.

44. Roy P. Basler, ed., *The Collected Works of Abraham Lincoln* (New Brunswick, NJ: Rutgers University Press, 1953), 35; "Northwestern Virginia Has Brought Grief and Shame to the State and to the South by Her Woeful Defection," qtd. by Walter H. Taylor, "A Quite Contrary View Of The Actions Of The West Virginians," in *Four Years With General Lee*, ed. James I. Robertson Jr. (Bloomington: Indiana University Press, 1962), 18.

CHAPTER 11

The Moderate Party of Rhode Island

Emily K. Lynch

Deeply rooted in their strong affinity for independence, Rhode Islanders pride themselves on their state's rich political history. The origins of their independence can be traced back to Roger Williams, the state's founder and first leader, and his deeply held beliefs regarding religious freedom. Because of Rhode Islanders' independent character, Rhode Island has not always acted in lockstep with other states. For example, Rhode Island did not ratify the Constitution until 1790, making it the last original colony to do so. It was during the 1700s when Rhode Island was nicknamed "Rogue Island,"[1] and, at times, Rhode Islanders have reflected this description by completely bypassing the main political parties with the election of two third-party governors in the 1800s (Law and Order Party and Union Party) and, more recently, the election of an independent governor in 2010.[2]

Independents are the largest group of registered voters in Rhode Island.[3] The large number of registered unaffiliated voters has greatly benefited the Rhode Island Democratic Party, to the chagrin of the Rhode Island Republican Party, since Democrats have held over 75 percent of the Rhode Island General Assembly seats over the past twenty years. The total amount of registered Republicans is less than one-third of the total amount of registered Democrats. This lack of party competition may have led to an extraordinary number of cases of corruption, which may further strengthen Rhode Islanders' apathy toward the main political parties.[4] The independent nature of the state of Rhode Island has also greatly contributed to the advent of the Moderate Party of Rhode Island, a third party that gained official party status with the state in 2009. Leaders of the Moderate Party took advantage of Rhode Island's current state of politics to reach out to the many independent voters and tackle corruption in the state. Despite the fact that the Moderate Party was an official party in Rhode Island for nearly ten years, the Moderate Party's future looks bleak based on the low levels of voter support for the Moderate gubernatorial candidate in the 2018 election. On February 5, 2019, the Moderate Party of Rhode Island was officially removed as a recognized political party in the state.[5]

This chapter explores the founding, current status, and future of the Moderate Party in Rhode Island. I begin with a brief description of the Moderate Party's political platform and how it differs from the main parties in the state. Next, I explore the main reasons why the Moderate Party exists in Rhode Island—including a discussion of Rhode Island's demographics and party organization. Finally, I examine the Moderate Party's current status in recent elections and its future prospects. The examination of the Moderate Party of Rhode Island contributes to a broader understanding of the US political party system and the factors that influence the growth of parties in the state and at a national level.

THE FOUNDING OF THE MODERATE PARTY

The Moderate Party of Rhode Island was founded by Ken Block, a businessperson who was ready to shake up Rhode Island politics. Block was born in Connecticut in 1965 and graduated from Dartmouth College with a computer science degree.[6] Block's background in writing software serves him well as the president of Simpatico Software Systems, a software company that analyzes large datasets to find inefficiencies and fraud, and Cross Alert Systems, a manufacturing company for intelligent traffic systems.[7] His background in running a software company in Rhode Island was an important factor in his forming a new political party.

In 2007, Block raised awareness about taxes and corruption in Rhode Island. Block discussed how his software business was negatively affected by the state's high tax levels in a letter to the editor of the *Providence Journal* in June 2007.[8] The Moderate Party informally began in December 2007 when Block created a party website, in part due to the positive feedback about the letter he wrote to the *Providence Journal*.[9] Five months later, he wrote another letter to the *Providence Journal* that outlined the immediate goals of the party and encouraged Rhode Islanders to visit the Moderate Party website or write to him to show their support.[10]

Several factors inspired Block to create a third party. As he raised in his 2007 letter to the editor, Block was most concerned with the high tax rate in Rhode Island and the comparably lower cost of living in Massachusetts—both of which he wanted to do something about.[11] Block summarized his impetus in forming the party by stating that "the core of the problem is this: Too much power has been concentrated in the hands of too few people for too long."[12] For example, there was an underfunded public employee benefit system and the absence of a strong statewide economic development strategy. Block also considered a major source of Rhode Island's political problems to be the unmatched power of the general assembly, controlled mostly by the speaker and Senate president.[13] Furthermore, Block posited that many of the Moderate Party supporters are "people who don't necessarily practice party politics, they don't like the status quo, they don't think it's working for them, and they want something different."[14]

Block and Arlene Violet, a former Rhode Island attorney general, formed the Moderate Party's executive committee in 2008. The Moderate Party was busy during their inaugural year. They endorsed thirteen Rhode Island General Assembly candidates, established a party platform, and held fundraising events.[15] That same year, Block formed a political action committee (PAC).[16] The Moderate Party of Rhode Island PAC was registered with the Rhode Island Board of Elections, and Block was chairman and treasurer of this PAC, which has been inactive since October 2012.[17] The Moderate Party of Rhode Island State Committee was recognized a year later and continues to be recognized by the state as a political party committee. Currently, this is the only active Moderate Party organization in Rhode Island.

Block faced major hurdles as he strived to gain official recognition for the Moderate Party. The first was that the Moderate Party was not affiliated with any national political party,[18] which may help with party recognition and resources. Also, the Moderate Party did not have the resources of the main political parties since they did not have any paid staff and no official office in 2009. The party was unable to successfully fundraise because all their efforts would focus on gathering signatures while the other officially recognized parties were able to fundraise freely without having to spend precious campaign time on signature collection.

Block argued that the process of becoming an officially recognized party in Rhode Island was unconstitutional. Rhode Island law did not allow parties to gather petition signatures until the beginning of an election year.[19] Rhode Island general laws allowed parties to be recognized if they 1) nominate a candidate for governor or president in the prior election and the candidate receives at least 5 percent of the vote or 2) follow a strict petition process. The Moderate Party did not nominate a candidate for Rhode Island governor or US president in the 2008 general election. The law also requires the petition to include a number of voters equal to 5 percent of the vote for governor or president in the previous election. Furthermore, all signatures needed to be obtained during the same year the political organization wanted to place the candidate on the ballot. This left a limited window: The Moderate Party had between January 1 and a June 1 deadline to obtain about 30,000 signatures (allowing for extra signatures in case some were declared fraudulent).

In February 2009, the Rhode Island American Civil Liberties Union (ACLU) filed a federal lawsuit against Rhode Island elections officials on behalf of the Moderate Party. First, the Moderate Party argued that it was too arduous to obtain enough signatures to equal 5 percent of the turnout in the previous election. Therefore, they asked for the required number of signatures to be reduced. Ultimately, the court decided that the 5 percent requirement was constitutional and that it was up to the general assembly to revise this threshold. Second, the Moderate Party sought to change the signature collection date time, because if they had to start gathering signatures on the first of January of the election year, they would have little time to prepare for the election. The court decided that the state had no compelling reason to limit the time period for a party to gather signatures. The state's concern was that the new party should use the most recent registration lists to avoid invalid signatures (including voters who moved or died). The court called the state's reasoning "nonsensical."[20] The court recognized that the major parties have an advantage over minor parties with the current set of laws. In conclusion, the US District Court decided:

> There is no question "[t]he American song is one best sung by a plurality of voices." R.I. Chapter of Nat'l Women's Political Caucus, Inc. v. Rhode Island Lottery Comm'n, 609 F. Supp. 1403, 1413 (D.R.I. 1985). Without justification, a January 1 start date unduly silences would-be singers in Rhode Island at a critical stage of the democratic process. Thus, in accordance with the foregoing, JUDGMENT will be entered (1) declaring that the January 1 start date for petition signature collection in R.I. Gen. Laws § 17-1-2(9)(iii) is unconstitutional; and (2) permanently enjoining Defendants from enforcing or applying the start date set forth in § 17-1-2(9)(iii) as a ground for rejecting or refusing to certify signatures collected by the Moderate Party for inclusion on the official Rhode Island election ballot in 2010.[21]

The US district judge ruled in favor of the party in May 2009. By the end of August 2009, the Moderate Party of Rhode Island gathered thirty-four thousand signatures and was officially recognized as a party.[22]

NATIONAL FACTORS AND THE MODERATE PARTY

Many national, state, and local factors have led to the formation, continuance, and electoral performance of the Moderate Party. Nationally, there were two forces that may have had an indirect effect on the development of the Moderate Party in Rhode Island. First, the Great Recession began at the same time the Moderate Party formed. Similar to the rest of the country, Rhode island's unemployment rate in January 2008 increased from 4.7 percent in January 2007 to 6.2 percent to 11.2 percent in January 2012, steadily dropping down to 4.5 percent in January 2018.[23] In reaction to the Obama Presidency and economic recession, the Tea Party movement formed in 2009 that highly criticized President Obama's handling of the recession and opposed government intervention. Because of the Tea Party factions, the Republican Party was being pulled farther to the right, which did not reflect the views of moderate Republicans and independents, especially independents in the Northeast. However, these Republicans and some independents may not have been happy with Democratic candidates, so they were looking for an alternative to the two-party system. The combination of the Great Recession and the Tea Party movement influenced politics throughout the nation. However, these national factors might have had a more pronounced influence on political parties in states like Rhode Island with their unique one-party status. Although national economic and political factors should not be ignored, state and local factors had a strong influence on the formation of the Moderate Party.

THE MODERATE PARTY PLATFORM

Block's overarching message within the Moderate Party platform was simple: reform the Rhode Island General Assembly. According to Block, the Moderate Party's "focus is the General Assembly, where the Party believes that current massive imbalance of power leads to poor legislating. We believe that good governance is the result of compromise and moderation, activities that do not occur when a single party has a 90% majority. That is why we have started this new party."[24] Block was not satisfied with either party— he did not like how the Rhode Island Democrats "had way too much power, it was very unbalanced, and when you have an imbalance of power, regardless of what color tie you wear, you usually end up with problems," and called the Republican Party in Rhode Island "dysfunctional."[25]

The Moderate Party of Rhode Island attempts to serve as a legitimate alternative to the two main parties in Rhode Island. This is apparent in the

Moderate Party's political platform that was published on their party website. The chairman's message states that "politicians should serve the best interests of the majority of the State's residents" while addressing the needs of the "moderate middle" by focusing on the four *E*s: economy, education, ethics, and the environment.[26]

The Moderate Party's first *E*, economy, is based on balancing the budget and pension reform. The party would like to reduce the budget deficit by ending waste and fraud, not by raising taxes. The party supports comprehensive pension reform because the unfunded pension liability is a debilitating issue to economic stability in Rhode Island. Once these issues are resolved, the party believes Rhode Island should look toward providing incentives to companies to relocate to the Ocean State.

The Moderate Party's second *E* is focused on education. The platform includes general plans for recruiting, evaluating, and retaining teachers. Other education reforms include developing a statewide model for a teacher's contract, incorporating vocational and technical education into Rhode Island schools, adding life skills in the school curriculum, and supporting special education. Finally, the Moderate Party supports increasing the number of charter schools (which is supported by the Rhode Island Republican Party) and supports effective preschool models (which is included in the Rhode Island Democratic Party platform). The inclusion of both Democratic- and Republican-supported policies underscores the unique middle position of the Moderate Party.

The Moderate Party's third *E* stands for ethics—specifically, ethical reforms in the legislative assembly. The platform includes specific reforms such as requiring the general assembly to publicize legislation at least thirty days before it is considered, ending the legislative grant process that allows off-budget payouts to organizations, not allowing legislators to take action on issues that favor their own businesses, prosecuting a legislator if he or she is casting a vote illegally or dishonestly, and ending the ability of the general assembly to create magistrate positions and exempting them from the judicial nominating committee process for judgeships. One of the initial goals of the Moderate Party was to end the "master lever," or one-line, straight-party voting, in Rhode Island. The party achieved this goal during the 2014 Rhode Island legislative session, when the state House and senate passed a bill that abolished the "master lever." Block was largely credited for leading the effort behind this legislation.[27]

Finally, since Rhode Island is the second most densely populated state in the country,[28] many of the Moderate Party's priorities focused on the final *E*, the environment. Much of the party platform for the environment is business-centric with a particular focus on land development. The party supports redevelopment in the state's urban areas, including brownfield land. The party also espouses the development in historic villages instead of forested areas, and the party supports zoning laws that encourage village-style development with smaller lot sizes. Additionally, the party supports the purchase and preservation of open spaces.

In stark contrast to the Moderate Party, the Rhode Island Republican and Democratic parties are much better organized, each having active partisan town or city committees throughout the state.[29] The main political parties also have well-developed websites and Facebook pages that provide current monthly meeting and event schedules. The Moderate Party's website does not list any past or future meetings under their "News and Events" tab. Although the Moderate Party has a Facebook page, the party does not have a space devoted to events. Though many of the issues on the Republican and Democratic party platform listed on their websites are similar to Moderate Party goals, issue prioritization varies among the political parties. The Moderate Party's website does not clearly show how their goals are different than other parties. The Moderate Party failed to use the internet as a tool to organize at the grassroots level and distinguish itself from the competition.

RHODE ISLAND: A ONE-PARTY STATE

Rhode Island is characterized as a one-party state because of Democratic Party strength in the general assembly. Rhode Island has been a one-party state since the Civil War, though initially with Republicans as the main party. This situation changed in 1935 when Democrats gained the majority in both houses while holding the governorship.[30] Since this election, Democrats have dominated the Rhode Island political scene.

Democrats have held most positions at the federal level. At the federal level, Rhode Islanders have favored Democrats since the 1930s, with the exception of Republicans John Chafee (elected in 1976) and his son Lincoln Chafee (appointed in 1999 and elected in 2000). Although Lincoln Chafee was a Republican, he was not considered a loyal party member in the US Senate, and he was the only senate Republican to vote against H.J. Res. 114, the Authorization for Use of Military Force Against Iraq Resolution of 2002.[31] Since 1941, Rhode Island has elected only two Republican US representatives: Claudine Schneider, serving from 1981 to 1991, and Ronald Machtley, serving from 1989 to 1995.

Although Democrats dominate Rhode Island politics at the federal level, the governorship has been held by a fair share of Republicans. Rhode Island consistently elected a Republican governor from 1984 until 2010, with the exception of the election of Democrat Bruce Sundlun, who served one term as governor from 1991 to 1995. In 2010, former Republican US senator Lincoln Chafee, running as an independent, was elected as Rhode Island's governor, but in 2013, toward the end of his term, Chafee switched party affiliations to Democrat.

Independent candidates have run for governor in Rhode Island before the emergence of the Moderate Party, but most do not fare well.[32] One independent, Robert Healey Jr., founded the Cool Moose Party in the 1990s, which is not an officially recognized party in Rhode Island. The Cool Moose Party platform focused on "less government intervention, a strict reading of the U.S. Constitution and fiscal conservatism."[33]

Healey gained more support than other third-party candidates in the past few decades. Healey ran for governor and lieutenant governor several times throughout the 1980s until his final run for governor under the Moderate Party ticket in 2014. Healey ran unsuccessfully for governor as an independent in 1986, winning 3 percent of the vote. Healey unsuccessfully ran for governor again in 1994, with 9 percent of the vote, and in 1998, with 6 percent of the vote. This was a time when Ross Perot, a third-party candidate, was popular at the national level, especially in the 1992 and 1996 presidential elections.[34] Although Healey did not win any of the elections, he was successful in his lawsuit against Rhode Island involving third-party candidates in primary elections.[35] Later, Healey ran for lieutenant governor in 2002, 2006, and 2010. During the 2010 election, Healey won 39 percent of the vote for lieutenant governor in 2010, with a campaign promise of abolishing the office if he won.[36] In 2014, Healey became the Moderate Party gubernatorial candidate and spent less than forty dollars on his campaign.[37]

Over the past twenty years, the Rhode Island General Assembly has remained a Democratic supermajority. From 2011 to 2012, Democrats held 76 percent of the senate seats, the lowest level of Democratic control in the twenty-year span (see Table 11.1). From 2005 to 2006, Democrats held 80 percent of the House seats, which was the lowest level of Democratic control during this twenty-year span. Democrats currently control over 80 percent of the House and senate. Despite the high levels of voters who register as unaffiliated in Rhode Island, an independent senator or representative is uncommon. The Rhode Island House and Senate each had four independent members from 1999 to 2019.

Democrats have a large advantage over Republicans and third-party members in Rhode Island, but the largest group of registered voters are independents. Many Rhode Islanders fall in the middle of the ideological

Table 11.1: Partisan Breakdown of the Rhode Island General Assembly

Session	House			Senate		
	Democrat	Republican	Independent	Democrat	Republican	Independent
1999–2000	86	13	1	42	8	0
2001–2002	85	15	0	44	6	0
2003–2004[a]	63	11	1	32	6	0
2005–2006	60	15	0	33	5	0
2007–2008	62	13	0	33	5	0
2009–2010	65	10	0	33	4	1
2011–2012	65	10	0	29	8	1
2013–2014	69	6	0	32	5	1
2015–2016	63	11	1	32	5	1
2017–2018	64	10	1	33	5	0
2019–2020	66	9	0	33	5	0

Source: Rhode Island Department of State.

[a]In 2003, the number of seats in the House and senate decreased (House: 100 to 75; Senate: 50 to 38).

spectrum. According to a recent Gallup poll, 40 percent of Rhode Islanders identified as moderate, ranking Rhode Island as tied with Utah for the fourth most moderate state.[38] Interestingly, there were more self-identified conservatives (29 percent) than liberals (25 percent), which does not reflect the small amount of registered Republicans and large size of registered Democrats. Independents increased in the 1970s through 1990s for several reasons: reduced patronage, leadership and rules reforms in the general assembly, an increase in the average income levels of Rhode Island residents, a shift from living in Providence to living in the suburbs, the semi-closed primary system, and political scandals reported by the *Providence Journal*.[39] Compared to other states, Rhode Island has had one of the highest shares of independent voters since the 1970s.[40] Currently, Rhode Island is one of only eight states that has more registered independents than registered Democrats or Republicans. Of those eight states, based on 2018 state party registrants, Rhode Island is the least politically competitive, due to the relative size of registered Democrats and Republicans.[41]

As of January 2, 2019, there were 320,096 registered Democrats in Rhode Island compared 97,625 Republicans. The largest group is comprised of unaffiliated voters, numbering 365,736 registered voters. [42] The Moderate Party had 4,004 registered voters, the largest number of voters were aged 18 to 30, followed by 30 to 40. About 1,600 residents over the age of 40 are registered as members of the Moderate Party. About two hundred and fifty more men than women are listed as a Moderate Party member (and another 655 Moderates who did not answer the gender question). There is a lack of polling data about the Moderate Party, perhaps because of the lack of political knowledge about the parties in Rhode Island. If a poll included a question about party identification, and included "Moderate" as an option, independents may choose this option because they believe they are centrist but not necessarily a registered member of the official Moderate Party.[43] Most public opinion polls will ask about a Moderate Party candidate. These polls will be discussed in the next section.

It is clear from the current party registration data that party affiliation is weak in Rhode Island. Some voters are still unsorted ideologically, since many older Democrats consist of Rockefeller Republicans and older Republicans are Reagan Democrats.[44] Scott MacKay, a reporter for Rhode Island Public Radio, and Maureen Moakley, professor at the University of Rhode Island, suggested that there could be more support for independent candidates when socially moderate and fiscally conservative Rhode Islanders are unhappy with either major-party candidate.[45] In a discussion about parties in Rhode Island in the *New York Times*, a Republican representative in the Rhode Island General Assembly, Brian Newberry, stated that "lots of Democrats here would be Republicans somewhere else, but they don't feel they can win without a 'D' next to their name."[46] Because of the one-party system in Rhode Island, "lawmakers in both parties get unusual latitude from their party bases for deviation from party orthodoxy."[47]

Several studies have placed Rhode Island at the top of the list of the most Democratic states, which has consequences for its level of polarization and elasticity. FiveThirtyEight's 2012 presidential voting index ranked Rhode Island as the fourth most Democratic state (behind Hawaii, Vermont, and New York).[48] FiveThirtyEight labeled Rhode Island as the second most elastic state in the country, because Rhode Island has many swing voters that consist of independent voters, and Rhode Island was ranked first in earlier elasticity score rankings.[49] If the swing voters are happy with the Democratic candidate, the Democrats will easily win the election. But if they are not happy with the Democratic candidate, then independents and Republicans could gather support for the best Republican or independent candidate.[50] Rhode Island is also the least polarized state, measured as having the least ideological differences between Republican and Democratic lawmakers, using roll-call voting data and survey data about a variety of economic, social, domestic, and foreign issues.[51] The "median Democrat in Rhode Island was more conservative than in all but 13 state legislatures."[52] These characteristics make party politics messier than other states. Legislative action would be more predictable based on a legislator's party status in other states that are more polarized and less elastic.

Rhode Island does not have large populations of individuals with characteristics that predict strong party affiliations, such as African Americans or evangelicals, but religion plays a large role in Rhode Island politics.[53] Roman Catholics are typically viewed as swing voters, and "the only group of Catholics that has been divided in recent elections is white Catholics who identify as moderate."[54] In 2014, Pew's Religious Landscape Study estimated that 42 percent of the Rhode Island population is Catholic (compared to the national average of 20 percent).[55] Rhode Island has the largest percentage of Catholics out of all the states.[56] Furthermore, Rhode Island racial demographics are very homogenous. Census estimates for 2018 show that whites make up 84 percent of the Rhode Island population.[57]

ELECTORAL HISTORY

The Moderate Party has fared poorly in elections. The following section includes a brief overview of public opinion polls and election results from several years (2010 to 2018) since the Moderate Party was recognized in 2009.

2010

Ken Block, the Moderate Party candidate for governor in 2010, was in a crowded race. The gubernatorial election was an open seat since Republican governor Donald Carcieri was completing his second term. Frank Caprio, the general treasurer under Carcieri, was the Democratic nominee. Caprio, a Democrat, won the general treasurer election in 2006 with 73 percent of the votes. Another colleague of Carcieri's, John Robitaille, his senior advisor of communications, ran on the Republican ticket. Lincoln Chafee, former Republican US Senator, ran for governor as an independent. In addition to these top four candidates, three independent gubernatorial candidates ran for office that year. In an October 2010 survey conducted by Fleming & Associates, Chafee was ahead with 33 percent support, Robitaille and Caprio were tied with 26 percent, and Block was polling at 4 percent.[58] Block garnered more support from men than women (6.2 percent versus 2.5 percent) and more support among the youngest group than the oldest respondents (ages 18 to 39: 6.4 percent; 60+: 1.8 percent). And, about the same number of Republicans and independents supported Block (6 percent and 6.7 percent, respectively), with little support from Democrats (1 percent).

Independent and Moderate candidates had more support at lower-level offices, such as lieutenant governor and attorney general. Elizabeth Roberts, a Democrat, ran against Robert Healey, an independent, and Robert Venturini, another independent in the lieutenant governor election. Fleming & Associates polls showed that Healey had sizeable support (35 percent) but slightly trailed Roberts (42 percent). Christopher Little, the Moderate Party candidate for attorney general, was polling at 12 percent support, behind Democrat Peter Kilmartin (33 percent) and Republican Erik Wallin (19 percent).

The Moderate Party may have had a slight chance to displace the weak Rhode Island Republican Party, but the difficulties remained as they do with any third party without the resources of the main parties. The Moderate Party was not as organized or well-funded, nor did they have the rich loyal ties common of the established political parties. Of the 342,940 votes cast for Rhode Island governor in 2010, the independent candidate, Lincoln Chafee, garnered 123,571 votes, winning the governorship. Instead of choosing a middle-of-the road candidate, Chafee may have won because Rhode Islanders wanted a governor more liberal than both the Democratic and Republican nominees.[59] John Robitaille, the Republican candidate, finished second with 114,911 votes followed by the Democratic candidate Frank Caprio with 78,896 votes, and then Moderate Party candidate Block was next with 22,146 votes (6.5 percent). In the lieutenant governor race, Healey won 39 percent of the vote, but it was not enough to beat Elizabeth Roberts. Christopher Little, a Moderate, lost the attorney general race with 14.4 percent of the votes.[60] In addition, four Moderate Party candidates ran for state representative seats and subsequently lost. Three candidates ran for representative seats in the Rhode Island General Assembly for Districts 19, 20, and 21, which cover Warwick and Cranston, the second and third largest cities in Rhode Island, respectively. In Districts 19 and 20, the Moderate Party candidates came in third behind the Democrat and Republican candidates. Richard Lavallee, the Moderate Party candidate for District 21 in Warwick, gained 39.6 percent of the vote because it was a two-party race without a Republican candidate. Thomas Browning, the only other Moderate Party candidate for the general assembly, ran for the District 36 representative seat (which includes the small towns of Charlestown, New Shoreham, South Kingstown, and Westerly) and lost to a Democrat but gained an impressive 36.9 percent of the vote because there was no Republican candidate. The final Moderate Party candidate ran for a seat on the Cranston Council for Ward 3. Joseph Paul Rhodes lost to a Democrat, yet he garnered more votes than the Republican candidate.

2012

The Moderate Party failed to recruit many candidates to run for general assembly seats. Similarly, the Republican Party failed to find candidates to run for all seats, and every year, dating back as early as the 1970s, a sizeable number of Democrats run in an unchallenged race.[61] In 2012, four Moderate Party candidates ran for local and state office. The Moderate candidate Nicholas S. Gelfuso lost to the Democratic candidate in the two-way race for the District 16 state senate seat in Central Falls and Pawtucket. In District 65 for East Providence, Joseph Botelho Jr., the Moderate Party candidate, lost to the Democratic candidate in a two-way race. A Moderate Party candidate was last in a race with six candidates, and all five of the Republican candidates earned seats on the town council of East Greenwich. South Kingstown residents elected four Democrats and one independent, leaving behind several other candidates, including Thomas Browning, who had run for the representative seat in 2010. Browning was ahead of one Republican candidate.

2014

Strategically, Block decided to run for governor in 2014 as a Republican. Block switched affiliations from the party that he founded because he felt Rhode Islanders did not know enough about the Moderate Party. He realized that starting a third party may not be an effective way to change Rhode Island politics.[62] Robert James Spooner decided to run as the Moderate Party candidate because he did not want to see the Moderate Party disappear. However, he withdrew from the race due to health issues.[63] Moderate Party chairperson William Gilbert appointed Healey to take Spooner's place. Healey became the Moderate Party's 2014 gubernatorial candidate when the Rhode Island Board of Elections ruled that his candidacy was legitimate, after objections made by the Republican Party.[64]

In 2014, Healey, running as the Moderate candidate, had 8.1 percent support in an October 2014 poll, with Democratic candidate Gina Raimondo, the general treasurer, in the lead (41.8 percent support), Cranston Mayor Allan Fung as the Republican candidate close behind (35.6 percent), and Kate Fletcher and Leon Kayarian (both independents with less than 1 percent) trailing behind Healey.[65] In the election, Raimondo won with 40.7 percent of the votes, Fung with 36 percent, and Healey with 21.4 percent of the vote. Healey's strong showing in this race may have been fueled by significant union support. Many municipal union members felt betrayed by Raimondo due to her recent stewardship, as state treasurer, of the state pension reform.[66]

There were few additional Moderate Party candidates in 2014. Other Moderate Party candidates included William Gilbert, running for lieutenant governor, earning 8.33 percent of the vote. The only other Moderate Party candidate was Paul Caianiello, who lost in a Rhode Island General Assembly race for representative in District 26, with 6.5 percent of the vote, falling behind the Republican and Democratic candidates.

2016

No Moderate Party candidates ran for general assembly seats in 2016. According to Gilbert, Moderate Party leaders decided that the best strategy was to put their efforts into preparing for the 2018 elections instead of focusing on the 2016 races. The Moderate Party attempted to build the party through monthly meetings, with thirty to forty members in attendance.[67]

2018

In 2018, Fleming & Associates conducted gubernatorial election polls for WPRI 12/Roger Williams University. A survey question asked: "If the election for governor was being held today and the candidates were Democrat Gina Raimondo, Republican Allan Fung, Moderate William Gilbert, Independents Anne Armstrong, Joe Trillo and Luis Muñoz, who would you vote for—Raimondo, Fung, Gilbert, Armstrong, Trillo or Muñoz?" Moderate Party candidate William Gilbert was polling at 1.7 percent in the final months leading up to the election, with the highest support in February (2.1 percent). Other third-party candidates ran for governor, including Anne Armstrong of the Compassion Party, who had the same amount of support as Gilbert in October, and Joe Trillo, an independent who gained a lot of publicity during the campaign (one newsworthy event was a boat mishap while campaigning off the Rhode Island shoreline) who was polling at 9.4 percent in October. Luis Munoz, an independent candidate, had 0.5 percent support in the October poll. The incumbent, Gina Raimondo (44.5 percent), and Republican challenger, Allan Fung (33.7 percent), were polling ahead of Gilbert and the independent candidates. In the same survey poll, 2.5 percent of the male respondents supported Gilbert versus 0.9 percent of female respondents. The age group with the largest supporter for Gilbert was the 18 to 39 age group, with 3.7 percent of the vote (versus 1.7 percent of the 40 to 59 age group and 0.7 percent of respondents aged 60+). There were slightly more Democrats (2.6 percent) than Republicans (1.7 percent) who said they would support the Moderate Party candidate.

While Gilbert's campaign platform focused on "The Four Es" of the Moderate Party, he also focused his attention on other policies. These policies included eliminating the minimum corporate tax; centralizing business inspections; creating enterprise zones to encourage business relocations to Rhode Island; coordinating regionalization of cities and towns; creating a statewide internship program for Rhode Island businesses, high schools, and colleges; decriminalizing recreational marijuana, and eliminating the lieutenant governor position (which Healey had advocated for in his campaigns).

The 2018 election results clearly revealed strong support for the Democratic incumbent, Gina Raimondo (52 percent), with Cranston mayor Allan Fung trailing (37.2 percent). The independent candidate Joseph Trillo (4.4 percent) was more popular than Gilbert (2.7 percent), and the other third-party candidates, independent Luis Daniel Munoz (1.7 percent) and Compassion Party candidate Anne Armstrong (1.1 percent), had the least support.

The lieutenant governor Moderate candidate Joel Hellmann was behind the other main party candidates, with 3.1 percent of the vote. Other Moderate Party candidates lost, with Rufus Bailey running for the Representative seat for District 51, earning 35 percent of the vote (versus a Democratic candidate earning 64 percent). In the school committee town of North Kingstown, Tony Jones lost with 24.9 percent of the vote.

THE FUTURE OF THE MODERATE PARTY

The Moderate Party is no longer recognized as an official Rhode Island party. According to an official order of the Board of Elections, and in accordance with Rhode Island law, the Rhode Island Moderate Party lost official party status because it did not earn 5 percent of the vote in the 2018 gubernatorial election. No Moderate Party members attended the Board of Elections meeting in protest.[68] Municipalities will have to inform registered Moderates that they will now be listed as "unaffiliated."[69] The party will have to circulate another petition if they would like to continue as an official party. Gilbert made it clear that the Moderate Party has not gone away.[70] Gilbert has been contacted by a third party with national recognition, but he is unsure if the Rhode Island Moderate Party's goals align with their goals. In the *Block v. Mollis* decision, the US District Court discussed the difficulties third parties face in remaining a viable party:

> The legislature has made continuous party status, similar to what the Democrats and Republicans enjoy, almost impossible to achieve without running a candidate for Governor in each cycle. Mr. Block's goal of being primarily a "General Assembly" party may prove to be overly optimistic because to do so will require a petition effort in each election cycle. Whether this is fair or good policy is not for this Court to decide. But it does show that the Plaintiffs' burden is even greater because it is an ongoing burden—one that would likely relegate them to a perpetual late start in the competition for money and votes, which in turn would ensure they never get too successful. This too is somewhat ironic given that the other "major" party—the Republican—is frequently unable to muster candidates for the General Assembly.[71]

The laws, carefully laid out in a one-party state, make it extremely challenging for a third party to gain power. The Moderate Party faced the same

Table 11.2: Straight Party Voting

	2010	2012	2014
Democrat	27,573	74,287	34,118
Moderate	6,441	9,295	7,042
Republican	11,781	21,128	11,180

Source: State of Rhode Island Board of Elections.

hurdles as the Republican Party, in that they were unable to find candidates to run in local and state elections. Only a handful of Moderate candidates ran for state and local offices, making it near impossible to build name recognition and trust with voters that they desperately needed.

Although William Gilbert fared worse in the 2018 election than Block or Healey in the 2010 and 2014 elections, respectively, trends in voter registration over time may indicate that support for the Moderate Party was slowly increasing. Upon the Moderate Party's inception in 2009, about six hundred residents had registered as members of the Moderate Party.[72] This number rose to about fifteen hundred registered Moderates in 2013.[73] In October 2018, a poll directed by John Della Volpe of Harvard for GoLocal Prov showed 6 percent of the survey respondents considered themselves affiliated with the Moderate Party.[74] By 2019, the number of registered Moderate Party members was just over four thousand.

Table 11.2 shows straight-party voting totals for the 2010, 2012, and 2014 elections before the "master lever" was abolished.[75] The numbers show two interesting patterns. First, the number of straight-party voters for the Moderate Party in each election greatly exceeded the estimated number of registered Moderate Party members at that time. Secondly, straight-party voting increased for the Moderate Party when comparing the 2010 and 2014 elections. The number of straight-party voting for the Democratic Party also increased, but it dropped for the Republican Party. There was a drop in the number of straight-party voters for all parties between 2012 and 2014, due to the large voter turnout during a presidential election. Another notable point is that thousands of voters used the "master lever" to vote for the Moderate Party in 2012 when there were only a handful of Moderate Party candidates in a few districts or towns. Ironically, Block used his own party's success in "master lever" voter turnout to prove a point, that residents were voting for a party without any associated Moderate Party candidates on the ballot.[76]

A large portion of Moderate Party members are young adults who have had less time to develop a deep loyalty to a specific political party. Perhaps if the Moderate Party had the chance to build up their party resources by fundraising and recruiting strong candidates they could become a more viable party.[77] Bill Gilbert, who lost the 2018 gubernatorial race, suggested that one of the reasons the Moderate Party failed to gain 5 percent of the votes needed to remain an officially recognized party was because of party polarization due to the "Trump effect."[78] Also, he believed that the Rhode Island media was to blame for the Moderate Party's poor performance. For example, Gilbert was excluded from the first televised debate because he did not meet some of the television company's invitation criteria, including having a campaign headquarters and accepting campaign contributions.[79]

The Moderate Party did contribute to the discussion of important issues in Rhode Island. In particular, the party was an integral part of successfully eliminating the "master lever" on election ballots.[80] This may be due to the ease at which the Moderate Party could communicate this concern about straight-ticket voting to the Rhode Island electorate because Block was a vocal opponent of the "master lever," making this a top reform issue for the party; he received a fair share of media publicity about it.[81] Some of the other ethics reforms on the Moderate Party platform are reforms that are more complicated issues that the general public may not easily grasp, such as the consequences of the legislative grant process that allows off-budget payouts to organizations. Better framing and messaging of specific policy goals would benefit the Moderate Party.

For the Moderate Party to survive in Rhode Island, it must act like the established parties and keep loyal voters. First and foremost, the Moderate Party must gain enough petition signatures so they are once again recognized as an official party and can recruit candidates. The party's efforts should turn to finding leaders who are willing and able to market the party with effective messages and reach out to the large group of independent voters, which means focusing on the socially moderate and fiscally conservative voters who seem to be searching for a political party in Rhode Island. Furthermore, party leaders must be willing to fundraise. The Moderate Party must also develop a stronger rationale for why the state needs a third party and how it is different than the Rhode Island Democratic and Republican parties. Without these efforts, the Moderate Party, already no longer officially recognized by the state, will cease to exist in any form in Rhode Island.

NOTES

1. Samantha Payne, "Rogue Island: The Last State to Ratify the Constitution," US National Archives: Pieces of History, accessed February 14, 2019, https://pro logue.blogs.archives.gov/2015/05/18/rogue-island-the-last-state-to-ratify-the-consti tution/.

2. David Gillespie, *Politics at the Periphery: Third Parties in Two-Party America* (Columbia: University of South Carolina Press, 1993).

3. From the January 2, 2019, Rhode Island Registered Voter File, provided by the Rhode Island Department of State.

4. Oguzhan Dincer and Michael Johnston, "Measuring Illegal and Legal Corruption in American States: Some Results from the Corruption in America Survey," Harvard University: Edmond J. Safra Center for Ethics, December 1, 2014, accessed February 14, 2019, https://ethics.harvard.edu/blog/measuring-illegal-and-legal -corruption-american-states-some-results-safra.

5. Based on the State of Rhode Island Board of Elections Order on February 5, 2019, shared with author via email by Miguel Nunez, the Deputy Director of Elections in Rhode Island, February 8, 2019.

6. Kate Nagle, "Ken Block to Run for Rhode Island Governor as Republican," GOLOCALProv, October 28, 2013, https://www.golocalprov.com/news/ken-block -to-run-for-rhode-island-governor-as-republican/.

7. "About," Simpatico Software, accessed January 14, 2020, http://simpatico software.com/about/ and http://www.crossalert.com/index.html.

8. Ken Block, "Less Onerous Taxes Only 10 Miles Away," *Providence Journal*, June 12, 2007, B-5.

9. Block v. Mollis, 618 F. Supp. 2d 142 (D.R.I. 2009)

10. Ken Block, "Rhode Island Needs a Moderate Party," *Providence Journal*, October 26, 2007, B-5.

11. Bill Bartholomew and Ken Block, "Ken Block (RI Political Watchdog, Businessman, Former Gubernatorial Candidate)," Newport Buzz: The Bartholomewtown Podcast, May 17, 2018, http://www.thenewportbuzz.com/the-bartholomew town-podcast-a-conversation-with-ri-political-watchdog-businessman-ken-block /15611.

12. Block, "Rhode Island," B-5.

13. Bartholomew and Block, "Ken Block."

14. Bartholomew and Block.

15. Block v. Mollis.

16. "Filing Reporting," State of Rhode Island and Providence Plantations Campaign Finance Electronic Reporting & Tracking System, accessed January 2019, http://www.ricampaignfinance.com/RIPublic/Filings.aspx.

17. "Filing Reporting," State of Rhode Island.)

18. Block v. Mollis.

19. Block v. Mollis.

20. Block v. Mollis, 7.

21. Block v. Mollis.

22. "Moderate Party," Internet Archive WayBack Machine, accessed January 14, 2020, https://web.archive .org/web/20121112082226/http://rhodeisland.onpolitix .com/parties/7/moderate -party.

23. "Rhode Island Historic Unemployment Rates Seasonally Adjusted," Labor Market Information, RI Department of Labor and Training, accessed January 14, 2020, http://www.dlt.ri.gov /lmi/laus/state/histadj.htm.

24. "Suit Filed Over Restrictive State Ballot Access Law," Open Government Voting Rights, American Civil Liberties Union of Rhode Island, February 3, 2009, http://www.riaclu.org/news/post/suit-filed-over-restrictive-state-ballot-access-law.

25. Bartholomew and Block, "Ken Block."

26. "Home," Moderate Party of Rhode Island, accessed January 14, 2020, http://rimoderateparty.org/.

27. Randal Edgar, "Bill Abolishing R.I.'s 'Master Lever' signed into law by Chafee," *Providence Journal*, July 2, 2014.

28. "Most Densely Populated U.S. States," World Atlas, April 25, 2017, accessed February 14, 2019, https://www.worldatlas.com/articles/most-densely-populated -u-s-states.html.

29. "General Reports," Rhode Island Campaign Finance, Rhode Island Board of Elections, accessed January 2019, http://www.ricampaignfinance.com/RIPublic /Reports.aspx.

30. Maureen Moakley and Elmer Cromwell, *Rhode Island Politics and Government* (Lincoln: University of Nebraska, 2001).

31. "Legislation and Records," Vote Statistics, United States Senate, accessed January 14, 2020, https://www.senate.gov/legislative/LIS/roll_call_lists/roll_call _vote_cfm.cfm?congress=107 &session=2&vote=00237#position.

32. "Rhode Island Political Parties," Vote Smart, accessed January 14, 2020, https://votesmart.org/political-parties/RI#.XDsod1xKg2w.

33. Jacqueline Tempera, "Cool Moose Party Founder Robert Healey, RI Original, Has Died," *Providence Journal*, March 21, 2016.

34. Lori Salotto, "Cool Moose Party Records," Rhode Island Historical Society, April 2001, accessed February 14, 2019, http://www.rihs.org/mssinv/Mss1058.htm.

35. Salotto, "Cool Moose"; Cool Moose Party v. State of Rhode Island, 98-1874, 98-1875 (1st Cir. 1999), accessed February 2019, https://caselaw.findlaw.com/us -1st-circuit/1260701.html.

36. Tempera, "Cool Moose Party"; "2010 General Election," State of Rhode Island Election Results, Board of Elections, accessed January 14, 2020, https://www .ri.gov/election/results /2010/general_election/.

37. Tempera, "Cool Moose Party."

38. Jeffrey M. Jones, "Conservatives Greatly Outnumber Liberals in 19 U.S. States," Gallup, February 22, 2019, https://news.gallup.com/poll/247016/conser vatives-greatly-outnumber-liberals-states.aspx.

39. Maureen Moakley and Elmer Cromwell, *Rhode Island Politics and Government* (Lincoln: University of Nebraska, 2001).

40. Moakley and Cromwell, *Rhode Island.*

41. Rhodes Cook, "Registering by Party: Where the Democrats and Republicans Are Ahead," University of Virginia's Center for Politics, Sabato's Crystal Ball, July 12, 2018, http://www.centerforpolitics.org/crystalball/articles/registering-by-party -where-the-democrats-and-republicans-are-ahead/. Neighbors Connecticut and Massachusetts are the closest, with Democrats outnumbering Republicans by almost 2:1 in Connecticut and 3:1 in Massachusetts.

42. From the January 2, 201,9 Rhode Island Registered Voter File, provided by the Rhode Island Department of State.

43. Joe Fleming, Fleming & Associates, which conducts political polls in Rhode Island, phone conversation with author, February 1, 2019.

44. Micah Cohen, "Rhode Island: The Most Elastic State," FiveThirtyEight, October 18, 2012, accessed February 14, 2019, https://fivethirtyeight.com/features /rhode-island-the-most-elastic-state/.

45. Cohen, "Rhode Island."

46. Josh Barro, "Welcome to Rhode Island, America's Least Polarized State," *New York Times*, August 14, 2014.

47. Barro, "Welcome to Rhode Island."

48. Cohen, "Rhode Island."

49. Nathaniel Rakich and Nate Silver, "Election Update: The Most (and Least) Elastic States and Districts," FiveThirtyEight, September 6, 2018, https://fivethirty eight.com/features/election-update-the-house-districts-that-swing-the-most-and-least -with-the-national-mood/; Cohen, "Rhode Island."

50. Nate Silver, "Swing Voters and Elastic States," FiveThirtyEight, May 21, 2012, https://fivethirtyeight.com/features/swing-voters-and-elastic-states/.

51. Boris Short, "Colorado Passes California for the Polarization Crown," Boris Shor (blog), January 6, 2017, https://research.bshor.com/blog/; Boris Shor and Nolan McCarty, "The Ideological Mapping of American Legislatures," *American Political Science Review* 105, no. 3 (2011): 530–551.

52. Barro, "Welcome to Rhode Island.".

53. Cohen, "Rhode Island."

54. "The Catholic Swing Vote," Pew Research Center, October 11, 2012, http://www.pewforum.org/2012/10/11/the-catholic-swing-vote/.

55. "Religious Landscape Study," Pew Research Center, accessed February 14, 2019, http://www.pewforum.org/religious-landscape-study/state/rhode-island/.

56. "U.S. States by Population of Catholics," World Atlas, October 25, 2017, https://www.worldatlas.com/articles/us-states-by-population-of-catholics.html.

57. "QuickFacts Rhode Island," United States Census Bureau, accessed January 2019, https://www.census.gov/quickfacts/ri.

58. Joe Fleming, Fleming & Associates, private email with author, February 1, 2019.

59. Barro, "Welcome to Rhode Island."

60. "Election 2010: Rhode Island," *New York Times*, accessed January 14, 2020, https://www.nytimes.com /elections/2010/results/rhode-island.html.

61. Maureen Moakley and Elmer Cornwell, *Rhode Island Politics and Government* (Lincoln: University of Nebraska Press, 2001), 137, tbl. 10.

62. Bartholomew and Block, "Ken Block."

63. Jessica Boisclair, "Spooner Jumped in to Keep Moderate Party Afloat," Valley Breeze, September 24, 2014, http://www.valleybreeze.com/2014-09-24/cumber land-lincoln-area/spooner-jumped-keep-moderate-party-afloat#.XEzKd1xKg2w.

64. Katherine Gregg, "Healey Wins GOP Challenge to His Moderate Party Candidacy for R.I. Governor/Poll," *Providence Journal*, September 17, 2014.

65. Joe Fleming, Fleming & Associates, private email with author, February 1, 2019.

66. Dylan Matthews, "Why Most Union Members Are Backing a Republican for Governor of Rhode Island," Vox, October 16, 2014, https://www.vox.com/2014/10 /16/6988457/union-rhode-island-raimondo-fung-taylor-mckee-afl-cio; Katharine Q. Seelye, "Defying Unions, Democrat Gina M. Raimondo Vies to become Rhode Island's First Female Governor," *New York Times*, September 14, 2014.

67. Bill Gilbert, private phone interview with author, March 6, 2019.

68. Patrick Anderson and Katherine Gregg, "Political Scene: Brown Academics' Study on R.I. Voter ID Law Raises Questions," *Providence Journal*, accessed February 14, 2019, https://www.providencejournal.com/news/20190210/political-scene -brown-academics-study-on-ri-voter-id-law-raises-questions.

69. "Moderate Party Loses Its Status as a Party in Rhode Island," *Providence Journal*, February 11, 2019, https://www.providencejournal.com/ZZ/news/20190211 /moderate-party-loses-its-status-as-party-in-rhode-island.

70. Bill Gilbert, private phone interview with author, March 6, 2019.

71. Block v. Mollis.

72. Block v. Mollis.

73. "Moderate Party Withers in RI, Fate of Many Parties," Turn to 10, September 16, 2015, https://turnto10.com/archive/moderate-party-withers-in-ri-fate of many -parties.

74. "GoLocalProv/Harvard's Della Volpe Poll: Raimondo Has Modest Lead over Fung, Trillo Big Factor," GOLOCALProv, October 12, 2018, https://www.go localprov.com/politics/golocalprov-harvards-della-volpe-poll-governors-race-nearly -a-dead-heat.

75. "General Reports," Rhode Island Campaign Finance, Rhode Island Board of Elections, accessed March 2019, http://www.elections.ri.gov/elections/prere sults/.

76. Michael McKinney, "Block Says 9,000 Voters Used Master Lever for Moderate Party—with No Party Candidates on Ballot," Politifact, February 22, 2013, https://www.politifact.com/rhode-island/statements/2013/feb/22/kenneth-block /block-says-moderate-party-has-lots-votes/.

77. Marjorie Randon Hershey, *Party Politics in America*, 11th ed. (New York: Pearson, 2005).

78. Bill Gilbert, private phone interview with author, March 6, 2019.

79. Katherine Gregg, "Moderate Party's Gilbert Protests His Exclusion from Gubernatorial Debate," *Providence Journal*, September 18, 2018, https://www.providencejournal.com/news/20180918/moderate-partys-gilbert-protests-his-exclusion-from-gubernatorial-debate.

80. Randal Edgar, "Bill Abolishing R.I.'s 'Master Lever' Signed into Law by Chafee," *Providence Journal*, July 2, 2014, https://www.providencejournal.com/breaking-news/content/20140702-bill-abolishing-r.i.s-master-lever-signed-into-law-by-chafee.ece.

81. For example, see McKinney, "Block says 9,000; Edgar, "Bill Abolishing."

CHAPTER 12

The United Utah Party

Richard Davis

The newest party described in this book is the United Utah Party. Like the American Party and the Moderate Party of Rhode Island, the United Utah Party is a centrist political party appealing to moderates who have become disenchanted with the extremism they see in the two major parties. Since it was formed only in May 2017, its electoral history is short. In fact, its history, generally, is short. This chapter will describe the party's electoral performance and appeal, as well as its future. But first, the party will be put into context through a discussion of the historical background of political parties, including minor parties, in Utah, as well as an analysis of the contemporary political environment that produced the United Utah Party.

HISTORICAL BACKGROUND

Utah is unique among states due to the strong influence of one religious denomination: the Church of Jesus Christ of Latter-day Saints (LDS), more frequently known as the Mormon Church. The state was founded by Mormon pioneers in 1847 and church members (today known as Latter-day Saints) still dominate the state's population as well as its governance. Six out of ten Utahns consider themselves Latter-day Saints, as do 90 percent of state legislators. Policies in which the LDS Church weighs in are usually adopted by Utah's governor and legislature.[1]

In the 1970s, the LDS Church began to take socially conservative positions on national cultural issues, including opposition to the Equal Rights Amendment and liberalized abortion laws. By the 1990s, the LDS Church began to oppose gay rights legislation and efforts to legalize same-sex marriage. Some church leaders also expressed opposition to federal government programs to foster economic conservatism among members.

This shift in the LDS Church's political engagement spilled over into Utah politics. At one time, Utah had been a bellwether state. Between 1920 and 1968, Utah had not voted with the winner of the presidential election in only one election (1960). However, from the 1970s on, Utah morphed into a reliably Republican-controlled state as Latter-day Saints identified with a Republican Party that mirrored the LDS Church's socially conservative issue stances, while Democrats generally opposed them.[2]

The increasingly lopsided nature of the competition between Republicans and Democrats meant that Utahns faced little or no electoral choice by the end of the twentieth century and the beginning of the twenty-first as Democrats' competitiveness across the state deteriorated. That was a dramatic departure from Utah's vigorous two-party competition that had occurred from statehood in 1896 until the 1970s. That two-party competition occasionally included other parties.

Indeed, minor parties have not been uncommon in Utah. Initially, it was the two major parties that were insignificant in Utah territorial politics. The largest political party in the Utah Territory during the middle-to-late 1800s was the People's Party, which was dominated by the LDS Church, while its opposition was the Liberal Party. It consisted primarily of those opposing the political dominance of the LDS Church. The two major parties did not form until the 1890s when the LDS Church called for the dismantling of the People's Party and the division of its members into the two major parties.[3]

An early successful minor party was the Socialist Party, which formed in the first decade of the twentieth century in Utah. The Socialists elected over one hundred public officials throughout the state between 1900 and 1920. The Socialist presidential candidate, Eugene Debs, received 8 percent of the vote in Utah in the 1912 election.[4]

In 1936, a group of citizens led by radio personality Father Charles Coughlin formed the Union Party to oppose President Franklin Roosevelt's reelection. A Utah chapter was created and petitioned to place the Union Party's candidate, William Lemke, on the ballot. The Union Party and its Utah branch disappeared after the 1936 election.[5]

The American Independent Party registered in Utah in conjunction with the candidacy of George Wallace in 1968 and won 6 percent of the vote. The 1972 candidate won approximately the same vote total. However, the party disappeared in Utah by the 1990s.

Ross Perot's independent candidacy took second place in Utah in 1992, beating Democratic candidate Bill Clinton. Four years later, Perot's Reform

Party won 10 percent. However, that party disappeared after disappointing results in the 2000 election.

Currently, in addition to United Utah, registered minor parties include the Libertarian Party, the Independent American Party, the Constitution Party, and the Green Party. The Libertarian Party has competed in Utah since the 1970s, although it has not won a partisan election. The Independent American Party and the Constitution Party are conservative parties— one regional in nature, while the other is national and runs presidential candidates. Neither has won elections in Utah. The most recent party, the Green Party, is the chapter of the national progressive party.

Utah requires political parties to gain at least 2 percent of the vote cast for a US Senate candidate or the aggregate of 2 percent of the vote for all congressional candidates. These minor parties typically barely cross that threshold. In 2018, both the Independent American Party and the Green Party did not do so and lost their ballot access.

THE CONTEMPORARY ENVIRONMENT FOR A NEW PARTY

The United Utah Party's organizers filed for official party status in Utah in May 2017. However, the origins of the party go back further, when several political leaders involved in the Democratic and Republican Parties met in the fall of 2016 to discuss a solution to the political situation in Utah. They had become disgruntled with the perceived extremism of the two major parties. One member of the group had been a Republican state legislator, while another had been a centrist Democratic gubernatorial candidate who had lost that year to a liberal candidate who, in turn, received only 28 percent of the vote in the general election. Yet another was a former Democratic county party chair who had run unsuccessfully for state party chair.[6]

Growing developments within the two major parties served as an impetus for the meeting. On one side, Utah Republicans had become dominated by two factions in continual conflict over the direction of the party. One faction consisted of more mainstream Republicans who were business oriented and shared national Republican economic views regarding tax cuts and less business regulation. Their leaders included former governor Mike Leavitt, former governor Jon Huntsman, and the late governor Olene Walker. On the other side were more socially conservative as well as more libertarian-leaning Republicans. Most were allied with the Eagle Forum, a socially conservative lobbying group initially founded by Phyllis Schlafly. It had become a powerful force within Utah Republican circles. Their leaders included US senator Mike Lee and US representative Jason Chaffetz.

The tensions in the Utah Republican Party led to an effort by the more mainstream faction to alter the nomination process to facilitate the nomination of more moderate candidates.[7] Utah's caucus/convention system rules nearly choked off competition within the party. More extremist delegates were able to defeat more moderate candidates at the convention and then deny them the opportunity to even compete in a primary because those candidates could not meet the 40 percent threshold to call a primary. That threshold, which was high for a convention system, led to the convention defeat of more moderate candidates, such as US senator Bob Bennett in 2010 and governor Olene Walker in 2004.

Calling their organization Count My Vote, the mainstream Republicans began the process of a citizen initiative to create a primary bypass mechanism that stripped the party caucus/convention process of the ability to determine a party nominee. After reaching a compromise with Utah legislators, the legislature passed a bill maintaining some power for the caucus/convention system but allowing candidates to bypass the convention and move straight to the primary after collecting a significant number of petition signatures.

The Utah Republican Party began a lengthy, contentious lawsuit intended to overturn the law and return the nomination process to its previous state. The suit split the party and led to dissatisfaction among many Republicans over the machinations of the two factions, particularly the extremists. Large donors began to withdraw funding from the party, and party registration fell as some people left the party in disgust. The GOP division weakened party ties and offered the environment for a new alternative.[8]

While Republicans experienced an increasingly powerful pull to the ideological right, Utah Democrats were affected by national trends tilting the Democratic Party to the ideological left. Utah Democrats were perceived as out of touch with Utah voters on issues such as abortion and same-sex marriage. Additionally, the quasisocialist economic positions of presidential candidate Bernie Sanders were gaining traction within the Utah Democratic Party, again in opposition to the economically moderate-to-conservative Utah electorate.[9]

Moreover, Democratic Party candidates often made statements or took actions that offended large segments of voters who belonged to the LDS Church. In 2016, the Democratic gubernatorial candidate sponsored a fundraising event in conjunction with a play that disparaged LDS beliefs.[10] In the same election, the party's US senate candidate used a debate at Brigham Young University, the LDS Church-owned university, to criticize the university's policies toward same-sex marriage.[11]

From the 1970s on, Utah increasingly became a one-party state. No Democrat had won statewide office since 1996. Indeed, since 2004, no Democratic candidate for statewide office had garnered more than one-third of the vote. For several decades, the legislature had been two-thirds to three-quarters Republican.

The imbalance in two-party competition had led Utah Democrats to be perceived as more insular and less responsive to the issue concerns of Utahns outside of traditionally Democratic areas within the state. As a result of the growing disconnect, Utah Democrats had largely written off their chances in most of the state outside of Salt Lake County—the largest county in the state and the one dominated by Salt Lake City. In 2018, for example, the party failed to run a candidate in one-fourth of state House districts outside Salt Lake County.

At the same time, Republicans had become increasingly dominant and confident. The party's arrogance reached the point that the expectation of continual victory allowed the elements of the Republican Party to conduct the bitter, public feud over the nomination process discussed above without real concern that Democrats could capitalize on GOP division. Some voters resented the party's tone-deafness on some issues because of the lack of need to appeal seriously for voter support.

Utah is known as a conservative state. However, the reality is more nuanced. Utah has a higher than average proportion of conservative voters. Yet Utah is among the top five states with the most moderates. Forty percent of Utah voters self-identify as moderate.[12]

Another impetus for the creation of the party was the 2016 presidential campaign when Utahns faced the task of choosing between the Democratic candidate Hillary Clinton, who was widely disliked in Utah, and the Republican candidate Donald Trump, who was viewed with great suspicion by many Utahns due to his personal character and history. After a search by conservatives for an alternative to Trump, Evan McMullin, a former CIA agent and congressional staffer, announced his candidacy on August 8, 2016.[13]

McMullin had ties to Utah: he was a graduate of Brigham Young University and a member of the state's dominant faith. Immediately, McMullin gained traction among Utah voters. Polls showed him closing in on the two major-party candidates, and, ultimately his ability to garner 21 percent in the final vote was a remarkable performance for a non-major-party candidate.[14] No independent candidate had done that well in a state since Perot's 1992 candidacy.

McMullin's ability to peel off a large segment of Utah voters from their traditional major-party affiliation and vote for a largely unknown candidate indicated that Utah voters might be open to future candidates at lower levels who were neither Republican nor Democrat. Admittedly, Utah voters remained reliably Republican at lower levels in 2016, but any crack in the hold of the two-party system was viewed as a possible opening for another political party.

The decision to form a new political party came in the midst of several months of discussion, which included small group meetings, focus groups, and a commissioned survey to gauge public interest in the idea. Satisfied that there was significant public desire for a centrist third-party option, United Utah Party organizers first formed a political action committee in April 2017 to collect signatures for ballot access. On May 22, party organizers held a press conference announcing their intention of forming the party and submitting signatures to the state within a few days.[15] After about six weeks of signature collection, they submitted two thousand and seven hundred signatures to the state elections office on May 25.

As mentioned previously, individuals seeking to form a new political party are required to gather two thousand petition signatures of individuals who indicate interest in joining the new party. The signature-gathering process allows a party to be placed on the ballot for the next general election, as well as to participate in primary elections if the party has contested candidates. However, as stated above, a party must reach a certain vote percentage to remain ballot worthy.

During the six weeks that the party organizers were gathering signatures, the first electoral opportunity for the new party occurred when a member of Congress resigned and the governor called a special election to fill the vacancy. The party decided to take advantage of that opportunity by fielding a candidate. However, the special election led to a federal court case that gave the new party sudden, unexpected publicity.

THE 2017 SPECIAL CONGRESSIONAL ELECTION

In April 2017, representative Jason Chaffetz hinted that he might resign from his seat within a few months. That warning allowed the governor to create a process for a special election to fill Chaffetz's seat. Since only one special Congressional election had occurred previously in the state's history (1928), legislation was vague on how an election would be conducted.

The day Chaffetz announced his resignation, the governor, in turn, announced a special election process for filling the seat. It included a calendar for filing and election dates. The legislature objected to the governor's schedule and urged him to call the legislature into special session to create the process. The governor refused, and the legislature was unable to affect the process.[16]

The governor's calendar required candidates for the special election to file by May 26—one week away from the governor's announcement—and forced the United Utah Party organizers to accelerate their signature-gathering process to meet that deadline.[17] However, by submitting its petition on May 25, the United Utah Party expected to field a candidate who would file on May 26. Jim Bennett, son of the late US senator Bob Bennett, announced on May 25 that he would file as a candidate for Congress.

However, when Bennett appeared at the state elections office to file, he was refused. He was told he could file as an unaffiliated candidate but not as a candidate of the United Utah Party because the office had not yet completed its verification of the signatures.[18] (The office ultimately took the full thirty days it was allowed by law to verify the new party's signatures and certify the party.[19]) The United Utah Party then sued in federal court to place Bennett on the ballot.[20] On August 2, a federal judge ruled that the state must certify Bennett. The judge also criticized the state elections office for taking thirty days to do something that could have been done in a day or two.[21]

The party's first candidate also succeeded in earning a place on the dais of the Utah Debate Commission (UDC) debate. The UDC, formed in 2013, is a consortium of media organizations and universities that sponsors and produces statewide and congressional district debates. Its debates are aired live on most television stations in the state. The commission set a threshold of 10 percent (plus or minus a 4 percent margin of error) in a UDC commissioned poll to participate in the debate. Since its inception, only candidates from the two major parties had qualified for the debate. However, Bennett earned 6 percent in the polls and became the first non-major-party candidate to appear.

PRESS COVERAGE

The party's initial news conference announcing its existence earned significant media coverage. New political party formation is not a common occurrence in the state. And a centrist political party was a first for Utah.

However, due to the state's reaction to Bennett's candidacy, what would have been a one-day story became a weeks-long story as the state resisted the formation of the new party and blocked the certification of its first congressional candidate. The legal struggle with the Utah elections office provided a relatively large amount of press coverage, particularly for a new party, until its resolution five weeks later. Bennett's challenge with the director of the office as he sought to file his candidacy received significant coverage in the news media, as did the party's lawsuit to force the state to recognize Bennett's candidacy. The party's fight with the Utah elections office and ultimate victory at the hands of a federal district judge garnered additional publicity.

Beyond the lawsuit and initial efforts to be recognized as a party and to have its first candidate certified, the party sought to raise awareness of itself by entering the public debate on various issues. Some of these efforts to gain traditional media coverage resulted in positive stories on the party. One such effort was the party's call for open primary elections. The Utah Republican Party's closed primary occasionally sparked public comment. This was particularly true in the summer of 2017 when a more moderate Republican candidate faced a more extreme candidate in the special congressional election primary, resulting in moderate groups calling for unaffiliated voters to register as Republicans to defeat the more conservative candidate. The party used the moment to call for open primaries by urging the state legislature to stop funding primary elections for political parties that refuse to open their primaries to all voters.[22] The party also announced its opposition to secret sexual harassment deals in Congress when that story broke in late 2017.[23]

In January 2019, the party called on the Utah legislature to end its practice of allowing secret bills that legislators would write but not release until just before the session ended.[24] The party also sought to influence the actions of the Utah legislature by proposing a set of political reforms such as term limits, campaign finance limits, and an independent redistricting commission. The party also urged its supporters to contact their representatives to oppose legislative efforts to overturn recent citizen initiatives.[25]

2018 ELECTORAL PERFORMANCE

Jim Bennett, the party's congressional candidate in 2017, earned 9 percent of the vote in the November general election. The outcome was well below the vote totals of the two major-party candidates but equal to the combined vote of all the other minor-party candidates. Like most non-major-party candidates, Bennett, who raised approximately $60,000, was vastly outspent by the two major-party candidates.

The party set its sights on 2018 and began fundraising, party organization-building, and candidate recruitment for the next election. Candidates announced their candidacies early in the year and gained attention as novelties. This was particularly true of the party's first two 2018 congressional candidates: Jan Garbett, coowner of a major Utah real estate developer, and Eric Eliason, a wealthy entrepreneur.[26]

By March 2018, the party had recruited three congressional candidates, a county commission candidate, and fifteen state legislative candidates. As is typical of minor parties, nearly all of the candidates lacked governmental or even campaign experience, although one candidate was a current city council member, while another was a former city council member. Two of the congressional candidates later withdrew. One did so for health reasons, which, under state law, allowed the party to replace her on the ballot. The other, Garbett, announced she needed to concentrate on her business and therefore could not be replaced.[27] Ultimately, the party fielded eighteen candidates in the 2018 election.

None of the party's 2018 candidates won. However, most performed better than other minor-party candidates. And some even performed better than Democrats had in previous two-way races with Republicans in those districts. Overall, the United Utah Party share of the vote in the eighteen races was approximately 10 percent. Where candidates waged active campaigns rather than simply serving as names on ballots, the vote share was 15 percent. In five races, no Democrat or Republican ran and the United Utah Party candidate ran head to head against the major-party candidate. In those races, the United Utah Party candidates averaged 34 percent of the vote, which was 3 to 7 percent higher than the Democratic candidate's historical average in that district. The best performance by a United Utah Party candidate was 39 percent in a two-way race, which was 7 percent higher than the typical Democratic performance in that state House district.

At the congressional level, the candidate who entered the race late as a replacement did not actively campaign and won only 2 percent of the vote. However, the other candidate, Eric Eliason, won 12 percent of the vote and earned the second highest vote total for a nonmajor party congressional candidate in the nation. He also was able to qualify for the Utah Debate Commission debate, making him only the second non-major-party candidate to qualify.[28]

ELECTORAL APPEAL

The United Utah Party sought to separate itself from both major parties by creating a platform that hewed to a centrist line, borrowing from more moderate Republican and Democratic issue positions, along with radical government reform proposals. For example, the party expressed support for significant increases in public education, which had been advocated for by both Democrats and moderate Republicans in Utah for many years. Utah has the lowest per-ratio expenditures in the nation. At the same time, the party took a moderate stance on immigration. They supported "an immigration system that respects the sanctity and dignity of families while enforcing the law."[29] Critics of the party panned the platform and labelled the "centrist" term meaningless. One editorial called the party "a conglomerate of disaffected persons" and termed its platform "broad and vague."[30]

The party's platform also called for specific political reforms such as campaign finance limits, term limits for elected officials, and an independent redistricting commission.[31] The party also sought to differentiate itself in the electoral process by favoring greater openness in public participation than was true for the two major parties. While both Republicans and Democrats had adopted the 40 percent threshold for calling a primary, the United Utah Party set theirs at 20 percent. That would reduce the power of convention delegates to block primary elections and give the public more of an opportunity to participate through a primary election in the nomination process. Also, the party opened its primary elections to all voters regardless of party affiliation. In Utah, the Democrats had an open primary, but the Republicans limited their primary to registered Republicans.

The party sought to appeal to three broad groups: moderate Republicans who were dissatisfied with a Republican Party that had adopted the person and policies of Donald Trump but also were uncomfortable in a state party that was increasingly becoming more conservative than they were, unaffiliated voters who were not strong partisans or ideologues and were swing voters in elections, and moderate Democrats who disliked the leftward tilt of the Democratic Party.

Who voted for the United Utah Party? In the 2018 election, the party fielded eighteen candidates who won between 1.5 and 39 percent of the vote in their respective races. In two-way races, the party's candidates captured the Democratic vote, since Democrats had no other alternative. However, they won approximately 10 percent of the traditional Republican vote as well. Without exit polling in a district, it is difficult to know whether these voters were Republicans or unaffiliated voters who typically voted Republican. The latter is more likely.

A 2017 poll by Dan Jones and Associates, a local polling firm, found that the greatest potential support for the political party came from voters who considered themselves "independents." Eighty-eight percent said they would seriously consider voting for a United Utah Party candidate. And 85 percent of self-identified "moderates" gave the same answer.[32] Given the appeal to unaffiliated voters, younger voters may be fertile ground for the United Utah Party. The Utah Foundation, a nonprofit concerned with Utah policy issues, found in a 2015 survey that millennials are more likely to consider themselves unaffiliated than are baby boomers.[33]

The party also targets women, particularly LDS women. Even though many of these women have been Republicans, they express dislike for President Trump and dissatisfaction with the Republican Party for supporting him. A new group—Mormon Women for Ethical Government—formed in the wake of the 2016 presidential election has voiced continual opposition to Trump and his policies.[34]

THE FUTURE

The United Utah Party has a short past. Whether it will have a long future is yet to be determined. Third parties typically have not exceeded single digits in state elections—and even then, only when there is only one major-party candidate in a race at a local level. The United Utah Party, however, has succeeded where other minor parties have failed. Jim Bennett received the largest share of the vote of any non-major-party candidate in Utah. Eric Eliason beat Bennett's record. The party jumped from nonexistence to the largest minor party in Utah in eighteen months.

However, the distance from minor-party to major-party status is still a big leap for the United Utah Party. To succeed, the party must count on the failure of Democrats to even run candidates in districts where the United Utah Party has the best chance to win. These are likely to be suburban legislative districts with younger populations where voters are less tied to either major political party.

The United Utah Party faces the challenge of establishing its niche within Utah politics but also responding to national political forces. To succeed, it must fight the wasted vote argument by winning elections or, at the least, displacing the Democratic Party as the second party in the state. It must convince more moderate voters—whether Democratic, Republican, or unaffiliated—that they can bolt from their existing parties and support a new party without the prospect of wasting their vote.

The United Utah Party must also respond to national political forces— both from the third-party and independent camps, as well as the national major political parties. The United Utah Party, unlike some other centrist state parties, so far has retained its independence from efforts to form a national third party. Nor is it associated with Unite America, the national group seeking to recruit and support independent candidates. The distinctiveness of the Utah electorate makes such a union potentially harmful to the party. For example, when Starbucks CEO Howard Schultz briefly ran for president as a "centrist independent" in 2020, he described himself as socially liberal and economically conservative. However, the Utah electorate is economically moderate and socially conservative. If Schultz had headed a United Utah Party ticket, taking positions on abortion and same-sex marriage that contradicted those of a majority of Utah voters, the party's electoral position could have been jeopardized—not only in the presidential race but also in down-ballot races.

The constant attention to national political parties weakens the position of the United Utah Party by forcing it to turn away from the state-centric issues it seeks to address. Maintaining a state-centric approach may be difficult in a national-oriented electorate. However, Utah's unique electorate makes such an approach necessary, and it allows the United Utah Party to target its message to a narrow and distinctive audience.

NOTES

1. Adam R. Brown, *Utah Politics and Government: American Democracy Among a Unique Electorate* (Lincoln: University of Nebraska Press, 2018), 92–96; Frank Newport, "Mississippi and Alabama Most Protestant States in U.S.: Rhode Island Is Most Catholic, Utah Most Mormon, and New York Most Jewish," Gallup, February 5, 2014, https://news.gallup.com/poll/167120/mississippi-alabama-protestant-states .aspx; Lee Davidson, "With Utah Legislature's Mormon Supermajority, Is It Representative of the People?" *Salt Lake Tribune*, December 12, 2016.

2. Brown, *Utah Politics*, 32–49.

3. Thomas G. Alexander, *Mormonism in Transition: A History of the Latter-day Saints, 1890–1930* (Urbana: University of Illinois Press, 1996), 7–8; G. Homer Durham, *The Development of Political Parties in Utah: The First Phase* (Salt Lake City: University of Utah Press, 1947).

4. John S. McCormick and John R. Sillito, *A History of Utah Radicalism: Startling, Socialistic, and Decidedly Revolutionary* (Logan: Utah State University Press, 2011).

5. Matthew Bowman, "'It Is Time We Do Something Radical': The Union Party in Utah," *Utah Historical Quarterly* 72 (Summer 2004): 253–270.

6. In full disclosure, the author of this chapter was one of those initial organizers of the party and later served as party chair.

7. Robert Gehrke, "Big Boost: Romney Backs Count My Vote," *Salt Lake Tribune*, February 24, 2014.)

8. Brian Grimmett, "Utah GOP to File Lawsuit Challenging SB 54," KUER, No-

vember 26, 2014, accessed February 1, 2019, http://www.kuer.org/post/utah-gop
-file-lawsuit-challenging-sb54#stream/0; Brian Mafly, "Feud in Utah GOP Over
Party Debt, SB 54 Lawsuit," KUTV, December 14, 2017, https://kutv.com/news
/local/feud-in-utah-gop-over-party-debt-sb-54-lawsuit.

9. Bob Bernick, "Utahns Mostly Believe Abortion Should be Illegal," Utah Pol-
icy.com, June 11, 2018, https://utahpolicy.com/index.php/features/today-at-utah
-policy/16914-utahns-mostly-believe-abortion-should-be-illegal;

10. Matt Canham, "Defending Fundraiser, Dem Hopeful Mike Weinholtz Says
'Saturday's Voyeur' Is Parody, Not Anti-Mormon Bigotry," *Salt Lake Tribune*, September 26, 2016.

11. "Welcome to the Utah Debate Commission," Utah Debate Commission Debate Archive, accessed January 14, 2020, http://www.utahdebatecommission.org.

12. Jeffrey M. Jones, "Conservatives Greatly Outnumber Liberals in 19 U.S.
States," Gallup, February 22, 2019, https://news.gallup.com/poll/247016/conser
vatives-greatly-outnumber-liberals-states.aspx.

13. Josh Rogin, "The Story Behind Evan McMullin's Run for President," *Washington Post*, August 22, 2016.)

14. "News Roundup: Trump-Clinton-McMullin Statistically Tied in New Utah
Poll," *Salt Lake Tribune*, October 12, 2016; Jack Healy, "Evan McMullin's Moonshot
White House Bid Has Utah's Attention," *New York Times*, October 14, 2016; "2016
General Election Results: Utah," Utah Elections Office, November 28, 2016,
https://elections.utah.gov/Media/Default/2016%20Election/2016%20General
%20Election%20-%20Statewide%20Canvass%203.pdf.

15. Dennis Romboy, "Frustrated Utah Republicans, Democrats Form a New
Centrist Political Party, *Deseret News*, May 22, 2017.

16. Lee Davidson, "Gov. Herbert to Utah Legislature: Forget Special Session,"
Salt Lake Tribune, May 18, 2017.)

17. Courtney Tanner and Lee Davidson, "Utah Sets Condensed Special Election
Calendar—and Its Already Started," *Salt Lake Tribune*, May 21, 2017.)

18. Courtney Tanner and Dan Harrie, "Jim Bennett Tries to Jump into Race for
Congress, but State Won't Let Him Under New Party's Banner," *Salt Lake Tribune*,
May 28, 2017.)

19. Julia Ritchey, "New Centrist Party Recognized by State Amid Lawsuit,"
KUER, June 27, 2017, http://www.kuer.org/post/new-centrist-party-recognized
-state-amid-lawsuit#stream/0.

20. Lisa Riley Roche, "Backers of New Utah Political Party Say They'll Sue to Get
Candidate in Congressional Race," KSL, June 17, 2017, https://www.ksl.com
/article/44671025.

21. Dennis Romboy, "Judge Orders State to Put United Utah Party Candidate
on Special Election Ballot," *Deseret News*, August 2, 2017.

22. Lee Davidson, "New Party Seeks to End State Funding for Closed Republican Primaries," *Salt Lake Tribune*, August 10, 2017.

23. Dennis Romboy, "Utah Rep. Mia Love Proposes to End Taxpayer-Funded

Sexual Harassment Settlements," KSL, December 2, 2017, https://www.ksl.com/ar
ticle/46209159.)

24. Christina Giardinelli, "The United Utah Party Pushes for all Legislative Bills
to be Made Public," *Salt Lake Tribune,* January 29, 2019.

25. "United Utah Announces Legislative Agenda," United Utah Party press release, January 31, 2019, https://www.unitedutah.org/united_utah_announces_leg
islative_agenda.

26. Preston Cathcart, "United Utah Party Candidates to Challenge 2 Congress-
men," *Deseret News,* February 13, 2018; Katie England, "Newly-formed United Utah
Party Announce Utah County Candidates," *Daily Herald,* February 15, 2018.

27. Ben Winslow, "United Utah Party Candidate Drops Out of Congressional
Race," Fox13, August 30, 2018, https://fox13now.com/2018/08/30/united-utah
-party-candidate-drops-out-of-congressional-race/.

28. "Democrat, United Utah Party Candidate, GOP Incumbent Debate," *Washington Times,* October 18, 2018.

29. "United Utah Party Platform," United Utah Party, accessed January 30,
2019, https://www.unitedutah.org/platform.

30. "Tribune Editorial: Curtis for Congress," *Salt Lake Tribune,* October 14,
2017.

31. Dennis Romboy, "Frustrated Utah Republicans, Democrats Form a New
Centrist Political Party, *Deseret News,* May 22, 2017.

32. Bryan Schott, "Utah Democrats and Independent Voters Would be Most
Likely to Vote for United Utah Party Candidates," Utah Policy.Com, June 28, 2017,
https://utahpolicy.com/index.php/features/today-at-utah-policy/13638-poll-utah
-democrats-and-independent-voters-would-be-most-likely-to-vote-for-united-utah-party
-candidates.

33. "Millennials and Boomers: Politics and Society (Part IV)," Utah Foundation,
July 14, 2015, http://www.utahfoundation.org/reports/millennials-and-boomers
-politics-and-society-part-iv/.

34. "Home," MWEG, Mormon Women for Ethical Government, accessed November 25, 2019, http://www.mormonwomenforethicalgovernment.org.

About the Contributors

C. Damien Arthur is the distinguished scholar and director of the Marshall University Center for Consumer Law and Education (CCLE), a partnership with the West Virginia University College of Law. Currently he is an assistant professor of public administration and policy at Marshall University. He is the coauthor of *Debating Immigration in the Age of Terrorism, Polarization, and Trump* (2017). He is currently writing the definitive biography of Senator Robert C. Byrd.

Gerald Benjamin is director of the Benjamin Center for Public Policy Initiatives and distinguished professor of political science at SUNY New Paltz. A Fulbright scholar, Benjamin has written or edited fifteen books and numerous articles as well as commented extensively on state and local government and regional governance with a special emphasis on New York.

Michael Catalano is currently a PhD student at Binghamton University (SUNY). His concentration is in American politics, with research interests in judicial institutions, political parties, and American political development. He resides in Endwell, New York, with his wife and their two children.

Richard A. Clucas is a professor of political science at Portland State University and the executive director of the Western Political Science Association. He has written extensively on democratic institutions, legislative politics, state government, and Oregon politics. Among recent works, he is the coeditor of *Governing Oregon: Continuity and Change* (2018).

Richard Davis is a professor of political science and director of the Office of Civic Engagement Leadership at Brigham Young University. He is the author of several books and articles on American politics and is the past president of the American Political Science Association's political communication section. In addition, he has been a political activist in his community.

Christopher J. Devine is an assistant professor of political science at the University of Dayton in Ohio. He is the coauthor of three books, including *Do Running Mates Matter?* (fall 2020, University Press of Kansas). His research has also been published in journals such as *Political Behavior, Political Psychology, Electoral Studies,* and *PS: Political Science and Politics,* and in media outlets such as the *Washington Post*'s Monkey Cage and FiveThirtyEight.

Melanie Freeze is a visiting assistant professor at Carleton College. Her research explores topics of political parties and polarization, the structure and change in political attitudes, and how individuals process information and communicate in polarized political climates.

Bertram Johnson is professor of political science at Middlebury College in Vermont. He is author of *Political Giving: Making Sense of Individual Campaign Contributions* (2013) as well as a number of articles and book chapters on US politics and state and local government. He is currently at work on a project examining how fires in state capitol buildings shaped the political history of various states.

Steve Lem is an associate professor and chairperson in the Department of Political Science at Kutztown University of Pennsylvania. His primary research agenda focuses on third-party candidate participation in US elections. He currently serves on the executive council of the Pennsylvania Political Science Association and has worked with several organizations to raise awareness of contemporary political issues around the state.

Edward Lynch is chair of political science at Hollins University in Roanoke, Virginia. He is the author of four books and numerous articles on politics, a contributor to The Hill, and a political analyst for the Roanoke NBC News affiliate. Besides his academic career, Lynch also worked on Capitol Hill and in the White House Office of Public Liaison.

Emily K. Lynch is a lecturer in political science at the University of Rhode Island, and she previously taught at Johnson & Wales University and Providence College. She served as an American Political Science Association congressional fellow for US senator Sheldon Whitehouse from 2013 to

2014 and worked on education policy for the senator. Her teaching and research interests include political psychology, public opinion, political communication, Congress, and political parties.

Joseph Phillips is a PhD candidate in political science at Pennsylvania State University. His work focuses on the causes and consequences of affective polarization in the electorate as well as life-cycle explanations of political attitudes and behavior.

Bilal Sekou is an associate professor of political science in Hillyer College at the University of Hartford. His research interests are racial politics, urban politics, and voting behavior. He has published articles on political participation by African Americans, election reforms, and public attitudes toward quality and integrated education in Connecticut. In addition, he has been a social and racial justice activist.

Index

A Connecticut Party, 9, 10, 11, 16 (table), 108
ACORN (Association of Community Organizations for Reform Now), 100, 108
Alaskan Independence Party, 10
America Elect, 17
American Independent Party (California), 8–9, 16 (table), 262
American Party, 2, 261
anarchist libertarians, 45
Anti-Masonic Party, 16 (table)
at-large elections, 71

Barkley, Dean, 182, 184, 190, 195, 196
Barr, Bob, 47–48
Barr, Roseanne, 123
Beck, Glenn, 93
Bennett, Jim, 267, 268, 271
Binion, Denise, 232, 233–234
Block, Ken, 239, 242, 243, 249–250, 251, 254
Bloc Quebecois (Canada), 21
Bloomberg, Michael, 103, 104, 165
Brexit referendum, 20
Britain, and minor-party dynamism, 19–20
Bryan, William Jennings, 1, 31
Buchanan, Patrick, 17, 89
Bull Moose Party. See Progressives
Bush, George H. W., 85
Bush, George W., 64, 87
Byrd, Robert C., 230–231
Cantor, Dan, 99, 102, 103–104, 114

Castle, Darrell, 93
centrist parties, era of, 16
Centrist Project, 18
Chafee, Lincoln, 244, 245, 249
Chaffetz, Jason, 263, 266
Church of Jesus Christ of Latter-day Saints, The, 261–262. See also Utah politics
Citizen Action of New York, 100
Clark, Ed, 46
Cleaver, Eldridge, 122
Clinton, Bill, 88–89
Clinton, Hillary, 265
Coalition Avenir Quebec (Canada), 21
coalition government, in Britain, 19
Connecticut Working Families Party
    Democratic Party and, 112, 113
    founding of, 108
    issues of, 109, 110–111
    in local races, 110–111
    prolabor campaign of, 112–113
    at state level, 111–114
    strategy of, 109–110
    See also Working Families Party
Conservative Caucus (CC), 85–86
Conservative Party (Britain), 19
Conservative Party (Canada), 20, 21
Conservative Party (New York), 153, 158, 167, 172
Conservatives (United States), 76
Constitutional Union Party, 5
Constitution Party
    ballot access and, 87–88
    campaigns of, 90, 93

Constitution Party, *continued*
  candidate recruitment, 15, 95
  Conservative Caucus (CC) and, 85–86
  electoral performance of, 86–87, 88,
    90, 94
  FEC recognition of, 86
  formation of, 2
  grassroots support, lack of, 94
  as interest group, 95–96
  legitimacy of, 95
  Libertarian Party and, 91, 92
  in Oregon, 213, 215, 216
  platform of, 90–92
  Republican Party and, 94, 95
  US Taxpayers Party and, 86, 90
  in Utah, 263
Cool Moose Party, 245
cross endorsement. *See* New York State
    politics
Cuomo, Andrew
  Liberal Party nomination of, 163
  as New York gubernatorial candidate,
    28, 153, 154 (table), 165
  third-party influence and, 176
  Women's Equality Party and, 105
  Working Families Party and, 104–106,
    160

debate rules, 31–32
de Blasio, Bill, 103–104, 105
Democratic–Farmer–Labor Party (DFL), 9
Democratic Party, 5, 17, 75–76, 77, 99
Dole, Bob, 86–87
Duverger, Maurice, 3, 69, 17, 141
Duverger's law, 3, 139, 140, 205

Eliason, Eric, 269, 271
elite recruitment, 84, 95

Farmer–Labor Party in Minnesota, 6, 9,
    10, 16 (table)
Federalists, 5
financial assistance, state-level, 30
fusion
  history of, 154–156
  Independent Party of Oregon and, 209
  minor parties, effect on, 30, 31, 150
  in New York, 31, 139, 154, 176
  state law and, 31, 155

Supreme Court decision on, 101
  in Vermont, 139–140
  voting, 100

geographic scope, 10
German Green Party (Die Grünen), 65,
    66
gerrymandering, 5, 7
Giardina, Denise, 226–227
Gilbert, William, 252, 253, 254, 255
Giuliani, Rudy, 102, 166
Gomes, Edwin A., 111–112
Gore, Al, 82, 227
Grassroots Legalize Cannabis Party, 197
Green Mountain Party, 138
Green Party (Canada), 21
Green Party (United States)
  Association of State Green Parties
    (ASGP) and, 68, 69
  Democratic Party and, 77
  division within, 66, 67
  electoral challenges of, 73, 74
  electoral performance of, 25, 66, 67,
    71–72
  formation of, 2, 65, 66
  future of, 78
  German Green Party (Die Grünen)
    and, 65–66
  Green Committees of Correspondence
    and, 66
  as Green Party of the United States
    (GPUS), 69
  as Greens/Green Party of the United
    States (G/GPSA), 66–67, 68
  Green Politics Network, creation of, 67
  major parties, impact on, 74, 77
  Mountain Party of West Virginia and,
    230
  in New York State, 101, 153, 156, 158,
    159
  party platform of, 66, 69, 76, 77
  Republican Party and, 76
  spoiler effect of, 64
  strengths and weaknesses of, 68, 78
  supporters of, 74–75
  in Utah, 263

Hall, Joshua M., 113
Hawkins, Howie, 153, 154 (table)

Healey, Robert, Jr., 245, 249, 250, 251
Hewitt, Jeff, 59, 61
Home Rule Party (Hawaii), 16 (table)
Horner, Tom, 30, 184, 196–197
Hospers, John, 46

Illinois Solidarity Party, 10, 16 (table)
Independence Party
    establishment of, 158
    in Minnesota, 3
    in New York, 101, 153, 156, 167, 169,
        172
    in Oregon, 2
Independence Party (IP) of Minnesota
    campaign funds and, 187–188, 188
        (fig.)
    candidate counts, 185–187, 186 (fig.),
        187 (fig.)
    electoral performance of, 183–187,
        195–196
    founding of, 181, 182
    Minnesota politics and, 196–197
    nonpartisan candidacies, support of,
        199n22
    PACs and, 183
    platform of, 183
    public finance and, 192–194, 193
        (fig.), 194 (table)
    Reform Party, affiliation with, 182
    as state-centric organization, 200n23
    status of, 190, 195
    See also Minnesota politics
Independent American Party, 263
Independent Democratic Conference
    (IDC), 106, 160
Independent Party of Oregon (IPO)
    automatic voter registration effect on,
        218
    ballot access, challenges to, 219
    campaign contributions and, 214–216,
        215 (fig.)
    candidates, number of, 213–214, 214
        (fig.)
    constituency of, 208
    Duverger's law and, 206, 213, 219
    electoral performance of, 216–217,
        218
    electoral reforms and, 206
    fusion voting and, 209

future of, 212–213, 218–219
    name, confusion caused by, 209, 219
    Oregon politics, role in, 218
    platform of, 208
    SB 326 and, 208
    status of, 205–206, 208, 209, 218
    as third option, 212, 217
    Working Families Party and, 216
    See also Oregon politics
independent voters, 25
interest articulation, 84, 95

Jackson, Jessie, 144, 148, 149 (table)
Johnson, Craig, 173–174
Johnson, Gary, 15, 23, 41–42, 48, 60
Johnson, Jesse, 230, 233–234
Jore, Rick, 94–95

Keyes, Alan, 15, 95
King, Angus, 6, 24
Koch, David, 46, 47, 165

Labour Party (Britain), 19
LaFollette, Robert, Sr., 11, 13
La Riva, Gloria, 126, 130
LDS Church. *See* Church of Jesus Christ of
    Latter-day Saints, The; Utah politics
left-right construct, 76
Legal Marijuana Now Party, 16 (table),
    197
Liberal Democrats (Britain), 19, 20
Liberal Party (New York), 9, 16 (table),
    159, 163
Liberals (Canada), 20
Liberals (United States), 76
libertarianism, 44
Libertarian National Committee (LNC),
    53
Libertarian Party (LP)
    anarchist libertarians and, 45
    electoral performance of, 14–15, 46–
        52, 49 (fig.), 50 (fig.), 51
        (table)
    formation of, 43–44
    future of, 61
    ideology of, 41–43
    libertarianism and, 44–46
    as long-term minor party, 13–14, 16
        (table)

Libertarian Party (LP), *continued*
in New York State, 101, 153, 156, 158,
159
in Oregon, 213, 214 (fig.), 215, 215
(fig.), 216
organization of, 52–53
Peace and Freedom Party and, 127,
129
platform of, 53–55, 60
policies of, 54–57, 57 (fig.)
policy preferences for members of, 55–
59, 58 (table)
state power, opposition of, 53
tensions within, 44–46, 47, 59, 60
as third choice, 41
in Utah, 263
in Vermont, 138
Liberty Union Party, 138, 143
London, Herb, 161, 163
long-term minor parties, 13–15

majority system with runoffs (France), 3
major parties
candidates of, 23, 24, 31, 78
supporters of, 18 (table), 27
third parties and, 83, 189
Manchin, Joe, 229–230
Marrou, Andre, 47
McMullin, Evan, 24, 187, 265–266
mechanical effect, 3, 69
Meek, Dan, 207
Meyer, William, 143
millennials, 26, 271
Miner, Stephanie, 153, 154 (table)
Minnesota politics, 189, 190–191, 197. *See
also* Independence Party (IP) of
Minnesota
minor parties
appeal of, 76
ballot access and, 87, 205
barriers to, 197, 189
candidates of, 25, 26, 27, 30, 78, 84
celebrities and, 28
in Connecticut, 108
developments in, 15
dynamism of, 19
electoral laws and, 189, 205
financing issues of, 29
formation of, 2

geographical area of focus of, 8
interest articulation and, 84
local governments and, 6, 139
longevity of, 10
major parties, impact on, 2, 83, 85
media and, 28
national, 16, 17
in New York State, 101
nominating petitions and, 87–88
political polarization and, 181
in senate elections, 82–83
in state legislatures, 24
support of, 17, 18 (table), 23, 26, 27
in 2016 presidential election, 23
uncontested elections and, 71
in Vermont, 140
winner-take-all voting systems and, 99,
189
See also long-term minor parties, short-
term minor parties
minor parties typology, 15, 16 (table)
moderate parties, 4
Moderate Party of Rhode Island
ACLU lawsuit on behalf of, 241
as alternative party, 242, 243
as centrist party, 17, 261
contributions of, 255
difficulties faced by, 240, 253–254
election laws, effect on, 240–241
electoral performance of, 249–252
founding of, 2, 239
"four Es" of, 243–244
future of, 239, 255
Great Recession and, 242
legislative assembly, focus on, 243
media and, 255
PAC of, 240
platform of, 242, 243, 252
polling data and, 247
Rhode Island General Assembly and,
242
State Committee of, 240
status of, 238, 239, 241, 253
straight-line voting and, 243, 254,
255
support for, 247, 254
Tea Party and, 242
"Trump effect" and, 255
See also Rhode Island politics

moderates, 17
Molinaro, Mark, 153, 154 (table)
Mormon Church. *See* Church of Jesus
    Christ of Latter-day Saints, The; Utah
    politics
Mountain Party of West Virginia
    agenda of, 223
    ballot access and, 229
    campaign spending and, 228
    debate inclusion and, 228–229, 233
    Democratic Party and, 228, 232
    efforts to expand, 230
    electoral performance of, 228, 230,
        231, 233
    environmental issues and, 227
    founding of, 223, 227, 228
    future of, 233, 234
    Green Party and, 15, 230
    policy issues of, 232
    state legislature and, 234
    voters and, 232, 234
    West Virginia politics and, 232
    See also West Virginia politics
multimember districts, 33, 139, 140, 141,
    150
multiparty systems, 3, 174–175
multiple-party nomination states, 100
"multi+" party system. *See* New York State
    politics
Murphy, Chris, 109

Nader, Ralph
    as Green Party candidate, 15, 67, 68
    Independent Party of Oregon and, 206
    primary election matching funds and,
        30
    in 2000 election, 23, 64, 75, 77, 82
Nathan, Tonie, 46
New Democratic Party (NDP; Canada),
    20, 21
New Left movement, 121, 124. *See also*
    Peace and Freedom Party (PFP;
    California)
New Party (NP), 99, 100–101. *See also*
    Working Families Party
New York State politics
    ballot complexity and, 175
    campaign finance reform commission
        and, 176

closed primaries and, 167, 169
cross endorsement and, 155–156, 165–
    167, 168 (table), 173–176
disaggregation and, 157
Fight for Tomorrow New York and,
    163
fusion and, 154–156, 163, 165, 173,
    176
independent bodies in, 156
minor-party endorsement and, 173
"multi+" party system, 153, 154, 160,
    166, 174
official parties in, 155–156
qualities of, 155–156
Supreme Court judges and, 169, 170
third parties and, 158, 160–163, 175,
    176
town elections and, 170–172, 171
    (table), 172 (table)
2018 gubernatorial election, 153–156,
    154 (table)
2018 Nineteenth Congressional District
    race, 163
vote splitting and, 165
Wilson-Pakula Act and, 156
Nixon, Cynthia, 28, 105, 160, 107
Nixon, Richard, 11–12, 43
Nolan, David, 43–44
nonpartisan ballots, 70–71

Obama, Barak, 229–230
one-party systems, 5
Oregon politics
    characteristics of, 206, 209–210, 217
    Democratic Party and, 212
    HB 2614 and, 207
    intolerance in, 211
    major-party requirements in, 206
    nonaffiliated voters and, 212
    Progressive movement and, 210
    SB 326, 208
    state election laws and, 211
    Vote-By-Mail and, 211
    See also Independent Party of Oregon
    (IPO)

Pacific Green Party, 213, 216
Parti Quebecois (Canada), 21
Paul, Ron, 14, 47, 48

Peace and Freedom Party (PFP; California)
activism and, 123–124, 129, 132
ballot access and, 125, 128
Black Panthers and, 121, 122
California Democratic Party v. Jones and, 129
Democratic Party and, 130
electoral performance of, 122, 128
factions within, 125–127
founding of, 121–122
future of, 130, 132
Green Party and, 130
influence of, 129
Libertarians and, 127, 129
New Left and, 124, 132
organization of, 125
People's Party and, 122
political platform of, 123–124
precariats and, 127
socialism and, 130
supporters of, 127
"top-two" primary impact on, 131
Penny, Tim, 184, 195 (fig.), 196
People's Party, 1, 8, 16 (table), 122, 123. *See also* Peace and Freedom Party (PFP; California)
People's Party (Utah), 262
Perot, Ross
Independence Party and, 158
Independence Party of Minnesota and, 181–182
influence of, 22
media and, 27
in 1992 election, 2, 31–32, 82, 189
public financing and, 29
Reform Party and, 8, 16
Utah and, 262–263
Phillips, Howard, 15, 85–86, 89
political socialization, 84
Populist Party, 6, 31
Populists. *See* People's Party (Utah)
Presidential Debate Commission, 32
Progressive Party (Vermont). *See* Vermont Progressive Party
Progressive Party (Wisconsin), 6, 9
Progressives (Bull Moose Party), 1, 7, 11, 12, 16 (table)

proportional representation systems (Europe), 3
psychological effect, 3, 5, 6–8, 7 (table), 13, 70
public financing policies, 29, 30

ranked-choice voting, 33
Reagan, Ronald, 12, 16
Reform Party
as centrist party, 16
Independence Party of Minnesota and, 182
national organization of, 8
New York and, 153, 155–156, 158, 167, 169
success and decline of, 16
Reform Party of Minnesota (RPMN), 182. *See also* Independence Party (IP) of Minnesota
regional parties, 10
Republican Party, 5, 8, 10, 17, 76, 93–94
Rhode Island politics
corruption in, 238
Democratic Party and, 238, 244, 245, 246 (table), 248
demographics of, 248
election laws and, 240–241, 253–254
independents in, 238, 245, 247
one-party system and, 244, 248
polarization of, 248
Republicans and, 244–245, 246 (table)
Rhode Island General Assembly and, 245
straight-party voting and, 254
tax rate and, 239–240
unaffiliated voters and, 247
See also Moderate Party of Rhode Island
Right to Life Party, 9, 16 (table), 159
Roosevelt, Theodore, 8, 11, 13

Sanders, Bernie
as Burlington mayor, 143
as democratic socialist, 130
as independent senator, 24
as Liberty Union candidate, 143
in 1988 Vermont gubernatorial election, 145
in 1990 congressional race, 145
Rainbow Coalition and, 143

Utah Democrats and, 264
Vermont Progressive Party and, 146
West Virginia and, 234–235
Working Families Party endorsement
    of, 107
Scottish Nationalist Party (Britain), 20
Serve America Movement (SAM), 17,
    101, 153, 155–156, 158, 159
Sharp, Larry, 153, 154 (table)
short-term/long-term dichotomy, 15
short-term minor parties, 11–12, 13–15
Shultz, Howard, 23, 272
single-member district plurality (SMDP)
    elections, 69, 70
Social Democrats (Britain), 19
social groups, 75
socialism, 130
Socialist Party, 6, 14
Socialist Party (Utah), 262
social media, 28–29
Southern Democrats, 5
state-centric minor parties, 9, 10, 15, 16
States' Rights Party (Dixiecrat), 8, 16
    (table)
Stein, Jill
    Green Party and, 72
    Mountain Party of West Virginia and,
        230
    primary election matching funds and,
        30
    in 2016 presidential election, 23, 41,
        64, 82

Teachout, Zephyr, 104, 105
third parties. *See* minor parties
three-party system, 5
Thurmond, Strom, 8, 11, 12
Trump, Donald, 17, 82, 87, 234–235, 265
two-and-a-half-party system (Canada), 20,
    21
two-party system, 4, 20, 24, 26

Union Party (Utah), 262
Unite America, 18, 272
United Kingdom Independent Party
    (UKIP), 20
United Party of Utah
    ballot access lawsuit of, 267
    as centrist party, 17, 261, 271–272
    debate access and, 267
    Democratic Party and, 271
    electoral performance of, 25, 268–269
    formation of, 2, 263, 265–266
    future of, 271
    media coverage and, 267–268
    national parties and, 272
    platform of, 268, 269–270
    signature-gathering efforts of, 266
    state-centric approach of, 272
    supporters of, 270–271
    in 2017 special election, 266–267
    wasted vote augment and, 271
    See also Utah politics
United Utah Party. *See* United Party of
    Utah
U'Ren, William, 210
US Taxpayers Party. *See* Constitution Party
Utah politics
    ballot access and, 263
    caucus/convention system of, 264
    The Church of Jesus Christ of Latter-
        day Saints influence on, 261–262
    Count My Vote and, 264
    Democratic Party and, 264
    Eagle Forum and, 263
    electorate of, 265, 272
    minor parties in, 262–263
    one-party state and, 265
    Republicans and, 262, 263–264, 265
    2017 special election and, 266–267
    two-party competition, history of, 262
    Utah Debate Commission and, 32, 267
    See also United Party of Utah

Vallone, Peter, Sr., 102
Ventura, Jesse
    Independence Party of Minnesota and,
        182, 184
    media coverage of, 27, 28, 184
    in 1998 gubernatorial debates, 32
    public finance and, 30, 192, 196
    Reform Party and, 9, 16
    struggles of, 195
    support of, 195–196
    vote share of, 195 (fig.)
    wasted-vote theory and, 6

Vermont politics
  activists and, 147
  Coalition for Responsible Government
    and, 143
  collective ballot listing and, 141–142
  Community Economic Development
    Office and, 147
  Democratic Party and, 148
  fusion in, 139–140, 150
  legislative districting of, 141
  minor parties in, 138, 140, 143
  multimember districts and, 139–142,
    150
  nuclear freeze campaign and, 144
  Progressive Coalition and, 143
  Progressive Vermont Alliance (PVA),
    144–145
  Rainbow Coalition and, 144, 148
  Republican Party and, 140
  town meetings, effect on, 142, 144,
    147, 150
  See also Vermont Progressive Party
Vermont Independent Party (VIP), 140
Vermont Progressive Party
  Democratic Party and, 31, 145
  founding of, 143
  grassroots organization and, 148
  growth of, 150
  leadership of, 150
  "new Vermonters" and, 148
  population growth and, 149, 149
    (table)
  success of, 138, 142, 145, 146, 147
  town meetings and, 150
  Vermont legislature and, 24
  wasted-vote theory and, 146–147
  See also Vermont politics

Walker, Bill, 6, 24
Walker, Olene, 263, 264
Wallace, George, 8, 11, 12, 13, 82
Weicker, Lowell, 6, 9, 10, 108
West Virginia Democratic Party
  coal industry and, 227
  Democratic Party (national) and, 225,
    229–230
  as moderate party, 225

  strength of, 224
  voter retention and, 233
  See also Mountain Party of West
    Virginia; West Virginia politics
West Virginia politics
  Climate Action Plan and, 229
  coal industry and, 227, 230
  conservatives and, 225
  mountaintop removal and, 227
  natural resource exploitation and, 223
  New Deal and, 224
  "Obama's War on Coal" and, 229
  polarization of, 229
  qualities of, 223
  Republican Party and, 224, 227, 233
  state legislators' ideology and, 226
    (fig.)
  unions and, 224
  See also Mountain Party of West
    Virginia; West Virginia Democratic
    Party
Whig Party, 5
Williams, Linda, 207
winner-take-all voting system, 99, 189
Wise, Bob, 228
Women's Equality Party, 107, 153, 156,
  158, 167, 169
Working Families Party
  Data and Field Services and, 103
  Democratic Party and, 167
  expansion of, 114
  founding of, 2, 99, 101–102, 158
  message of, 110
  New Party and, 99–101
  in New York City, 102–104
  in New York State elections, 104, 169,
    172
  in Oregon, 213
  strategy of, 100
  tensions within, 107, 160
  unions and, 102
  vision of, 114
  See also Connecticut Working Families
    Party

Zuckerman, David, 24, 145, 148, 149, 149
  (table), 150